BEYOND NATIONALISM

BEYOND NATIONALISM

A Social and Political History of the Habsburg Officer Corps, 1848–1918

István Deák

OXFORD UNIVERSITY PRESS
New York   Oxford
1992

Oxford University Press

Oxford   New York   Toronto
Delhi   Bombay   Calcutta   Madras   Karachi
Kuala Lumpur   Singapore   Hong Kong   Tokyo
Nairobi   Dar es Salaam   Cape Town
Melbourne   Auckland

and associated companies in
Berlin   Ibadan

Copyright © 1990 by Oxford University Press, Inc.

First published in 1990 by Oxford University Press, Inc.,
200 Madison Avenue, New York, New York 10016

First issued as an Oxford University Press Paperback, 1992

Oxford is a registered trademark of Oxford University Press

Library of Congress Cataloging-in-Publication Data
Deák, István.
Beyond nationalism : a social and political history of the
Habsburg officer corps, 1848–1918 / István Deák.
p. cm. Includes index.
ISBN 0-19-504505-X
ISBN 0-19-504506-8 (pbk)
1. Austro-Hungarian Monarchy. Heer—Officers—History.
2. Sociology, Military—Hungary. 3. Sociology, Military—Austria.
I. Title. UB415.A8D43 1990
306.2'7'09436—dc20   89–9389   CIP

Some segments of this book appeared in a tentative form in the following publications:

"The Education of Habsburg Army Officers 1848–1914," in Béla K. Király and Walter Scott
Dillard, eds., *The East Central European Officer Corps 1740–1920s: Social Origins, Selection, Education, and Training* ("War and Society in East Central Europe," XXIV; Social
Science Monographs, Atlantic Research and Publications, Inc. Distributed by Columbia University Press, 1988), pp. 73–98.

"The Habsburg Army in Memoir Literature," in Solomon Wank et al. eds., *The Mirror of
History: Essays in Honor of Fritz Fellner* (Santa Barbara and Oxford: ABC-CLIO, 1988), pp.
68–89.

"Latter Day Knights: Officer's Honor and Duelling in the Austro-Hungarian Army," *Österreichische Osthefte* 28 (1986): 311–27.

"Pacesetters of Integration: Jewish Officers in the Habsburg Monarchy," *East European Politics
and Societies* 3 (Winter 1989): 22–50.

I am grateful to the editors of these books and journals for having allowed me to try out my
ideas on their expert readerships.

2 4 6 8 9 7 5 3 1

Printed in the United States of America
on acid-free paper

To my wife, daughter, and sister

Preface

To be a youth in Hungary in the 1930s meant to live with the memories, triumphs, defeats, paraphernalia, and lingering nostalgia attached to the Habsburg monarchy. Soldiers wore the uniforms, carried the flags, and—this being impoverished little Hungary—still shouldered the rifles of the defunct Austro-Hungarian army. True, the Royal Palace on Budapest's Castle Hill no longer housed a monarch, for the Hungarian parliament had dethroned the Habsburg dynasty in 1921. Legally, however, Hungary was still a kingdom, and Regent Miklós Horthy, who had assumed the monarch's place, wore the uniform of an Austro-Hungarian admiral and at grand parades was flanked by Habsburg Archduke Joseph, bedecked in the uniform of an Austro-Hungarian field marshal. Everywhere one could feel the Habsburg past: in the grandiose public buildings, the cast-iron railroad stations, the "Schönbrunn yellow" military barracks, and the ornate apartment houses, mostly built under Francis Joseph and bearing plaques commemorating his reign. It was manifest in the Budapest boulevards—subsequently rechristened in honor of Lenin and his comrades—bearing the names of Habsburg rulers and their consorts; in the graceful Danube bridges (one named for Francis Joseph and another for his wife, Elizabeth); in the dazzling public spectacles which, we were told, reflected ancient Hungarian customs but which, we know today, stemmed mostly from the age of Francis Joseph. Veterans of the World War marched solemnly behind regimental flags or pushed themselves, legless, in pitiful wooden carts. On the street corners stood bemedaled beggars with shaking heads; "Doberdo," they used to stutter, referring to the rocky plateau on the Italian front, where so many had suffered shell shock.

There were the campaign ribbons in my father's drawer and the two silver medals, which he had earned for acts of bravery that he never wanted to discuss. There was also the heavy iron canteen, glazed in green, with a large shell-torn hole in the middle, which I regarded with religious reverence, for I sensed, however dimly, that had my father not happened to wear it on his hip that day, I might never have been born.

We lived and breathed the monarchy and the war. Our schoolbooks taught us that Austria-Hungary had been a marvelously strong, happy, and peaceful place, in which one could travel hundreds upon hundreds of miles without a passport, though the Austrian half of Austria-Hungary had really been a foreign country to us Hungarians, and the Austrians not truly our friends. We were taught that our king had been a good ruler, though back in 1849 he had hanged the bravest Hungarian patriots, and though there could be no question of our having another king from the same family. We were taught that Czechs, Slovaks, Serbs, Croats, Romanians, Ruthenes, Poles, Italians, and German-Austrians had fought shoulder to shoulder with us in the World War, though most of these nations had always been our enemies, and though the Romanians as well as the Czechs had been quite particularly cowardly and vile. We were taught that many Jews fought bravely in the war, though Jewish people were considered the bane of the country. We were taught that our soldiers had won great victories in the war until stabbed in the back, in 1918, by the pacifists, Freemasons, socialists, and Czechs. We were further taught that the Magyars were the best soldiers in the world, despite the fact that Hungary had not won a single war since the fifteenth century. And, finally, we were told that Hungary had been a great and sovereign kingdom within Austria-Hungary, and that it had suffered a terrible injustice after 1918 when it was deprived of two-thirds of its territory. Clearly, as youths it was our sacred duty and the goal of our life to redress this injustice and to recover the lost provinces from our neighbors: Romania, Yugoslavia, Czechoslovakia, and Austria. Nor did the memory of the Habsburg monarchy fade completely during World War II: when Hitler's soldiers crossed the country in the spring of 1941 to attack Yugoslavia, we were told that the Germans had been our brothers-in-arms during World War I, and that Yugoslavia, whose Serbs had been our enemies in that same war, deserved its sorry fate. Never mind that Hungary had concluded a treaty of eternal friendship with Yugoslavia shortly before the German attack.

In June 1941, Hungary's warlike tradition appeared to experience a rebirth when its army joined in the German attack on the Soviet Union. But the war soon became unpopular, and an entire Hungarian army was lost on the Don River. As the old officers gradually faded away, they were replaced by cocky young men, many of them National Socialists, who bore less and less resemblance to the former Habsburg officers. Then there were the anti-Semitic laws, which turned Jewish veterans of the Great War into pariahs and decorated Habsburg officers into forced laborers. But even then, as well as in the horrifying Eichmann days of 1944 when Jewish women, children, and war invalids were herded into cattle cars for deportation, some dim remnants of the Habsburg tradition and of the tolerant practices of the Habsburg military could be made out. Even the Hungarian Nazis, operating in the winter of 1944–1945, exempted the most highly decorated Jewish war veterans—a mere handful, it is true—from the anti-Semitic laws.

With the installation of Communist rule in Hungary around 1948, an official reevaluation of Habsburg history and World War I began. The Habsburgs and the old elites were transformed in the textbooks into feudal-capitalist oppressors, Habsburg-Hungary into a semicolony of Western capitalism, and the First World War into an imperialist conflict. I left Hungary in the middle of this reeducation process, and it was not until the 1960s that I rediscovered my interest, as a teacher of history in the

United States, in the Habsburg monarchy. Still later, in the 1980s, I became fasci-
nated with the Habsburg army and with what I began to see as the undocumented
role of the Habsburg army officer corps. Earlier, while doing research in the Vienna
War Archive on the Hungarian revolution of 1848–1849 and its leader Louis
Kossuth, I came upon the marvelously rich materials it contained on all aspects of
Habsburg military history, particularly the men in service to the emperor. The
documents highlighted the harrowing dilemma confronted by the soldiers of the
1848–1849 revolutions and wars as to whether to continue to serve the emperor or
to enter the service of the nation into which they had been born. The documents also
made clear—in contradiction to my education—that in 1848–1849 at least as many
Hungarian officers remained loyal to the Habsburg dynasty as joined the camp of
Louis Kossuth. I discovered that it was the Habsburg army and the officer corps in
particular that had bonded the empire at that time; furthermore, that it was primarily
the officers who held the monarchy together until 1918.

Who were the men who made up this strange, multitongued, multiconfessional,
supranational band? I was determined to find out. The present study is the result of a
decision, made in Vienna some eight years ago, to write their history.

Acknowledgments

To realize a book of even this modest scope, a veritable army of collaborators appears to be a basic requirement. The little army that slowly came into being on my behalf was made up of historians, archivists, librarians, graduate students, foundation directors, editors, relatives, and friends who had helped formulate my goals, assisted me in my research, did statistical analyses on my behalf, provided me with funds, published the partial results of my research, allowed me to present papers on the Habsburg army at conferences and public lectures, interviewed me on radio and television, read both the unfinished and the completed manuscript, or prepared it for publication. Shamefully, I cannot even recall all the names of my recruits, yet I would like to thank each in turn. Let me try to move from country to country and thank at least those who had helped me most.

In Austria I owe particular gratitude to Drs. Peter Broucek and Rainer Egger as well as to other members of the Vienna *Kriegsarchiv,* including its director, Dr. Walter Wagner. I am no less grateful to the head of the Military Scientific Section in the Austrian Ministry of Defense, Dr. Othmar Tuider, and two of his collaborators, Professor Manfried Rauchensteiner and Dr. Erwin A. Schmidl. The latter in particular has helped me consistently during the many years of our friendship: I admire his industry and talent. I also wish to thank Franz Steip, who assisted me during one of my sojourns in Vienna. In that country, moreover, I received valuable assistance from the grand old man of Austrian military history, Johann Christoph Allmayer-Beck, and from Professors Moritz Csáky, Horst Haselsteiner, the late Ludwig Gogolák, and Drs. Waltraud Heindl and Walter Lukan. The latter published my article on the officers in the journal *Österreichische Osthefte.* I am greatly indebted to Dr. Peter Urbanitsch for having allowed me to read, in manuscript form, the monumental *Die bewaffnete Macht,* of which he is coeditor, and who read and corrected the manuscript of my book. I wish also to express my thanks to the historian Dr. Peter Schmidtbauer, who helped me evaluate the personal records of the Habsburg officers.

I should mention as well the historian Liviu Maior of the University of Cluj-

Napoca in Romania and the sociologist Viktor Kárády in Paris. The number of Hungarians who helped me is almost embarrassingly long, making me feel as if the entire Hungarian intellectual community had been mobilized to bring my research to a successful conclusion. Here are some names: the sociologists Gyula Benda and László Füstös; the young historians Péter Dippold and Mária Csicskó, who did research for me on the Hungarian officers of noble origin; the late György Ránki who, as director of the Institute of History of the Hungarian Academy of Sciences, offered me hospitality as well as advice, and who invited me to various scholarly conferences; Ferenc Glatz, Ránki's successor as director of the Institute and now Hungary's minister of education, who published two of my short papers on the officers in the journal *História;* Zoltán Szász of the same institute, who arranged for some financial support; Gábor Bona of the Hungarian Institute of Military History; my friends, Péter Hanák and Tibor Hajdu, both outstanding historians; and Colonel Kálmán Kéri of the pre–World War II Hungarian army, who began his military career under the Habsburgs and who suffered persecution under the Stalinists. Kálmán Kéri spent long hours with me, recounting his youth and career, sharing the results of his research, and infecting me with his enthusiasm for the multinational Habsburg army.

All this does not exhaust the list of Hungarians who have assisted me. Let me mention Károly Tóth, who helped code my data on the officers, Zoltán Vas and the staff of the computer center at the University of Szeged in Hungary, and my friends, Mária M. Kovács and György Bence, who read the manuscript. My brother-in-law, Pál Veress, and my sister, Éva, helped in many ways. Finally, there are the two young Hungarian sociologists, Drs. András Ungár and Antal Örkény, who have adopted my project as their own, voluntarily spending many hours coding and programming the data on my randomly selected 1200 officers. It is not their fault that relatively little of the mass of material they have provided has actually made it in the book. I have stubbornly resisted their calls for such refined things as a cluster analysis, preferring to relate stories and even anecdotes where scientific data may have been more warranted. I thank them both, and I hope that we shall have the opportunity to work together, at a later date, on a more scientific analysis of my data.

I am grateful to the Canadian historian Nándor F. Dreisziger for having invited me to the Royal Military College at Kingston, Ontario. In the United States, I want to thank Professor Béla K. Király, who invited me to several conferences he organized on "War and Society in Eastern Europe," and who published some of my writings on the Habsburg army; Professor Daniel Chirot, who published a piece of mine in *East European Politics and Societies,* and Professor Sol Wank, who published another piece; Professors Gunther E. Rothenberg, Gary Cohen, and Ferenc Fehér, as well as my former students, Drs. Peter Black and Leonard Smith, all of whom read and corrected the manuscript; the staff of the Institute on East Central Europe at Columbia University, and quite particularly John Micgiel, the administrator of the Institute. Robert Scott read the manuscript many times and used his editorial talents to smooth out my style, and Valur Ingimundarson helped me with the index and the galleys. At Oxford University Press, both Nancy Lane and Paul Schlotthauer treated my manuscript with particular good will and care.

I am grateful to the director and staff of the Wilson Center in Washington, D.C., where I spent a happy semester in 1986, working on the book. Similar thanks are due the Fulbright-Hays Commission in Washington, D.C., and to IREX in Princeton, for providing me with fellowships and for arranging my repeated research trips to Austria and east central Europe. Vivian Abbot, Livia Plaks, and Margit Serényi, all at IREX, are among those who helped me most.

My wife Gloria also helped substantially although she was occupied with her own two-volume work in art history. I think of her with love as I do of my daughter Éva.

New York   I. D.
December 1989

Contents

BEYOND NATIONALISM

Introduction

In March 1848, the Habsburg monarchy consisted of a myriad of kingdoms, principalities, duchies, margravates, counties, baronies, and lordships. This conglomerate of territorial entities, and the varied peoples inhabiting them, were presided over by a sickly, somewhat retarded, and benevolent monarch. Like the Habsburg rulers before him, Emperor-King Ferdinand was theoretically absolute in his authority yet bound by the historical rights and privileges of each of his domains. Before his throne paraded continual delegations of national politicians, each demanding a greater share of rights for his own constituency. All professed undying loyalty to His Imperial and Apostolic Royal Majesty, while casting covetous eyes on the lands of their neighbors in the realm and furtive glances at whatever foreign power might be enlisted to support their aspirations.

In October 1918, seventy years later, the Habsburg monarchy consisted of only two major political entities, Austria and Hungary. Each included a great number of the old historic provinces, some with a measure of autonomy, others without, but none of the nationalities inhabiting those provinces was concerned about recognizing the authority of the dynasty. Instead, their leaders were readying themselves either to join a neighboring power or to create their own independent state, all the while laying claim to the territory of their neighbors inside Austria-Hungary. Presiding over the dissolution of the monarchy was an earnest, devout, and benevolent young man, Emperor-King Charles, who, though sworn to uphold the constitutions of both Austria and Hungary, also claimed divine sanction for his authority.

In March 1848, the Habsburg monarchy was subjected to the greatest internal crisis theretofore known in the course of its long and complex history, but it was able to overcome that challenge within the next year and a half. The next great crisis, however, occasioned by World War I, was to prove fatal. In the intervening years, the monarchy passed through many difficult episodes, but startlingly, it managed to survive, and even thrive at least economically and culturally, leaving an indelible mark on the ethos of its various subject peoples. Such prolonged survival in the face of overwhelming odds was assured by two factors: the presence of the multinational Habsburg army and the sixty-eight-year reign of Emperor-King Francis Joseph. That this diligent, upright, judicious, seemingly cold, and rather unimaginative prince succeeded in holding the monarchy together was due in large part to the magic of his longevity, but also to the loyalty and devotion of his army. The latter was there at the dynasty's side in March 1848, and it was still there at the beginning of November 1918, even after the breakup of the monarchy itself.

With its massive presence in every province, the army was the most important all-monarchical institution in the realm. In 1867, that realm was divided into two politically equal parts: Austria (which, until 1916, went by a much more complicated name) and Hungary. Because Francis Joseph was simultaneously emperor of Austria and king of Hungary, and because he had sworn, in 1867, to abide by both constitutions, he represented, in his very person, the conflicting interests as well as the unity of the two sovereign states. A few common institutions remained, but none so ubiquitous as the Joint Army (so called to distinguish it from the separate "national" armies—hereinafter referred to as National Guards—of Austria and Hungary).

Along with a common monarch and a joint army, the two states possessed a common foreign service, but the latter was, by its very nature, not a significant presence within the monarchy. There was also a joint ministry of finance, but it was charged merely with administering the budgets of the foreign service, armed forces, and a few other joint financial institutions. The common navy, quite obviously, was not visible in most parts of the realm. Finally, even the rank and file of the Joint Army must be eliminated from the list of great all-monarchical institutions, since, following the introduction of universal military service in 1868, the men were on active duty for an average of only three years, too little time to shed an ethnic identity for a supranational one. Hence, we are left with the army officers and, to a lesser degree, noncommissioned officers, for whom service was a lifetime proposition.

The officers were the nerve center and spiritual essence of the army. Each of them, of course, had his own particular—or, very often, mixed—ethnic origin, but for them service to the monarch was the basic commitment, overruling all other considerations. The officers saw themselves even more as direct subjects of Francis Joseph than of the monarchy, if only because, by 1900, there was not a single officer in active service who had not received his commission from that ruler and sworn personal fealty to him. This ultimate connection between officer and monarch, taken in conjunction with Francis Joseph's own military training, and his predilection for military regalia, fortified the identification of each officer with the highest levels of the state. It offered a further incentive to the officer corps to act as the guardian of the multinational monarchy.

The aim of this book is to analyze the social and ethnic origin of the officers, their reasons for entering service, their education, training, and ideology, their way of life and peculiar customs, their role in politics, culture, and society, the evolution of the officer corps between 1848 and 1918, its relations with the civilian authority, its responsibility for the survival and for the ultimate breakup of the monarchy, and, finally, its impact on the post-1918 history of east central Europe. The officers will be studied as individuals but also in their collectivity as a corporation or caste. They were a unique phenomenon in a unique European state, but an attempt will also be made here to place them within the great family of imperial and national officer corps and armies.

While many parallel cases of multiethnic armies could be proposed, almost none would stand up to the test. The British and the French military made ample use of colonial troops but did not amalgamate them with units from the *métropole;* they simply delegated career officers and noncoms to command the colonial regiments. The army of the Ottoman Empire was as mixed ethnically as that of the Habsburg monarchy, but one had to be a Muslim to serve in the regular units or to make a career. The army of the Russian Empire was dominated by the Russian nationality and Eastern Orthodoxy. Nor does the Soviet army resemble the defunct Austro-Hungarian army; even though about half of the Soviet population is made up of non-Russians, the language of the army is Russian and Russian alone, with scarce regard for the sensibilities of other ethnic groups. Moreover, the Soviet army practices "extraterritoriality," meaning that soldiers are generally stationed faraway from their home territory. Finally, the Soviet army discriminates against its non-Slavic minorities. In the words of two experts: "Combat units [in the Soviet army] are staffed by a clear majority of soldiers from the Slavic nationalities, usually 80 percent or more. Noncombat units usually contain 70 to 90 percent or more non-Slavs, especially Central Asians and Caucasians. Non-Slavs who serve in combat units often are relegated to support roles, such as in the kitchen or in the ware-houses."[1]

Probably only one major army, that of the Indian republic, could be said truly to resemble the Habsburg. It, too, is a multinational force, with no dominant ethnic group and a barely dominant religion; it uses a language or, rather, several languages of convenience; it suffers from the overrepresentation in its officer corps of certain confessional and ethnic groups, such as the Sikhs; and it preaches a supranational all-Indian ideology designed to override all ethnic, religious, and local considerations.

The Austro-Hungarian Joint Army used a language of convenience—German. It was the language of command and service, and the mother tongue of an absolute majority of its officers, but it was not the language of instruction or of communication with the rank and file, except in German-speaking units. In other units, the "regimental language" (or languages) was that of the ordinary soldiers and, as in today's Indian army, the Habsburg officer was required to learn to speak the language of his men. The peoples of the monarchy and hence its soldiers spoke ten major and scores of minor languages. Moreover, there was a vast discrepancy between the everyday languages of the officers and those of the rank and file. The latter were recruited more or less evenly from all nationalities, but the former included a much higher proportion of those groups with a tradition of military service and loyalty to the House of Austria or those with a relatively larger educated stratum.

To assess the influence of an army and its officers on a country's politics, society, economy, or culture requires caution. Existing views range all the way from such sweeping assertions as the statement that in Prussia "the army was not so much for the state, as the state for the army" to such modest views as the notion that in modern democracies the army is the obedient tool of the government and of the people who have elected that government. Some observers see a "military-industrial complex" in every capitalist state; others maintain that the foremost socialist state, the Soviet Union, exists solely for the purpose of military expansion. Military writers, for their part, tend to underplay the role of the army in state and society; for them, the army has always been a loyal, much neglected, and badly misunderstood instrument of those in power. Quite often, they see the army and its officers as the victims of reckless and irresponsible civilians.

There can be no doubt that the military, as a social institution and as a pressure group, has played a crucial role in modern history, a role that has hitherto been insufficiently explored, partly because of the reluctance of historians and intellectuals in general to deal with what they see as an unappealing body of men. The brutality, seeming aimlessness, and utter boredom of military life in peacetime repels almost as much as the carnage of war. Social historians study workers, peasants, maids, prostitutes, or slaves rather than such elite groups as an officer corps. Military historians concentrate on strategy, armaments, and campaigns; political historians study the politics of the generals. Only in recent years has the social history of the military emerged as a respectable discipline, resulting in several fine studies of the military as a factor in society, as well as studies of the life of officers and men.

Like the two other great dynastic empires, Prussia/Germany and Russia, the Habsburg monarchy was a militaristic state: the rulers of these countries viewed themselves first and foremost as soldiers. They accorded army officers an exalted status in society; imperial propaganda held up the officers as examples for all to follow; military service and a readiness to die in defense of the monarchy were proclaimed a fundamental duty and the supreme virtue; the authoritarian practices of the army and military discipline in general were imposed upon large segments of civilian society, from railroad men to schoolchildren and farm laborers, and the wearing of uniforms, often complete with a dagger or a sword, was a mark of distinction imposed upon and coveted by bureaucrats, students, and other groups. Finally, the officers' code of honor, putatively derived from the medieval concept of knighthood, was the accepted norm, at first among the nobles alone but later among all educated men.

Unlike German society, however, Austro-Hungarian society was distinctly un-warlike. Up to about the middle of the nineteenth century, political decisions were made by the ruler, by the imperial bureaucracy, and by the representatives of the nobility assembled in their several diets. Thereafter, political power passed increasingly into the hands of the governments of Austria and Hungary, their respective bureaucracies, and the two parliaments, in which the officer corps had neither representation—except for some retired officers—nor any real political clout. Throughout the period under examination, the military budget of Austria-Hungary was proportionally the smallest of all the European great powers. It is an apt comment on the political weakness of the army that, when Austro-Hungarian entrepreneurs finally discovered the financial benefits of military provisioning in the early twentieth century, the two governments and parliaments voted far more money, proportionally, for the equipping of a rather useless navy than for the army, despite the bitter protest of the military high command. The reason, aside from imperialist dreams, was that the construction and outfitting of battleships brought greater and more immediate benefits to heavy industry and the banks than did the equipping of the army. It can be argued, however, that sometime after 1906 the army's influence on politics began to grow, and that this influence, marked by an aggressiveness born of despair, may well have been one of the reasons for the monarchy's collapse.

If the Austro-Hungarian army's influence on politics and the economy was limited, its influence on the lifestyle and culture of the monarchy's population can hardly be overstated. Military service was the most formative experience in the life of the common man. The army took its recruits to faraway places, taught them personal hygiene as well as reading and writing, and inculcated in them a type of personal behavior that made the discharged soldier easily recognizable. The army experience may well have been brutal, but it was likewise unforgettable. As for the officers, their ideology and lifestyle penetrated an ever-widening circle of middle-class civilians thanks to the creation, in 1868, of a reserve officer corps. Whether a positive or a negative hero, the officer was a conspicuous figure on the dramatic stage, in operettas, novels, and the press, reflecting society's profound involvement with the officer corps on telling levels of fantasy and reality, and, through the officers, with the monarch and the monarchy.

The armed forces of the great European dynastic states traditionally served a dual purpose: to preserve the empire by preventing or suppressing domestic revolts and to enhance the glory of the ruling house in foreign wars. It is the thesis of this study that between 1848 and 1914, the army of the Habsburg dynasty accomplished the first task admirably, maintaining the empire merely by its presence and having to combat a major domestic revolt only in the first year of the period in question. But the army failed in its second task, decisively losing the two major wars that it fought. The war of 1859 against France and Sardinia and the war of 1866 against Prussia and Italy brought humiliation to the emperor and the loss of a few provinces. It is true that in 1878 the army was able to enrich the House of Austria by conquering Bosnia-Hercegovina, but only after a difficult struggle against the determined opposition of poorly armed guerrillas.

The peacetime successes and wartime failures of the Habsburg army between 1848 and 1914 were the result of many factors, most of them unrelated to the efficiency of the military. Domestic peace was assured among other things by growing prosperity, an industrial revolution, and the conservative loyalty and political simplicity of the peasants who provided the army with most of its recruits. Wartime defeat was brought about by the relative backwardness of the Austro-Hungarian economy and society, a paucity of funds, and the superior military leadership of France in 1859 and Prussia in 1866. But the dichotomy between domestic success and wartime failure was amplified by the fact that the army was trained and equipped primarily to maintain order at home. Military education and the ideology of the officer corps were well suited to stabilizing the monarchy within; they were far less useful for imperial expansion. Francis Joseph came to recognize this clearly, but only after he had lost two wars. In fact, the emperor became so sensitive to the role of his soldiers as representatives of monarchical grandeur that he stubbornly insisted on preserving traditional splendor even when it was clearly detrimental to wartime efficiency. Contemporaries and historians have tended to ascribe this to a lack of imagination, and even stupidity, but the emperor was probably correct in his sense that a cavalry squadron in gold-braided uniform, a military band playing a Sunday concert in every town of the empire, or a magnificent military parade on a feast day could contribute powerfully to a public sense of immutable stability.

In an age when the monarchy's inhabitants were inundated by every conceivable type of nationalist and social propaganda, when parliamentary deputies engaged in fist fights rather than legislation, the army and its foremost soldier, the emperor, offered a vision of peace, order, tolerance, and continuity. Only after the emperor had become very old, early in the twentieth century, did the army undergo a drastic reorganization under new leadership. It was then finally being trained for modern warfare and imperialist expansion. Contemporary domestic and international tensions, caused at least in part by army policy, drove the monarchy's political and military leaders to risk war as a means of diminishing those tensions.

Until the early years of the twentieth century, the education, training, and ideology of the officer corps were well suited to the emperor's domestic goals. The officers asked no questions; they were generally incorruptible; and they commanded respect. By contrast, the new military leadership created early in the twentieth century was increasingly politicized, often critical of the state, at once overly confident and overly pessimistic, and therefore more and more willing to seek spiritual and moral refuge in all-out war. By adopting its program in attacking Serbia in July 1914, the monarchy spelled its doom.

The two chapters that follow immediately sum up, in chronological order, the history of the army, with particular emphasis on the period between 1848 and 1914. This survey is followed by several chapters on key aspects of the life and mentality of the officers and, finally, two chapters on the Habsburg officers during and after World War I.

Throughout, the book attempts to demonstrate the uniqueness of the Habsburg officer corps as an institution that succeeded in preserving the multinational monarchy without applying more than a minimum of force. The achievement of this near-miracle was due to the fact that the officer corps was both a closed and an open institution: closed, because the officers, often themselves the sons of soldiers and living a life of political isolation, constituted a solid caste and a well-defined interest group, and because those officers who had been recruited from the lower classes, always a substantial group, felt a special loyalty to the army that had given them dignity and a special social status; but open, too, because of career officers' ready acceptance and ideological inspiration of thousands of reserve officers, drawn from the educated strata of the monarchy's myriad nationalities.

I hope to demonstrate as well that the officers and the army were a remarkably cohesive institution, at least until the second year of the First World War, when, because of the near annihilation of the pre-1914 standing army, fighting had to be shouldered by hastily trained men. One might even argue that the rest of the war was no longer the business of professionals but of a citizens' militia. Finally, I venture to show how the limited intellectual horizon of Francis Joseph was, paradoxically, a boon both to the army and to the peoples of the monarchy. A more imaginative and enterprising monarch might have exposed the officer corps to novel political ideas and influences, thereby hastening the collapse of the military edifice and thus of the monarchy as well. It is not easy to see what benefit its peoples would have derived from such a precipitous development, considering that even the relatively late collapse in 1918 brought no change for the better. The postwar successor states, which claimed to be based on national self-determination but were in reality almost all multinational states, showed little of the ethnic indifference of the emperor and the Habsburg army. Their economic weakness, social troubles, and mutual hatreds gave birth to a series of tragedies from which the peoples of the region have yet to recover.

Throughout, I hope to make apparent the historical dilemma presented by the disappearance of the supranational Habsburg dynasty. Clearly, the monarchy can never be reconstituted and, indeed, nothing could be more alien to a modern, Western lifestyle than a court and an army imbued by feudal values. But today, as we begin to accommodate the idea of a gradual disappearance of nation-states, to be replaced by a supranational state (at least in western Europe), it is worth remembering that the nation-states of central and east central Europe are likewise not an absolute historical given, that theirs, in fact, has been a very brief history. Two hundred years ago, there was not a single nation-state in the region, and one hundred years ago, only a few. In viewing the shifting scene of today's east central Europe, an area marked by economic backwardness, ethnic antagonisms, and moves toward democracy, it is of value to reexamine the Habsburg experiment, characterized, as it was, by a fundamentally decent administration, unheard-of liberties, economic progress, and a lack of political boundaries between the Carpathian mountains and the Swiss Alps. I am convinced that we can find here a positive lesson while the post-1918 history of the central and east central European nation-states can only show us what to avoid.

As already suggested, the story of the Habsburg army is played out against a background of enormous political, ethnic, and institutional complexity that owed what cohesion it had to the overarching authority of the ruling Habsburg dynasty. In the interest of clarity, it therefore seems essential, at the outset, to provide some overview of that dynastic establishment, of the varied peoples who inhabited its lands, and of the rank order and organizational structure of the army. This will be followed by a description of the rich archival and printed statistical sources that serve as the fundamental basis of this study. This study, of course, also draws upon a variety of other sources: memoirs, historical literature, and even belles-lettres. In the interests of brevity, however, detailed discussion of these sources has been relegated to an appendix.

A Note on the Dynasty and Its Peoples

The Habsburg family is known to have flourished as feudal lords in what is today Switzerland as early as the tenth century; Austria as a territorial unit is older still. The two were joined, however, only in the last decades of the thirteenth century, when Rudolph of Habsburg, elected German king and head of the Holy Roman Empire, gained possession of the Duchy of Austria, a Babenberg legacy. Since that time the word *Austria* has been a most confusing term, designating over time a dynasty as well as a territory of wildly varying size and importance.[2] In the sixteenth century, the House of Austria was the world's foremost ruling family, with possessions as far-flung as Hungary, Bohemia, the Netherlands, Spain, Mexico, Peru, and the Philippines. "Austria," as a geographical and political term, applied, alternately, to the old Duchy of Austria, around Vienna and to the west of the city, and to the Habsburg possessions in central and east central Europe. Today, of course, it is the name of a small republic.

After 1526, the Habsburgs wore the crowns, among others, of Spain, Bohemia, and Hungary, and they were also regularly elected, with a brief interruption in the eighteenth century, as heads of the Holy Roman Empire. However, in the sixteenth century, the Habsburg domains were divided between a "German" and a "Spanish" branch, the latter dying out in 1700.[3]

In 1806, Emperor Francis resigned himself to the liquidation of the Holy Roman Empire, but until 1866, the head of the Habsburg family continued to function as president of the German Confederation or Bund, an incoherent association of independent states. Hence, until 1866, the Habsburgs had a legal claim—and a keen desire—to meddle in the affairs of Germany. Nonetheless, what concerns us here is not so much the role the Habsburgs played as suzerains or presidents of the federation of German states as the authority they exercised over their family possessions in central and east central Europe.

In 1804, Francis adopted the title of Austrian emperor, and until 1867, the Austrian Empire or Austria included the following lands:

1. The so-called Hereditary Provinces, consisting of the archduchies of Lower Austria (capital: Vienna) and Upper Austria (capital: Linz); the Princely County of Tyrol with the Land of Voralberg; and the duchies of Salzburg, Styria, Carinthia, and Carniola. The latter province is now in Yugoslavia, as are the southern parts of Styria and Carinthia, whereas the southern half of the Tyrol is now part of Italy. The rest of the Hereditary Provinces constitute, along with a small part of the old Kingdom of Hungary, the territories of the Austrian Republic.

2. The lands of the Czech crown, namely, the Kingdom of Bohemia, the Margravate of Moravia, and the Duchy of Silesia, all of which are now in Czechoslovakia, except for a small section of Silesia that is part of Poland.

3. The Adriatic littoral (including Trieste) and the Kingdom of Dalmatia, both of which are in Yugoslavia today, except for a small piece in Italy.

4. The Kingdom of Lombardy (capital: Milan) and the former Venetian Republic, which now belong to Italy.

5. The Kingdoms of Galicia and Lodomeria, divided today between Poland and the Soviet Union, and the Duchy of Bukovina, now partly in the Soviet Union and partly in Romania.

6. Finally, the lands of the Hungarian Holy Crown, namely, the Kingdom of Hungary, the Grand Duchy of Transylvania, and the Kingdom of Croatia-Slavonia, the latter including the separately administered Military Border, or Grenze. Today these lands are divided among Hungary, Czechoslovakia, Romania, Yugoslavia, Austria, and the Soviet Union.

The Habsburgs lost Lombardy in 1859 and Venetia in 1866. In 1866 they were also expelled from the German Confederation, now dominated by a victorious Prussia. A year later, Francis Joseph was obliged to divide the Austrian Empire into halves, one centered in Vienna, the other in Budapest. Although joined by a number of common institutions, each half was now sovereign. This Dual Monarchy did not even have a capital, although Vienna continued to be regarded as such, and the emperor-king was legally bound to divide his attention equally between the two halves.

What were the two states called? The question is more complex than it might seem. Because its constituent provinces could agree on next to nothing, not even on a sensible name, the Dual Monarchy's non-Hungarian half was officially designated as "the Kingdoms and Lands Represented in the Reichsrat," the Reichsrat, or Imperial Council, being the parliament that met in Vienna. The other half of the Dual Monarchy went by the simpler name of "Lands of the Hungarian Holy Crown," and it included the Kingdom of Hungary, Transylvania (now united with Hungary), and the subordinate Kingdom of Croatia-Slavonia.

To complicate matters further, in 1878 the armies of the Dual Monarchy occupied the Turkish provinces of Bosnia and Hercegovina, although the region was not formally annexed until 1908. Attached simultaneously to both halves of the Dual Monarchy and administered by the joint minister of finance, Bosnia-Hercegovina was treated as a common acquisition, thus forming a third, though less than autonomous, part of the Dual Monarchy.

Obviously, we cannot—nor did anyone at the time—refer to the two halves of the Dual Monarchy by their ridiculously cumbersome official names. Instead, it became customary to talk of Cisleithania and Transleithania, from the small Leitha River east of Vienna which separated Hungary (Transleithania) from the other part. But these names, too, sound anachronistic and cumbersome today, and so the term "Austria" will be used here for that part of the monarchy which centered in Vienna, and "Hungary" for that part centering in Budapest. When referring to the two halves jointly, I shall use the terms "Dual Monarchy," "Austria-Hungary," or "Habsburg monarchy."*

Thus there was an Austria, by which people meant the part of the Dual Monarchy that was neither Hungary nor Bosnia-Hercegovina, but there was also a German-Austria, a term designating the Hereditary Provinces, and there were also Lower and Upper Austria, the two provinces around Vienna and Linz. If all this sounds complicated, so was administrative life in Austria-Hungary, to the point that statistics were generally drawn up separately for Austria, Hungary, and Bosnia-Hercegovina. Many statistics referring to the monarchy as a whole in this study represent either my own computations or those of other historians.

The monarchy was inhabited by eleven major and sundry smaller nationalities. While only a handful of Hungarians (Magyars) and Slovaks lived in Austria, and only a few Czechs, Poles, Slovenes, and Italians in Hungary, the other major ethnic

*Even though this is done again and again in Western history books, it would be incorrect to talk of a "Habsburg Empire" or "Austro-Hungarian Empire," because, after 1867, only Austria was an empire; Hungary was a kingdom or rather, two kingdoms. Nor would it do to write "Austrian Empire," as is so often done, because in Austria-Hungary the term was used exclusively to designate that part of the monarchy which was neither Hungary nor Bosnia-Hercegovina.

Table I.1. Population of the Habsburg Monarchy, 1910

Territory	Absolute Number	Percentage
Austria	28,571,934	55.6
Hungary	20,886,487	40.6
Bosnia-Hercegovina	1,931,802	3.8
Total	51,390,223	100.0

groups were well represented in both states. In fact, the cardinal rules of the monarchy's history were that ethnic and political frontiers did not coincide, and that its diverse nationalities were scattered pell-mell throughout its territories. After 1918, the so-called successor states valiantly strove to end this unhappy state of affairs, and they succeeded to a large degree, thanks to the use of such modern techniques as forced assimilation, persecution, and expulsion. In the entire Habsburg monarchy, only German-speaking Salzburg, Upper Austria, and Voralberg as well as the predominantly Serbo-Croatian-speaking Bosnia-Hercegovina can be said to have been monolingual lands. It should be noted, however, that Bosnia-Hercegovina had, and still has, terrible problems because of the division of its population into Catholic, Orthodox, and Muslim groups. All the other provinces included one or more ethnic minorities, unless they were, like the Bukovina, veritable mosaics of peoples. Moreover, most ethnic groups could be found simultaneously in several provinces, and even outside the monarchy. Serbo-Croatian speakers, for example, lived in southern Hungary, Croatia-Slavonia, Bosnia-Hercegovina, the Adriatic littoral, and Dalmatia, as well as in the independent Serbian Kingdom and the Ottoman Empire.

The totals in Tables I.1 and I.2, the result of my own computations, represent a less than perfect combination of the Austrian, Hungarian, and Bosnia-Hercegovinian statistics because I could not take into account the relatively small number of Czechs, Poles, and Slovenes in Hungary, and the Slovaks and Magyars in Austria. Consequently, these people fell into the "others" category, as did such small ethnic groups as Armenians, Greeks, Bulgarians, Albanians, Turks, and Gypsies. On the other hand, I was able to include in their appropriate national groups those non-Bosnians (mostly soldiers and bureaucrats) who resided in Bosnia-Hercegovina. All in all, it suffices to know that the so-called dominant nationalities, the Germans and the Magyars, together constituted 43 percent of the total population, the Slavs 45 percent, and the rest 12 percent.*

Some provinces were much more heterogeneous than others. Among those of most mixed nationality we find Silesia (with a population of 776,000 in 1914), in which 47 percent were counted as Germans, 30 percent as Poles, and 23 percent as Czechs; Galicia (population 8,812,000 in 1914), with 54 percent Poles, 43 percent

*Hungarians call themselves the Magyar nation and their country, Magyarország. In Hungary, all the inhabitants of the country, whether Hungarian-speaking or non-Hungarian-speaking, are called *magyarok* (Magyars). Nevertheless, I have opted for the practice—intensely disliked by many Hungarians—of differentiating between ethnic Hungarians and the others by writing Magyars in specific reference to the first group, and Hungarians in reference to all the inhabitants of the Hungarian kingdom.

Table I.2. Nationalities of the Habsburg Monarchy, 1910

Nationality	Absolute Number	Percentage
Germans	12,006,521	23.36
Czechs	6,442,133	12.54
Slovaks	1,967,970	3.83
Poles	4,976,804	9.68
Ruthenes (Ukrainians)	3,997,831	7.78
Slovenes	1,255,620	2.44
Serbs and Croats	4,380,891	8.52
Italians	768,422	1.50
Romanians	3,224,147	6.27
Hungarians (Magyars)	10,056,315	19.57
Others	2,313,569	4.51
Total	51,390,223	100.00

Ruthenes, and 3 percent Germans; and the Bukovina (population 818,000 in 1914), in which 42 percent spoke Ruthene, 32 percent Romanian, 21 percent German, and 5 percent other languages. Hungary—excluding Croatia-Slavonia but including the Adriatic city of Fiume—had a population of 18,261,533 in 1910, 54 percent of which spoke Hungarian, 16 percent Romanian, 11 percent German, 11 percent Slovak, 4 percent Serbo-Croatian, 3 percent Ruthene, and 1 percent some other language.*

Note that the methods of compiling ethnic statistic differed in the two halves of the monarchy, the Austrian census-takers inquiring about "language of communication" (*Umgangssprache*) and the Hungarians about "mother tongue" (*Muttersprache*—in Hungarian, *anyanyelv*). Since "language of communication" referred to that language which a person used most frequently in everyday life, it is clear that assimilation, mostly into a locally dominant nationality was more readily accepted in Austria than in Hungary. And yet, the Hungarian government was particularly keen to prove that the Magyars formed an absolute majority in their kingdom. Note, too, that Jews were not recognized as a separate nationality, and that Jews generally reported as their nationality the ethnic group into which they felt they were best integrated: in Galicia, Polish; in Hungary, Magyar; in Bohemia and Moravia, Czech or German. Yiddish-speaking Jews generally reported (or were counted) as Poles in Galicia, and as Germans in the Bukovina. Confessional statistics show that in 1910 Jews constituted 4.4 percent (2,258,013 people) of the monarchy's total population.

*The major sources for the above statistical tables and computations were Sixtus von Reden, *Österreich-Ungarn. Die Donaumonarchie in historischen Dokumenten* (Salzburg, 1984); *Hof- und Staatshandbuch der österreichisch-ungarischen Monarchie für das Jahr 1914*, XL (Vienna, 1914); *A Magyar Szent Korona Országainak 1910.évi népszámlálása* (The 1910 census of the Lands of the Hungarian Holy Crown), Part VI (Budapest, 1920); *Statistische Rückblicke aus Österreich* (Vienna, 1913); as well as Adam Wandruszka and Peter Urbanitsch, eds., *Die Völker des Reiches* ("Die Habsburgermonarchie 1848–1918," vol. 3; Vienna, 1980). Almost incredibly, the last work, although otherwise invaluable and containing hundreds of statistical compilations on its 1,471 pages, offers no comprehensive ethnic breakdown on the monarchy's total population.

It is important to remember that in the nineteenth century, despite wild nationalist agitation, many people were still unconscious of their nationality, especially in the less-developed eastern provinces. When questioned, some reported that they were "from here" or indicated a province or a county as their fatherland. Millions spoke two or more languages indiscriminately. That a large proportion of the monarchy's inhabitants were uncertain of their nationality or were ready to change it instantly is suggested by the vastly different and contradictory ethnic statistics published in the successor states after 1918. This means that despite the undoubted honesty of the monarchy's census-takers and statisticians, all data regarding nationality must be treated with skepticism. The same caution must apply to official military statistics on ethnicity, as we shall see later.

Place names in the monarchy reflected the same ethnic complexity. Thousands of communities, rivers, and mountains had two, three, or even four names, most of them in popular usage, others imposed by the authorities. Consequently, no matter which term historians use, they are bound here and there to wound someone's sense of national pride. Because this is a book on the German-speaking Joint Army, I shall be using German place names when available and not completely anachronistic. Thus, I shall write "Lemberg," not the Polish "Lwów," the Ukrainian "Lviv," or the Russian "Lvov." When a place has a commonly accepted English name, such as Prague or Vienna, this is the form that will be used. Our difficulties are compounded, however, by the army's catering to Hungarian sensibilities after 1867, which means that official Joint Army publications concerning Hungary consistently used Hungarian place names. Thus I shall be writing "Kassa," not the German "Kaschau" or the Slovak "Košice," even though this town is today in Slovakia. A multilingual nomenclature in Appendix II should satisfy the reader's curiosity in this respect.

As regards personal names, I shall again strictly adhere to military practice, as reflected in the Joint Army's annually published officers' rank list or *Militär-Schematismus*. This rank list carefully reproduced the ethnic spelling of family names (thus referring to the South Slav field marshal as "Boroević" and not the German "Boroewitsch"), but it translated all first names into German, resulting, for example, in my father's being listed as Stephan rather than István Deák. Officers' rank lists published by the Hungarian National Guard or honvédség rendered all first names in Hungarian, except for Croatian officers, whose first names appeared in Serbo-Croatian.

If all this sounds complicated, consider that in the Austrian parliament fist fights erupted over the proper ethnic name of one small town or another, and that in the Hungarian parliament one would have been denounced as a traitor for referring to Francis Joseph as emperor rather than king.

On Ranks and Titles

Officers' ranks will often be noted in the text; they will be rendered in English, except in the case of generals, whose ranks differed confusingly from those used in the U.S. and British armies. For example, an Austro-Hungarian general with the

Table I.3. Ranks in the Habsburg Army (after 1908)

Rank Category		Rank	Approximate U.S. Equivalent	Usual Field Assignment
General officers	I	Feldmarschall	General of the Army (five-star)	Group of armies
	II	Generaloberst (introduced in 1915)	General (four-star)	Army (100–200,000)
	III	General der Infanterie; General der Kavallerie; Feldzeugmeister (artillery, engineers)	Lieutenant general (three-star)	Army or Corps (30–40,000)
	IV	Feldmarschalleutnant	Major general (two-star)	Division (15–20,000)
	V	Generalmajor	Brigadier general (one-star)	Brigade (2 regiments; 6–8,000)
Field-grade officers	VI	Oberst	Colonel	Regiment (3–4,000)
	VII	Oberstleutnant	Lieutenant colonel	Independent battalion or deputy regimental commander
	VIII	Major	Major	Battalion (1,000)
Subalterns	IX	Hauptmann Rittmeister (cavalry, train)	Captain	Company (200–250)
	X	Oberleutnant	First lieutenant	Deputy company commander or commander of platoon
	XI	Leutnant	Second lieutenant	Platoon (50)
Ensigns	XII	Fähnrich	—	Platoon

splendid rank of Feldmarschalleutnant had, in reality, only two stars and was consequently merely equal to a British or U.S. major general. A Habsburg Generalmajor wore one star and was therefore at the same level as a U.S. brigadier general or a British brigadier. I include here a table of Austro-Hungarian officers' ranks, along with their approximate command responsibilities and U.S. equivalents (table I.3).

Naval officers and those serving in special branches of the army had ranks different from those listed in table I.3, but all were fitted neatly into the overall rank categories. Thus, an admiral was in the same third-ranking category as a three-star army general; a Linienschiffskapitän was equal to an army colonel, and a Linienschiffsleutnant to an army captain. Medical officers, chaplains, judge advocates, and other military officials such as technical personnel had their own fancy ranks, with a Feldbischof (military bishop) being equivalent to a Feldmarschalleutnant, the Feldrabbiner der IX. Rangklasse (military rabbi, IX. rank category) and Regimentsarzt (regimental medical officer) having the rank of captain, the Militärbaurechnungsakzessist (accounting clerk in the military construction office) being ranked with an army lieutenant, and the Abteilungsvorstand des Marine-hydro-

Table I.4. Subalterns (*Oberoffiziere*) in the Habsburg Army

Rank Category	Before 1850	1850–1866	1867–1868	1869–1907	1908–1918
IX	Hauptmann	Hauptmann I. Classe	Hauptmann I. Classe	Hauptmann I. Classe	Hauptmann (Ritt-meister in cavalry and train)
IX	Capitän-Leutnant	Hauptmann II. Classe	Hauptmann II. Classe	Hauptmann II. Classe	
X	Oberleutnant	Oberleutnant	Oberleutnant	Oberleutnant	Oberleutnant
XI	Unterleutnant	Unterleutnant I. Classe			
XI	Fähnrich	Unterleutnant II. Classe	Unterleutnant	Leutnant	Leutnant
XII	Cadet	Cadet	Cadet	Cadet-Offiziers-Stellvertreter	Fähnrich

graphischen Amtes (section head in the naval hydrographical office) with a lieutenant colonel.

The ranks of army subalterns changed often and bewilderingly between 1848 and 1914, as illustrated in table I.4.

The strict hierarchical order of the officer corps manifested itself in countless ways, among other things in the appellation due the various ranks. Two-star generals and above were to be addressed as *Exzellenz;* field-grade officers were entitled to a *Hochwohlgeboren* (highly well-born); whereas those below the rank of captain had to be satisfied with a mere *Wohlgeboren.* Every military rank corresponded to one in the civil service, but as we shall see later, civil servants received more money. Also, quite surprisingly for a state in which officers had automatic access to the imperial-royal court but civil servants did not, civilian authorities enjoyed precedence over military ones at official ceremonies, religious services, and religious processions. As the military handbook noted, only in a garrison church was the high military authority allowed to occupy the choice pews normally reserved for the civilian leadership.[4]

On Army Units and the Command Structure

The heart of a traditional army was the regiment, and in this book many more references will be made to it than to any other unit. First formed in the seventeenth century by military entrepreneurs, great lords, or diets, regiments were distinguished by individual customs, distinctive uniform, and the self-contained life of their officer corps. In the early days, a regiment was under the authority of its owner or Regimentsinhaber. He decided whom the unit would serve, for how long, and for what pay; he had absolute judicial authority; he named and promoted the officers; he authorized or forbade marriages; he paid the officers and the rank and file; and he was the only source of pensions. The colonel acting as his deputy merely oversaw the everyday operations of the regiment.

All this was to change in the eighteenth century as regiments were gradually subjected to central authority, symbolized by the adding of a number to their name and their adoption of the uniform of their supreme warlord, the emperor. By 1868, the regimental proprietors or "colonels-in-chief" had lost the last vestiges of their authority, whether administrative, economic, or judicial. After that date, the regimental proprietor, whether a foreign prince, Habsburg archduke, great aristocrat, or, as was increasingly the case, a superannuated general, had scarcely any privileges other than the fact that the regiment bore his name (either in perpetuity or temporarily) and the right to don, on solemn occasions, the uniform of the regiment. The real authority was now the colonel, but he, in turn, had become a paid servant of the state, a mere military functionary.

Throughout the course of this transformation, the regimental officer corps made strenuous efforts to preserve something of the tradition and the individuality of their units. The 8th Bohemian Dragoons were entitled to march unannounced across the grounds of the imperial palace once a year. In addition, their commander had the right to appear before the emperor, unannounced and dressed for combat. The 14th Bohemian Dragoons were exempted from the compulsory rule (until 1869) to wear a moustache. The 28th Bohemian Theodor Graf Baillet de Latour Infantry engaged only blond officers, at least until the middle of the nineteenth century. In the 7th Carl Freiherr Kress von Kressenstein Chevaux-légers (light cavalry) Regiment all the officers sported a beard. Others were entitled to a small distinctive mark on their flags. Nonetheless, by the second half of the nineteenth century, all regiments wore garb issued by the Ministry of War, and the main distinction among them was the service arm to which they belonged, such as infantry, cavalry, or artillery. True, in the infantry and cavalry there was also the distinction of the regimental "facing color" and the "button color" on the collars and cuffs of their uniform, but it took a superbly trained eye to distinguish, let us say, between the "imperial yellow" facing color and "yellow metal" button color of the 2nd Alexander I, Kaiser von Russland Infantry Regiment, and the "sulphur yellow" facing color and "yellow metal" button color of the 16th General Giesl von Gieslingen Infantry Regiment. Still, these minute differences and, of course, the tradition of the regiment, were considered to be of supreme importance, and an officer's loyalty was always to his regiment, not to his company, battalion, division, or army corps. The regiment was said to be the officer's family even after 1868, when promotion was no longer within the regiment but within the arm of service as a whole.

The regimental officer corps protected the "honor of the regiment," and no one could serve in the regiment, or marry, or retain his rank without the consent of the regimental officers' assembly. By the end of the nineteenth century, however, some of these regimental rights had become merely symbolic. And, even though some regiments were definitely more respectable and honorable than others, the Habsburg army never developed a system of guards regiments, those elite formations so characteristic of the British, Russian, and Prussian armies.

All this does not mean that regiments were always kept together, or that each regiment was self-contained. On the contrary, before the reform period, the regiment's two trained battalions, known as Linienbataillone, were usually stationed faraway from regimental headquarters, and regiments seldom marched into battle as

Table I.5. Armed Forces of the Habsburg Monarchy, 1900

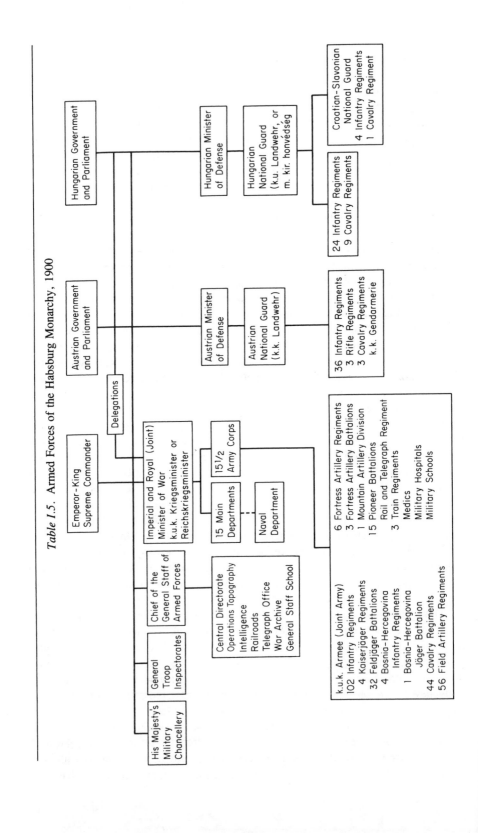

a single unit. After the 1880s, as we shall see, regiments were usually kept near their recruiting bases but even so were dispersed territorially. The smallest administrative unit was the company, of which there were about sixteen in a regiment. The smallest self-contained strategic force was the division, which comprised several regiments as well as specialized formations. An army division could fight a battle unaided, but a regiment, made up only of infantrymen, or cavalry, or artillery, could not. Still, an officer was at all times identified by his regiment or, in the case of the light infantry (Jäger) and some technical formations, by his independent battalion. All this gave the regimental commander great prestige and extraordinary moral responsibility.[5]

This book will also refer occasionally to army organization and the command structure. Both changed frequently and, after 1868, they became immensely complicated, partly because of the control exercised—via the so-called Delegations—of the Austrian and Hungarian parliaments over the armed forces, and partly because of the creation, in 1868, of the National Guards. In table I.5, presented for later reference, I have attempted to show how the system was constructed, but it is impossible to illustrate all the complexities graphically. For instance, the chief of the general staff of the armed forces (Chef des Generalstabes der gesammten bewaffneten Macht), administratively subordinated to the joint minister of war, was operational head not only of the Joint Army but also of the National Guards, but his administrative superior, the joint minister of war, had no authority over the National Guards.

The Archival Evidence

Centuries of bureaucratic punctiliousness have left their mark in a truly marvelous mass of documentation on the Habsburg army and its officer corps. In the eighteenth century, when much of the monarchy was still wallowing in the chaos created by amateurish elected administrations, well-trained military officials were already piling up mountains of paper on the life and activities of the soldiers. They registered the vital statistics of millions of recruits, issued absurdly detailed instructions to the troops, recorded the proceedings of courts-martial, filed petitions from soldiers and their widows and orphans, and corresponded extensively with the civilian authorities. Most important, however, for the purposes of this monograph, the military bureaucracy assembled minutely detailed information on every officer who wore the emperor's uniform from the reign of Maria Theresa to the end of the First World War.

The officer's *Conduite-Liste* (rechristened *Qualifikations-Liste* in the mid-nineteenth century) was updated each year and recorded such data as his name and noble predicate (if any); his place and date of birth; his legal domicile; his confessional affiliation and any changes in same; his father's occupation; his education and training (including a list of all schools and professional courses attended, grades received, and occasionally a complete transcript); his marital status and, if married, the value and nature of the marriage bond (*Heiratskaution,* a deposit made to the treasury by the bride or the groom, the interest on which was paid out to the married couple); the number, age, and sex of this children and whether or not the military authorities had already taken care of their education; his financial circumstances, including his private income and the total amount and nature of his indebtedness. There followed a complete description of the officer's professional career, including all promotions and transfers as well as changes in the location of his regiment; his familiarity with the different provinces, rivers, and mountains of the realm; his foreign travels; his special skills and aptitude, if any, for music and fine arts; and his familiarity with languages spoken inside and outside the monarchy, along with an annual evaluation of his mastery of them. The records also contained the annual evaluations, by the officer's superiors, of his ability to lead his men, get along with his comrades, and show proper respect to his commanders. They also evaluated his skill in riding, fencing, and target shooting, his proclivity for drinking or gambling, and, in general, his demeanor as an officer and a gentleman. They took into account his suitability for such special tasks as mapping, teaching, and general staff work; the rate at which he should be promoted and whether he qualified for higher command posts; the state of his health; his ability to withstand the rigors of a campaign; his battlefield valor; the citations and decorations he had received; and any breaches of discipline or appearances before the officers' court of honor or courts-martial.

Commanders were given precise instructions regarding the completion of the *Qualifikations-Listen,* which had to be brought up to date by September 30 of each year, with a copy sent to the Ministry of War. The evaluation was performed by a commission made up of the officer's superiors, with the lowest-ranking member of the commission presenting the first opinion. The record had to be signed by every commission member, but brigade and division commanders usually merely indicated that they were not personally acquainted with the officer in question. Colonels and generals were evaluated on a special form, known as the *Hauptberichte.* Dissenting opinions had to be entered and signed separately. The reports were secret, but an officer had to be warned in writing of all correctable shortcomings. He was also told if, as a result of inadequacy, he had been assigned a lower spot on the seniority list.[6]

At the same time, these voluminous personal records, often amounting to dozens of folio sheets, leave many questions unanswered. During the premodern period (that is, before 1868) in particular, they often simply list a father's occupation as "nobleman," "burgher," or "soldier"; even later it was sometimes simply described as "farmer," "merchant," or "official," without any further specification. The names of an officer's mother and wife were scarcely ever recorded; references to his wealth and private income were generally incomplete, and the true reasons for any sudden pensioning or resignation can only be inferred from earlier comments made by superiors. The date of an officer's death was recorded only occasionally, as an afterthought, and then always in pencil. Among other things, it quickly became clear to me that evaluations of language skills had to be treated with caution. Military law formally prescribed a serious penalty—no promotion—for those officers who failed the demanding task of mastering the regimental language or languages. Hence, it is not surprising that sooner or later officers' language skills were almost invariably judged "adequate for the needs of service."

It also became evident to me that one had to read between the lines in most comments on performance, both general and specific, which as a rule ranged from "fairly good" to "excellent," the accepted custom apparently being to damn with faint praise. A "good shot" was a poor marksman indeed, and a "fairly good rider" did not know how to ride a horse. A colonel judged "well qualified to command a regiment" would somehow never be entrusted with such a responsibility; one had to be "eminently qualified." Clearly the Austrian army was plagued by the same kind of inflation of grades as are U.S. Army effectiveness reports or American college reports today. At the same time, there must have been a great deal of bias, prejudice, and personal enmity hidden behind some of these conventional phrases. The frequency of biased evaluations cannot be determined, of course; the fact remains, however, that each and every annual evaluation had to be signed by an officer's superiors, from the company commander all the way up to the general commanding his division. One must assume that the opinion of one's immediate superior was generally accepted by the higher-ups, although there were also many instances of dissenting opinions, always spelled out in writing.

These personal documents have one other major deficiency, irritating to the researcher but no doubt a real blessing to contemporaries. Neither the older *Conduite-Listen* nor the newer *Qualifikations-Listen* contain the slightest reference to an officer's ethnic origin or mother tongue, such considerations being of no importance to the antinationalist Habsburg army. This information can only be inferred from other sources.

The records have been carefully preserved in the Vienna War Archive, where they fill some 4,500 large boxes in a vast and dismal casemate. Despite their evident shortcomings, they are an inestimable historical source of which I have attempted to make good use.

The method I chose for drawing a collective portrait of the officers was to concentrate on two cohorts, those who were career lieutenants in 1870 and those who held this rank in 1900. Since the first generation was born generally between 1840 and 1850 and the second between 1870 and 1880, the careers of the two groups embrace virtually the entire period under investigation here. A random selection was made of every tenth lieutenant in each group, as culled from the rank lists of officers contained in the *Militärschematismen* for the years 1871 and 1901. Because each list contained the names of approximately 5,000 career lieutenants, the result was a representative sample of approximately 500 (486 and 517, to be precise) from each group. Much of what will be said in this monograph is based on an analysis of the 1,000-odd lieutenants.

Such a method has its advantages and disadvantages. Obviously, some lieutenants were considerably older than others, the maximum age being fifty-one and the minimum eighteen in the 1870 cohort, and forty-six and nineteen in the 1900 cohort, but these extremes were very exceptional. My earlier attempt to select from the *Militärschematismen* only lieutenants who had been commissioned in the same year had to be abandoned, because in some branches of service the number of lieutenants commissioned fluctuated wildly from year to year.

My final list includes a random sample of all those who belonged to the combat forces: the infantry, light infantry (Jäger), cavalry, artillery, engineers and other technical branches, transports (Train), medics,* gendarmerie, and horse-farm staff. I also included representatives of those military officials (Militärbeamten) who were attached to the combat branches, namely medical officers, judge advocates, and troop accountants (Truppen-Rechnungsführer).† I excluded the reserve officers, who were in reality civilians. I also excluded the chaplains, who were attached to the combat branches but whose confessional affiliation was a given and would have weakened my statistics on the confessional makeup of the corps.

Some concessions to reality had to be made: by 1900, medical officers and judge advocates—now all boasting a university education—began their careers as first lieutenants rather than lieutenants; these, then, were the ones included in my selection.

Other problems presented themselves. After 1907 the traditional *Qualifikations-Listen* were replaced with a shorter and less revealing questionnaire, and during World War I, *Qualifikations-Listen* were not maintained at all; instead, a much shorter *Vormerkungsblatt* (preparatory sheet) was drawn up hastily by frontline commanders. This means that whereas the records of the 1870 generation are virtually complete (only a handful of those who had been lieutenants in 1870 continued to serve after 1914), the records of the 1900 cohorts are uneven and incomplete, although the latter make more exciting reading.

Subalterns, such as a lieutenant, were still on probation, and many of those who fell into the random sample proved to have very brief careers, resigning within a year or two. Obviously, a representative sample of field-grade officers (majors, lieutenant colonels, and colonels) or a complete list of generals would have been equally possible as the focus for my study, but this would have offered merely a look at an elite within an elite. The method I have selected ought to show both the kind of men who became officers in the Habsburg army and the kind who made a genuine career of the military.

Next to the officers' personal records, the most important body of data for this study is found in Austrian and Hungarian statistical publications, all of them very thorough and reliable. Their primary source of information was the census, carried out at ten-year intervals beginning in 1780 and perfected in the second half of the nineteenth century. The armed forces, as the oldest and largest bureaucratic organization in the monarchy, compiled and published its own detailed statistics. The most important, the *Militär-Statistisches Jahrbuch,* was issued, for some unknown reason, only for the years 1870–1911. Compiled and published by the Third Section of the Joint War Ministry's Technical and Administrative Military Committee,‡ each

---

*Medics, a relatively small service arm, were in charge of giving first aid and of transporting wounded and ill soldiers to the hospital. They are not to be confused with the medical corps, made up of university-trained medical officers.

†Defined in the best Germanic bureaucratic style as *Militärgeistlichkeit, die dem Soldatenstande nicht angehörenden Offiziere, die Militärbeamten, und die sonstigen im Heeresverbande befindlichen, im Gagebezuge stehenden Personen,* military officialdom included, among others, the chaplains, medical officers, judge advocates, troop accountants, commissioners, technicians, general accountants, and civilian teachers at military schools. Not all of them had officer's rank, although those in whom we are primarily interested did, namely, the chaplains, doctors, judges, and troop accountants.

‡After 1890, the Ministry of War was no longer called the k.k. [*kaiserlich-königliches*, imperial-royal] Reichs-Kriegs-Ministerium but the k.u.k. [*kaiserliches und königliches*] Reichskriegsministerium,

yearbook contained several hundred pages and reported in extraordinary detail on, among other things, the health and physical condition of the recruits, their vital statistics and civilian occupation, and the reasons for the rejection of some. Detailed statistics were provided, moreover, on casualties suffered by the troops and the number and nature of illnesses, suicides, desertions, courts-martial, prison sentences, and executions. The figures were compiled by recruiting district but also cumulatively, in absolute numbers and in percentages.

The military yearbooks reported in detail on military schools, cadets, and, last but not least, the officer corps, including the number and proportion of those on active duty, in the reserve, and in retirement, the age breakdown of these groups by rank and service branch, their careers in relation to the schools or special training courses they had attended, and the military campaigns in which they had participated. Also recorded were the officers' confessional and ethnic breakdown—the latter only between 1897 and 1911—the numbers and proportion of each such group in the different arms of service, the number and nature of promotions, and the number of those who had left service, along with the reasons for their departure. Unfortunately, not every one of these statistical analyses was provided every year, and nowhere, in the yearbooks themselves or in the archives, does there seem to be a written explanation of the methods used in compiling the statistics.

I have looked at other kinds of archival sources, of course, among them the papers of the War Ministry, the military schools, and the military courts. I was able, for example, to locate the court-martial records of almost every officer in my sample who was tried for one reason or another. In addition, I examined the records of a great number of other interesting trials involving officers that I was able to identify using a contemporary index of court-martial proceedings between 1896 and 1915.

Work in the Vienna War Archive was complemented by research in the Budapest War Archive. In the latter, I was able to assemble, among other things, a random selection of two hundred honvéd (Hungarian National Guard) officers. This sample consists of two equal-sized groups: those who were lieutenants in 1880 and those in 1900. Here, too, some concessions had to be made to reality. In 1870, the honvéd army, established only two years earlier, was still in the process of formation. Hence, my choice of the generation of 1880 instead. Even a cursory examination reveals that honvéd lieutenants lagged significantly behind their counterparts in the Joint Army in terms of training, experience, travel, and linguistic skill but not in social standing, many honvéd officers having been recruited from among the Hungarian nobility. It is also clear, however, that by 1900 the honvéd army had become much more like the Joint Army.

This undertaking necessitated several research trips to Vienna and Budapest and many months of work in the two war archives. Even so, I am painfully aware that thousands of documents relating to the life of the officers have had to be left untouched. Nor have I been able so much as to cast a glance at the military archives

---

and in 1910, it was renamed k.u.k. Kriegsministerium. Both of these seemingly meaningless changes marked a Hungarian political victory, for the addition of the conjunction *und* was as important from a Hungarian point of view as the omission of the word Reich. They underlined the Hungarian claim that the two halves of the monarchy were joined by mutual agreement only, and that Hungary was most definitely not part of the Reich, or empire.

of Czechoslovakia, Poland, Romania, Yugoslavia, and Italy, all of which house large quantities of material relating to the Habsburg army. At the Paris peace conference following World War I, it was decided that each of the successor states would have the right to cull from the Vienna central archives all documents that referred specifically to its domestic affairs. The result was chaos. Because it was impossible to oversee the vast documentary collections in the several Vienna central archives, and because it was extremely difficult to distinguish between documents of national and supranational character, records were removed from Vienna more or less at random. In the case of the *Qualifikations-Listen,* the records of officers who ended up serving in the army of one of the successor states were sometimes left in Vienna, other times transported to the war archives of the new state, and in still other cases were divided between the two. To give but one example, the personal records of my father, a first lieutenant in the reserve, who served in a Joint Army fortress artillery regiment during World War I, were taken to Budapest after the war, but the papers which referred to his brief training in Vienna as a searchlight specialist remained in Austria.

A final remark on the physical condition and legibility of the documents. Unlike many printed publications from around the turn of the twentieth century, which are rapidly crumbling, these archival papers are in mint condition. The texts were handwritten, of course, until after 1900, when typewritten documents began to make their appearance. German handwriting (*Deutsche Schrift*) has its problems, but documents written or copied by the scribes are quite legible, as are most other official papers written by officers and NCOs, all of whom were drilled in calligraphy.

1

From the Turkish Wars
to the Revolutions of 1848:
An Early History

Feudal Levies, Border Troops, and the Army
of the Enlightened Despots

The European standing armies originated from such motley forces as feudal levies, mercenary companies, town and peasant militias, and princely body guards, none of which was permanent in character. The levies and militias went home, the mercenaries turned into bandits, the standing armies of the Renaissance princes had to be disbanded because of lack of money as well as the unwillingness of noble estates to tolerate their presence. The Habsburg possessions were no exception to this rule; they even provided a perfect example of reckless princely ambition, estate hostility, and desperate shortage of funds. The sixteenth-century Habsburgs were obliged to dissipate their energies in fighting simultaneously against the Ottomans, the French, the German Protestant princes, the unruly nobles in their own domains, and often their own troops. For all this, there was never enough money. The estates regularly denied their ruler the necessary funds, often on religious grounds, and the ruler spent his meager resources on winning followers and on ruinously expensive marriage contracts. So the Habsburgs borrowed, from the Fuggers and the Welsers in the sixteenth century, and from Jewish army agents and such military entrepreneurs as Albert of Wallenstein in the next. The bankers were ruined in the process, and when Wallenstein became too powerful, he was assassinated (in 1634) at the suggestion of Emperor Ferdinand II, perhaps the first instance of the legendary "Habsburg ingratitude" that was to mark relations between the ruler and his great captains well into World War I.

According to Gunther E. Rothenberg, the history of the early Habsburg army can be divided into three periods: (1) from 1522 to about 1625, when certain basic institutions were established; (2) the seventeenth and early eighteenth centuries, when the standing army slowly became a reality and Austria became a great power; and (3) from 1744 to 1815, when the military was transformed into a reliable state instrument capable of withstanding the strain of the Prussian and French wars.[1]

Strangely, the first permanent military institution in the Habsburg realm was not a standing army but a craggy line of frontier defenses, begun in 1522 to ward off the Ottomans; it was manned by mercenaries, local militia, and most significantly, armed peasants organized into military colonies. This was the famous Military Border (Militärgrenze), which cut across Croatia-Slavonia and Hungary but which, following the expulsion of the Turks at the end of the seventeenth century, was permanently shifted to the southern border of these two countries. Eventually, the Border expanded to cover the entire southern frontier, extending from the highlands above the Adriatic to the Eastern Carpathians, deep inside present-day Romania. Controlled directly from Vienna until its dissolution in 1881, the Grenze was essential for the survival of the monarchy, but it was also a source of recurring conflict with the Hungarian, Transylvanian, and Croatian estates, who claimed the Military Border for themselves.

At first, the Grenze was more of an irritant than a blessing. Made up in large part of Christian refugees from the Balkans, the Border Guards or Grenzer fought not only the Turks but one another, neighboring landowners, and the Habsburgs. When dispatched to participate in European campaigns, they made themselves notorious for plundering. Only in the mid-eighteenth century, under Maria Theresa, were the Grenzer finally disciplined and organized into eighteen infantry regiments, eleven of which were in Croatia-Slavonia. These regiments were more than military units; they constituted distinct territorial entities, each subdivided into smaller territories called companies. The officers in charge were both military commanders and governors responsible for the economy, social organization, and educational system of their territory. The inhabitants of the Military Border, including women and children, were legal subjects of the regiment, which strictly regulated their lives. Service obligation extended to every adult male, and it consisted of active duty in the line battalions, manning the watchtowers of the Border, guarding the line (Kontumazlinie) established to ward off the cholera and the plague, being on call to repel incursions from the south, and for older men, forming a reserve of last resort.

In exchange for these services, the Grenzer enjoyed many privileges. The roads and public buildings in their area were constructed by army engineers (with Grenzer labor it is true, a much resented corvée); their sons were given free elementary-school education and, if talented, were sent to cadet schools and could become officers. The Grenzer were not serfs and therefore recognized no feudal lord; they owed no obligation in labor, cash, or kind to any landowner. Unlike the other peasants in the Lands of the Hungarian Holy Crown, they were not under the authority of the noble-dominated county administrations. They enjoyed confessional freedom even in the early period when peasants elsewhere were obliged to embrace the confession practiced by their lord. In Croatia-Slavonia, the Grenzer were allowed to preserve their ancestral social organization, the zadruga, an extended family under the authority of a patriarch. The lands of the zadruga were inalienable and remained in the family. Still, these privileges were not universally appreciated, for discipline was harsh; the Grenzer regiments were poor, often suffering famine, and if the military colonies were of true benefit to refugees from the Balkans and to many Serbian, Croatian, and Romanian peasants (which did not prevent them from revolting from time to time), they were considered enslavement by others. The Székelys (or Seklers), for instance, a free Hungarian tribe in eastern Transylvania, revolted bloodily in 1764 after Maria Theresa transformed a part of their ancestral land into two Grenzer regiments.

In its final version, the Militärgrenze comprised an ethnic mosaic of Catholic Croats, Orthodox Serbs, German and Romanian settlers in the Banat region, and Romanians as well as Seklers in Transylvania. There were even a few Grenzer cavalry regiments, and a battalion of Serbian river guards in southern Hungary.[2]

The Court War Council, or Hofkriegsrat, was the second lasting military institution to emerge in the monarchy.[3] Created by Emperor Ferdinand I in 1556, this mixed military-civilian body survived until 1848, when its place was taken by the Ministry of War. Following a period of instability in the sixteenth century, when there were three competing court war councils, the Hofkriegsrat was placed in charge of the entire military administration, recruitment, and the conduct of war. At all times, the Court War Council (as well as its successor, the Ministry of War) struggled with provincial opposition to the concept of a centralized military bureaucracy. The independent German princes of the Holy Roman Empire never submitted to its authority, nor did several provinces within the Habsburg possessions. The Hungarians in particular regarded the association of their kingdom with the rest of the monarchy as one between sovereign states, and they insisted on voting their own military budget and raising their own recruits. Yet at least in regard to Bohemia, a major breakthrough was achieved during the Thirty Years' War, when the Czech nobles were defeated at the Battle of White Mountain in 1620, and the so-called Revised Land Ordinance of 1627 deprived the Bohemian estates of their military rights. Thereafter, the Hofkriegsrat gradually established its absolute authority over most of the Austrian Hereditary Provinces as well as Bohemia, Moravia, and Silesia.

In time, a fundamental and lasting division emerged between those Habsburg possessions in which the Hofkriegsrat was more or less free to raise recruits and those, such as Hungary, Transylvania, "Civil Croatia," the Tyrol, and the Austrian Netherlands (after 1714), in which recruitment and military appropriations remained the privilege of the local diets.

There were, in the seventeenth and early eighteenth centuries, some great Habsburg captains, such as Wallenstein, who served the Habsburg throne in the Thirty Years' War, and Count Raimondo Montecuccoli, who defeated the Turks at St. Gotthard in 1664. Most notable was the great Eugene of Savoy, who helped liberate Hungary from the Ottomans at the end of the seventeenth century and defeated the Turks in the war of 1716–1718. In the intervening period, he won resounding victories, with the British general Marlborough, over the French in the War of the Spanish Succession (1701–1714). But the Austrian standing army remained ill-organized and demonstrated a near-fatal weakness in the Turkish wars of 1738–1739 and against Frederick the Great after 1740.

Finally, it was Maria Theresa (reigning in 1740–1780 as "king" of Hungary and Bohemia) who, assisted by talented advisers, created a genuine standing army that was able to stop the Prussians. Patched together from a few already functioning Habsburg regiments, mercenary formations, and units raised by various estates and great aristocrats, Maria Theresa's new army numbered up to 200,000 men in peacetime, and it came to be supported by a fine artillery that remained the pride of the Habsburg forces until the very end. The army was divided into permanently established regiments, each with its own number as well as name; German was made the universal language of command and service; the troops were provided with uniforms and interchangeable weapons; a military academy and technical schools were established; and drill and discipline were standardized, as were military justice, medical care, military education, and the commissioning of officers. No less important for the future of the army, Maria Theresa—who was obliged to wage wars against the German princes and who personally could not become emperor—took the first steps toward making her forces "Austrian" as opposed to German. When her husband was crowned emperor in 1745, she ordered that her army be called "imperial-royal" (*kaiserlich-königliche Armee* or *k.k. Armee*), and that the black and yellow Habsburg colors be displayed in her forces to signify the political unity of her family possessions.[4]

All this did not mean the end of domestic difficulties. Recruitment remained uneven, with Hungary, the Tyrol, northern Italy, and the Austrian Netherlands (Belgium) continuing to contribute less than their share. Although the monarchy had lost most of Silesia, its richest province, to Frederick the Great, the Habsburg lands were becoming increasingly prosperous. Nonetheless, military appropriations remained grossly inadequate. The acquisition of Galicia in 1772 and the Bukovina in 1775 remained—for a long time—more of a financial and political burden than benefit. Nor could Maria Theresa or her son Joseph II (who became co-regent in 1765) decide where the monarchy's foreign interests lay. They insisted on preserving the Habsburg presence in Germany and Italy, yet they also participated in the partition of Poland, and Joseph in particular attempted to compete with Russia in southeastern Europe. The result was a further dissipation of energy, and because there were now no commanders of the caliber of Eugene of Savoy, there were bloody defeats: in the Seven Years' War against Prussia between 1756 and 1763, and in Joseph's unfortunate Turkish war of 1788–1789. Joseph's attempts to modernize and centralize everything in his realm, from the administration and the educational system to the military establishment and the rights of peasants led to provincial resistance and a virtual state of war in Hungary and Belgium. He died in 1790, a self-confessed failure, but left behind a tradition of bureaucratic centralism forever associated with his name. "Josephinism" had become markedly progressive under his rule, but later it lost much of its original ideological content and came to mean not only bureaucratic efficiency but also punctiliousness.*

*Archduke Charles, the Austrian commander in chief between 1806 and 1809, cited as an example the case of a Kürassier (heavy cavalry) officer who had petitioned the Hofkriegsrat for a remuneration of six Dukats, termed a "Douceur," for having done service with his own horse for twelve years. At the end, the horse was shot out from under the officer, but still he had seen no money. The officer's request had gone through twenty-six hands before it reached the emperor; then, on its way back, it went again through the hands of twenty-two bureaucrats, for a total of forty-eight. (Georg Nitsche, *Österreichisches Soldatentum im Rahmen deutscher Geschichte* [Berlin-Leipzig, 1937], pp. 139–40.) There was also the case of the Lower Austrian General-Militär-Commando requesting authorization to buy a cat to hunt mice. The request had passed through forty-eight hands before permission was graciously granted. (Manfried Rauchensteiner, *Kaiser Franz und Erzherzog Carl. Dynastie und Heerwesen in Österreich 1796–1809* [Vienna, 1972], p. 62.)

The French revolutionary and Napoleonic wars proved to be a supreme test for the monarchy. There were many setbacks, of course, at Jemappes, Fleurus, Lodi, Arcola, Rivoli, Mantua, Marengo, Hohenlinden, Austerlitz, and Wagram, but as early as 1796 Archduke Charles triumphed over the French in two consecutive battles fought in Germany and in 1798 General Melas defeated the French in Italy. Then there was Archduke Charles's victory at Aspern in 1809, the first setback Napoleon suffered in a large-scale battle.[5] Throughout, the Austrian troops suffered from an excess of drill and a lack of purpose, but when a purpose was finally found in defense of the homeland, as in the Tyrol in 1809, Emperor Francis (1792–1835) was forced to cool the national ardor of his subjects because he could not afford the luxury of patriotism in a state based on dynastic loyalty.

Toward the end of the Napoleonic Wars, Austria contributed the largest force, 300,000 men, to the campaign against France, which entitled it to name the supreme allied commander, Field Marshal Prince Karl Schwarzenberg. The Austrian Empire (as the state came to be known in 1804) had successfully weathered the Jacobin agitation of the revolutionary years and repeated invasions by the French. Dissension in the armed forces had been minimal, and the handful of Hungarian officers who had plotted for national independence and perhaps even a republic were executed or imprisoned in 1795. In the last years of the war, a militia or Landwehr was created in German-Austria and the Bohemian lands (not, of course, in Hungary), but this "people's army" never assumed the importance of its Prussian counterpart, and it was permanently suspended in 1831. The only lasting innovation was a reorganized general staff. Created under Maria Theresa in 1758 and clumsily named General-Quartiermeister-Stab, this minuscule institution was heartily disliked by the generals, who preferred dash and drill to planning and thinking, and it remained in a very subordinate position—as we shall later see—until the second half of the nineteenth century.[6]

From the Congress of Vienna to the Crisis of the Old Order, 1815–1848

The Austrian Empire emerged from the Napoleonic wars with its prestige greatly enhanced. Vienna acted as host to the postwar peace conference, and the Austrian chancellor, Metternich, was widely recognized as "the coachman of Europe." The unregretted loss of Belgium to the king of the Netherlands was amply compensated for by the acquisition of the Archbishopric of Salzburg and the former Republic of Venice, which included Dalmatia. The glamour of the Congress of Vienna, however, could barely hide the growing gap between the Austrian and West European economies, and the treasury was nearly empty. Still, Metternich wanted Austria to play the role of Europe's policeman, and he loaded the federal fortresses in Germany as well as those in the Italian client states with Austrian garrisons. In 1820–1821, Habsburg troops marched into Naples; in 1831, there were military expeditions to central Italy; and in 1846, the Austrians suppressed a Polish revolution in the tiny Republic of Cracow, which they then proceeded to annex.

Austria's international commitments required a strong army, but for that there

was not enough money. Moreover, when Count Anton Kolowrat gained a commanding voice in domestic affairs in 1826, the government itself set out to trim the sails
of the armed forces: the first but certainly not the last instance in modern Austrian
history of a civilian leadership's hostility to the military. As Gunther E. Rothenberg
shows, in 1817 the army still received half of the total revenues; by 1830 it received
only 23 percent.[7] Thus, even though the army had a theoretical strength of about
400,000 men, which would have made it a respectable force for an empire of about
thirty million, there were never more than 250,000 men on active duty at any one
time. The others had been furloughed to fend for themselves, and even those in
service were often released, particularly during harvest time, so as to free the army
from the burden of feeding them.

More than ever, the emphasis was on spit and polish, partly because of the
conservatism of the generals but also because parades cost far less than warlike
training. An infantryman was provided with only twenty rounds of ammunition
annually, which meant that he rarely if ever fired a live bullet while in training. (It is
true that one round plus wear and tear on the barrel cost as much as a soldier's daily
ration.)[8] In most provinces recruitment was now based on selective conscription
which, according to the law of 1827, exempted all noblemen, priests, houseowners,
farmowners, educated people, and those with a respectable profession. In addition,
those who could afford it paid a hefty exemption tax of between five hundred and
eight hundred gulden. Because the authorities had the right to send undesirables to
the colors, this meant that it was mainly the poor who served.

The term of service varied depending on the province, but in 1845 it was
reduced to a uniform eight years throughout the empire. Hungary (but since 1815 no
longer the Tyrol) still insisted on the principle of voluntary enlistment.[9] In practice,
those who were enlisted there were the ones unable to avoid the recruiting sergeants
and the local authorities. Discipline was harsh even by contemporary European
standards and the housing of the soldiers was quite abysmal. But at least the troops
were fed adequately. The regiments were on the move almost incessantly, partly in
answer to political and military needs, but increasingly also so as to prevent frater-
nization with the civilians.

The ethnic and social composition of the officer corps, as we shall see later, had
not changed drastically from the eighteenth century: part noble, part non-noble; part
German and part Hungarian, Slavic, Italian, and Romanian, with a heavy admixture
of foreigners. The corps was socially privileged yet grossly underpaid and badly
neglected. There were, before 1848, about ten thousand officers, who found the
promotion process even slower than in the other armies of Europe as well as open to
abuses, although less so than, for instance, in the British army. But in this period, as
in all others, the army was quite indifferent to the ethnic background of the officers
and surprisingly, too, to their social origin, except for ruling princes and the aristocracy. And even though Roman Catholicism was the religion of the army's supreme
commander, an officer's confessional allegiance and religious devotion were considered quite immaterial for promotion. The officers were unpolitical, and when the
revolution came, in 1848, it definitely did not originate from army ranks. There had
been a few small conspiracies among Italian and Polish officers, but these had been

suppressed without difficulty. Even so, beginning in March 1848, the army faced the greatest or, better to say, the only internal crisis in its history.

The Great Army Crisis of 1848–1849

The Austrian revolutions began in mid-March in response to the February revolutions in Paris.[10] Within a few days, central authority had collapsed, Metternich had fled to England, and various traditional provincial legislatures as well as self-appointed national committees had exacted sweeping concessions from Emperor-King Ferdinand (1835–1848). The revolutions proclaimed universal fraternity and a united struggle against reactionary tyranny, but because the national goals of the various political groups overlapped badly, the revolutionaries inevitably came into conflict. Students and burghers in Vienna clamored for the democratic transformation of the monarchy, but also for the unification of such parts of the monarchy as had once been in the Holy Roman Empire with the progressive Great German Reich that seemed on the verge of creation. Revolutionaries in Milan and Venice worked for the creation of a progressive and unified Italian state that would have included several areas claimed by the German-Austrians for the future great German state. Liberal reformers in Prague desired a unified Czech state that would have included millions of German-speakers, yet Czech patriots would not hear of the inclusion of their lands in the future German state (which was the goal of the German nationalists). The Hungarian political leaders sought their country's reunification with Transylvania and the transformation of the lands of the Hungarian Holy Crown into a modern, liberal, unitary, and Magyar-dominated state, but this conflicted with the interests of the Croatian revolutionaries, who wanted a sovereign state for themselves, and with the stirrings of Slovak, Romanian, and Serbian political movements that desired autonomy within Hungary or even a possible unification with their brothers in Bohemia, Moldavia-Wallachia, and the Serbian principality, respectively. And one could easily go on!

The empire seemed about to collapse. A few generals were prepared to put up a determined resistance, but they received contradictory orders from the emperor or no orders at all. So, following some initial violence, the generals allowed their troops to be driven out of Vienna. In other places, such as Budapest and Prague, army units kept to their barracks and attempted to remain neutral.

To make matters worse, on March 23, Charles Albert, king of Piedmont-Sardinia, declared war on Austria, and his army, together with local revolutionaries, pushed the Austrian army out of Lombardy. In Venice, a republic was declared, and the local Austrian governor surrendered power to the revolutionary leader Daniele Manin.

Of the entire Habsburg army, only units stationed in northern Italy had been on a war footing in March 1848, and they had even been reinforced prior to the revolutionary outbreaks. Even so, their commander, Field Marshal Count Josef Radetzky, had a total of only seventy-three thousand men at his disposal, including noncombatants and the fortress garrisons. His forces included about twenty thousand Italians, most of whom were soon lost because of desertions or because they had been stationed in Venice.[11] But Radetzky, then eighty-two, was a brilliant general, with a well-deserved renown dating back to the Napoleonic Wars, and he did not give up easily. His greatest asset was his popularity among his troops and among the Italian peasants. The latter tended to see him as their protector against the aristocratic Italian revolutionaries, who were very often their landlords. Nor did the peasants care much for the urban political movement led by intellectuals, a phenomenon typical not only of northern Italian but of other areas in the empire as well, and one that proved, ultimately, to be the salvation of the dynasty. Radetzky withdrew his forces into the Quadrilateral, the four great Austrian fortresses protecting the Alps and prepared for a counterattack. Meanwhile, he urged the Austrian government, which was a creation of the revolution but in its composition still rather conservative and dynastically loyal, not to make any concessions to Piedmont nor any more concessions to the domestic revolutionaries.

For the time being, nothing could stop the bewildered authorities in Vienna— the Austrian government and whoever else cared to speak in the name of the emperor—from granting various constitutions and other concessions to the long line of aggressive petitioners who had come to court. The most important of the concessions was the constitution granted to Hungary, which recognized the country's right to reunite with Transylvania, to exercise genuine suzerainty over Croatia-Slavonia, and eventually even to reincorporate the Military Border into Hungary. The constitution made Hungarian the official language of the new unified state; it introduced sweeping liberal reforms; and it set up a constitutional government responsible to a soon-to-be-elected popular parliament. Hungary was granted its own financial administration, its own minister of war, and even a foreign ministry. Yet the constitution left completely unclear how the two foreign services and the two military establishments, in Vienna and in Budapest, were to coordinate their actions. As a further major concession, the Hungarians gained the right to make all Habsburg troops stationed in the Hungarian lands swear an oath of allegiance to the Hungarian constitution. This placed these soldiers under the authority of the Hungarian minister of war. But it was not made clear whether there should now be an exchange of regiments, with those originating from Hungary and Transylvania being returned there, and the non-Hungarian units being sent away. In any case, Radetzky would not hear of such an arrangement, and even though he granted leave to one of his cavalry colonels to assume the post of Hungarian minister of war, he kept the Hungarian troops under his command, just as he held back the Croatian Grenzer and all others.[12]

The Austrian armed forces were at that time administratively divided into twelve major territorial commands, the so-called General-Militär-Commanden, each one headed by a senior general. Of those, five now fell, theoretically, under the authority of the Hungarian government. The situation was no better with regard to the army regiments. Of the thirty-five Cisleithanian or so-called German infantry regiments, six were in Italy at that time, and four were in Hungary. Of the fifteen Hungarian and Transylvanian infantry regiments, six were stationed in Austria and four in Italy. Of the eight Italian infantry regiments, half were stationed outside northern Italy.

The same complex situation applied to the cavalry. Of the twenty-five "German" cavalry regiments (which included units consisting of Czechs, Poles, Ruthenes, and Slovenes, of course), thirteen were serving at that time in Hungary. On the other hand, of the twelve Hungarian hussar regiments, only six were stationed in the Hungarian lands.[13] Command authority over these regiments and the question of their loyalty became burning issues, for the initially almost bloodless revolutions soon deteriorated into a series of civil wars and, by the fall of 1848, into a full-scale war between Austria and Hungary. Moreover, the schematic listing of regimental distribution above does not even begin to tell the whole story, for in reality, it accounts for the territorial presence only of the trained first and second battalions of each regiment. Yet there was also a third battalion, composed mainly of young soldiers, which was generally stationed in the regiment's own recruiting area. In addition, each infantry regiment had had the obligation to surrender two companies of select tall soldiers to the special Grenadier battalions, made up of men from several regiments. The Grenadiere rarely served in the same place as the first, second, or third battalions of their own regiments. This meant that all infantry regiments and most of the cavalry units were divided, some more so than others, and when the civil wars and then war between Austria and Hungary broke out, diverse battalions of the same regiment could be found in both camps, sometimes even opposing one another.* Small wonder, then, that when the war was finally over and the Austrian military historians had to account for the events, they invariably found some units, no matter how small, from each regiment which had fought for and not against the emperor. Their bravery and loyalty were consequently extolled, while the actions of the others were conveniently forgotten.

Bloody conflicts in parts of the monarchy other than northern Italy began in June in Prague, when Field Marshal Prince Alfred Windisch-Graetz crushed a local radical revolt there. This was the beginning of the military counterrevolution, but it would be many months before the army could take matters in hand. True, on July 24, Radetzky annihilated the Piedmontese at Custozza; he then reconquered Lombardy and, on August 9, forced Charles Albert to accept an armistice. But for the time being this Austrian success had no serious repercussions in the rest of the monarchy. In Vienna, revolutionary students were in power, not the Austrian gov-

---

*Here are but a few examples. In 1848–1849, the First and Second Battalions as well as the two Grenadier companies of the Hungarian 19th Schwarzenberg Infantry Regiment (hereafter abbreviated as IR) waged war for the emperor in Italy, while the Third Battalion waged war against the emperor in Hungary. The same situation prevailed in the Hungarian 32nd Este IR, except that in this case the Grenadiere were also on the Hungarian side. In the Lombardian 23rd Ceccopieri IR, the First and Second Battalions participated in the campaign against Hungary, while the Third Battalion, stationed in Italy, went over to the revolutionary side. In the Lombardian 44th Erzherzog Albrecht IR, the First and Second Battalions joined the Italian revolution, but the Third Battalion, although it was also stationed in Italy, remained loyal to its sovereign.

Among the twelve Hungarian hussar regiments, the 5th, 7th, and 8th fought for the emperor in Italy; the 10th and 11th were divided between the Austrian and Hungarian causes. The 1st, 2nd, 3rd, 4th, 6th, 9th, and the majority of the 12th Hussar Regiments made war on the Hungarian side. (Alphons Freiherr von Wrede, *Geschichte der k. und k. Wehrmacht. Die Regimenter, Corps, Branchen und Anstalten von 1618 bis Ende des XIX Jahrhunderts*, 5 vols. [Vienna, 1898–1905], vols. I, III).

ernment, and back in May the emperor and court had fled to the Tyrol. There was thus still no central authority. Meanwhile, the Serbs and then the Croats had rebelled against Hungary.

Serbian political agitation began in the spring of 1848, at the same time as that of the other nationalist movements, and it aimed at the official recognition of the Orthodox Serbs as an autonomous ethnic-religious entity within Hungary.[14] However, because Ferdinand had surrendered all rights in Hungary to the newly constituted Hungarian government, the Serbian delegations went away from Vienna empty-handed. This led to a radicalization of attitudes, soon to be reinforced by military and political assistance from the neighboring principality of Serbia, an autonomous state under nominal Ottoman suzerainty. The Serbian leaders now began to nurture expansionist ambitions, claiming virtually all of southern Hungary for themselves, and late in May they revolted openly against the Budapest government. The bulk of the rebel forces was made up of Grenzer units who resented their submission to the authority of the Hungarian minister of war. The Budapest government ordered imperial-royal regulars and Hungarian National Guards, a newly constituted militia, against the Serbs. At first, the regulars were willing to fight a rebellion which appeared to be fomented from abroad, but matters became more complicated when it turned out that the Grenzer were led by Habsburg officers, and that they carried the imperial-royal flag. Now Habsburg troops fought one another, with those on the Serbian side generally gaining the upper hand. Meanwhile, officers in both camps despised the "lawyers," "scribblers," and "radical mob" in Vienna as well as Budapest.

The conflict in the South quickly deteriorated into mutual massacre, with Serbian Grenzer and peasants killing Hungarians, German colonists, and Romanian peasants, and the Hungarian National Guards responding in kind. Nothing illustrates better the confusion of the period and the moral dilemma of the imperial-royal officers than the adventures of Colonel Baron Friedrich Blomberg, whose story I allow myself to borrow from my book on Louis Kossuth and the Hungarian Revolution of 1848–1849.[15]

In the summer of 1848, Blomberg, himself an Austro-German, was in charge of a Polish lancer (Uhlan or Ulan) cavalry regiment stationed in the Banat, a prosperous region of southern Hungary inhabited by a hopelessly mixed population of Germans, Magyars, Orthodox and Catholic Serbs, Romanians, and Bulgarians. Threatened by Serbian rebels, Blomberg turned to his commanding general for instructions. The general, although personally opposed to the Budapest government, instructed the colonel to combat the Grenzer and foreign volunteers, as did the local Hungarian government commissioner, who happened to be a Serb. Blomberg did fight, successfully, but when the leader of the Serbian rebels, a Habsburg army colonel of Austro-German nationality, begged Blomberg to think of his duty to the emperor rather than his duty to the king (the two were one and the same person, of course), Blomberg ordered his Poles out of the region. He thereby left his German co-nationals, who happened to be loyal to Hungary, to the fury of the Serbs. Much disturbed, Blomberg wrote to the Austrian minister of war, General Count Theodor Baillet de la Tour: "Have pity on us, recall us from this place of uncertainty. We can no longer bear this terrible dilemma."[16] But Blomberg was not recalled, because, as he was subsequently reminded by the Austrian minister, his regiment had been placed under Hungarian authority. Instead, Blomberg was ordered "to consult his conscience." The area formerly under his protection was occupied by the Serbs, with accompanying brutality and plunder, but it was liberated twice by the Hungarians, first under the command of a former Habsburg officer of Serbian nationality, and then under a Polish general.

It might be worth noting that both Blomberg and his erstwhile opponent on the Serbian side, Colonel Ferdinand Mayerhofer, later became generals in the Habsburg army; whereas the Hungarian government commissioner, Sebő Vukovics (or Vukovič), and the Polish general, József Bem, fled into exile at the end of the war, and the Hungarian commander of Serbian nationality, General János Damjanich (or Damjanič), was hanged by the Austrians.

The Serbian revolt was powerfully assisted by a simultaneous Croatian political movement and rebellion against Hungary.[17] The Croatian situation was vastly different from that of the Serbs, because the Kingdom of Croatia-Slavonia had been a recognized legal entity before 1848, and because the leader of the Croats, Josip Jelačić, was an imperial-royal general. He had been recently appointed by Ferdinand as governor (*Ban*) of so-called Civil Croatia and, simultaneously, as commanding general of the Zagreb General-Militär-Commando. His dual appointment was due to the court's desire both to weaken the Hungarian influence in Croatia-Slavonia and to guarantee the continued loyalty of the Croatian Grenzer. Jelačić proved to be a bitter enemy of the Hungarians, a loyal Habsburg subject, and a Croatian patriot—in that order. Under him, the progressive Croatian national revolution turned into a powerful movement for the preservation of the monarchy and the destruction of Hungarian sovereignty.

As governor of Civil Croatia, Jelačić immediately renounced any obedience to the Hungarian prime minister and, as commanding general in Croatia, to the Hungarian minister of war. The Hungarians thereupon declared him a rebel, seconded by the emperor-king. Under intense Hungarian pressure, Ferdinand even went so far as to deprive Jelačić of all his posts in June. But the Croatian leader disobeyed the order, not the first instance in 1848 (Radetzky had preceded him) of a Habsburg general's ignoring the command of his imperial master in what he perceived to be the interest of the monarchy. Secretly encouraged by some members of the court and by Baillet de la Tour, Jelačić mobilized the Croatian Grenzer and, on September 11, marched into Hungary.

The Hungarians, who were now effectively if not yet officially led by Louis Kossuth, the minister of finance in the constitutional government, ordered a Habsburg general to march against the rebel Jelačić. The split within the army appeared final. But Generalmajor Franz Ottinger was reluctant to fight his comrades-in-arms; instead, he withdrew his forces from the Hungarian-Croatian border, and then resigned and went over to Jelačić, taking with him a number of non-Hungarian units. Kossuth now experimented with another general, this one a Magyar, but was no more successful. Finally, a third Habsburg officer, Generalmajor János Móga, also a Magyar, was willing to make a stand. His motley forces, composed of imperial-royal regulars, a few battalions of the newly created honvéd national army and Hungarian National Guards (in reality, poorly armed peasants) stopped the Croatian Grenzer on September 29 at Pákozd, not far from Budapest. The decisive element in this encounter seems to have been the artillery, manned on both sides by the Czech cannoneers of the 5th Prague Artillery Regiment. Because the Czechs in the Hungarian camp outgunned their comrades from the same regiment in the Croatian camp, the Hungarian revolution was able to continue.[18]

A three-day truce was declared between the "Royal Hungarian and the Imperial-Royal Croatian Armies," and Jelačić took advantage of the lull to withdraw in the direction of Austria. He later asserted that he had been in a hurry because on October 6 another radical revolution had broken out in Vienna; the emperor (who had returned to Vienna in August) had fled again (this time to Olmütz in Moravia); Latour* had been hanged on a lamppost, and the imperial army had once again been driven out of the capital.

The Vienna October revolution was a turning point in Habsburg history. It disillusioned the moderate revolutionaries and the burghers of the city; it caused the peasants in Austria and Bohemia-Moravia to turn against the urban revolutions, and it permitted Field Marshal Windisch-Graetz to take matters in hand. He assembled a powerful army in Bohemia, transported it by rail to Lower Austria and, reinforced by Jelačić's Croats, stormed the capital on October 31. A day before, at Schwechat, near Vienna, the imperial troops defeated the pitifully small Hungarian army that had followed Jelačić and had, rather hesitantly, penetrated into Austrian territory.

The Grenzer were now allowed to ransack the capital, and a state of siege was declared there, to last until 1853. Some revolutionary leaders were executed, including the commander of Vienna, Wenzel Cäsar Messenhauser, a former Habsburg first lieutenant.

The political break between Austria and Hungary was now complete, although this did not prevent the military institutions of the two countries from cooperating repeatedly for several more weeks. Nor did it prevent the Hungarian minister of war from issuing orders and promoting officers in the name of His Majesty the King for many months to come.

On October 3, an imperial-royal manifesto outlawed both the Hungarian parliament and the National Defense Committee, the executive body that now functioned as the government of Hungary. Ferdinand placed Hungary under a military plenipotentiary. From that time on, all Habsburg officers in Hungarian service were traitors and rebels. This did not, however, prevent the Austrian military authorities from receiving some defectors from the Hungarian ranks with open arms, even several months later, while imprisoning others. The Hungarians defied the manifesto and organized for war. Kossuth became virtual dictator of the country, under the supervision of the parliament, and he placed a thirty-year-old former first lieutenant of the Imperial-Royal 12th Hussar Regiment, Arthur Görgey, in command of the Hungarian forces facing the Austrian army in western Hungary.[19]

This, then, was the situation late in the fall of 1848. The revolutionary movement had been suppressed everywhere, including an abortive Polish revolt at Lemberg in October; the Piedmontese had been driven out of Lombardy; and only

---

*The real name of the Austrian minister of war was Baillet de la Tour, but he was popularly known— and hated—as Latour.

Venice and Hungary continued to resist. Austria now had a new, powerful prime minister in the person of General Prince Felix Schwarzenberg; Radetzky was in control in northern Italy; and Windisch-Graetz had been put in command of the coming campaign against Hungary.

The Austrian armies invaded Hungary from all sides in December; they occupied Budapest in January but were unable to conquer the whole country. In a short period of time, Kossuth succeeded in setting up a national army of close to 200,000 men and, in the spring of 1849, following a series of brilliant victories, the Hungarians reconquered Budapest. By May both Hungary and Transylvania were nearly free of Austrian troops. The victorious Hungarian campaign in Transylvania had been led by József Bem, a Polish general and exiled revolutionary; the campaign in Hungary proper by Görgey and other, mostly junior, Habsburg officers.

Fearing ultimate defeat, the new emperor Francis Joseph (Ferdinand had graciously abdicated in December) sought and received Russian military assistance in May 1849.[20] This was a great error on the part of Austria, because it undermined forever the reputation of the Habsburg army and because, in all likelihood, the Austrians alone could have prevailed over the Hungarians. In Italy, Radetzky had easily smashed a second Piedmontese attack in March; Venice was being besieged and would surrender in August. Elements of nearly all the Habsburg regiments were now marching on Hungary, and the energetic new Austrian commander there, Feldzeugmeister Baron Ludwig Haynau, had 175,000 troops at his disposal. Nor was there any shortage of recruits and even of volunteers on the Austrian side. It turned out that the majority of the monarchy's inhabitants—Germans, Czechs, Serbs, Romanians, and even Poles, as well as the peasants in general—preferred Austrian absolutism and Austrian ethnic tolerance to nationality conflict and the urban or aristocratic revolutionaries.

In any case, now the Russians too were on the scene, and the allied armies, some 360,000 strong, gradually drove the 170,000 honvéd troops into the southeast corner of Hungary. War weariness had set in among the Hungarian population even before the arrival of the tsarist armies. Görgey surrendered in August, and the last Hungarian fortress pulled down the national flag early in October.

The Austrians exacted rather brutal revenge after the war, court-martialling 498 former Habsburg officers, among them 24 imperial-royal generals. About 40 officers (but none of the old army generals) were executed; most of the others were given harsh prison sentences. Retribution affected thousands of civilians as well.[21]

There is no trace of the army leaders' having attempted to analyze the causes of this unique crisis in the officer corps, so we must attempt to do it for them. The constitutional arrangement between Hungary and the emperor-king had placed about one-third of the Habsburg forces under Hungarian authority. By the time a Habsburg officer in Hungary discovered that he had been obeying the wrong authority, it was too late. He had taken an oath to the Hungarian constitution, he was receiving his pay from Budapest, he had been promoted by the Hungarians—in the name of the king, of course—and he was being watched by Hungarian political commissioners. Until the autumn, resignation or retirement was relatively easy; afterward the officer trying to resign risked arrest by the Hungarian authorities. Or, if he succeeded in going over to the Austrians, he risked arrest by the Austrian authorities. Besides, even after the promulgation of the October 3 manifesto, it was not quite clear whether staying in the Hungarian army was truly illegal. The Budapest government assured the officers that the manifesto was a forgery perpetrated by the king's evil advisers, or that it had been coaxed out of the king. Many career officers in the Hungarian national army persisted in never reporting to the "illegal" National Defense Committee, but only to Colonel (now General) Lázár Mészáros, the Royal Hungarian minister of war.

After all this has been said, it still remains true that for an officer to remain on the Hungarian side was a matter of individual decision. At least one thousand officers, or about 10 percent of the Habsburg officer corps, elected to do so, even after the Hungarian parliament had officially "dethroned the House of Habsburg-Lorraine" on April 14, 1849, and had acclaimed Kossuth governor-president of the country.

Far from all the rebel officers were ethnic Hungarians. The Hungarian military historian Gábor Bona has calculated that of the 830 field-grade and general officers of the honvéd army (the vast majority of them Habsburg regulars), 571, or 68.8 percent, were Magyar; 129 or 15.5 percent, German; 35 or 4.2 percent, Polish; and 31 or 3.6 percent, Serbian or Croatian.[22]

Of the fourteen Hungarian rebel commanders tried by the Austrians at Arad fortress in Hungary, thirteen of whom were hanged or shot, one was a German from outside Austria, one a German-Austrian, two Germans from Hungary, one a Croat, one a Serb, and two Magyars of Armenian descent. Of the five "pure" Magyars, not every one could speak or understand Hungarian. Their composite portrait is remarkable for its lack of uniformity.

The ages of the fourteen ranged from thirty to fifty-seven; their prerevolutionary army ranks, from lieutenant to colonel. Five were infantrymen, one an army engineer, and eight were from the cavalry. Most had been in active service before the war; three had resigned earlier but reenlisted in 1848 at the behest of the Hungarian government. One was Greek Orthodox, one Calvinist, and the others Catholic. One of the generals, Count Karl Leiningen-Westerburg, came from a princely family in Hesse; another general belonged to the Hungarian aristocracy but knew no Hungarian; yet another was an enormously wealthy landowner. The rest of the defendants had little or no private wealth. Several had brothers in the Austrian army; two had fathers and uncles who were Habsburg generals. None of the Arad defendants was politically active before the war. Some were promoted rapidly in the old army; most had moved up slowly. None had had any trouble with the Habsburg military authorities. Before the military court, they argued that they had only been doing their duty in the posts in which the king had placed them. Even on the point of death and in private correspondence, several asserted they had been loyal Habsburg subjects. "I have always been a devoted subject of the House of Austria—and I shall die as such, because I served Hungary only so as to benefit Austria," wrote General Ernő Kiss to his daughter a day before his execution. "You know how I have landed in this catastrophic situation, against my best convictions, despite all the love I feel for the Ruler and for the Fatherland," wrote General Ernst Ritter Poelt von Poeltenberg, then already under sentence of death, to his father in Austria. Poelt von Poeltenberg, a German Austrian with no knowledge of Hungarian, had been a captain in a Hungarian hussar regiment before the war. The word Fatherland in his letter undoubtedly referred to the Austrian Empire, not to Hungary.[23]

What, then, motivated these officers? One of them, General Nagysándor, was a republican; another, Leiningen, was a liberal who felt that the fight for a united Germany would be best advanced by serving in Kossuth's army. He also felt deeply attached to Hungary, thanks to his marriage to a Hungarian noblewoman. While in the national army, all the generals voiced Hungarian patriotic sentiments; when in Austrian prison, many spoke or wrote otherwise. In view of the peculiar circumstances, both types of behavior could be considered meaningless. What is certain is that most, but again not all, strove mightily for rapid promotion in the national army, and that they enjoyed the opportunity to exchange the command of platoons and companies for the command of brigades, divisions, and army corps. Some even thought that, by surrendering, not to the Austrians but to the Russians, as most of them did, they would have an excellent chance to be taken into the tsarist army and even be promoted.

And yet, it would be wrong to call these men mercenaries and opportunists. The tradition of free, untrammeled service was common to the officers. They viewed themselves as spiritual heirs of Eugene of Savoy, who had demonstrated his diverse ethnic origin and his indifference to nationality by signing his name in three languages: "Eugenio von Savoie." Hundreds of foreigners served in the Habsburg forces at that time, quite particularly in the Hungarian hussar regiments, and few people considered this to be abnormal or unusual.* Hundreds of Habsburg officers served more than one master during their lifetimes. Capital punishment for treason was a professional risk one took unwillingly, of course, yet many took it nonetheless.

The fundamental reason for the presence of one thousand Habsburg officers in the Hungarian army was most likely neither Hungarian patriotism nor even career-seeking but loyalty to one's regiment, the officer's true fatherland, or, if not that, then devotion to a charismatic commander. The Hungarian cavalry regiments undoubtedly formed such a "fatherland," and commanders of the caliber of Arthur Görgey were such charismatic leaders. This quiet, cold, often ruthless young cavalry lieutenant, who had resigned his commission three years before the war, exercised a tremendous attraction even on career officers far ahead of him in experience and seniority. Thanks to the personal intervention of Tsar Nicholas, Görgey went unpunished after the war. It is a historical irony that he became the unwitting cause of the execution or imprisonment of hundreds of officers who had followed him blindly into surrender, rather than escaping abroad, as did hundreds not under his command.

Obviously, the rank and file had much less say in the matter than the officers. Many soldiers, perhaps even a majority, had only the vaguest notion of which side they were on. It was indeed difficult to understand a situation such as that of the

---

*Only the radical military critic, Daniel Fenner von Fenneberg, himself a former officer, protested the presence of so many foreigners in the Habsburg officer corps, not on national grounds but because of the special privileges in promotion allegedly enjoyed by these Englishmen, Belgians, Frenchmen, Swedes, and non-Austrian Germans. ([Daniel] Fenner von Fenneberg, *Österreich und seine Armee* [Leipzig, 1842], pp. 96–98.)

summer of 1848, when, in the words of Count Majláth, a Hungarian aristocrat: "The King of Hungary declared war on the King of Croatia, and the Emperor of Austria remained neutral, and all three monarchs were one and the same person."[24] And yet, many ordinary soldiers did make individual political decisions during the war. For instance, most of Radetzky's Italian soldiers deserted early during the campaign; some even mutinied against the Austrians.[25] In the Hungarian war, too, there were many cases of individual soldiers' changing sides or rebelling against their officers. In some of Hungary's great fortresses, where officers' councils had to make crucial decisions for or against the Hungarian government, ordinary soldiers occasionally participated in the process, and in at least one case, that of the great fortress of Peterwardein in Slavonia, the Hungarian rank and file forcibly prevented the officers from surrendering to the Austrians.

During the war, the armies of Austria and Hungary consisted of a great majority of conscripts. Both the Austrian occupation forces in Hungary and the Hungarian authorities impressed young men into service without regard to nationality. But both sides also received thousands of volunteers. Slovak miners, as well as German artisans and students formed some of the best battalions of the honvéd army. On the other hand, peasants of all nationalities formed the backbone of the Habsburg infantry and cavalry.

In the final analysis, the most characteristic feature of the revolutions and of the war was bewilderment. For one thing, it was often impossible to distinguish between friendly and enemy soldiers. The newly created honvéd battalions were provided with new, distinctive flags and uniforms, but the Habsburg regulars on the Hungarian side generally carried the old flag and wore the traditional uniforms, which sometimes led to catastrophic misunderstandings. In desperation, Windisch-Graetz ordered his soldiers to wear a white ribbon on their shakos; the Hungarians replied with a red ribbon. Now it looked as if the two opponents were engaged in peacetime maneuvers, but still the confusion continued, because the trumpet and drum signals had remained identical, and so had the drill and, generally, the language of command.

And yet, again, all was not confusion. Despite the opéra bouffe appearance of the whole affair, this was a most serious war, with up to 50,000 infantry, sixty squadrons of cavalry and hundreds of guns engaged in a single encounter, and with a total of 100,000 killed. Ultimately, the monarchy was saved by determined generals such as Radetzky, Windisch-Graetz, Jelačić, and Haynau, and by the 9,000-odd career officers (perhaps 2,000 of whom hailed from Hungary) who had remained in the emperor's service throughout the war. For these officers, there was the comforting feeling that by fighting the revolutionaries and the Hungarians they were fighting for domestic peace, an end to ethnic conflict and class war. And because the aristocracy as well as the middle classes, whether German, Magyar, Polish, or Italian, had proven themselves unreliable, there was also the comforting feeling that of the entire social elite only they, the officers, had proven themselves worthy to the dynasty. Few officers doubted that, after so many years of gross neglect, they would finally receive their just reward as the most distinguished estate in the realm.

The legacies of the revolution and of the Hungarian war were, of course, legion. Instead of prostrating the country, the defeat shifted Hungarian strivings to the social and political scene, where great successes had been achieved already before 1848. In 1867, the Hungarian nobility, the backbone of the Hungarian national movement, would win a great belated victory. There was also the legacy of the Habsburg military experience with the honvéd army, much more democratic in style and national in its ideology. These experiences hastened reforms in the Austrian army and led to a growing awareness of the nationality question.

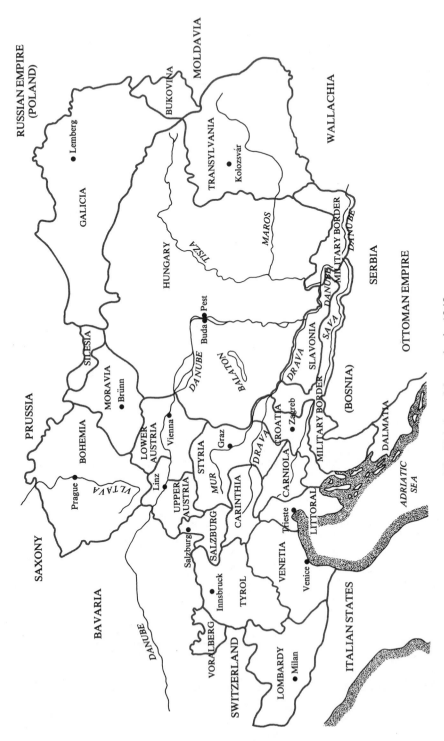

The Habsburg Monarchy in 1848

RUSSIAN EMPIRE
(POLAND)

MOLDAVIA

BUKOVINA

WALLACHIA

GALICIA

• Lemberg

TRANSYLVANIA

Kolozsvár •

MAROS

TISZA

HUNGARY

MILITARY BORDER

DANUBE

SERBIA

SILESIA

PRUSSIA

MORAVIA

Brünn •

BALATON

Pest

Buda •

DANUBE

DANUBE

SAVA

OTTOMAN EMPIRE

SAXONY

BOHEMIA

Prague •

LOWER
AUSTRIA

Vienna •

Linz •

VLTAVA

DANUBE

STYRIA

Graz •

DRAVA

SLAVONIA

(BOSNIA)

CROATIA

Zagreb •

MILITARY BORDER

BAVARIA

UPPER
AUSTRIA

SALZBURG

Salzburg •

MUR

CARINTHIA

CARNIOLA

DALMATIA

Trieste

LITTORAL

ADRIATIC
SEA

DANUBE

VORALBERG

Innsbruck •

TYROL

VENETIA

Venice •

SWITZERLAND

LOMBARDY

Milan •

ITALIAN STATES

2

Absolutism, Liberal Reform, and the Ideology of Preventive War: The Army between 1850 and 1914

The Decade of Imperial Absolutism and the Defeat at Solferino, 1850–1859

It was indeed a powerful and proud army that emerged from the revolutionary wars.[1] In 1850, when Austria nearly went to war over Prussia's occupation of the Principality of Hesse, the monarchy was able to mobilize a well-armed force of 450,000. The outnumbered Prussians backed down; they evacuated Hesse and signed the humiliating "Olmütz Punctation."[2]

The humbling of Prussia fit well into Prime Minister Schwarzenberg's plan of a great German Reich under Austrian leadership. This was not to be, of course; instead, Schwarzenberg's power policy led to the collapse of the conservative Austro-Prussian alliance. Schwarzenberg died in 1852, but his legacy of dynamism in the conduct of foreign policy was not abandoned. During the Crimean War, Austria came close to entering the conflict against Russia, in a blatant act of ingratitude, on the side of the Franco-British-Sardinian-Ottoman alliance. This time about half a million men were mobilized at ruinous expense, and between 1854 and 1856 a large Austrian force occupied the Danubian principalities of Moldavia and Wallachia.[3] Austria gained nothing in the Paris Peace Treaty ending the Crimean War. Moreover, it not only lost Russian friendship but was now faced by a self-confident Sardinia to the south, and a freshly established, soon irredentist Romania to the east. It should be noted that a much more aggressive role in this reckless maneuvering was played by the young emperor and his political advisers than by the top military leaders, who were aghast at the crumbling of the conservative dynastic alliance of the three "Northern Courts."

At home, a brief period of constitutional rule (weakened in any case by the fact that much of the empire was under martial law) soon came to an end with the imposition of an absolutist regime. The army itself had been under the emperor's personal command since 1849. Francis Joseph, the first soldier-emperor since Joseph II (and, as we shall soon see, not much more effective than the latter as a

43

battle commander), hoped to base his empire on the twin pillars of a personally loyal bureaucracy and army.

In the last seven decades of their existence, both the monarchy and army were so intimately linked to the person of Francis Joseph that a history of neither institution can be complete without some consideration of his personal character.[4]

The oldest son of Archduke Francis Charles and the grandson of Emperor Francis, Francis Joseph was born in 1830. He was thus only eighteen when he ascended the throne in December 1848, after his energetic mother, the Bavarian princess Sophie, Prime Minister Schwarzenberg, and the monarchy's leading generals had forced his uncle, Emperor Ferdinand, to resign. The dramatic events of 1848 shaped the character of Francis Joseph's sixty-eight-year rule. Placed on the throne by an act of questionable legality in order to save the old order based on tradition and law, he indeed became the supreme guardian of legitimacy in his realm, but did not scruple, at least in his younger years, to do away, by imperial fiat, with several constitutions and laws. In the war against Hungary, he rode at the head of his victorious troops at the battle at Győr, but Hungarian successes also forced him to write a humiliating plea for assistance to Tsar Nicholas. Thus, while Francis Joseph fancied himself a popular and successful military commander, he also experienced, at nineteen, the very real limits of his power.

Urged on by his mother and principal advisers, Francis Joseph at first imagined he could be, simultaneously, ruler, prime minister, and supreme military commander of his unified and centralized realm. Yet despite his conceit and stubbornness, he gradually came to understand that Austria was backward, internally divided, and militarily weak. To save what could be saved, he accepted the constitutional arrangement of 1867, which, among other things, made a former Hungarian revolutionary, Count Gyula (Julius) Andrássy, Sr., the prime minister of half of the monarchy. Once hanged in effigy by an Austrian executioner, Andrássy, the "*beau pendu,*" went on to become the foreign minister of what was known after 1867 as the Dual Monarchy. Unwilling to experiment any further, Francis Joseph clung stubbornly to the Austro-Hungarian Compromise, even when its continuation manifestly doomed his realm.

Francis Joseph was widely recognized as Europe's last *grand seigneur:* infinitely polite and infinitely aloof, he nevertheless had the personal tastes of a petty bourgeois. He married and forever loved a magnificent and beautiful princess, the Bavarian Elizabeth, but because his marriage was extremely unhappy, he consoled himself with a commoner actress, Katherine Schratt, whose tastes and lifestyle were equally petty bourgeois. The emperor was punctual, considerate, honest, reliable, unimaginative, boring, and, most important for his peoples, religiously and ethnically tolerant. It made no difference to him whether a subject was a German, Hungarian, or Slav, so long as the subject did his duty. With the same humility and grace that he accepted the blessings of the pope, he accepted the blessings of a rabbi or of a Muslim cleric. At military parades, he asked the same innocuous questions of an aristocratic cavalry officer and a Ruthenian batman, and he rewarded all who merited recognition without regard to origin. But he scolded only officers.

The legends about Francis Joseph are legion and, amazingly, almost all of them are true. He could become terribly agitated over the slightest imperfection in the uniform of an archduke or the smallest mistake committed at a military parade, but he was uninterested in strategy and refused to inspect his rapidly growing navy because, as he freely admitted, he understood nothing of naval matters and could not have cared less. He enjoyed riding trains, because trains were familiar to him from his youth, but he would not talk on the telephone or ride an elevator.* Francis Joseph refused to discard his worn-out uniforms; he preferred a Spartan lifestyle, and he expected the same of his servants, among whom he counted cabinet ministers. But he spent untold millions from his own purse on the arts, on relief of the poor, on his servants in financial distress, and on his insanely prodigal wife. More important, having pursued a disastrous personal policy in his youth, Francis Joseph came to understand his intellectual limitations and willingly vested power in others, making certain that the fundamental interests of his house, the tenets of decency, and the rule of law would be respected. His was indeed a *Rechtsstaat,* at least after the 1860s, a state based on respect for the law. Moreover, following the catastrophic Austro-Prussian War of 1866, Francis Joseph wished to see no more major armed conflicts, and he preferred his army to remain a splendid spectacle. But he also wished to preserve the great traditions of his doomed house, and so he personally made the decision to go to war in 1914, asserting: "If we must perish, we should do so with honor."

In the 1850s, Francis Joseph was still inexperienced and brash, and he engaged in too many experiments. As for the military, he at first restricted the constitutional Ministry of War—an unpleasant reminder of the recent revolutions—to purely administrative matters and then abolished it altogether in 1853. In place of the ministry, he set up an army high command, which he also abolished in 1860, replacing it with a resurrected war ministry. Having made himself supreme commander in the early 1850s, he enlarged the power and responsibility of his personal military cabinet, the *Militärzentralkanzlei,* and entrusted it to Feldmarschalleutnant Count Karl Ludwig Grünne, his first-adjutant-general. All through Francis Joseph's reign, the military cabinet would coexist uneasily with the Ministry of War and with the general staff. The latter had been reduced to a minimum in the 1850s but would become increasingly important after 1867. It is true, however, that the emperor's military cabinet never assumed the same importance as its counterpart in Wilhelmian Germany. Nor did the general staff ever overshadow the constitutional Ministry of War in Austria-Hungary to the extent that it did in the Second Reich.[5]

In the 1850s, Grünne was the most important soldier in the realm; some called him the real ruler of the monarchy.[6] This was not true, for Francis Joseph—and Archduchess Sophie—often went their own way, and the influence of such politicians as Foreign Minister Count Karl Buol, Police Minister Baron Johann Kempen (himself a soldier), and Minister of Interior Baron Alexander Bach should not be underestimated. In any case, Grünne's elevation to a position of power was a great mistake, for this haughty aristocrat (among haughty aristocrats) was an inex-

---

*When his favorite soldier, General Beck, then already in retirement, broke his arm, the eighty-four-year-old emperor preferred to climb three flights to visit him rather than take the elevator. Stories about the aged Francis Joseph's conflicts with the telephone are no less frequent and amusing. (On the elevator incident, see Edmund von Glaise-Horstenau, *Franz Josephs Weggefährte. Das Leben des Generalstabschefs Grafen Beck* [Zurich-Leipzig-Vienna, 1930], p. 442.)

perienced soldier and a poor politician. He improved neither the living conditions nor the combat readiness of the troops. "I can always find lieutenants at 24 gulden a month," he snapped at a group of subalterns who had appeared before him to beg for a raise.[7] Admittedly, during Grünne's tenure military appropriations at least remained stable: 123,030,000 gulden, or 36.1 percent of the state budget in 1857, as opposed to 62,068,000 gulden, or 37.3 percent of total state expenditures in 1847, but as usual, too much of this went to pay the military administration and too little to the troops. In 1860, for instance (just one year after Grünne's dismissal), 48.4 percent of the Austrian military appropriations was devoted to administrative expenses; in that same year the proportion was 42 percent in France, and 43 percent in Prussia.[8]

Internal security absorbed large sums of money. The events of 1848–1849 had demonstrated that the regular army in Austria—as in France and Prussia, for that matter—was morally and technically unprepared to deal with popular uprisings. In 1848, the standing orders for the troops had been to fire directly into the mob without warning if threatened. The soldiers were not trained to handle demonstrations and consequently did their best to avoid direct confrontations. When they occasionally used their weapons, as did the besieged Hungarian Grenadiere in Vienna on March 13, 1848, it only helped to fan the flames of rebellion. The bourgeois National Guards who replaced the regular army in Vienna proved to be more efficient and more brutal, as, for instance, on August 22, 1848, when they killed 22 lower-class demonstrators in Vienna and wounded another 340. Naturally, the postwar regime would not hear of burghers in uniform, and so, in 1850, the Gendarmerie was set up, a paramilitary force which became a permanent feature in the life of the monarchy's inhabitants.[9] Eventually expanded in number to nineteen regiments, the gendarmes (and special military police), were a select force: well paid, well trained, and universally hated. Their ruthlessness was notorious, but considering that the state of siege had ended everywhere in 1854, their presence was indispensable to a regime deeply unpopular in many of its lands, at least until the 1860s. The gendarmes hunted down political conspirators in Hungary, Transylvania, and northern Italy. They also made short shrift of the "patriotic bandits" who infested the countryside; indeed, until this congerie of military deserters, former honvéd army soldiers, and plain outlaws could be eliminated, it was difficult if not impossible to build railroads and factories in the eastern half of the monarchy.

Aside from the creation of the Gendarmerie, the 1850s saw few military reforms. Universal military service was introduced in 1858, but only in theory. A general staff school, the Kriegsschule, was created in 1852, and the higher military commands were reshuffled repeatedly, but ideology, training, and living conditions remained essentially the same.

By the late 1850s, the political situation in northern Italy had become untenable. It mattered little that the Austrian administration of Lombardy and Venetia was more lenient and efficient than those of the independent Italian states. The educated classes were all for *Risorgimento,* and the Austrian occupation forces lived as in enemy territory. In 1857, Radetzky, then ninety, was finally prevailed upon to retire, but his successor, Feldzeugmeister Count Franz Gyulai, had neither Radetzky's genius nor his charisma. Rather, this aristocrat of Hungarian origin was a martinet of the worst sort, and he was indisputably stupid.[10]

A war with France and Sardinia had long been in the making. In 1858, at Plombières, Napoleon III and Sardinian Prime Minister Count Camillo Cavour agreed to expel the Austrians from Italy, and soon thereafter, the Sardinians set out to provoke Austria into a declaration of war. The monarchy rose to the challenge, but without adequate diplomatic and military preparation. Grünne and the leading generals objected to sending an ultimatum to Sardinia, but it was dispatched nevertheless, on April 23, 1859, and three days later the two countries were at war.[11] As plotted by Cavour and Napoleon III, France immediately joined in the fray.

The bulk of the French forces would not be arriving until the end of May, which offered Gyulai's 107,000 combat troops an excellent opportunity to attack and destroy the weaker Sardinians.[12] But Gyulai wasted several weeks marching and countermarching; meanwhile, provisions failed to reach the hungry soldiers, who, in their heavy clothing, suffered badly from the heat. The Adjutanten-Corps, created in 1856 and made up mostly of amateurish aristocrats, undermined the work of the more professional but smaller and unrespected general staff, and the corps commanders (with one exception all aristocrats) quarreled among themselves. Thus, the army waited for the arrival of the French and, on June 4 at Magenta, suffered heavy losses in an indecisive battle. Gyulai, easily discouraged, ordered his troops back to the line of Austrian fortresses, where he was replaced by no lesser personalities than Francis Joseph and Grünne, who had assumed command of the troops. Nonetheless, the feuding continued, now between Grünne and Feldzeugmeister Baron Heinrich Hess, the talented chief of the general staff. When the army finally sallied forth from the fortresses under the personal command of Francis Joseph, it met with terrible defeat, at Solferino on June 24. Of the 160,000 Austrians involved in the battle, at least 22,000 were wounded or killed.*[13] The sight of the carnage inspired the Swiss Henri Dunant to found the Red Cross.

Fearing Prussian intervention and a European war, Napoleon III and Francis Joseph signed a preliminary peace at Villafranca on July 11. By that treaty, Austria ceded Lombardy to France, which in turn ceded the province to Sardinia. The Austrians still retained Venetia and with it, a foothold in Italy, but the monarchy was no longer able to prevent the eventuality it had long feared: within two years, local revolutions had swept away the Italian principalities, including several Austrian client-states, and Italy was united under Victor Emmanuel II, the Sardinian king. Aside from Venetia, only Papal Rome remained separate, under the protection of French troops. Having acquired Russia and Romania as potential enemies in the Crimean War, Austria was now also saddled with the problem of an irredentist Italy.

Historians agree that defeat in 1859 was facilitated by the ineptitude of Gyulai, Grünne, and Francis Joseph, by confusion in the high command, by the superior organization and élan of the French army, and by the rifled guns of the French artillery. However, as I have tried to show elsewhere, I cannot quite agree with the

---

*Note that statistical data on the number of soldiers participating in this battle and on the number of casualties vary according to the source. But, then, so do the statistical data on any battle.

widely held opinion that the defeat also owed something to the disloyalty of the monarchy's Italians and Hungarians.[14] No doubt, the high command was deeply suspicious of several nationalities, and it diverted some of the best units to control the provinces, especially Hungary. It is also true that the Franco-Sardinians encouraged desertion by creating a Hungarian Legion and an exile Hungarian National Directorate, headed by Louis Kossuth. Thousands of Italian soldiers and many Hungarians did go over to the enemy, but the Italian deserters originated more from the Lombardian than the Venetian, Friulian, and South Tyrolian regiments. The Lombards fought the war in home territory; they found it easy to disappear among the civilians. Things were more difficult for the other Italians and for the non-Italians, and thus the great majority of Italians, Magyars, Poles, and Croats, whether loyal or disloyal, remained with their units. They suffered heavy casualties and received a significant number of medals for bravery. Nor did the civilian population engage in any kind of revolutionary activity. On the contrary, in Hungary two volunteer regiments of hussars were set up to help the emperor.

During the war, the French captured thousands of Austrian soldiers of every conceivable nationality, and some Hungarian prisoners of war did in fact volunteer for Kossuth's Legion. But for most other Hungarian prisoners, the Legion was just another army into which they had been forcibly inducted. The French units had been given orders to dispatch to Legion headquarters all the prisoners of war who were found wearing tight or "Hungarian" trousers (as opposed to the wide slacks worn by the "German" regiments). Ironically, the Croatian regulars and Grenzer also wore tight Hungarian trousers, and thus the Croats, those dedicated enemies of the Hungarian national cause, found themselves thrown into the Hungarian Legion. No wonder, then, that the desertion rate from the Legion ran as high as that from the Austrian army. In any case, the Legion saw no action in the war. No less ironically, because the Croats had a reputation among the French for not taking prisoners, surrendering Hungarians were often killed in the mistaken belief that they were Croats.

The 1859 war ended with the Austrian army's reserve still large enough to have continued the fight for some time. This was small consolation, however, in the face of widespread recognition that something was very wrong with the forces. Calls for army reform were added to the growing clamor for the monarchy's economic, moral, and political rejuvenation. The next few years were to prove the empire's ability to remodel its economy and political structure, but not—for the time being—its army.

Constitutional Experiments and the Defeat
at Königgrätz, 1860–1866

The 1859 war led to a purge of the high command. The emperor personally eliminated himself, resolving never again to assume the command of an army. He dismissed Gyulai, Grünne, and dozens of others. Archduke Albrecht (son of Charles, the victor at Aspern), who had shown great determination in 1848 and who, as commanding general in Hungary, had proven himself equally tough, assumed increasingly important military posts.[15] Feldmarschalleutnant (later Feld-zeugmeister) Ludwig von Benedek, an untitled nobleman and a Lutheran, was made commanding general in Hungary and, simultaneously, chief of the Austrian general staff, another proof, incidentally, of the relative insignificance of the general staff at that time. Benedek was born in Hungary; he had a Magyar name, and he spoke good Hungarian, but he had no interest in the Hungarian national cause. He distinguished himself in 1849 in the Hungarian campaign, and again in 1859 at Solferino, where he commanded a corps made up mostly of Magyars and won his part of the battle by defeating the opposing Sardinians. The latter feat made him popular in the army and the idol of the Vienna press. But Benedek was no Radetzky, as he would amply prove in 1866, and, as a strategist, he was far less imaginative than Hess, whom he had replaced as chief of the General-Quartiermeister-Stab. Following in the hallowed Austrian military tradition, Benedek despised learning; he looked askance at the Prussian general staff's practice of meticulous planning, and he swore by the practice of élan, that is, frontal attack with the bayonet.[16]

Benedek was actually not the sole survivor of the purges; several other generals less successful in 1859 than he also escaped dismissal. The officer corps as a whole was not purged, but its members were offered a bonus if they chose to resign their commissions; about eight hundred took advantage of the opportunity.[17] The measure was in fact of dubious value, since those who resigned were often the ones with enough drive and talent to find employment with the rapidly growing railroads or in industry. For the first time, nobles began to leave the corps, and the new middle class was not sufficiently motivated to replace them. The pay of junior officers remained abysmally low, as we shall see later, and thus there was now a shortage of officers as well as, incidentally, of trained NCOs.

The war of 1859 put an end to the absolutistic experiment in Austria. As long as the empire was strong, or at least appeared to be so, the government could dispense with popular support. Now it was necessary to win followers; therefore, in 1860, Francis Joseph promulgated the so-called October Diploma, which created a central parliament in Vienna (with limited authority, it is true) and resurrected the provincial diets. These measures were expected to please provincial interests, particularly those of the Hungarians, who had always been the monarchy's biggest problem. The Hungarians did indeed avail themselves of the opportunity, re-creating their parliament and restoring the autonomous county administrations, but only in order to struggle even more effectively for the restoration of the 1848 constitution and Hungarian sovereignty. Some Hungarian politicians, especially the newly amnestied former exiles and political prisoners, wanted to go even further. They strove for complete independence, which in turn would have permitted complete Magyar domination of the kingdom. At least the great majority of Hungarians no longer advocated an armed struggle, however. Meanwhile, the German-Austrian liberals, who were unconditional centralists, rejected the October Diploma with its implied threat of federalism.

The battle lines were clearly drawn and remained essentially unchanged until the monarchy's dissolution. Federalization of any kind met with the determined opposition of the German-Austrian politicians, who were painfully aware of their numerical minority in the monarchy and were therefore loath to cede any shred of German cultural, economic, and political primacy. They would be joined in their advocacy of centralism by the Hungarians, and would be to an even greater extent after 1867, although the centralist strivings of the latter were focused not on Vienna but on Budapest. Opposed to them were the empire's smaller national groups whose hopes lay in the promotion of a more federal scheme.

Roughly speaking, two political camps were taking shape in the monarchy. In the first camp, Germans of many political shadings, from Pan-German nationalist to liberal to socialist, formed a very uneasy alliance with the Hungarian political parties. The Magyars had no excessive love for the German-Austrians, whom they tended to view as inhabitants of a foreign country, but they had even less liking for the Slavs and Romanians. In the second camp were assembled the Czech, Croatian, Serbian, Ruthenian, Romanian, and Italian politicians, who, no matter what their social program and political ideology, favored small provincial autonomies. In this struggle, the Slavs often benefited from the support of such unlikely allies as the conservative aristocrats, bureaucrats, officers, and Catholic high clergy, in other words, "Old Austrian" Habsburg loyalists who judged German and Hungarian nationalism to be more dangerous for the monarchy than Slavic nationalism. But as time advanced, more and more of these "Old Austrians" became "national," and embraced one or another of these local national movements. At the end, only the officers would continue to be true to the idea of a unified monarchy.

There were, in addition, a number of specific alliances and enmities. For example, Polish political leaders tended to support the Vienna government, whether liberal or conservative, federalist or centralist, so long as the government allowed Poles to dominate the Ruthenes in Galicia. Or the Serbs in Hungary, who alternately allied themselves with the Croats and looked for Magyar support against Croatian political ambitions. Or, finally, the Italians in Dalmatia, who were generally loyal to Austria out of fear of the Croatian majority in that province. All in all, whatever the emperor attempted to do was bound to meet with the determined opposition of a great number of political groups.

Because the system created in 1860 proved unworkable, the emperor in February 1861 issued a patent greatly increasing the power of a new bicameral legislature in Vienna and concomitantly reducing the authority of the provincial diets.[18] Among other things, the patent vested the central parliament with control over military expenditures. This pleased the German-Austrian liberals, but they still resented the need to share power with the imperial bureaucracy and strove to be completely free to implement a program of liberal reform, emancipation, and modernization. As for the Hungarians, they rejected outright the notion of an all-monarchial central parliament; nor were the other national politicians enchanted. Nevertheless, thanks to the support of the imperial bureaucracy and the German-Austrian liberals, the new system functioned for about four years, allowing for spectacular economic progress. No less important, the cabinet of Anton Ritter von Schmerling almost managed to balance the budget, probably a first in Habsburg history. This meant, however, cutting military expenditures, from 179 million gulden in 1861 to 96 million in 1865.[19] The consequences for the monarchy were disastrous.

The army was grossly underfinanced, and yet was asked to suppress irredentist agitation in the Italian-inhabited provinces, to keep the Hungarians in check, and to fight two wars to preserve the Habsburg presence in Germany and Italy. In theory, the army's peacetime size was 600,000, and its mobilization strength 850,000, but in reality no more than 374,000 men were in active service in 1865.[20]

Thanks to the Olmütz Punctation of 1850, Austrian primacy in the German Confederation had been preserved, but after Bismarck became the minister president of Prussia in 1862, it was only a matter of time before this primacy would be challenged. Economically, Prussia had long predominated in northern Germany through the so-called Customs Union. For the time being, however, Austria and Prussia managed to cooperate in an unauthorized "federal execution" against the Danish king. A conflict over the famous and devilishly complex Schleswig-Holstein question led to the invasion of Denmark by a joint Austro-Prussian expeditionary force on February 1, 1864. The small Danish army resisted heroically, but the war was over by October of the same year.[21]

The Habsburg army corps under Feldmarschalleutnant Ludwig von Gablenz distinguished itself and won a decisive victory by storming the heavily fortified Danish ramparts at Oversee. Prussian and Austrian observers pointed out the prohibitive cost of such frontal assaults, but their warnings were ignored in the general exultation, with the argument that "everything [can] be achieved with the bayonet."[22]

It is easy to fault the Austrian commanders for driving their men headlong into concentrated enemy fire, but it should be remembered that the army was made up largely of illiterate peasants, who could hardly be taught to employ individual initiative or take part in complex maneuvers.* In Denmark in 1864, and again in the war of 1866, Austria paid a heavy price for having exempted the moneyed and educated classes from conscription.

Trouble between the two allies began immediately after the Danish War, when Bismarck set out systematically to provoke Francis Joseph into a declaration of war, not in order to destroy Austria but to rid himself of the Austrian presence in Germany. In the developing conflict, most German states sided with Austria against Prussia, but their military assistance, except for that of Saxony, was useless. Meanwhile, Bismarck had secured the active intervention of Italy on his side.

The story of the Seven Weeks' War of 1866, a true turning point in European history, is well known.[23] In terms of population, Francis Joseph had the upper hand: his empire of 35 million, supported by numerous allies, faced 18 million Prussians. But the combat forces were roughly equal. Since over 100,000 Austrians had to be kept in the South to face the Italians, only some 175,000 Austrians and 32,000 Saxons met the 254,000 Prussian invaders in Bohemia.[24] The Austrian cavalry and

---

*In 1865, the proportion of literate recruits was estimated at less than 10 percent; in the Prussian army the proportion was over 90 percent. (Heinz Helmert, *Militärsystem und Streitkräfte im deutschen Bund am Vorabend des preussisch-österr. Krieges von 1866* [Berlin, 1964], pp. 64–65.) In the Habsburg army it was common practice to teach recruits the difference between left and right by tying hay to their left leg and straw to the right. The cadence "hay-straw, hay-straw" seems to have worked wonders. As late as 1889, an Austrian military writer noted that many recruits were unaware of their family name. (Alfons Danzer et al., *Unter den Fahnen. Die Völker Österreich-Ungarns in Waffen* [Prague-Vienna-Leipzig, 1889], p. 200.)

artillery were on a par with those of the Prussians, but the infantry was notably inferior in training, tactics, equipment, and, probably, dedication. On the other hand, the Austrians were on home territory, and foreign observers, among them Friedrich Engels, confidently predicted an Austrian victory.

A number of factors, overlooked by the observers, militated in favor of Prussia: universal conscription, introduced there during the Napoleonic Wars; Krupp's rifled cast-iron cannon; the breech-loading needle gun, which allowed a rifleman to fire rapidly and from a prone position, while his Austrian counterpart had to stand to load his albeit more accurate muzzle-loading Lorenz rifle; the superior training and precise planning of the Prussian general staff, as contrasted with the happy-go-lucky attitude of the Austrians; the skilled use the Prussians made of railroads and telegraph; the ethnic homogeneity and warlike tradition of the Prussians; and, last but not least, the tremendous qualitative difference between Helmuth von Moltke, the Prussian commander, and Benedek, the Austrian. The former was a military genius, calm and self-confident; the latter was a hesitant, weak-willed pessimist.

Benedek accepted the command of the Northern Army only because he had been ordered to do so by his beloved sovereign, and Francis Joseph appointed Benedek only because of public pressure. Archduke Albrecht would have been a better choice, and, ironically, the same Vienna press that before the war had clamored for the appointment of the "liberal" Benedek, the "people's soldier," hinted openly after its conclusion that his appointment had reflected the emperor's desire to spare a member of his own family the humiliation of certain defeat. In reality, before Königgrätz, Francis Joseph was as confident of victory as the Vienna press and nearly everyone else in the monarchy.

Prussia and Italy declared war on Austria on June 18, 1866; eleven days later, the invading Prussians destroyed the Austrian I Army Corps at Gitschin. Because of this and other bad news from the battle lines, Benedek decided to withdraw his main army to Moravia, there to await the Prussians. The tactic might have worked, but Benedek was already so dispirited that he begged his emperor to make peace immediately. The request was rejected in an imperial telegram, which Benedek misunderstood as an order to seek a decisive encounter. Loyally, he marched out of Olmütz, confronted the Prussians at Königgrätz in the early days of July, and was thoroughly trounced. It was the largest battle fought theretofore in modern history, involving about half a million combatants. The outcome was decided by the unexpected arrival of the Prussian Second Army, hurrying to the aid of the other two Prussian armies.[25]

At first, the Austrians withdrew in good order, but then panic broke out, and a headlong flight ensued. Only the artillery's self-sacrifice saved Benedek's army from complete annihilation. Austrian casualties at Königgrätz numbered 1,313 officers and 41,499 men killed, missing, wounded, or captured; Prussian casualties amounted to only 359 officers and 8,794 men.[26] Yet despite the general mood of dejection in the Austrian camp, the war was not yet lost. Benedek still disposed of 180,000 troops, and in northern Italy, where 110,000 Austrians were pitted against 260,000 Italian regulars and Garibaldi's 40,000 volunteers, Archduke Albrecht had won a decisive victory at Custozza on June 28.[27] Triumph in the South was completed on July 20 at Lissa, where Vice-Admiral Wilhelm von Tegetthoff overwhelmed a much larger Italian fleet.

On July 10, Albrecht assumed command of all the Austrian forces and established a creditable defensive line along the Danube, which was reinforced with troops rushed north from Italy. Suddenly, there were many volunteers to help defend Austria; nor did Bismarck have any success with his half-hearted attempt to spread the flame of revolution to northern Hungary by sending a Hungarian Legion there. In fact, Hungary's unofficial leader, Ferenc Deák (no relative of mine), went out of his way to reassure the emperor that his Hungarian countrymen would not exploit the monarchy's distress. To top it all, the Prussians had to worry about cholera in their ranks as well as about the rumored plans of Napoleon III to rush to the aid of Austria.

It was Francis Joseph who decided to put an end to the bloodshed, a decision strongly influenced by the Vienna municipality's request that the capital be declared an open city. On July 26, at Prague, peace was concluded with Prussia, enabling Austria to deal with Italian guerrilla incursions into Austrian territory. To everyone's surprise, including that of William I of Prussia, Bismarck had wanted no territorial concessions from Austria. Instead, he annexed Hannover, Hesse, and a few other German states, replaced the old German Confederation with a Prussian-dominated North German Confederation, and forced the South German states to enter into a military alliance with the king of Prussia. The centuries-old Habsburg presence in Germany had come to an end.

The Italian side of the war dragged on for a few more weeks, but Francis Joseph had already ceded Venetia to the French, who, in turn, ceded the province to Italy. True, Venetia had been promised to France before the war; true, too, the Austrians had been most unpopular in that province. Still, the cession of Venetia was a great blow to the soldiers who had done so well in the Italian war. Ironically, before the outbreak of hostilities, the king of Italy had offered to buy Venetia and the Italian-inhabited parts of the South Tyrol for the hefty sum of 400 million Austrian gulden.[28] His honor offended, Francis Joseph had indignantly rejected the offer; now, he had to give away Venetia for nothing.

The Austrians had also been pushed out of Italy, but to Italian eyes, the process was not complete. For the next fifty years, Italian politics concentrated on redeeming oppressed brethren in Dalmatia, Trieste, Friulia, and the South Tyrol, all areas inhabited by a very mixed population.

Court-martial proceedings were instituted after the war against Benedek and his two inept aides, Generals Henikstein and Krismanić. In the end, Francis Joseph quashed the proceedings against Benedek, but not without the publication of a court-inspired press report on Benedek's "guilt" and the emperor's "generosity." The unfortunate Feldzeugmeister went into retirement, never to say or write a word in his own defense. He would become a symbol of indignation over what officers perceived to be the imperial court's and public's ingratitude toward a long-suffering army.

Reform and Consolidation, 1867–1897

Rather than destroying the Habsburg monarchy and annexing its German-speaking provinces, Bismarck opted for a "Little German" solution and proceeded to win over Austria as an ally and junior partner. He urged the monarchy's leaders to find a solution to their domestic problems, especially the most pressing of all, the Hungarian problem. Francis Joseph himself was so conscious of the need for a thorough political reorganization that he had begun negotiating with the Hungarians a year before the Austro-Prussian conflict. The principal dramatis personae in this often acrimonious and painful affair were Ferenc Deák; Count Andrássy; Colonel Friedrich von Beck, then the head of the emperor's military cabinet; Archduke Albrecht; Empress Elizabeth; and, joining them somewhat later, Baron Friedrich Ferdinand Beust, the new Austrian foreign minister. It is worth noting that none of them was a Slav or a German-Austrian. Beust was a Saxon refugee; Beck came from the Rhineland; Elizabeth was a Bavarian; Andrássy as well as Deák were Hungarians; and Albrecht was a Habsburg with a profound personal commitment to family tradition and an equal hatred for all nationalisms, including German nationalism.

The most difficult problem of the *Ausgleich* (Compromise) negotiations was that of the armed forces.[29] The Hungarians were pressing for complete military sovereignty; they were ready to provide for a common defense but not for a unitary army. They wanted to resurrect the national honvéd army, complete with the uniforms and insignia of the 1848–1849 revolution, as well as with Hungarian as the language of command and service. This the emperor rejected categorically. Deák and Andrássy were prepared to make substantial concessions on the army question, but they had to tread carefully because of their own vigorous domestic opposition, which regarded even a personal union between Austria and Hungary as a major concession. The passionately Magyarophile (and, reputedly, passionately Andrássyphile) Elizabeth urged her husband to accommodate the Hungarians; Beust and Beck, the latter more reluctantly, were inclined toward a compromise; only Archduke Albrecht held out as long as he could for an all-monarchical, unitary army.[30]

The Compromise Agreement, as finally worked out in 1867, took the form of two distinct laws, one Austrian and the other Hungarian, as well as a series of temporary economic agreements. Austria and Hungary each had its own constitution and a cabinet directly responsible to the legislature. There were, however, to be three ministries in common, one to administer the Common or Joint Army, another for the conduct of foreign affairs, and a third to handle the finances of the two other joint ministries. The agreement on economic cooperation included the creation of a common bank of issue and a customs union. Unlike the compromise on the ministers, the economic agreements were revokable and had to be renegotiated every ten years. Hungary's initial contribution to common expenses was set at 30 percent, a figure which slightly underestimated the country's national income. Forever after, the Austrians kept pressing for an increase in the proportional Hungarian contribution, with the result that by 1907 it had risen to 36.4 percent. The Hungarian kingdom itself was divided into two parts: Hungary proper (which had been reunited with Transylvania), and the much smaller Kingdom of Croatia-Slavonia. In 1868, the Hungarians and Croats concluded their own compromise, the so-called Nagodba, which left the Croats dissatisfied.

Finally, it should be noted that as a result of the Compromise both the Austrian and the Hungarian parliaments each delegated sixty of their members (forty from the lower chamber and twenty from the upper house, with the Hungarian delegation including eight Croats) to handle matters of common interest. The two delegations met semiannually, alternating between Vienna and Budapest. They listened to the reports of the joint ministers and decided on how the common budget should be spent. Characteristically, even though the two delegations met in the same building, they sat separately and communicated only in writing. In practice, each delegation acted as a mouthpiece of its own parliament and government. In the Hungarian case, this meant a forceful representation of the majority party; in the Austrian case, it meant confusion, because a lasting majority could never be formed in the Vienna Reichsrat.[31]

After 1867, important affairs of the Dual Monarchy were conducted in direct meetings between the two prime ministers, or between the emperor-king and one or both of his prime ministers, or, finally, at the sessions of a "joint council of ministers," consisting of the ruler, the two prime ministers, the foreign minister (who acted as unofficial chancellor of the Dual Monarchy), the joint ministers of war and finance, and whomever else the council cared to invite to its deliberations.[32]

The Compromise Agreement did not satisfy anybody, which assured its survival. Although they themselves would never admit it, the principal beneficiaries of the new system were the German-Austrian and Hungarian social and political elites. The Slavs, Romanians, and Italians were more legitimately dissatisfied, but they were restrained by the reality of growing prosperity and, at least in the Austrian Empire, by the repeated concessions made to nationality interests. In Hungary, forceful administrative methods achieved the same results.

After 1867, developments diverged markedly in the two halves of the Dual Monarchy. In Austria, political equality was granted gradually to the elites of the various nationalities and, with the introduction of universal suffrage in 1907, even to the lower social classes. The result was repeated crises of the Austrian parlimentary system and its replacement, time and again, by near-dictatorial cabinets made up of bureaucrats. In Hungary, the Magyar-speaking oligarchy remained in firm control throughout the Dualistic period, but it was prepared to co-opt many newcomers: less willingly if they originated from among the Magyar peasantry, more eagerly if they hailed from the German and Slavic minorities or the Jewish community. The consequence was the survival of a vigorous Hungarian parliamentary system.

Because of Austrian disunity and the unified will of the Hungarian political leadership, at least as regards the major problems of the monarchy, the Hungarians came to exercise a dominant influence on Austro-Hungarian foreign policy. The same cannot be said of their influence on the military, but the army did remain subordinate to the political leadership. In any case, however, both Hungarian and Austrian political influences were mitigated by the independent will of the ruler, who preserved extensive prerogatives in the conduct of foreign and military policy.

The military provisions of the Compromise were formulated into an Austrian and a Hungarian law, both adopted in 1868. Because these laws also dissatisfied nearly everybody, they likewise survived essentially unchanged until 1918. The two laws provided for a joint army and a joint navy under a minister of war, as well as for three national guards or Landwehre: Austrian, Hungarian, and Croatian-Slavonian. Because the last of these was a mere annex of the Hungarian Landwehr or honvédség, there were only two "national" ministers of defense, the Austrian and the Hungarian. The National Guards wore a modified version of the Joint Army uniform, but the Hungarian and Croatian National Guards displayed their own national insignia and swore allegiance not to the emperor but to the king and constitution. The Joint Army's and the Austrian National Guard's language of command and service was German, that of the honvédség, Hungarian, and that of the Croatian-Slavonian Hrvatsko Domobrantsvo, Serbo-Croatian.

Provisions were made for all cadres to learn the languages spoken by the troops, but this requirement was generally ignored in the Hungarian National Guard. The Croatian-Slavonian National Guard faced no such problems, since in none of its battalions did the proportion of non–Serbo-Croatian speakers exceed 20 percent, the minimum required for a unit to be recognized as multilingual.

The same two military laws of 1868 introduced universal conscription, with the proviso that nearly 80 percent of the conscripts be inducted into the Joint Army and Navy, and that the rest be evenly divided between the Austrian and Hungarian National Guards.* The purchase of exemptions was abolished, military age was set at twenty, and the duration of active service in the Joint Army was set at three years, to be followed by seven years in the reserve, and then two years in the reserves of the National Guards. Conscripts who had entered the National Guards directly did active service for two years, followed by ten years in the reserves.

The National Guards were at first perceived as second-line formations, and they did not have artillery and technical branches of their own until 1912. However, because the Hungarian politicians diligently strove to improve the quality of the honvédség, the Austrian National Guard also followed suit, albeit reluctantly. As a result, the National Guard infantry and cavalry were often better equipped than their counterparts in the Joint Army, although the prestige and quality of National Guard officers continued to lag behind that of the Joint Army officers.

The annual intake of recruits was divided by lot. Those drawing the highest numbers were inducted into the Joint Army or into one of the National Guards; those with a middle number were assigned to a special formation, called the Ersatzreserve, in which, after 1882, the training period was set at eight weeks, to be repeated once a year for a period of ten years. Those drawing the lowest numbers were assigned after 1886 to an *arrière garde,* called the Landsturm.

The Ersatzreserve included not only those who had drawn a middle number but also seminarians, teachers, teacher-trainees, owners of inherited land, and the less than perfectly fit. Military training in the Ersatzreserve was nearly worthless and yet, in 1914, its units would play a crucial role in replenishing the decimated regular formations at the front. As for the Landsturm, this paper organization included individuals who had received no training at all as well as veterans (up to the age of forty-two) of active service formations. In World War I, the Landsturm would also

---

*To be precise, universal conscription was not immediately extended to all parts of the monarchy. The Tyrol, Trieste, and the area around Cattaro and Ragusa in southern Dalmatia were exempted, and when an attempt was made, in 1869, to introduce universal conscription in southern Dalmatia, there was a bloody upheaval.

come to life, with entire army divisions of this third-rate formation being rushed to the front, there to suffer terrible casualties.

The military laws of 1868 set the annual intake of conscripts to the Joint Army at 95,400 (56,000 from Austria and less than 40,000 from Hungary). An additional 20,000 recruits were assigned to the National Guards. New military laws adopted in 1889 increased the annual intake of conscripts into the Joint Army to 103,000. In addition, after 1889, 12,500 recruits were drafted directly into the Hungarian and 10,000 into the Austrian National Guard each year. The annual total of 125,500 recruits remained unchanged until 1912, even though the monarchy's population had increased in the meantime from 42 to 52 million. Because the military laws were renewable every ten years, the two parliaments saw to it that the Austro-Hungarian standing army remained proportionally smallest of any of the Continental great powers. In fact, the gap was widening constantly.[33]

In Hungarian eyes, the military laws of 1868 were merely provisional and, for the next five decades, the Budapest parliament witnessed sustained agitation for the expansion of the Hungarian National Guard to include all soldiers originating from Hungary. If this could not be achieved, it was hoped at least that Hungarian could be the language of command and service in every Joint Army regiment originating from Hungary. In this respect, there was no difference between the goals of the liberal Government Party (or Party of 1867) and the equally liberal National Opposition Party (known also as the Party of 1848 or Independence Party), except that the Government Party was prepared to move more slowly. So it came to be that, in a parliament where nearly everyone wanted to see the separation of the armed forces into two parts and the creation of a genuine Hungarian national army (about half of which would be made up of non-Magyar speakers, of course), every decennial debate of the military bill led to shouting matches and mutual accusations of treason. Meanwhile, students, members of the middle class, and artisans ran riot in Budapest, especially in the years 1888–1889 and 1903–1906, demanding that the accursed black and yellow Habsburg colors and the double-headed eagles be removed from all military signposts. Simultaneously, Croatian demonstrators in Zagreb vented their fury on the Hungarian national insignia.

The exasperating debates on "army language" obscured all other issues, yet all this did not prevent the Hungarian kingdom from flourishing economically as well as in the fields of education, health care, and culture. It is nevertheless ironic that a political and social elite which badly needed the backing of the monarchy's armed forces against the Croats, the national minorities, irredentist neighbors, and working-class as well as peasant unrest, should have devoted so much energy to weakening that army. For no matter what the Hungarian politicians said then and what many Hungarian historians have been saying since that time, an independent Hungarian army would have been unable to preserve what the Hungarians officially termed the "Hungarian Empire."

Political life displayed little more sanity in the Austrian half of the Dual Monarchy. In the Vienna Reichsrat, German liberals, Pan-Germans, and German-Austrian Social Democrats vied with Czech liberals, radicals, and socialists, and with Italian, Slovene, Ruthenian, and Romanian nationalists in railing against the "feudal," "reactionary," "Germanic," "Hungarophile," "Pro-Slav," "Judaized,"

"Jesuit-dominated," "corrupt," "inefficient," and "spendthrift" army. The Czech deputies in particular clamored for their own national guard on the Hungarian model or, short of that, for the adoption of Czech as the language of command and service in regiments originating from the Czech lands. Nothing came of these demands, even though the system seemed always on the verge of collapse. In fact, the World War I joke that the situation in the Habsburg monarchy was "hopeless but not serious" (as opposed to the German Reich, where "the situation was serious but not hopeless") accurately described the Dual Monarchy and the position of its army.

The army laws of 1868 were never invalidated but, gradually, additional concessions were made to nationalist sentiment as well as to practical considerations. In 1882, the territorial principle was introduced in the Joint Army, meaning that thenceforth the monarchy's fifteen and a half army corps each drew their conscripts from a specifically defined territory. The incessant migrations of the first-line battalions had ended much earlier; now even trained units spent more and more time at or near their home base. This saved expenses along with pleasing the Hungarians, but it deprived the officers of an opportunity to learn about the lands they were expected to defend. In 1881, for instance, out of the forty-one Joint Army infantry regiments originating from Hungary, only fourteen were in Austria, and eight did occupation duty in newly acquired and commonly administered Bosnia-Hercegovina. In the same year, out of the thirty-nine Joint Army infantry regiments originating from Austria, not a single one was stationed in Hungary. In 1897, of the 188 Joint Army infantry battalions originating from Hungary, only 17 were in Austria and 24 in Bosnia-Hercegovina. In the same year, of the 18 Hungarian cavalry regiments in the Joint Army, 5 were in Austria, but not a single Austrian cavalry regiment was stationed in Hungary.[34] Subsequently, there would be other concessions made to Hungarian national sentiment.

The National Guards were territorial and stationary from the start. Their battalions (National Guard regiments were created only in 1890) took their conscripts from narrowly defined recruiting districts where the units were permanently stationed. This meant that the National Guard officers were often unfamiliar even with their own half of the monarchy. And yet, after all this has been said, it should be stressed that the separation of the armed forces into three (or four) independent sections never led to a truly dangerous situation. The commander in chief of each of the National Guards was a Habsburg archduke, and the Guards proved their loyalty repeatedly, by their determined action against local rioters, during the campaign to occupy Bosnia-Hercegovina, and, most important, during World War I. In sum, the military system created in 1868 had many drawbacks and only one merit: it endured.

In 1868 and in subsequent years, a wave of reforms swept through the armed forces. Among other things, the last remnants of the venality in the officers' promotion system were abolished. The Military Border, a truly outmoded institution, was gradually dismantled, all its regiments being incorporated into the regular infantry by 1873. The latter operation did not proceed without major complications and a good deal of hostility between the Hungarians and the Croats, but it was accomplished nevertheless. The last Grenzer revolt took place in 1871, when some NCOs and ordinary soldiers of the 3rd Ogulin Regiment conspired to set up a Croatian national army and, eventually, an independent South Slav state. The mutineers killed a few of their officers, but they were promptly subdued by Grenzer companies loyal to Baron Anton Mollinary, the commanding general in Croatia-Slavonia and himself a child of the Border. Eight years later, Mollinary resigned, however, because of what he perceived as ruthless Hungarian interference in Croatian affairs.[35]

Military reform involved making the soldiers' uniforms more practical, modernizing their equipment, and setting up a number of new arms' manufactures. Military hospitals and homes for invalids were constructed, as were scores of new barracks which, even though they look dark and forbidding today, represented a vast improvement over the former monasteries whose tenants had been evicted by Joseph II or the peasant cottages in which many soldiers had been billeted. For the first time, enlisted men on maneuvers had their food prepared in mobile kitchens. Their pay improved as well, although not too noticeably. In 1889, for instance, an enlisted man had to make do with six kreuzers daily. After deductions for such things as laundry, tobacco, salve for his feet, grease for his rifle, and a clean scarf for his neck, this left him with four-fifths of a kreuzer per day, the equivalent of approximately one-third of a contemporary U.S. cent.[36]

In this period, too, the military schools were reorganized, and their curriculum modernized; advanced training courses were created for talented officers; the pay and pensions of officers and NCOs were improved; and provisions were made for their widows and orphans. Finally, a reserve officer corps was established, to which only educated civilians had access. More will be said about all this at a later point in this study.

Two men provided the driving force behind these and other reforms: General Baron Franz John, minister of war, 1866–1868, and chief of the general staff, 1866–1869 and 1874–1876; and General Baron Franz Kuhn von Kuhnenfeld, minister of war, 1868–1874.[37]*

Both John and Kuhn were "liberal centralists," which meant that they believed in an enlightened, unified military administration. Of the two, Kuhn was the more aggressively anticonservative. He introduced humanistic subjects in the curriculum of military schools; he managed to suppress, albeit temporarily, the general staff, which he judged to be elitist; and he tried his best to turn the officer corps into a middle-class institution, imbued with bourgeois-liberal ideals. Both John and Kuhn were opposed from the very start by Archduke Albrecht, who, for reasons personal and ideological, wanted to restrict the Ministry of War to the mere handling of administrative affairs. It was Albrecht who caused the resignation of John in 1868 and Kuhn in 1874, but the archduke was not all-powerful either. Despite his vigorous protests, the position of commander in chief was abolished in 1869, and thereafter he had to be satisfied with the role of inspector-general of the army. Albrecht was the monarchy's sole peacetime field marshal, but when he became old and nearly blind, this great soldier lost much of his former influence and power.

Albrecht was not alone in opposing the two successive liberal war ministers.

---

*Note that, unlike Gyulai and Grünne, John and Kuhn were not aristocrats; unlike Benedek, they were not even noblemen. The sons of low-ranking officers, John and Kuhn received their baronial title (Freiherr) as a result of having been awarded the Maria Theresa Order for exceptional bravery.

The general staff, the emperor's military cabinet, and the adjutant general's office all resented the power of the ministry as well. Yet all three institutions, as well as the Ministry of War, were gradually subdued by Friedrich Beck, who came to enjoy the sovereign's confidence to a greater extent and for a longer period of time than any other general before or after him.[38]

Beck, who was born in 1830, the same year as Francis Joseph, came to the fore at the battle of Königgrätz while still a mere colonel and the emperor's adjutant. In 1867, he was made head of the emperor's military cabinet; in 1874, adjutant general; and in 1881, at the age of fifty-one, chief of the general staff. He retained this last post until 1906, when, at seventy-six, he was finally forced to retire. Beck actually survived his imperial master, dying in 1920 at the age of ninety. This quiet, cautious, enormously dedicated middle-class German (who, however, married into an aristocratic family) became, in time, the emperor's friend. Francis Joseph shook hands with Beck occasionally, and, when very old, the two men sometimes conversed while sitting. The public referred to Beck as the *Vize-Kaiser,* and he was surrounded by nearly the same ceremony as the emperor-king. Francis Joseph liked to take Beck's advice, which was invariably to avoid war. With regard to the conduct of military affairs, Beck occupied a middle position; he thought nothing of Kuhn's liberal experiments and, even though his heart was on the conservative side, he also quietly obstructed Albrecht's reactionary policy.

As "chief of the general staff of the entire armed forces," Beck mitigated the many-sided internal army conflict. He saw to it that the Ministry of War would be in sole charge of military organization, administration, justice, education, and procurement, as well as relations with the two parliaments. The general staff he entrusted with military planning, operations, intelligence, and transport in case of mobilization. Some said that, under Beck, the general staff—an institution ignored by the two constitutions—became much too powerful. It is true that the general staff substituted for a high command of the armed forces, and that its subordination to the constitutional Ministry of War had become, under Beck, more and more nominal. At the same time, however, there was a real need for a unified command, at least in case of war. Beck attempted simultaneously to modernize the army and to preserve its ancient supranational ideology.

The final arbitrator between the differing factions was, however, not Beck, but the emperor-king, who successfully drowned all controversies in a sea of paper. At once courteous and distant, Francis Joseph easily reduced all claimants to size. He granted over a hundred audiences weekly, receiving all visitors, be they archdukes, cabinet members, or the poorest of the poor, in the same atmosphere of dignity and carefully orchestrated ritual. Standing at attention, the emperor-king caused his visitors to adopt the same military posture and to report to him briefly and precisely. Those who misbehaved in the slightest were dismissed before their allotted time with a barely perceptible click of the heels or a nod of the imperial head. In his august presence, all passions and hatreds were reduced to mere ceremonial and bureaucratic routine.

The Habsburg monarchy had never known such a long period of peace as that between 1867 and 1914. For career soldiers this was, of course, a mixed blessing. Except for a lucky minority who participated in the localized military operations on the monarchy's southern borders, an entire generation of officers went through the ranks without seeing combat. If commissioned in 1870, for instance, an officer would retire in 1910, at the age of sixty, having experienced nothing but drill, parades, and the customary autumn maneuvers. There, the enemy wore red or blue insignia, and even the most exhilarating cavalry charge could be stopped by a contemptuous general staff officer equipped with a white armband. All this was very frustrating, but not nearly as frustrating as the slow advance of officers up the promotional ladder, a fate so different from the glorious careers carved out by the preceding generation on the battlefields of Hungary, Solferino, or Königgrätz.

What campaigns were there during these long years of general peace? In 1869, the inhabitants of the mountainous Krisvosije region in southern Dalmatia revolted against the introduction of universal conscription and in support of their hallowed right to bear arms. It took several months for eighteen infantry battalions and a number of other units to force a semisurrender from the thousand-odd insurgents. In exchange, the rebels gained all that they had fought for, at least temporarily.[39] In 1878–1879 came the occupation of Bosnia-Hercegovina, a far more serious affair, involving some 270,000 soldiers, and then, in 1881, another revolt in the Krisvosije region, as well as in newly occupied Bosnia-Hercegovina.[40] But that was all.

In all these campaigns, the troops proved reliable and loyal, and the high command less than superbly efficient. All in all, however, at the cost of a great deal of brutality, rape, burning, and hanging when engaged in search-and-destroy operations, the Austro-Hungarians succeeded in "pacifying" these areas, which was more than the Germans and Italians could do in World War II. The Balkan expeditions between 1869 and 1881 also demonstrated that local enmities, such as those between Catholics and Muslims, could best be handled by "native" generals: the Austro-Hungarian commander of every one of those military expeditions was himself a South Slav.

The monarchy's Balkan involvement was a natural corollary to Austria-Hungary's exclusion from Germany and Italy. There had been a last opportunity, during the Franco-Prussian War of 1870–1871, for Austria to reappear on the German scene and avenge Königgrätz. Indeed, negotiations to that effect were begun between Francis Joseph and Napoleon III as early as 1867. Three years later, Foreign Minister Beust, Archduke Albrecht, and Minister of War Kuhn pushed for armed intervention on the French side, but Prime Minister Andrássy opposed the move, since for him, as for all Hungarians, the tsar, not Bismarck, was the real enemy. As would happen again and again, public opinion in the monarchy was wildly divided, with the Czechs and other Slavs favoring war against Prussia, and the majority of German-Austrians as well as the Hungarians rooting for Bismarck. Because both Chief of the General Staff John and General Beck advised restraint, the now-cautious Francis Joseph opted for armed neutrality. Thus, the monarchy looked on impotently as France was defeated and a German Empire proclaimed, despite the fact, as Kuhn and others pointed out, that the monarchy would have been able to mobilize 600,000 men against Prussia. It is a stimulating exercise to wonder whether an Austro-Hungarian attack on Prussia in 1870 could have changed the history of Germany and thus also of the world.[41]

In 1871 Andrássy replaced Beust as foreign minister, thus hastening Habsburg-

Hohenzollern reconciliation, motivated chiefly by Vienna's fear of Russia. The Russian menace had actually been the primary reason for Francis Joseph's refusal to go to war in 1870. Three years later, Bismarck arranged for a renewed alliance between Russia, Prussia, and Austria-Hungary, but in 1875 grave difficulties arose between Austria-Hungary and Russia over the issue of the Balkans.

In June of that year, the inhabitants of Bosnia and Hercegovina revolted against their Ottoman overlords. The uprising had been encouraged by Austro-Hungarian propaganda and arms shipments. The Serbian principality, in theory a vassal state of the Ottomans, joined in the insurrection almost immediately, followed, in 1876, by Montenegro and the Bulgarian provinces of the Ottoman Empire. However, rather than collapsing immediately, as had been generally expected, the Turks drowned the Bulgarian insurrection in a sea of blood and, in September 1876, they destroyed the Serbian army. This caused great excitement in Russia, where the elite was imbued with Pan-Slavic ideas, and in April 1877 Tsar Alexander II felt obliged to declare war on the sultan.

Following some unexpectedly strong Turkish resistance, the Russian army arrived at the outskirts of Constantinople in March of 1878; in the same month, the Ottomans sued for an armistice and, at San Stefano, they signed a treaty amounting to their exclusion from the Balkans and a complete Russian takeover. The other great powers found such a resolution intolerable, however, and they forced the Russians to the negotiating table at the Congress of Berlin in June-July 1878.[42] The Congress awarded complete independence to an enlarged Romania and Serbia, and it authorized Austria-Hungary to occupy Bosnia and Hercegovina as well as to garrison the Sanjak of Novi Bazar, a strip of land between Serbia and Montenegro. There existed a tentative agreement between Andrássy and Russian Foreign Minister Ignatiev regarding the division of the spoils in the Balkans, but now, as a consequence of Berlin, the Russians felt cheated, for they had made no territorial gains and the Austro-Hungarians had.

The Balkan War had momentous consequences. From that time on, Romania and Serbia would exercise an ever-increasing attraction on their co-nationals in the monarchy; it mattered little that, for the time being, both countries were in a very subordinate position to Austria-Hungary. The Russians, for their part, could not forget their humiliation at Berlin, which they attributed more to Andrássy than to Bismarck or Disraeli. The monarchy's mandate in Bosnia-Hercegovina would lead inevitably to a conflict with Serbia, which claimed the provinces on the basis of historic right and nationality. Finally, it became clear to all observers that the monarchy's relative success at Berlin would have been impossible without German political support.

At home, public opinion had again been divided, with the Hungarians rooting for the Ottomans, and the Czechs and the South Slavs for Russia. The army leadership itself was split between a conservative pro-Russian faction under Albrecht and those who desired a war with the tsar. Again it was Beck who had advised caution by pointing to the possibility of Italy's falling upon Austria-Hungary from the rear, not the first or the last instance of aggressive Austro-Hungarian war plans being overruled by the real or imagined threat of a two-front war.

The occupation of Bosnia-Hercegovina promised to be an easy affair. "All we need is two companies of soldiers, accompanied by a regimental music band," Andrássy is alleged to have boasted. Instead, the Austro-Hungarians encountered the strong resistance of 90,000 Turkish regulars and a large part of the Muslim population.[43] The Christian population, traditionally under the thumb of Muslim landowners, generally welcomed or even helped the invaders. The campaign lasted from July 29 to October 20, 1878, and, according to official statistics, it cost 5,198 Austro-Hungarian casualties. The actual figures seem to have been closer to 3,300 dead, 6,700 wounded, and 110,000 sick.[44] The financial costs were considerable and aroused great commotion in the two parliaments.

At first, the two occupied provinces were under military administration, with a considerable difference in treatment between the two. In Bosnia, Feldzeugmeister Baron Josef Philippović von Philippsberg, a Catholic Croat from a Grenzer family, behaved rather brutally toward the Muslim rebels and would not allow the restoration of communal administrations. In November 1878, Francis Joseph replaced him with a more lenient commander. In Hercegovina, Feldmarschalleutnant Baron Stephan Jovanović, another Catholic Croat from a Grenzer family, quickly reconstituted the local administrations, a policy which gradually became that employed in both provinces. Thereafter, Austro-Hungarian rule in Bosnia-Hercegovina was characterized by cooperation between the authorities and the Muslim landowners. This, in turn, tended to alienate the Christian peasants.

Treated as a commonly acquired colony, the two backward provinces, lacking roads, schools, and hospitals, became a model of enlightened administration, rapid economic progress, and slowly growing local autonomy. Physical improvements were the achievement largely of army engineers; a posting to Bosnia-Hercegovina became a challenge for the monarchy's most ambitious officers. As part of the process of emancipation, the army soon created a few local volunteer Bosnian-Hercegovinian Jäger battalions. Later, universal conscription was introduced in the two provinces, and the volunteer battalions were transformed into regular infantry regiments. By 1894, there were four Bosnian-Hercegovinian infantry regiments, to be complemented in 1903 by an independent Jäger battalion. The Bosniaken, as they were popularly called, counted among the monarchy's best and most reliable soldiers.[45]

Following the occupation of Bosnia-Hercegovina, all seemed well with the monarchy. Both Austria and Hungary enjoyed, at last, a stable government, under Count Eduard Taaffe (1879–1893) in Vienna and Kálmán (Coloman) Tisza (1875–1890) in Budapest. In 1879, the Dual Alliance was signed with Germany, providing for German protection against a Russian attack on Austria-Hungary, but no obligation of Austro-Hungarian help in case of a French attack on Germany. And yet, despite this secret treaty whose essence was no secret at all, the three great conservative empires, Russia, Germany, and Austria-Hungary, renewed their alliance in 1881 and again in 1884. Italy joined the Dual Alliance in 1882, and Romania in 1883. Because Serbia behaved as a client state at that time, the monarchy was at peace with, or even allied to, all of its neighbors. The future seemed assured.

More important, despite periodic setbacks, as in 1873, for instance, there was extraordinary economic development which led in turn to other improvements. In 1869, 67.2 percent of the Austrian population was engaged in agriculture, and in

Hungary, 80 percent. By 1910, the proportion of agriculturalists had fallen to 53.1 percent and 66.7 percent, respectively. Between 1864 and 1866, Hungary produced an annual average of 1,720,000 tons of wheat and 200,000 tons of sugar beets; between 1911 and 1913, the annual average was 4,910,000 tons of wheat and 4,333,000 tons of sugar beets, the latter representing a twentyfold increase. Bosnia-Hercegovina's wheat production more than doubled between 1897 and 1913.

In 1881, Austro-Hungarian industry consumed 520,000 tons of pig iron; in 1911, 2,150,000 tons. The index of industrial production in Austria more than tripled between 1880 and 1913; in Hungary, the increase was even greater. In 1870, the total length of Austro-Hungarian railroads was 9,600 kilometers; in 1880, 18,500 kilometers; and in 1900, 36,300 kilometers. This meant a railroad density (relative to the number of inhabitants) near that of Germany and Great Britain, exceeding that of Belgium, and far exceeding that of Italy. In 1848, the accumulated capital of Hungarian credit institutions totaled 3.7 million kronen; in 1867, 28.8 million kronen; in 1890, 348.5 million kronen; and in 1913, more than 2.5 billion kronen. Between 1901 and 1905, the mortality rate of infants under one year of age was 21.5 percent, a far better percentage than that of Russia and nearly as good as that of Prussia (19 percent), although less good than that of France (15.9 percent) and Great Britain (13.2 percent). In 1911–1912, there were 1,705 elementary-school pupils for every 10,000 inhabitants in Austria, and 1,319 in Hungary. The comparative figures were 1,581 in Germany, 1,435 in France, 980 in Italy, and only 370 in Russia.[46]

The budget in both Austria and Hungary had been balanced since the mid-1880s, and in 1892 the monarchy went over to the gold standard. Yet military expenditures did not keep pace with economic growth. In 1868, the budget of the Joint Army totaled 190 million kronen; in 1882, 268 million kronen; and in 1910, 436 million kronen. Considering the vastly increased cost of armaments and the slight inflation, this was far from enough. Only naval expenditures increased significantly, from 15.9 million kronen in 1868 to 98.9 million in 1910.[47] The Joint Army's rank and file in active service grew almost imperceptibly, from 290,500 in 1872 to 327,600 in 1910. To put it differently, while the monarchy's population increased by 48.5 percent between 1870 and 1914, its military expenditures grew by only 14 percent. True, in 1883, the number of infantry regiments was increased from 80 to 102, but this meant a change only in cadres, not in the total number of effectives.

In 1906, the Dual Monarchy conscripted 0.29 percent of its population; Russia, 0.35 percent; Germany, 0.47 percent; and France 0.75 percent.[48] This means that, after 1867, Austria-Hungary was no longer a military great power, not because it would have been economically unable to preserve this status but because it did not spend enough money. The reason for the shortage of funds was political or, better to say, national.

The most determined opposition to the 1867 Compromise came from the Czech nationalists, who felt cheated out of a good thing and who, as a consequence, boycotted the Reichsrat for the next twelve years. The discontent of the Czech politicians spilled out into the streets, and martial law had to be imposed in Prague in 1868. Three years later, the Austrian government attempted to placate the Poles and the Czechs by granting limited political autonomy to Galicia and to the Czech lands. This was successful in Galicia, because the Ruthenian leadership was too weak to protest Polish supremacy, but in the Czech lands, the prospect of provincial autonomy met with the determined opposition of the German minority. In 1871, the Budapest government vetoed the idea of a Bohemian autonomy because it would not hear of replacing the dualistic with a trialistic system. Thereafter, the dynasty could no longer count on the unconditional loyalty of the Czechs, which was all the more serious because, meanwhile, the Czech middle class had gradually acquired a command position in the economy and in the politics of the Czech lands. Put on the defensive, the thitherto dominant German minority in Bohemia and Moravia looked for support no longer to the Vienna government but to the German-Austrian political parties. The Czech-German conflict became a permanent feature in the life of the empire.

True, in 1879, the government of Count Taaffe persuaded the Czech deputies to return to the Reichsrat, but this again met with the determined opposition of the German political parties. By the 1880s, German-Austrian liberalism was on the decline, to be replaced, at least in part, by the Pan-German movement, which opposed not only excessive military expenditures, as the liberals had, but also the monarchy in its entirety. Led by Georg Ritter von Schönerer, the Pan-Germans abominated the army and regarded its German-speaking officers as renegades and traitors. The Social Democratic movement, which arose in the 1870s, was no less antiarmy, although of course on different ideological grounds.

In 1885–1886, a new crisis erupted in the Balkans, starting with a brief war between Serbia and Bulgaria, the latter a client state of Russia. Only the monarchy's ultimatum saved the defeated Serbs from ruin. There followed a political turmoil in Bulgaria and, once again, Europe hovered on the brink of a great war.* In Vienna, a war party, headed by Crown Prince Rudolf agitated for a preemptive strike against Russia but, again, the war plans were deflated by the caution of Francis Joseph and Beck, with the latter arguing that neither the German allies nor the public at home could be trusted absolutely, and that, in any case, the army was not ready for war.[49] Thus, for once, domestic difficulties proved to be a great blessing for the monarchy as they helped to avert a suicidal military adventure. But the alliance of the three emperors was not renewed in 1887 and, at home, political trouble continued unabated.

In 1889, the decennial army-law debates turned into a far more vicious affair than they had been in 1879. By then, the Hungarian public was in an uproar over previous attempts by the Joint Army command in Budapest to honor the memory of some Austrian heroes of the 1848–1849 war. The army bill, as presented in the Hungarian parliament, greatly aggravated the situation. The issue at stake was, of course, the language of command in the Joint Army, but also the obligation of candidates for a reserve officer's commission to pass a German-language test. Once again, Francis Joseph turned down the Hungarian demands, for he understood only

---

*Note that Alexander of Battenberg, the deposed prince of Bulgaria, entered the Austro-Hungarian army following his ouster in 1886, and that his successor on the Bulgarian throne, Ferdinand of Coburg, had been a career officer in the Habsburg army.

too well that the division of the armed forces into two parts would bring about inevitable division into many more parts and thus the dissolution of the monarchy. There were wild street scenes in the Hungarian cities, and even though the army law was finally passed (thanks to the efforts of Prime Minister Kálmán Tisza, who was nearly lynched in the process), the little goodwill that had existed between the army high command and the Hungarian politicians had now evaporated.[50] To give only one example, the Budapest government in 1890 forbade the transfer of Bosnian units through Hungary on the way to Vienna, with the strange argument that the passing through of "alien" troops was forbidden by the Hungarian constitution. So the Bosnian troops of Austria-Hungary had to be transported by sea so as to participate at a great parade honoring the birthday of the Austro-Hungarian sovereign.[51]

Things went from bad to worse when, following the suicide of Crown Prince Rudolf in 1889, Archduke Francis Ferdinand became—informally, although officially only in 1896—heir to the throne. Rudolf had been alternately exuberantly pro-Magyar and violently anti-Magyar, as befitted his passionate temperament and his confused politics. Francis Ferdinand was a man of absolute principles, which augured ill for the future. After all, only someone prepared to make compromises could possibly preside over this maddeningly complex system. A bigoted Catholic, an anti-Semite, and an absolutist, the archduke hated the Hungarians because he saw them as the chief troublemakers of the monarchy, and because he believed that the liberal Hungarian leaders were tools in the hands of the Jews and of international capitalism. Another reason for Francis Ferdinand's passionate hatred of the Magyars was that, unlike Francis Joseph, Rudolf, and most other Habsburgs, he had no talent for languages. Unable to master the intricate Magyar tongue, Francis Ferdinand felt deeply offended when, as a young colonel in charge of a Hungarian hussar regiment, he had to endure his officers speaking Hungarian in his presence. Yet, according to Habsburg military tradition, it was perfectly correct procedure for officers to use the regimental language when not giving orders.[52]

In 1882 and again in 1884, there were violent workers' demonstrations in Vienna and, although—unlike the nationalist movements—workers' agitation never seriously threatened the monarchy, there was now also a "Red Scare." In the same period, the Austrian police uncovered a few minor anarchist plots, which frightened the army into ordering its officers to sign an affidavit guaranteeing that they did not belong to, nor would ever join, a secret society.[53]

Count Taaffe's policy of keeping everyone in the empire, including the Austro-Germans, "in a state of mild discontent" prolonged his tenure in office but, quite obviously, solved nothing. In 1893, after new riots had erupted in Bohemia, Francis Joseph finally dismissed Taaffe.* Three years earlier, Prime Minister Kálmán Tisza had also resigned in Hungary; this left the monarchy without its most skilled and forceful leaders. The era of stable governments in both Austria and Hungary was over.

Again and again, troops had to be called out to put down rioters, which ended in

---

*In the course of these riots, the unreliable 28th Prague k.u.k. Infantry Regiment had to be transferred from the Bohemian capital to Linz in Upper-Austria. The same regiment went over to the Russians on the Carpathian front in April 1915. (Edmund von Glaise-Horstenau, *Franz Josephs Weggefährte. Das Leben des Generalstabschefs Grafen Beck* [Zurich-Leipzig-Vienna, 1930], p. 358.)

the regular stationing of large military forces in Prague, Vienna, Graz, and Budapest. The garrisons consisted, in part, of Bosnian soldiers, who could not possibly understand what all the excitement was about. Replacing the now defunct Grenzer with these new cossacks proved to be an effective measure, but the Hungarian, German, and Czech nationalists, especially the students, now began to feel and act as if under foreign occupation.[54]

All this makes a dismal story, even though worse was to come. Still, it must be kept in mind that the importance of political demonstrations was vastly exaggerated by the contemporary press and, later, by historians. The majority of the monarchy's inhabitants remained unaffected by the political turmoil. For the peasantry, the passing through of a cavalry squadron, and for townspeople, the Sunday noon concerts offered by the regimental music band remained the most colorful events of their lives. In the eyes of the majority, nothing had changed: the emperor-king sat in the Hofburg or at Schönbrunn, and his periodic outings to hunt chamois in the Alps were celebrated in adulatory tones by the same press that systematically excoriated His Majesty's governments as a gang of thieves, national traitors, and murderers.

The Crisis of the Dual Monarchy and the Army, 1897–1906

In 1895 Archduke Albrecht, the last statesman and general who still thought in purely dynastic terms, died. "If the army is split," he once wrote to Crown Prince Rudolf, "then its spirit will become degraded, the dynasty will be lost, and Austria will exist no more."[55] After Albrecht, General Beck acted as the unofficial head of the entire military establishment. Beck's policy was that of Francis Joseph: to uphold the Compromise Agreement as the only viable solution for the continuation of the monarchy. But in the ensuing decade, it was precisely this Compromise which was most severely challenged from all sides.

In the same year that Albrecht died, Count Kasimir Badeni, a Polish aristocrat of Italian origin, became prime minister of Austria. It was now Badeni's turn to tackle the problems of electoral reform in the empire and linguistic relations in Bohemia. In 1896, the Austrian suffrage was extended to a so-called Fifth Curia, which gave the vote to millions more adult males, although because of the tiered system of suffrage, their votes counted for less than the votes cast in the higher Curiae. The ensuing elections produced the usual divided Reichsrat, now complemented by fourteen Social Democrats. It was to this assembly that Badeni presented, in 1897, his plan to create a bilingual administration in Bohemia and to oblige all Bohemian Beamten to learn Czech and German within the next three years. Nothing could have been more reasonable in a province where the majority of the inhabitants spoke Czech and the minority German; still, the result was bedlam. Since many German functionaries neither knew nor cared to learn Czech, the German parties organized violent protest demonstrations and, in the Reichsrat, they engaged in paralyzing obstruction. As a last resort, Badeni attempted to change the house rules, driving the Social Democrats and the German nationalists into a tactical alliance against him. On November 26, their combined forces assaulted and demolished the presidential rostrum. The police had to be called in to evict the enraged deputies, an act which the German press, including the liberal and generally loyal *Neue Freie Presse,* characterized as "bloody tyranny."[56]

The German protest took its most violent form in Graz, a city near the linguistic border with the Slavs and, hence, a center of militant German nationalism. In the face of the upheaval, the governor of Styria appealed for military assistance; the local corps commander obliged and, on November 27, army units found themselves facing a raging mob led by students. Attacked, the officers of the 2nd Bosnian-Hercegovinian Infantry Regiment ordered their troops to fire. One person was killed and several others were wounded. The ensuing funeral turned into an enormous antiarmy demonstration. Speakers denounced the "black and yellow Moslem mercenaries," and the Graz municipal council officially deplored the presence of "foreigners." Elements of the 7th Carinthian Infantry Regiment, who eventually replaced the Bosnians, were welcomed as national liberators.[57]

The fact that many of the leading student demonstrators were reserve officers or reserve officer candidates was a particularly hard blow to the morale of the career officers, the majority of whom were themselves Germans. Officers had been called traitors in the streets of German-speaking cities, and if they were no longer welcome there, where could they expect to be? Once again, it was demonstrated that educated Germans were among the least loyal elements in the monarchy. The same students who, while in military uniform, sang the imperial anthem, sang the Reich German "Wacht am Rhein" in their fraternities and swore allegiance there not to Francis Joseph but to the German kaiser.[58]

The emperor and the high command were infuriated: thirty-three student reserve officers and ensigns were subsequently stripped of their rank by military courts of honor.[59] The unfortunate Badeni was dismissed in the same year, and his language reform was gradually abandoned. This, in turn, led to violent Czech counterprotests in Prague, and the destruction of German as well as Jewish property.* Nor did German demonstrations cease for another three years. In 1898, new clashes erupted in Graz between the troops and German nationalists; meanwhile, Bohemian recruits were instructed by Czech nationalists to answer "*zde*" instead of the required "*hier*" when their names were called.

Because the Reichsrat was paralyzed, successive cabinets, made up of civil servants, found it necessary to govern dictatorially, invoking the much-decried 14th or Emergency Article of the Constitution. In 1902, however, seemingly by a miracle, a working majority was pieced together in the Reichsrat, encouraging the joint minister of war to request a modest increase in the number of recruits. Now it was the turn of the Hungarian public to run wild. The ensuing crisis, lasting for several years, led to near-civil-war conditions in that country. At least that was what the Hungarian government and press insisted would ensue unless the ruler surrendered to Hungarian interests on the military question.

Ever since the resignation of Kálmán Tisza in 1890, Hungarian prime ministers had attempted to make political capital for themselves by demanding concessions from Vienna in return for their support for the Joint Army. They endorsed such

---

*Jews in Prague usually spoke German and were consequently often the targets of Czech nationalist fury. Not that this endeared the Jews to the Bohemian Germans.

demands of the Opposition as the compulsory transfer of Hungarian officers to Hungarian regiments and the weeding out of Austrians from Hungarian units; the easing of the German-language requirement for Hungarian officer candidates; the training of Hungarian cadets exclusively in Hungarian military schools; the recognition of Hungarian as an official military language; and the use of the Hungarian flag and insignia in Hungarian units. Some of these demands were manifestly unrealistic, as the Hungarians knew only too well, for they threatened the survival of the armed forces, and—as the French military attaché pointed out in his report to Paris in 1903—there were simply not enough Hungarian officers to command all the units originating from Hungary.[60] Although Hungarian politicians never openly differentiated between the Magyar and non-Magyar career officers who happened to be Hungarian citizens, in fact non-Magyars, for the largest part Germans, formed the majority of this group. Most of these officers had no desire to transfer to a Hungarian unit, nor, as it soon became evident, did most of the Magyar officers.

Hungarian agitation is made understandable, nonetheless, by the somewhat justified concern—as Gunther Rothenberg points out—that when Francis Ferdinand succeeded to the throne, he would attempt to abrogate the Compromise Agreement.[61] Thus, a repetition of the 1848 scenario was in the offing: the Hungarians wished to strengthen their sovereignty and national defenses in case the monarchy collapsed or, if not, then in case the Austrians attempted to subvert the Compromise Agreement. The Austrians in turn prepared to prevent the secession of Hungary, an eventuality that seemed increasingly likely.

Repeated government crises in Hungary in 1903, always over the army question, ultimately led Francis Joseph to issue, on September 16, his notorious Chłopy Army Order, which upheld the unity of the Joint Army in a language that the Hungarians found intolerable. It stated, among other things: "My entire armed forces . . . are imbued with that spirit of unity and harmony which respects every national characteristic and is able to solve all antagonisms so as to utilize the individual qualities of each ethnic group for the benefit of all."This seemingly harmless statement flew in the face of the Hungarian view that theirs was not just one of the many nationalities but that Hungary, with its several ethnic groups, constituted a sovereign nation in equal partnership with Austria and its multiple ethnic groups. Worse still, the term "ethnic group" (*Volksstamm*) was translated into Hungarian as "tribal group" (*néptörzs*), an unforgivable insult in Hungarian eyes.[62]

The ensuing parliamentary storm in Budapest surpassed any of the earlier ones, and even though Francis Joseph ended up by making real concessions to Hungarian interests on the army question (for instance, allowing Hungarian officers to transfer to Hungarian regiments and ordering that the Hungarian flag be hoisted next to the imperial flag on Joint Army military buildings in Hungary), the Hungarians could no longer be satisfied.

In November 1903, István Tisza, the son of Kálmán, became prime minister. This man of uncommon ability and strength was ready to save the Dual Monarchy, but not without further concessions to Hungarian interests.[63] His essentially positive intentions were misunderstood: in Austria, they were seen as manifestations of Magyar chauvinism, and in Hungary, they were interpreted as an abject surrender to

Austrian interests. Tisza now adopted the desperate expedient of dissolving the parliament in Budapest and ordering new national elections. In January 1905, he was overwhelmingly defeated; it was the first victory—despite all electoral gerrymandering—by the National Opposition. On June 18, 1905, Francis Joseph appointed General Baron Géza Fejérváry, commander of the Hungarian Noble Bodyguards, as prime minister. Because Fejérváry enjoyed no parliamentary support, and because the Hungarian Constitution lacked an emergency provision for government by decree, an extralegal situation had been created.

For several years, the Hungarian opposition had demanded that taxes not be paid and recruits not be conscripted; this now became the official policy of the Hungarian parliament. Everything began to look again as it had in 1848, even the fact that the Croats were pressing for an end to their own Compromise Agreement with Hungary, and that the threat of violent conflict between Hungarians and Croats loomed large.

The hopelessness of the parliamentary situation in both Austria and Hungary even led the sovereign to toy with the idea of universal suffrage, in the hope that social reforms favored by the lower classes would sweep away the nationalism of the middle classes. This would have meant, in effect, a monarchical alliance with Social Democracy and the populist Christian Socials.

The Hungarian minister of interior officially proposed suffrage reform in December 1905 and, three months later, General Fejérváry forcibly dissolved parliament with the help of a battalion of Hungarian National Guards. The possibility of an open break with Austria seemed likely. General Beck had already developed plans for an armed invasion of Hungary, the famous "Fall U [Ungarn]," but nothing of the sort happened.[64] It was clear that this time the honvéd army men would not fight against their comrades-in-arms, and that both the national minorities and the organized workers had more faith in the ruler than in the socially conservative and ethnically intolerant National Opposition. As a result, the thitherto intransigent opposition parties, led by Ferenc Kossuth, the opportunistic and weak son of Louis Kossuth, suddenly gave in. In April 1906, the several independence parties concluded a pact with the king: in exchange for their promise to vote for a new budget and an army bill providing for the raising of recruits, the king allowed the oppositionist coalition to form a government. The Hungarian constitutional crisis was over, but so was the last opportunity to reform the country in a way that could have satisfied the aspirations of the nationalities and the lower classes.

Political reform proved much more successful in Austria, where Prime Minister Max Wladimir Beck introduced universal suffrage at the end of 1906. The ensuing Reichsrat elections brought success to the Christian Socials (ninety-eight mandates) and the Social Democrats (eighty-seven mandates), as well as the relative weakening of those parties whose only program was nationalism.[65] Austria had become a truly democratic state, which—as later events would show—did not make it any more governable.

The year 1906 was a momentous one in the history of the monarchy. In October, the energetic and aggressive Count Aloys Lexa von Aehrenthal became foreign minister and, a month later, Conrad von Hötzendorf replaced Beck as chief of the general staff. Beck had served his emperor for sixty years, and his departure was as symbolic as the fact that, at the army maneuvers in the same year, an armored car made its appearance. But, as legend has it, Francis Joseph dismissed it as a gadget of no real military value because it frightened the horses.[66]*

The appointments of Aehrenthal and Conrad were due to the influence of Francis Ferdinand, the "rash fool" whom Francis Joseph despised. Thenceforth, more dynamic men were to be in charge of the monarchy, a necessary and yet dangerous development, as the international situation grew increasingly more threatening and complex.

On the Way to War

Internationally, the 1890s and early 1900s were a relatively quiet period for the monarchy, allowing it to ride out the domestic storms. The German alliance stood strong; Russia was preoccupied in the Far East, and Italy in Abyssinia. Europe was engaged in a colonial race, in which Francis Joseph himself had never expressed the slightest interest. Nor did Francis Ferdinand, otherwise a bully and a fierce militarist, manifest any desire for territorial expansion and foreign adventures. On the contrary, he hoped to renew the conservative dynastic alliance with Russia so as better to control revolutionary agitation in both monarchies. His main concern was with the threat of Hungarian secession, and he surrounded himself at his headquarters in Belvedere Palace with a coterie of military and political advisers whom he instructed to devise plans for the drastic reorganization of the realm. Some of these plans were indeed ingenious, calling for the creation of a United States of Austria, or a People's Austria, but, of course, nothing was to come of any of them.[67]

The only concrete result of all this planning and of the intrigues of the "Belvedere Cabal" was the fierce distrust of the emperor and of the Hungarian politicians. As it was, Francis Joseph would not forgive the heir apparent's morganatic marriage to Countess Sophie Chotek in 1900 which, aside from undermining the emperor's absolute authority over his family, threatened to split the monarchy as well. The Hungarian Constitution knew nothing of morganatic marriage and, hence, it was legally possible for Francis Ferdinand's offspring to succeed to the Hungarian throne. Habsburg family law forbade such a succession in the Austrian possessions. True, before his marriage, the heir apparent had formally renounced any claims to the throne on behalf of his children, but it was a renunciation made under duress, and it appeased neither uncle nor nephew. As for the Hungarians, they were galled by the heir apparent's predilection for crossing Hungary in his railroad car with curtains drawn and by his refusal to inspect a Hungarian regiment.[68]

Francis Ferdinand had strong opinions, one of which was that war had to be avoided, but he was not always consistent. How else are we to explain his favoring

---

*In 1906 also, the first motorcar units were established, even though three years earlier General Beck had declared motorcars to be "a pretty pastime for aristocratic lazybones and Jewish sportsmen [but] of no use for the army." (Erwin A. Schmidl, "From Paardeberg to Przemysl: Austria-Hungary and the Lessons of the Anglo-Boer War, 1899–1902," in Jay Stone and Erwin A. Schmidl, *The Boer War and the Military Reforms* ["War and Society in East Central Europe," vol. 28; Lanham, Md.-New York-London, 1988], p. 291.)

of the appointment of Conrad, who was certainly not one to shy away from the idea of war? The new chief of staff was right, of course, in his pessimistic assessment of foreign developments. In 1903, Serbian army officers massacred pro-Austrian King Alexander Obrenovich and his spouse and placed a Karageorgevich prince on the throne instead. Thenceforth, Serbian policy aimed at unification with those parts of the Dual Monarchy which were inhabited by South Slavs. It did not help matters that, between 1904 and 1909, the monarchy was engaged in a customs conflict with Serbia. Conrad was also quite correct in arguing that, far from being a reliable ally, Italy was the monarchy's secret enemy.

Franz Conrad von Hötzendorf was born in 1852 and was thus General Beck's junior by twenty-two years. Unlike the Reich German Beck, he was a true German-Austrian, and again unlike Beck, whose brilliant career was due at least in part to his friendship with the emperor, Conrad had achieved his success through pure ambition and talent.[69] A product of the Austrian general staff school, Conrad was a thinking man's soldier. His war experience was understandably minimal: he had participated in the Balkan campaigns of 1878–1879 and 1882. Meticulous, caring, and charismatic, he had called attention to himself by his writings on military tactics and by turning the 1st k.u.k. Infantry Regiment, which he commanded between 1895 and 1899, into a model formation. Thereafter, he rose quickly from one command to another, winning a host of admirers, who swore by this "modern" general.

Actually, it is not easy from the vantage point of the present to understand Conrad's legendary fame or to appreciate his much-acclaimed foresight. True, he recognized the dangers threatening the monarchy, but in this he was certainly not alone. And even if he was correct about Italian, Serbian, and Romanian enmity toward the monarchy, it was not to mean that military aggression on their part was inevitable. Irredentism did threaten the integrity of the monarchy, but Conrad greatly exaggerated the menace of secession. The Romanian minority was powerless under Hungarian rule; the Italian minority in Austria was very small and not uniformly disloyal, and most of the Croatian, Bosnian, and even Serbian politicians in Austria-Hungary, although far from satisfied with their current situation, were afraid of Great Serbian imperialism and preferred autonomy within the monarchy to unification with the Serbian kingdom.

Conrad recognized very early the importance of such things as camouflage uniforms, modern technology, massed artillery, and mountain warfare. He turned both the general staff school and the general staff into superior institutions, placing equal emphasis on learning, command ability, and physical conditioning. But even though he well understood the impact of firepower, he still insisted on the decisive importance of massed infantry attack with the bayonet, arguing that even though losses were bound to be terrible, superior élan would always carry the day. True, in this respect, he was no different from the other European generals of the period. Come 1914, Conrad would make catastrophic strategic errors, which once again did not set him apart from most other generals of his day. What made Conrad unique in Europe was his profound pessimism about the state he served. Despairing of the future, he advocated preventive war, first against Serbia and then, increasingly, against Italy. This infuriated the emperor as well as Francis Ferdinand, and he was dismissed in December 1911. He was reinstated a year later, however, at the insistence of his fellow generals, and so it was Conrad who led the monarchy into war in 1914.

Foreign political crisis came in 1908, following the Young Turk revolt in Constantinople, which heralded the rejuvenation and "nationalization" of the thitherto decrepit multinational Ottoman Empire. Among other things, the Young Turks claimed sovereignty over Bosnia-Hercegovina. To prevent the loss of the two provinces and to gain the friendship of Russia, Foreign Minister Aehrenthal proposed a division of the Balkans into a Russian and an Austro-Hungarian sphere of interest to Russian Foreign Minister Alexander Izvolsky. In the course of these complex and controversial negotiations, Austria-Hungary formally annexed Bosnia-Hercegovina, but Russian ambitions in the Dardanelles were frustrated by Great Britain and the other great powers. The Russians were indignant over the one-sided annexation, and so were the Western powers, which had not been consulted. As for Serbia, its indignation knew no bounds and, from that time on, Serbian politics aimed at undermining the Dual Monarchy through propaganda, disinformation, and, as planned by some Serbian officers, assassination.

Had it been up to Conrad, the Serbian outcry would have been answered with an Austrian invasion. He argued, quite correctly, that Russia, recently defeated by Japan and barely recovered from a major revolution, would be unable to help the Serbs. Yet Conrad's plan to crush and then annex Serbia did not take into account the fact that the monarchy's Slavic majority opposed the idea of aggression against brother Serbs, or that the last thing Austria-Hungary needed was more Slavs within its boundaries. Since Francis Joseph, Francis Ferdinand, and Aehrenthal would not accept Conrad's proposal, there was to be no war in 1908.

The annexation crisis was finally resolved by Germany's unconditional support of its only true ally. In March 1909, Serbia was obliged to issue a declaration that the annexation had not infringed upon its rights; that the Serbian army would be reduced to its peacetime effectives; and that official anti-Austrian propaganda would cease. It was a humiliation that neither Serbia nor its protector, the Russian Empire, could easily forget.[70]

During the crisis, the Habsburg army was partially mobilized, not without a few embarrassing ethnic incidents (of which more in chapter 11) that should have served as a warning. More important, the crisis had shown that, for the first time in modern Habsburg history, the military command—not only Conrad but others as well—was in ideological opposition to the emperor, something that would have been inconceivable in the days of General Beck. An ever-increasing number of younger generals and general staff officers were now voicing social Darwinist sentiments. For Conrad, it meant a struggle for survival between states; for others, it meant a struggle between the superior Germanic and the inferior Slavic race. "The recognition of the struggle for existence as the basic principle of all events on this earth"— Conrad wrote—"is the only real and rational basis for policy making. . . . Whoever remains blind to the mounting danger, or whoever recognizes [the danger] but remains too indolent to arm himself, and is too undecided to deliver the blow at the proper moment, deserves his fate." Influenced not only by Darwin but also by Nietzsche, Conrad held to a philosophy of activism, asserting: "The will to live creates and dominates the world; its inevitable consequence is the struggle for life."[71] Conrad wanted to wage war to save the multinational monarchy; some of his colleagues, and an increasing number of politicians, wanted to wage war to save the monarchy, and because war appeared to them as the goal of life and the ultimate proof of German racial superiority.

Unfortunately for the monarchy, Aehrenthal died in 1912, to be replaced by the less respected Count Berchtold.[72] Under him, irresponsible lesser officials of the Ballhausplatz (the Austro-Hungarian foreign ministry), were able to proceed at will, helping to lay the foundations for the tragedy of 1914. Because the very old emperor devoted himself increasingly to his only true passion, everyday bureaucratic routine, Francis Ferdinand remained nearly alone in opposing the war party.

The domestic situation too gave cause for worry. In 1908, Austria's thitherto successful reforming prime minister, Baron Beck, resigned, to be replaced by another series of civil service prime ministers. The great celebrations of the sixtieth anniversary of Francis Joseph's reign in 1908 were used by Germans and Czechs in Prague as an occasion to clash violently, with the result that martial law had to be imposed on the city again. The Austrian elections of 1911 again produced an unworkable Reichsrat, profoundly divided along national and ideological lines. Now even the internationalist Social Democrats were split into mutually hostile national groups. Clearly, the central European political parties were not ready for democracy.[73]

The international situation heated up with the Moroccan crisis in 1911 and, more threateningly for the monarchy, with the Balkan wars of 1912 and 1913. In the first of these wars, Serbia, Greece, and Bulgaria fell upon and defeated the Turks. In the second war, Serbia, Greece, Romania, and even the Ottoman Empire fell upon and defeated Bulgaria, which had grabbed too much in the first conflict. As a result of these conflicts, the Ottoman Empire was virtually excluded from the Balkans, and the monarchy's potential enemies, Romania and Serbia, had made considerable territorial gains. True, an Austro-Hungarian ultimatum had stopped a Serbian drive to seize Albania but, as in 1908, this proved to be a Pyrrhic victory. The two partial mobilizations, in 1908 and in 1912–1913, cost the monarchy a total of one billion kronen.[74]

The two governments and parliaments finally came around to the realization that the monarchy's defenses needed strengthening. The drive to that effect was led by István Tisza, whose liberal party had regained strength in Hungary. The War Services Act of 1912, adopted in both parts of the monarchy, provided for emergency measures in case of a war, putting all labor, goods, and services at the disposal of the state. Also, the annual recruit contingent was increased from 139,000 to 181,000. Meanwhile, Minister of War Auffenberg secretly and illegally ordered twelve batteries of the later-famous 30.5 cm heavy mortars from the Škoda Works in Bohemia and took other steps to strengthen the armed forces. But, as it soon turned out, these measures had come far too late.[75]

In June 1914, Francis Ferdinand decided to attend military maneuvers in Bosnia-Hercegovina, not as heir to the throne but as inspector general of the armed forces. This way, he could take along his wife and let her enjoy the respect owed the spouse of a commanding general. The result was that not the police but the military,

Table 2.1. Defense Appropriations of the Great Powers (Index Numbers)

	France	Russia	Germany	Italy	Austria-Hungary
1890 ($ millions)	100 (142)	100 (145)	100 (121)	100 (79)	100 (64)
1900	98	141	139	99	106
1910	132	215	169	154	140
1914	139	304	365	178	284

Source: Paul M. Kennedy, "The First World War and the International Power System," *International Security* 9, no. 1 (Summer 1984): 8.

inexperienced in security matters, had to shoulder responsibility for Francis Ferdinand's safety in Sarajevo.

The Sarajevo murder on June 28 succeeded because of Austro-Hungarian negligence and because of a series of unfortunate misunderstandings and accidents. The assassin Gavrilo Princip and his friends were, for the most part, poverty-stricken Bosnian students, imbued with anarchistic and patriotic ideals. Yet there can be no doubt about the involvement in the plot of Artamonov, the Russian military attaché in Belgrade, and of a great number of Serbian officers. Artamonov had provided the money, and the officers had trained, equipped, and transported the would-be murderers. The Serbian government had foreknowledge of the plot but, fearing the conspirators, failed to warn Vienna.

With the most determined opponent of war, Francis Ferdinand, out of the way, the Austro-Hungarian war party could now proceed with its plans. The responsibility for the decision to make war lay, aside from the German government and Great General Staff, with Conrad, Minister of War Krobatin, Berchtold, a number of diplomats, and Austrian Prime Minister Stürgkh. Only the Hungarian prime minister, István Tisza, favored a diplomatic solution, but he too abandoned his opposition once he became convinced that Hungary's indispensable ally, the German Reich, favored a violent solution.[76] The final responsibility for what happened lay, however, with Francis Joseph, who, although greatly relieved that Francis Ferdinand was dead and sensing that the monarchy was doomed, nevertheless consented to the issuing of an unacceptable ultimatum.* He signed the fatal mobilization order so as to preserve the dignity of the house.

When war was declared on Serbia, on July 28, 1914, the monarchy's armed forces consisted of 414,000 enlisted men and noncommissioned officers. Mobilization brought in 2,846,000 more men, including reservists and the class of 1914, making a grand total of 3,260,000 soldiers. They were led by fewer than 60,000 officers. As far as military appropriations are concerned, table 2.1, shows that Austro-Hungarian military appropriations in 1890 were lower than those of Italy, a far weaker power in terms of population and economic production. Even thereafter,

---

*It was when he heard of the assassination that the emperor uttered words testifying to his capacity for callousness and dynastic fanaticism: "This is terrible! The Almighty does not let himself be provoked! . . . A higher authority has now restored the order, which I was regrettably unable to preserve." Quoted in Albert Freiherr von Margutti, *Kaiser Franz Joseph. Persönliche Erinnerungen* (Vienna-Leipzig, 1924), pp. 138–39.

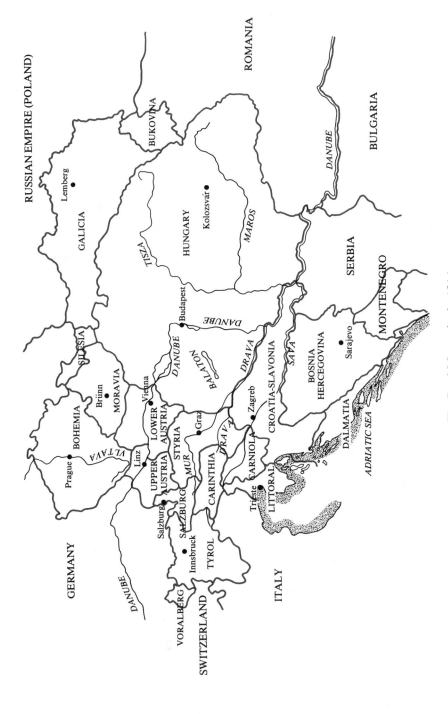

The Dual Monarchy in 1914

Austro-Hungarian military appropriations grew very slowly. The quantitative jump after 1910 (in reality after 1912) could not possible change things drastically by 1914. Conrad was not far off the mark when he argued, in 1907, that the monarchy did not need to send representatives to the Second Hague Conference on Disarmament since it was already in a state of permanent disarmament.

I shall attempt to show in chapter 11 that the officers did their duty in the Great War, but there were too few of them to command such an enormous mass of men. First, however, we shall undertake a study of the officers themselves: their education, training, lifestyle, ideology, and confessional and ethnic origin, as well as the nature of their careers.[77]

3

The Making of Future Officers

Cadets, Students, and Schools in Prereform Times

The transformation of the Habsburg officer corps from a group of disorderly noblemen and mercenaries at the moment of its creation in the seventeenth century into
a centrally controlled professional caste in the late 1860s was a long and uncertain
process. Well into the nineteenth century, the recruitment and training of future
officers was a most confusing affair, and only slowly and fitfully did a unified
system begin to take shape.

There were many ways, around 1850, for a young man to become an officer, the
least common of which was through regular schooling. The average troop officer
attained his commission by entering a regiment directly, but even this straightforward proposition covered a variety of scenarios. He could, as an ordinary conscript,
rise through the ranks (*von der Pike auf*); the prerequisite for this was battlefield
valor, and thousands followed that route.

Then there was the special situation enjoyed by the inhabitants of the eighteen
Grenzer regiments (remember that these regiments were not only military but also
administrative and territorial entities), where compulsory elementary education had
existed since Maria Theresa's time. Supervised by the colonels and captains of the
regiment, the sons (and, to a lesser extent, daughters) of these peasant-soldiers were
taught to read and write in their native tongue and in German, usually by a noncommissioned officer. If talented or well connected, a boy was then sent to a higher-
level Grenzschule, where he paid no tuition. He was by then a bona fide soldier,
regardless of his age. If judged sufficiently talented once more, he could now go on
to a military academy or join a Grenzer regiment as a cadet, with the expectation of
making it to a noncommissioned or even commissioned rank. Some of the most
famous Habsburg generals began their careers in this fashion.

A boy could also enlist voluntarily and, provided he was able to pay for his
uniform and equipment (which made him an *expropriis Gemeiner*), he could entertain the hope of being admitted one day into the cadet corps of the regiment. Or, he

could complete an elementary military school (Unter- and Obererziehungshaus), generally reserved for the sons of noncommissioned officers and lower civil servants, and enter a regiment as a cadet, with a fair chance of becoming an officer. Alternatively, he could enter a regiment directly as a cadet, usually at the age of fourteen or fifteen, and then hope for a commission.

Even among such cadets there was a bewildering variety. "Imperial cadets" received monthly pay from the state and had the right to every third lieutenant's position to open up in the regiment. The others were "regimental cadets," more often than not boys who had been the despair of their parents. The admission examination to a regimental cadet corps, if there happened to be one, was usually quite farcical. One cadet-applicant, aged seventeen, was asked by his examiners to name the emperor and the emperor's predecessor and to write a fictional letter to his parents asking for permission to join the regiment.

The trouble was that many units took in a vast number of cadets (the 3rd Infantry Regiment, for instance, had forty-two in 1841), and yet there were years in which not a single position became available in the officer corps of the regiment. Even when there happened to be an opening, it was often filled by an outsider brought in by the colonel or the regimental proprietor. So cadets waited, grew old, and, meanwhile, were sometimes taught nothing.[1]

There were, however, also a few higher military schools, established at an earlier date, which trained the elite of the officer corps. Among these professional institutions were a number of middle-level schools, known as Schul-Compagnien, which took most of their students from the military elementary schools. Theoretically, the school companies were for training noncommissioned officers, but the better students could make it to the level of officer. Some of the school companies, for instance, the Pionier-Schule at Tulln in Lower Austria, achieved extraordinary fame,[2] but the most prestigious institutions were the two military academies, one for infantry and cavalry, and the other for the technical branches.

Albert of Wallenstein founded the first Austrian military academy in 1624, but the school did not survive its creator. In 1666, Baron Richthausen von Chaos established a school for military engineers in Vienna, and in 1717 Eugene of Savoy turned that school into a regular academy for military engineers (k.k. Ingenieurakademie). A private institution until 1852, the academy charged an annual tuition of 1,000 gulden (equal to a contemporary $400, a very large sum), a cost which was later increasingly assumed for the students by private donors and the provincial estates.[3]

The first state-supported higher military schools were set up by Maria Theresa in the 1750s, but her aim was less to train officers than to provide for military orphans, the sons of deserving officers, and the younger sons of the minor landed nobility—a concern that was to preoccupy the Habsburg rulers until the last days of the empire. Her best schools were actually not schools at all, but the units of the Hungarian and Italian Noble Bodyguards, established in Vienna and Milan, respectively, which provided a general education to a few dozen sons of penniless Hungarian and Italian noblemen. This rudimentary system of military education was subsequently expanded by Joseph II and his successors, so that by the mid-nineteenth century there were a number of military schools with well-established traditions. Foremost among them was the Military Academy at Wiener Neustadt, near Vienna, which supplied the army with its best-educated infantry, Jäger, and cavalry officers, and continues to train the officers of the Austrian army today.[4]

Until the mid-nineteenth century, the Military Academy took in an annual contingent of a hundred boys eleven to twelve years of age and kept them for seven or eight years before commissioning them as second lieutenants. Less-deserving students were supposed to become noncommissioned officers, but graduates were in fact almost invariably commissioned. The students were primarily the sons of officers; in theory, the lower the rank of the father, the more likely his son was to be admitted to a "free place," which meant room and board as well as a little pocket money. In practice, as one critic of the Austrian army wrote in 1842, he, the son of a two-star general, was admitted automatically to a free place.[5] Some students had "half-free" places, and a few paid the full fee, which amounted to 800 gulden per year. This sum, the equivalent of a captain's annual basic salary, was one that only foreign princes, landowning aristocrats, and the very rich bourgeoisie could afford to pay.

The academy was under the command of a general, and the majority of its teachers were officers, but before 1852, particularly in lower classes, much of the teaching was done by Piarist (Calasantian) fathers. In fact, the academy was a curious cross between a monastery and a barracks. At first only Catholics were admitted, but later Protestants as well. Mass was celebrated every day; later it was replaced by a brief prayer rattled off at great speed. Religion seems to have played only a very minor role in the life of the students; religious instruction was treated as a necessary bore, typically offered by a Czech padre whose Bohemian accent was a frequent source of amusement to memoirists.[6] Religious services were a formality, as much a part of the pomp and circumstance of an officer's life as grand parades, guard duty at the imperial place, and solemn military funerals.

The curriculum emphasized theoretical knowledge; mathematics and geometry counted for four points; German and French for two; and history, geography, and natural history for only one. Fencing, gymnastics, and music counted for nothing— at least until the 1850s. The students treated the professors of important subjects, all military men, with respect, and the teachers of unimportant subjects, often priests or civilians, with a good deal of contempt. The burden of classwork was enormous, amounting to thirty-five to thirty-eight hours weekly. About sixty subjects were taught, all under strict supervision and iron discipline.

The students at the Military Academy slept in the same meticulous order that regulated their waking hours: always in their own platoon and arranged by height. Reveille was at five or six in the morning, and from that moment on every movement of the students was scrupulously controlled. They marched in close order to the washroom under the supervision of a "class sergeant" (Klassenfeldwebel or Inspectionsorgan, generally an elderly NCO) to wash in cold water with a few soap bits kept in a small bag; a hot bath was provided only once a month.[7] Then came mass, a breakfast of black bread and water (in winter, warm milk), and, finally, work in the classroom. Lunch and dinner were quite sumptuous; in general, the students ate better and lived more comfortably, despite everything, than they had at home or would again as junior officers.

Study consisted mostly of memorization, followed, later in the afternoon, by a walk in the academy park. There was the "Grand Tour" on Sundays and the "Little Tour" on weekdays, performed in close order, with one class marching fifty to a hundred feet behind the other, always on the same path, every day of the year. One alumnus calculated that he had walked the Grand Tour five hundred times and the Little Tour three thousand.[8] The students, called *Zöglinge,* never saw the rest of the enormous park, where hunting and forestry were practiced on a broad scale.

Classes were strictly separated; even the members of parallel sections were forbidden to meet. Brothers at the same school were allowed to get together once a month, and then for only an hour.[9] When classes did meet, it was usually to fight one of those famous battles—recounted in so many memoirs—in which furniture was destroyed or set afire and a few participants ended up in the hospital. Curfew was strictly enforced, and leaves were granted with great reluctance. Honor students were occasionally allowed to eat out, but only on Sunday afternoons and only if invited and accompanied. Vacation was in September, but if the family was faraway (as it often was), or if it lacked the money to pay for travel (as it often did), or if the student was under interdict (as most were), then there was no vacation. The official *Reglement* emphasized the basic principle of early-nineteenth-century education: "The young people are to be prevented from following their natural inclination toward laziness."[10] Thus, some students were never allowed to leave the academy. Even Sunday mornings were devoted to work, but, this being a Catholic country, there were several religious holidays. When finally commissioned after seven or eight years of virtual imprisonment, the graduates often felt utterly lost in the great world. There were legendary stories of a young lieutenant who, upon arriving in Vienna, which he had never seen, was afraid to step off the sidewalk and could not find his hotel because he was unable to conceive of more than one hotel in a town.[11] And such people were expected to take over platoons of raw recruits in some remote corner of the monarchy!

Entertainment at the academy consisted of mild games and the far more brutal illegal rumbles. Smoking was prohibited but practiced in secret. There were occasional trips to the local theater to see specially expurgated plays. Reading material was scarce and censored. Before 1867, the discovery of a copy of Goethe's *Goetz von Berlichingen* in one's trunk could be cause for summons before the company commander; a copy of *Werther* could lead to incarceration, and one of the poems of Heine to incarceration and enforced fasting. The reading of Schiller, a far more irreverent poet than Goethe, was encouraged, perhaps because so many of Schiller's heroes were soldiers.[12] James Fenimore Cooper's Leatherstocking tales seems to have been the favorite reading of the younger students. Correspondence was supervised, as were the rare authorized visits of family members. Punishments were varied and imaginative, ranging from no dinner to eight days' imprisonment in a dark cell with a wooden bunk, bread-and-water rations, and "light irons," the latter to be removed every third night. Much more feared was lashing (*Schilling*), carried out under medical supervision and often resulting in hospitalization. Quitting school was extremely difficult, and expulsions were rare.

The students' unwritten code of behavior was in clear conflict with the official code, foreshadowing the two conflicting sets of norms that officers would have to live by. Much divided among themselves, the students presented a united front to the authorities. Complaining to a supervisor or informing on one's comrades was seen as the worst of crimes, and one was expected to suffer bullying without a murmur. The freshmen, called "Benjamins," were routinely mistreated by the seniors, called *Burgherren* (lords of the castle). The bullying of students entering the academy from civilian life (called *Philister*) was particularly odious, whereas the *Fisolen* (Austrian for "green beans"), who came from the lower-level military schools, generally knew how to defend themselves.

A sense of camaraderie must have helped, as did homoeroticism. The memoirists are very shy on the subject, but at least two of them mention that there were many "romantic friendships" which had "the character of love affairs." Older boys tried to choose their beloved ones, called *Schmalzel,* from the younger classes and risked severe punishment to spend a few minutes with them. At the very least, they could cast longing eyes at each other. The weaker or more effeminate partner in such a relationship was commonly referred to as *die Dame*. Permission to hold hands or walk arm in arm at one of the rare excursions counted as a supreme favor. The cadets spent every free moment in the morning pomading their hair (pork fat would do if nothing else was available) and sprinkling themselves with strictly forbidden perfume. These friendships should not necessarily be interpreted in a physical sense, there being in fact little opportunity for that kind of contact. Rather, the passion felt for one's *Schmalzel* probably represented the only affectionate relationship many boys had enjoyed since they had turned six or seven. However, Oscar Teuber, a writer of very popular military reminiscences, does mention rather casually that at the Military Academy it was possible to bribe the warden for permission to join a friend in the punishment cell, "for the pleasures of sweet intimacy." That the authorities closed their eyes to such special friendships is shown by the fact that the class sergeant sometimes admonished the students to choose their *Schmalzel* from among their own classmates.[13]

The memoirists are unanimous not only in their description of the discipline and the terror but also in their emphasis on the enthusiasm, youthful idealism, and ethical purity of the students. For them, the memoirists claim, the emperor was a demigod, and so were the supervising officers, with whom they had, incidentally, little contact. The students had more mixed feelings toward their teachers (officer teachers could send a student to jail), and they professed boundless contempt for the class sergeants, whom they called *Fetzen* (rags that served as a foot soldier's substitute for socks). The sergeants, mostly highly decorated war heroes of lower-class origin, shared their quarters with the students; they nagged—but were not allowed to punish—the students and were terrorized by them in turn. Beating up the sergeant in the dark of night seems to have been a favorite pastime. The sergeants endured because of the prospect of an officer's commission at the end of their long stay, but it is an apt comment on the vast class difference between future officers and enlisted men that the students' brutalization of the *Fetzen,* the only non-gentlemen with whom they were in contact, was so casually tolerated.[14]

Ideological training at the Military Academy in mid-nineteenth century was, for a modern point of view, incredibly primitive, and perhaps precisely for that reason, very effective. The teaching of history consisted mainly of a listing of the great deeds of former Habsburg rulers; military history consisted more or less of the same thing. One of the most important subjects was military writing style, in which calligraphy was considered equally as important as the memorization of the complex formulae by which the higher-ups were to be addressed.[15] It was perfectly good form to conclude a petition to His All-Highest Majesty with the fervent wish "to expire in deepest reverence at the feet of His Most August Presence."[16] God, Emperor, and Fatherland were mentioned in the same breath (the earlier formula had been "Throne and Altar"), but the meaning of "Fatherland" was never defined. Nor could it be, considering the fact that Austria was never truly unified.

The students hailed from all parts of the monarchy. The majority of them had German-speaking parents, but this did not necessarily mean that they were German. In fact, the students sometimes distinguished between those who used "Army-German" (*Armeedeutsch*) at home, regardless of their family's ethnic origin, and genuine German nationals. During the Franco-Prussian war, when the Austrian military was aching to avenge Königgrätz, the students ostracized and often mistreated the ethnic Germans in their midst. There were many conflicts between the so-called *Einfach-Österreicher* (plain Austrians), or *Armeedeutschen* (Army Germans), and the ethnic Germans, whom their opponents referred to as "Prussians." Croats were called *Krowaten* or *Krowatowitsche,* and their protection was often sought, because these boys from Grenzer families were reputedly stronger and more mature than the others. Ethnic Hungarians or Magyars were also much sought after because of the sumptuous food packages they received from home.* Poles had a reputation for being wealthy aristocrats and poor students; Czechs, Italians (*Katzelmacher*), and Romanians were all seen in the light of their national stereotypes. In the first year, a student was forbidden to speak his mother tongue, and some students were forced to relearn their native languages later in courses offered by the school.[17]

Officers, noncommissioned officers, officials, and teachers tended to use German in everyday speech whatever their mother tongue, but, as I shall demonstrate later, the Germans among the Military Academy graduates did not make a better career for themselves than the non-Germans. On the other hand, the academy graduates considerably outpaced the graduates of other schools and officers without a formal education. Admission policy definitely favored the well connected, but at the academy itself there seems to have been no favoritism or discrimination.

The language of education and communication at the academy was, as at all the other military schools (before 1868), German. The students were spared the burden of Latin and Greek but had to learn French, "Bohemian" (that is, Czech), and either Hungarian or Italian (replaced after 1866 by Polish)—apparently all taught quite badly.[18]

In the 1850s, exercise and sports counted for little in the life of the students—

---

*Later in the century, the popularity of the Magyar students would decline considerably because of their growing nationalism, exclusiveness, and the tendency of some Magyars to speak Hungarian in front of the others. On this see, among others, Peter Broucek, ed., *Ein General im Zwielicht. Die Erinnerungen Edmund Glaises von Horstenau,* 3 vols. (Vienna-Cologne-Graz, 1980–1987), 1:103–4; and Ernst Palombini, Freiherr von Jedina, "Erinnerungen," unpublished manuscript, Kriegsarchiv, Vienna, B/959, pp. 84–94.

they would become important later. Gymnastics were considered lower class in any case. Fencing, riding, and dance instruction, on the other hand, were required and popular.

The day of liberation came on August 18, the emperor's birthday, when the young lieutenants were commissioned. For the occasion, the army proved as generous to the graduates as it would be stingy toward them later as commissioned officers, providing them with uniforms, silver, elegant linen, and luxurious underwear. At midcentury, the average worth of these gifts was calculated at nine hundred gulden, but the gala uniform of some cavalry regiments alone could cost a thousand.[19] Later there would be fewer such benefits. Before commissioning, the students usually visited a tailor to have the collars on their uniforms heightened: this was a source of dandy pride for them, and an irregularity much disliked by the military authorities.

The ceremony of commissioning (*Ausmusterung*) is invariably described by the alumni "as the greatest day in my life," and most of them must have been sincere in shouting the academy's motto: *"Treu bis in den Tod!"* (Faithful unto death!). The Military Academy had probably not treated them much worse than they would have been in any other establishment. Nor was strict discipline unknown to youngsters who came, for the most part, from military families. They had learned to be gentlemen, which would count for more than anything else in the regiment. Of politics they knew nothing; they took their absolute devotion to the ruler for granted. There was now one more walk in the park, in freely formed groups at last; from there, the road led directly to the troops.

The Military Academy trained, as it has been noted, the cream of the infantry and cavalry officer corps. The Engineering Academy, founded by Eugene of Savoy, was actually two academies, one for gunners and another for engineers. It changed its name and location a number of times but consistently turned out highly qualified artillerymen, builders, and sappers. Its graduates demonstrated superior knowledge, formed exclusive castes, and were well respected. Socially, they were more middle class than the Military Academy graduates, and they provided central Europe with some of its foremost scientists and technical innovators.

The 1850s and 1860s: A Period of Transition

The war of 1848–1849, in which a hastily organized Hungarian national army nearly defeated the imperial forces, led to demands for military reform, especially in the area of education. The schools were reorganized in successive waves, but not until the Compromise of 1867 and the concurrent triumph of liberalism were substantial reforms introduced.

The first changes were in fact quite superficial. For instance, in the 1850s, the three academies, the Military Academy at Wiener Neustadt, the Engineering Academy (Genieakademie) at Klosterbruck bei Znaim, and the Artillery Academy at Olmütz, transferred their first four classes to four new cadet institutes (Kadetteninstitute) in which boys between the ages of eleven and fifteen prepared for entry into the academies. The new system increased to 800 the number of well-educated military students available for admission to the academies. The latter now functioned as senior high schools and trained a total number of 720 students—450 at Wiener Neustadt and 135 at each of the two technical academies, among them many entrants from nonelite preparatory schools.[20] At least as many officer candidates were still trained in the Schul-Compagnien, and many more came through the regimental cadet companies. Discipline became even more stringent in all the schools. Students were locked up in their institutions; they were spied on and were expected to spy on others. The aim was to turn them into obedient and hardy warriors. For example, an imperial regulation of 1859 stipulated that the students' sleeping quarters at all institutions be kept at a temperature of 8 degrees Reaumur (10 degrees Celsius) at night, and that the mess halls be practically unheated. Only the infirmary and the classroom were to be warmed to a blissful 19 degrees Celsius.[21]

The military defeats of 1859 and 1866 increased the impetus for fundamental political change in the monarchy and, with it, a reform of the system of military education. The Battle of Königgrätz in 1866 was widely interpreted as a victory of the Prussian school system over the Austrian. (The French were to draw similar conclusions from their defeat at Sedan in 1870). Austrian military observers as well as the civilian press admiringly compared the self-reliant Prussian junior officer with the heedlessly heroic, overdisciplined, and militarily ignorant Austrian officer, and stressed the urgent need for a new type of officer who could lead a new kind of army.

Incredibly, in at least one memorable case, the students took reform into their own hands. In January 1867, when the commander of the cadet institute at Marburg, Styria, ordered the lashing of lazy students in addition to, as theretofore, those guilty of serious infractions, the older students (boys of fourteen and fifteen) conspired to make a revolution. On February 1, when the students were armed with rifles (without bullets) and bayonets for field exercises, they took over a building, set up barricades, and chanted revolutionary slogans. When they nearly stabbed the commanding colonel who had tried to negotiate, a Jäger battalion was ordered to surround the building. Unfortunately for the students, although the food supply they had assembled was adequate for a long siege, the question of water had been overlooked in the excitement. They surrendered by midnight of the same day in exchange for the promise of a partial amnesty and the abolition of lashing for insufficient diligence. Although there had been an orgy of destruction in the building, practically no one was punished or expelled from the institution. Almost as if in response to the revolt, corporal punishment was abolished at all military schools in October 1868, and—in a further major concession—students were now permitted to keep a significant part of the pocket money sent by their parents.[22]

Military Education in the Liberal Dual Monarchy

The 1867 Compromise resulted, as noted above, in the creation of four separate armed forces in the monarchy. All four military establishments had their own schools, and while the Hungarians (and Croats) insisted that Hungarian (or Croatian) be spoken in their national forces and national military schools, the Joint Army and the Austrian National Guard continued the old anational or supranational tradition. What concerns us here are the military schools of the Joint Army.

The fundamental principle of the new system was that all officers should receive a military-school training. By requiring a certain measure of education from everyone, the new system closed the door to ambitious enlisted men and noncommissioned officers, but their sons were still welcome in the military schools and thus also in the officer corps.

After the last great reform of military education, devised by Colonel Adolph von Wurmb in 1874, there were three types of schools for training career officers: academies, cadet schools (Kadettenschulen), and schools for the professional retraining of reserve officers. Still at the top of the system were the military academies, which drew their students primarily from specially established military preparatory high schools (Militär-Unterrealschulen and Militär-Oberrealschulen). Civilian high-school students could also be admitted to the academies at the age of seventeen, that is, before they had earned their *Matura* (high-school graduation certificate). The academies offered a three-year curriculum which led to commissioning as a full lieutenant. (The rank of lieutenant second class no longer existed).

The Military Academy supplied the army with one out of every eight infantry officers, while the ratio in the cavalry was one out of every two; most of the other officers came from the newly established cadet schools, four-year institutions whose graduates entered the army not as officers but as ensigns (Kadet-Offiziers-Stellvertreter, known after 1908 as Fähnriche). Their commissioning as lieutenants usually followed one or two years of army service.

There were, in 1900, only two Joint Army military academies, the Military Academy at Wiener Neustadt and the Technical Military Academy at Vienna. There were eighteen (later nineteen) cadet schools, one each for the cavalry, artillery, and engineers, and fifteen (later sixteen) for the less prestigious infantry. Whereas the academies took in an annual contingent of about 250 freshmen, the cadet schools were ready to admit about 1,000 youngsters annually; in practice, however, there were never enough students. Tuition at the cadet schools was half that at the academies, but in both types of institutions the majority of students paid nothing. The academies admitted the talented and the well connected, which more or less amounts to saying that they admitted the sons of the military and civil-service elites. The Military Academy class of 1874 included, among its ninety-five graduates, seventy-one sons of officers, the son of a military official, and thirteen sons of civil servants, a total of eighty-five young men whose fathers were in state service. With 90 percent of the graduates coming from a military or civil-service background, the occupation of the fathers of the remaining 10 percent seems almost immaterial. In any case, they included four estate owners, a rentier, a Protestant minister, three professionals, and a peasant. Of the ninety-five graduates, twenty-eight (or 30 percent) had a noble predicate (five barons, two Ritter, and twenty-one from the lower nobility), but except for the two Polish Ritter and a few Austrian, Hungarian, and Polish untitled nobles, these boys were not from the old nobility. Rather, they were the sons of ennobled officers and officials.[23] In brief, in the 1870s, the primary function of the Military Academy at Wiener Neustadt was to train the sons of upper-echelon officers and civil servants. To cite another example, out of eighty randomly selected students at the military preparatory high school at Mährisch-Weisskirchen, in 1899, nine boys were the sons of generals or admirals.[24]

By the turn of the century, however, new elements were represented at the elite military schools, and by the eve of World War I, the social composition of the Military Academy had changed significantly. Of the 133 graduates (plus one Chinese) of the class of 1913, only 50 (37.6 percent) were sons of officers; another 6 were sons of noncommissioned officers (in 1874, none had been), and 11 were sons of military officials (in 1874, 1 had been). Thus sons of military men constituted only half (67) of the class. Even if we add to this the surprisingly large number (32) whose fathers were civil servants, the entire state service made up only 74.4 percent (99 students) of the class (in 1874 it had been 90 percent).* The occupations of the other fathers are not without interest; they included five estate owners, a rentier, a factory director, a hotel owner, a wholesale merchant, nine professionals (including an artist), four merchants, four business employees, four artisans, two farmers, and a doorman. Clearly, the class of 1913 was less representative of the officer corps and of state service in general than the class of 1874 had been. Furthermore, it included a goodly number of boys of lower-middle-class background. Characteristically, it had only 1 titled nobleman, a baron whose father was a two-star general and whose aristocratic title represented a mark of personal distinction. There were also 2 Ritter, and 29 lower nobles, almost all from the new or service nobility.[25]

The graduates of the military academies had a good chance of making it into the general staff and thus ending up as generals. The students at the cadet schools were trained to serve with the troops, but crossing over from one type of school and career into another was quite common, and many a poor cadet-school student went on to the general staff and from there to a general's rank.[26]

The third road to a professional career led through a reserve-officer's commission. The Austrian and the Hungarian military laws of 1868 enabled conscripts with a high-school education or its equivalent to serve one year instead of three. By creating this institution, the liberal Austrian and Hungarian governments hoped to fill the officer corps with educated civilians in uniform as well as to attract the bourgeoisie to the military profession. The "one-year volunteer" (*Einjährig Freiwilliger*) was a conscript just like the ordinary recruits, but he enjoyed many privileges, and he alone qualified for reserve-officer school. Once he had completed his brief training, the "volunteer" was usually made a noncommissioned cadet officer with a good chance of becoming an ensign in three years and later a lieutenant in the reserve. Subsequently, if he wished and qualified, the reserve lieutenant could attend a special course to make him a career officer. Between 1883 and

---

*There seems to have been nothing unique about the situation at the Austro-Hungarian Military Academy. At the Royal Prussian Cadet Corps between 1871 and 1918, two-thirds of the cadets were sons of army officers, and fully 77 percent of the fathers earned their livelihood in the king's service. (John Moncure, "The Royal Prussian Cadet Corps 1871–1918: A Prosopographical Approach," in Béla K. Király and Walter Scott Dillard, eds., *The East Central European Officer Corps, 1740–1920s: Social Origins, Selection, Education, and Training* ["East European Monographs," No. 241; New York, 1988], p. 65.)

October 1914, the Joint Army commissioned 16,000 career infantry and Jäger lieutenants: 13,700 came from the professional military schools and only 2,300 from the reserve officer corps. Thus the liberals' hope of altering the composition and ideology of the career officer corps through the influx of educated civilians did not materialize.[27]

Students at the military preparatory schools and at the academies were overburdened with courses. They were expected to acquire a combined humanistic and scientific erudition (minus Latin and Greek) and to complement it with such subjects as public law, economics, astronomy, geodesics, the building of fortifications, terrain drawing, the major languages spoken in the monarchy, the handling of complex weapons, field exercises, drill, tactics, strategy, horseback riding, fencing, swimming, dancing, and athletics. History continued to be taught in accordance with the official dictum that "thought-provoking [*reflektierende*] or critical presentations are to be avoided; on the other hand, every opportunity must be used to strengthen the patriotic and military consciousness [*Gesinnung*] of the pupils."[28] The military schools had no special textbooks in the humanities and social sciences. History books continued merely to rattle off lists of Roman and Germanic rulers and euphorically recount the great deeds of Habsburg princes. The quality of teaching varied a good deal, even though the army had set up teacher-training schools. Specialists came from the general staff and the higher military technical institutions; humanities, social sciences, and languages were often taught by officers who were frustrated poets or writers.

In the race for good grades, crucial for admission to a desirable regiment or to the elite Jäger, Military Academy students lost or scarcely developed any interest in ethical or religious problems, civic duties, and social or political culture. But at least now there was more freedom. Long gone were the stern Calasantian fathers, the daily mass, and the compulsory confession. The class sergeant had vanished in 1868, along with fasting, corporal punishment, and imprisonment in a darkened cell. Students at the academy were now free to smoke, to keep their pocket money, to stay out on Sunday, to go to the theater, to write uncensored letters, to read nearly anything they liked, to cultivate the arts, and to walk anywhere in the park. Hazing by upperclassmen remained, however, as did the dual moral standard. Instead of the airs of a bully, students now tended to display an air of cultural superiority that made them obnoxious not only to their liberal and socialist critics but often also to their comrades in the cadet schools. Only one thing seems to have remained common to all military students, no matter where they were trained: their devotion to Francis Joseph, the only supreme commander they, their fathers, and sometimes even their grandfathers had known.

The cadet schools came much closer to being egalitarian establishments, if not in spirit then at least in the cultural and social background of their pupils. Because there were never enough applicants, a junior-high-school average of *genügend* (satisfactory), the lowest passing grade, sufficed for admission to an infantry cadet school. Failure in Latin and Greek was discounted, and the compulsory entrance examination was treated as a farce.[29] Thus the cadets were often those who had not made it into the Gymnasium or whose parents were too poor to pay the costs of a civilian senior high school. Yet even the lowly infantry cadet schools seemed to demand the impossible of their students. In February 1893, Anton Lehár, brother of the composer Franz Lehár, received generally excellent grades in the following assessed qualities and courses for the first semester of his fourth year at the Vienna infantry cadet school: comportment, industry, ability, character, behavior, accoutrement, German, Hungarian, French, geography, history, arithmetic and algebra, geometry, geometric design, practical geometry, physics, chemistry, calligraphy, freehand drawing, service regulations, drill regulations, army organization, weaponry, terrain study and terrain drawing, tactics, military engineering, fortifications and fortress warfare, military administration and business style, field exercises and the training of troops, gymnastics, fencing, service rules and proper conduct (*Anstandslehre*), singing, music, and social dance. Interestingly, Lehár was given no religious instruction in his senior year.[30]

The military schools of the Joint Army remained stubbornly indifferent to the social background (except in the case of archdukes), ethnicity, and religion of their students, and I have not come across any complaints about intramural discrimination.

The language of education and communication at the Joint Army schools was still German, but the first cracks in the system began to appear when Hungarian students insisted on the use of their language in public, and in 1904, when the Hungarian government succeeded in introducing Hungarian as a compulsory language at Wiener Neustadt. Joint Army schools located in Hungary were now obliged to teach a number of subjects in Hungarian, even to students who did not come from that country. Moreover, pupils born in Hungary had to learn Hungarian no matter where they studied.[31]

The army high command feared Hungarian separatism; the Hungarian government worried about the anti-Dualism of the army and the underrepresentation of Hungarians in the officer corps and the military schools. In reality, between 1867 and 1914, Hungarians made considerable advances at the military schools and thus ultimately in the officer corps as well. In the academic year 1880–1881, the Joint Army had a total of 2,033 military students; of these, only 395 had been born in Hungary (not including Croatia-Slavonia and the port city of Fiume), a number representing only 19.4 percent of military students at a time when Hungarian citizens constituted 36.2 percent of the monarchy's total population.[32] Worse still, a large part of these Hungarian-born students were in reality Saxons, Zipsers, and Swabians—that is, members of the German minority in Hungary. Other so-called Hungarians were ethnic Serbs or Romanians. By the beginning of the twentieth century, however, this situation had changed dramatically. Not only did the Hungarian National Guard now have its own military academy, the Ludovika Akadémia, as well as a military preparatory high school and two infantry cadet schools, where the overwhelming majority of students were native speakers,[33] but the proportion of Magyars in the Joint Army schools now surpassed, for the first time, the proportion of ethnic Hungarians in the monarchy's total population. In 1911–1912, the Joint Army had 4,380 military students; 960 of them, or 21.9 percent, were native speakers of Hungarian,[34] this at a time when Magyars constituted about 18 percent of the monarchy's total population.* Magyar representation in the Joint Army military schools was in 1911–1912 greater than the proportion of all Hungarian-born students, whether Magyars, Germans, Serbs, or Romanians, had been in 1881. This was due to such factors as the rapid growth of a Magyar educated elite, the generous fellowships provided by the Hungarian government and wealthy patrons to Magyar officer candidates, and the Hungarian nationalist desire to "conquer" the army, which contrasted strangely with the parallel nationalist goal of putting an end to the Joint Army.

Two obstacles remained to establishing complete Hungarian parity with Austria in military affairs. One was the chronic underrepresentation of ethnic Hungarian teachers in the Joint Army military schools, although the introduction of compulsory Hungarian in many schools offered a partial remedy for this shortcoming. The other was the uneven distribution of Magyar students in the different military schools. The Military Academy at Wiener Neustadt always had a disproportionate number of Magyar students preparing for the cavalry branch; on the other hand, there were almost no ethnic Hungarians in the artillery or the other technical schools. As late as 1897, the Artillery Cadet School at Vienna did not have a single Hungarian-born student. In 1899, there was one such student, apparently quite unqualified.[35] But by 1912, the Hungarian National Guard had finally obtained an artillery branch and had set up an artillery section at its academy. Simultaneously, Magyars were becoming more conspicuous in the artillery and technical schools of the Joint Army. There would have been nothing wrong with the Hungarians' developing an interest in all aspects of military service had not the Hungarian leadership aimed at splitting up the Joint Army. In Hungarian eyes, every Hungarian-born cadet of the Joint Army was a future commander in His Apostolic Majesty's Royal Hungarian forces. Clearly, the Joint Army was fighting a losing battle, even in terms of military education.

Not only Hungary but all the kingdoms and provinces of the Dual Monarchy were unevenly represented in the Joint Army military schools. In 1880–1881, for instance, the greatest number of students came, proportionally (in descending order) from Lower Austria (including Vienna), with an almost purely German population; Silesia, with a mixed German, Polish, and Czech population; and Moravia, with a majority of Czechs and a respectable minority (29 percent) of Germans. The lowest number of students came, proportionally (also in descending order) from the Tyrol and Voralberg, with a majority of Germans and a large minority (38 percent) of Italians; Hungary, with an ethnic admixture of Magyars, Romanians, Germans, Slovaks, Serbs, and Ruthenes; and Galicia, with a mixed Polish and Ruthene population. In 1880–1881, the Lower Austrian representation in the military schools was proportionally almost six times that of the Galician and five times that of the Hungarian.[36] By the turn of the twentieth century, however, the balance had begun to change in favor of the primarily Slavic and Hungarian provinces and kingdoms.

---

*One of the more dubious achievements of the Hungarian government was to have the Joint War Ministry inquire into the ethnic background of the military students. How these data were compiled (whether, for instance, cadets or their parents were asked about their mother tongue) remains unclear.

Most disturbing, from the point of view of the military high command, was the dwindling number of military students in the two decades preceding World War I. Between 1897 and 1911, the two military academies maintained a total enrollment of about 650, but at the nineteen cadet schools enrollment fell from 3,333 in 1897 to 2,279 in 1907 and to 1,864 in 1911. True, enrollment at the military preparatory schools had increased from 1,293 in 1897 to 1,694 in 1911, but this showed only that a large number of youngsters were taking advantage of the free middle-level education offered at these Realschulen, without any intention of pursuing a military career. Following the introduction of expanded military budgets in 1912, there was a new growth in student enrollment, but like the military budget increase, it came too late to provide for the needs of the Great War. Clearly, in the years immediately preceding World War I, an officer's career in the Joint Army was beginning to appeal to fewer and fewer young men.[37]

World War I brought inevitable changes in the life of the military students as well as a great number of reform projects. Students were commissioned early to replace the subalterns killed at the front. The Military Academy graduated 134 lieutenants in 1913; of these, 40 (30 percent) died in the war, the majority during its first weeks. Another 27 graduates (20.3 percent) were captured, and 2 were badly wounded: thus 69 graduates (51.9 percent) were lost.[38]

The school reforms aimed at further liberalization and at establishing equality between the academies and the cadet schools, but there was no time to institute these changes.[39] During the first two years of the war, the students were well provided for, but then hunger gradually set in. Nor was there much heating. News from the front was kept from the students, one reason, perhaps, for the continuing absence of nationality conflict at the schools. When the monarchy collapsed, some students did not know where to go; the soldiers' sons, in particular, had no idea of which country they were the citizens. In November of 1918, after Emperor-King Charles had been abandoned even by his noble bodyguards, student companies from the Military Academy and the Traiskirchen artillery school mounted guard at the Schönbrunn Palace to protect their former ruler from the revolutionaries. Then Charles withdrew to a hunting lodge in Austria and, on December 2, 1918, the last Habsburg army military students handed over their equipment and horses to the Vienna city police. From there, they dispersed to their new fatherlands.[40]

Military education in the Habsburg monarchy changed with the changing times. Under Maria Theresa, students were separated into noblemen and commoners, but even the latter enjoyed six-course dinners, wine, and the service of lackeys. In the post-Napoleonic restoration period, the students were locked up, spied upon, and treated as potential troublemakers; the subjects they were taught were treated as supplements to religion and ethics. In the absolutistic era after 1849, the students were trained to be brave, rough, practical soldiers. In the post-1867 period, they were brought up to be educated men and leaders. At all times, the students' devotion to the monarch was taken for granted, and there is no evidence to show that more than a small minority wavered in their near-religious attachment to the ruling house. The students were offered an enormous amount of scientific and practical knowledge, particularly after 1867. What they were never taught—either from the standpoint of grasping the complexities of the Habsburg realm, or from the standpoint of cultural enrichment—was the folklore, customs, problems, and aspirations of the monarchy's many peoples. But such sociocultural considerations were not part of any nineteenth-century academic curriculum, whether at Sandhurst, St. Cyr, Berlin-Lichterfelde, St. Petersburg, or Wiener Neustadt. Officer trainees were taught to lead masses of men, not to be concerned with the peculiarities of their individualism.

Appendix: Theresan Military Academy at Wiener Neustadt in 1912–1913

Excerpts from the *Jahresbericht der k. und k. Militärakademie in Wiener Neustadt, 1912/13* (Wiener Neustadt, 1913), pp. 75–78:

Teachers, supervisors and administrators, 55; of these, teaching personnel, 42 (teacher : student ratio, 1 : 10).

Students, first year, 150; second year, 150; third year, 138; total, 438. Of these, commissioned on August 18, 1913, 134; 82 (including 1 Chinese) to the joint infantry and Jäger, 34 to the joint cavalry, 15 to the National Guard infantry, 3 to the National Guard cavalry.

Table 3A.1. Religious Distribution of Students

Religious Affiliation	Number	Percentage
Roman Catholic	381	87.0
Greek Catholic (Uniate)	4	0.9
Greek Orthodox	20	4.5
Lutheran	23	5.3
Reformed (Calvinist)	5	1.1
Jewish	3	0.7
Confucian	2	0.5
Total	438	100.0

Table 3A.2. Distribution of Students by Domicile

Home Territory	Number	Percentage
Alpine provinces	115	26.3
Carniola and Adriatic littoral	16	3.7
Bohemia, Moravia, and Austrian Silesia	136	31.0
Galicia and the Bukovina	33	7.5
Lands of the Hungarian Holy Crown	136	31.0
Foreigners	2	0.5
Total	438	100.0

Note (1) that even though Bohemia, Moravia, and Silesia (today mostly in the Czechoslovak Republic) provided 136 students, only 28 of them had Czech as their mother tongue, and (2) that of the 136 students from Hungary and Croatia-Slavonia, only 71 considered Hungarian to be their mother tongue.

Table 3A.3. Distribution of Students by Mother Tongue

Nationality	Number	Percentage
Germans	277	63.2
"Czechoslavs" (*Tschechoslawen*)	28	6.4
Poles	16	3.7
Ruthenes	1	0.2
South Slavs (Serbs, Croats, and Slovenes)	35	8.0
Italians	5	1.1
Romanians	3	0.7
Magyars (*Magyaren*)	71	16.2
Chinese	2	0.5
Total	438	100.0

Table 3A.4. Distribution of Students by Previous Academic Preparation

School Attended	Number	Percentage
Civilian high schools (Realschulen, Gymnasien, Realgymnasien)	144	32.9
Military preparatory schools (Militär-Oberrealschulen)	229	52.3
Cadet schools (Kadettenschulen)	65	14.8
Total	438	100.0
Of total, acquired a high school graduation certificate (*Matura*)	162	

Table 3A.5. Distribution of Students by Payment Categories (*Platzkategorien*)

	Number	Percentage
Paid nothing	411	93.8
Paid partial or full fees	27	6.2
Total	438	100.0

Table 3A.6. Citizenship of Students Admitted in 1912–1913

Citizenship	Number	Percentage
Austrian	97	64.7
Hungarian	53	35.3
Total	150	100.0

Table 3A.7. Student Grades for 1912–1913

Grade	Number	Percentage
Excellent (*Vorzugsschüler*)	63	14.4
Very good	165	37.7
Good	185	42.2
Satisfactory	4	0.9
Unsatisfactory	1	0.2
Other	20	4.6
Total	438	100.0

4

Life in the Regiment

Reporting to the Garrison

Shortly before graduation, Military Academy students were allowed to indicate which regiment they wished to join, though their choice would not necessarily be accepted. In theory, the wishes of the foremost students were to be honored; in reality, much depended on the influence of fathers and relatives. It should be remembered that in the prereform period, students at the higher military schools constituted only a minority of those who would become officers, and that only this minority enjoyed the theoretical privilege of choosing. The others, whether enlisted men on the rise or cadets, had taken their oath as soldiers long ago and were already serving in a regiment. Our discussion here, however, will focus mainly on the post-1868 period, when, with the minor exception of reserve officers turned professional, all new career officers came from the academies or cadet schools. They had been sworn in only on graduation day: the academy students as full-fledged lieutenants and the cadet school students as ensigns.

Cavalry graduates of the Military Academy had a particularly delicate task in choosing their regiment; while all cavalry units, whether Dragoner, Husaren, or Ulanen, were socially desirable, there were subtle differences between them. The problem was not so much the location of a regiment—all cavalrymen could count on spending many years near the Russian border in Galicia—as it was the tradition and social composition of the regimental officer corps. There was, as we shall see later, a pecking order among aristocratic cavalry regiments. It was not the same thing to serve with, say, the 7th Dragoner, where almost everyone was a baron or a count, as with the 8th Ulanen, where only a minority were.

Gunners and engineers were less concerned with noble titles than with the quality of the regiment. But even among the gunners, there was a marked social distinction between the field artillery (Feldartillerie), where all the officers were mounted, and the fortress artillery (Festungsartillerie), where only those with the rank of captain and above were assigned a mount. In fact, field artillery officers alone were accepted by the cavalry as equals.

95

Our main concern is with the infantry officers, who formed the bulk of the corps and for whom the choice of a regiment could mean the difference between a tolerable and an intolerable existence. At the very outset this group faced an immediate and decisive selection process, with the best and the best-connected graduates among them being posted to a Jäger battalion (or even better, to the famous Tiroler Jäger-Regiment; later four regiments), while the rest had to be content with one of the regular infantry regiments. When the son of Baron Franz von Trotta in Joseph Roth's *Radetzky March* expresses the amazing wish to exchange his Ulan regiment for an infantry unit, the distraught father uses his good connections at court to have his son posted to a Jäger battalion.[1] Even though, by the second half of the nineteenth century, the Jäger barely differed from the regular infantry in training and equipment, there remained their distinctive plumed hat, their tradition of bravery, the higher quality of the men they recruited from the western provinces, and the inherited prestige of the Jäger officers.

In the regular infantry, what counted most was the location of a regiment, the ethnic composition and literacy of its men, and the quality of its officers. Most young officer candidates simply had to sweat out graduation day, when they were finally notified of their assignments. A six-week vacation followed, then a trip to a new post and, often, to disappointment. Alighting at the railroad station in his very best uniform, a young officer frequently found that the garrison was still many miles away, down a dusty or muddy road, and, at least in the eastern provinces of the monarchy, that no one had come to meet him but an Orthodox Jew, who offered to take the new arrival to regimental headquarters in his shabby one-nag wagon. The Jew seemed to know all about the young officer: his name, his future quarters, and the company he would be assigned to. He was the famous *Möbeljud* or "Furniture Jew," a self-appointed business agent who attached himself to a unit and provided the officers with private accommodations, furniture, civilian clothing, and women, all for a modest honorarium. The butt of many jokes, the *Möbeljud* must nevertheless have appeared to the young officer as an angel in kaftan and sideburns; this, at least, is how he emerges from the memoirs.[2]*

The reception that awaited the new arrival at the garrison varied from the gruff to the amiable, but, nearly always, the young officer found his assigned quarters most inadequate. Ensigns were housed several to a room; lieutenants were offered their own quarters, complete with the services of a batman, but with very little or no furniture. Even before the era of reforms the batman was given a cot, table, chair, and shelf for the small room he occupied within the officer's quarters, but the lieutenant found that

> not the smallest piece of furniture encumbered the space that was to be the officer's home, and the new arrival blessed his predecessor for every nail left in the wall. This way he could avoid the unpleasantness of having to lay his shako and overcoat on the floor.[3]

Solicitous company commanders provided a new arrival with a cot and bed linen, complete with bedbugs. The real comforts were furnished by the *Möbeljud*. The

---

*Note that, until at least the 1850s, each regiment had an official agent, a civilian, who was located in Vienna. This *Agent* is not to be confused, of course, with the *Möbeljud*.

first improvements came in 1851 and, after that date, the subalterns no longer confronted empty quarters in the barracks; they were now furnished, by imperial order, with a bed, bed linen, blankets, a closet, a trunk, two tables, and four stools, all of painted soft wood. There was even a night table, an "ordinary mirror," a washstand, a carafe, a drinking glass, and a chamber pot.[4] The trouble was that the barracks constructed in great numbers in the 1850s were designed as fortresses from which to control the population and were, as a result, damp, dark, and forbidding affairs. Real improvements came only in the 1870s when a vigorous program of barrack construction began: relatively bright, hygienic, often widely spaced buildings which improved living conditions immensely, as did the introduction of officers' mess halls, better hospitals, retirement homes for invalids, resort houses at famous spas, and, last but not least, an increasing number of well-constructed military schools intended for the sons and daughters of the soldiers.

Those who could afford it rented a room in town, or several subalterns would team up to rent an apartment. This gave the young subalterns unheard-of freedom, especially as they soon found that service was far from onerous, usually demanding one's presence only from seven to eleven in the morning, and from two to five in the afternoon.[5] There should have been ample time to enjoy what was invariably described in propagandistic military literature as *Die schöne, wilde* (or *goldene*) *Leutnantszeit*, the lovely, wild lieutenant's existence. Memoir writers use the term with the same regularity, quite often in ironical quotation marks.

There was, however, not only pleasure but much to worry about as well. An academy graduate sometimes found that he constituted a minority of one in the company's officer corps; the rest were, in prereform days, former enlisted men and other semieducated types and, in the postreform period, the scarcely more refined graduates of the cadet schools.[6] Barely twenty years of age, the new subaltern was confronted with middle-aged lieutenants and first lieutenants (again, mostly in the prereform era), many of them embittered alcoholics. If he was an aristocrat in an infantry unit (and there were many of these), he felt the envy and suspiciousness of his comrades; if a commoner in a cavalry regiment, he inevitably felt snubbed.

Yet the Habsburg army also practiced a custom that proved to be a great equalizer, unique among the dynastic armies of Europe. This was the well-established tradition of officers' addressing and conversing with one another in the familiar second person singular form, using *Du* (thou) rather than the more formal *Sie*. The importance of this custom is shown by the fact that it is discussed by most military writers. It was indeed an extraordinary phenomenon in a society where children rarely addressed their parents in this form, or husbands their wives. *Duzen* was originally an aristocratic custom, testifying to the unity of the great noble families through their elevated status and matrimonial ties.

The practice of using *thou* in unofficial contacts (almost never in service) began among Habsburg army officers during the Napoleonic Wars. It was a distinctive feature of Radetzky's Army of Italy, and it came into general use in the post-1849 absolutist period, when the officers felt that they and they alone had saved the monarchy and therefore constituted the true first estate of the realm. There were some exceptions to the rule, in conservative regiments or in truly awkward situations, such as when a young lieutenant had to address a field-grade officer or a general. Besides, individual officers made a sport of using the *Du* only selectively. There was also the absolute obligation to add a person's rank to the *Du: "Du, Herr Leutnant," "Du, Exzellenz."* Nonetheless, this intimate form of address contributed as much to the officers' esprit de corps as did their code of honor (of which more will be said later). Toward the end of the nineteenth century, with the influx of reserve officers, the practice was increasingly difficult to maintain, but maintained it was, even if it led to such strange scenes as an aristocratic cavalry captain jumping up from his seat, shaking hands with, and saying *thou* to, say, a Jewish reserve lieutenant (in private life a shopkeeper) from the transportation corps. During World War I, the custom resulted in so many painful incidents with Reich German officers that Austro-Hungarian officers were finally forbidden to introduce themselves to their German colleagues when they found themselves in the same railroad compartment.[7]

No sooner had he arrived than a young lieutenant was ordered to take over the Mannschaftsschule, the classroom instruction of the company's young recruits. In the Habsburg army, unlike in the Prussian, all instruction was provided by officers rather than NCOs. Indeed, noncommissioned officers generally played a less important official role in the Austro-Hungarian armed forces than in the Prussian or the Reich German. Needless to say, experienced master sergeants—and there never seemed to be enough of them—often had to substitute for the subalterns, in the classroom or on the training ground, if for no other reason than because they were more likely to speak the language of the men than were the officers.

To face a classroom full of peasant lads and address them in their mother tongue must have been a harrowing experience. Chances were slim, indeed, that the young lieutenant would speak their language (or languages) well enough to teach them how to read and write (in what language anyway: German or their own tongue?), or to explain the intricacies of weaponry and the proper way to address one's superiors. I have noted already that every military student was taught several languages: German (not always his mother tongue) and two other major languages spoken in the monarchy as well as French. These courses, however, were usually taught by indifferent military men, and they earned the student fewer points than science or the military subjects. It did little good anyway for the young lieutenant to speak Polish, for instance, in a Galician regiment, if the men happened to speak Ruthene, Hucul, Goral, Lemko, Bojko, or some other dialect common to Galician peasants. And even if the officer was lucky enough to be a German-Austrian in a German-speaking regiment, chances were that he understood very little of the Tyrolean or Transylvanian Saxon dialect spoken by the men. Nor did German-speaking soldiers necessarily understand his educated High German. Yet, as the memoir writers assure us, the young lieutenant would succeed somehow, mostly with the assistance of a noncommissioned officer, and with the use of *Kauderwelsch,* the linguistic mélange that passed for a means of communication in the Habsburg army.[8]*

---

*Some officers were luckier than others. General Urbański, who was born and grew up in Dalmatia, learned Polish and German from his soldier-father; Italian from his mother; an Italian-Slavic *Kauderwelsch,* called *ponaški* ("our language"), from the servants; and some Hungarian from his father's batman. (August von Urbański, "Das Tornisterkind. Lebenserinnerungen," unpublished manuscript, Kriegsarchiv, Vienna, 5/58. Nr. 4, p. 4.)

Commanding a Multilingual Army

The Habsburg armed forces accorded official status to about ten or eleven languages spoken by their rank and file. Even after the "Bohemian" and "Moravian" tongues on the one hand, and Serbian and Croatian on the other ceased to be treated as separate languages, German, Hungarian, Czech, Slovak, Polish, Ruthene (Ukrainian), Serbo-Croatian, Slovene, Romanian, and Italian continued to enjoy recognition as "national languages." Their use was compulsory for the officers and NCOs, provided that they were spoken by at least 20 percent of the rank and file within a given military unit. Only some eighty major commands, such as "Right," "Left," "Halt," "At ease," and "Fire," were issued in German; the rest were given in the national language or languages of the unit. How this was achieved in practice is one of the more comic sides of Austro-Hungarian military life: picture an officer or NCO first barking his command in German and then switching to one, two, three, or even four other languages to explain more precisely what he had in mind, or to instruct, harangue, or curse his men.

The overwhelming majority of the Habsburg army units were multilingual. In the summer of 1914, for instance, only 142 major military formations (regiments and independent battalions) were considered monolingual. In 162 units two languages were spoken; in 24 units, three languages; and there were even a few units where four languages were in use. Of the 142 monolingual units, only 31 were German-speaking, which meant that less than 10 percent of all the officers were in the enviable position of being able to address their soldiers in the same language they had used to issue their words of command. Or, to put it differently, more than 90 percent of the officers were obliged to communicate in at least one language other than German.[9]

The military authorities expected linguistic proficiency on the part of the officers. The accepted minimum was what the *Qualifikations-Listen* termed "adequate for the needs of service" (*zum Dienstgebrauch genügend*), something between "native fluency" (*vollkommenes Sprachkenntnis*) and an "inadequate" or "poor" (*notdürftiges*) knowledge. Familiarity with the regimental language or languages had to be demonstrated before a commission which met within three years after an officer's entry into his unit. If he failed the examination, he was usually granted a two-year grace period, but if he failed again he was set back on the promotion list with the remark, "unqualified for the time being" (*zur Zeit nicht geeignet*). At this point, he could try to transfer to another regiment or might even resign his commission. In practice, almost every officer was sooner or later found to possess adequate linguistic knowledge, but those who took longer lost precious years of opportunity for promotion.

Unlike the military schools, the army did virtually nothing to help its officers learn a new language. Only in a few regiments, and then mostly toward the end of the nineteenth century, were language handbooks containing a rudimentary grammar and a list of indispensable expressions printed up for the use of officers.[10]

Beginning in 1870, the army occasionally published statistics on its officers' familiarity with languages. These data indicate that most officers spoke an average of two languages besides German, and that linguistic abilities improved gradually. They also show that the particular languages known changed over time, in accordance with the monarchy's territorial expansion or contraction and the gradual ethnic transformation of the officer corps.

As the statistics in Table 4.1 show, the officers spoke more languages in 1904 than in 1870 (a total of 154.5 percent versus 136.89 percent). The advance of Hungarian reflects both the increasing presence of Magyar officers in the Joint Army and the gradual adoption of Hungarian as a compulsory language in several military schools. Czech had replaced Italian as the officers' most likely second language, less because of the increasing proportion of Czechs in the officer corps than because of the general usefulness of Czech as a language for communication with all Slavic soldiers. Of course, only a minority of Slavic-speaking officers had a perfect command of any Slavic language; the majority were content to speak the notorious *Armee-Slawisch,* best translated as pidgin-Slavic, in which Czech words predominated. In older *Qualifikations-Listen* one often encounters the note that a given officer spoke "Slavic" (*Slawisch*), without any further specification. Anecdotes about what this "Army Slavic" really consisted of were a favorite theme of memoir writers and military humorists. General August von Urbański quotes a soldiers' song in *Armee-Slawisch,* in this case a mixture of Czech and German, in which the lyrics refer to the heroism of one Franz Javurek, a Czech gunner at the battle of Königgrätz in 1866. Beginning as follows, "*A u kanonu stàl—a furt jen ladovál*" (He stood by the gun—and loaded it incessantly), the song recounts how Javurek continued to do his duty, long after being decapitated by a Prussian cannonball.[11]

Linguistic ability varied enormously among the several service branches, reflecting the differing ethnic composition of the troops and officers in each. Because Polish and Hungarian officers and men were heavily overrepresented in the cavalry,

Table 4.1. Familiarity of Career Officers with Languages (Other than German) Spoken in the Habsburg Army, 1870 and 1904 (Percentages)

1870		1904	
Language	Percentage	Language	Percentage
1. Italian	32.76	1. Czech	47.0
2. Czech	30.18	2. Hungarian	33.6
3. Hungarian	19.77	3. Polish	19.3
4. Polish	17.62	4. Serbocroatian	15.3
5. Serbocroatian	17.36*	5. Romanian	8.8
6. Romanian	8.95	6. Italian	8.5
7. Ruthene	5.14	7. Ruthene	7.8
8. Slovene	5.11	8. Slovene	7.3
9. Slovak	—*	9. Slovak	6.9

Source: Militär-Statistisches Jahrbuch für das Jahr 1870, Part I (Vienna, 1872), p. 222; and *Militär-Statistisches Jahrbuch für das Jahr 1904* (Vienna, 1905), p. 146.

*In 1870, Serbian (6.41 percent) and Croatian (10.95 percent) were still listed separately; on the other hand, Slovak was not yet a recognized national language.

Table 4.2. Familiarity of Career Officers with French, 1870 and 1904 (Percentages)

1870		1904	
Officer Category	Percentage	Officer Category	Percentage
General staff	92.36	General staff	63.9
Cavalry	38.34	Cavalry	38.5
Artillery	21.80	Jäger	17.7
Jäger	20.97	Field artillery	14.4*
Infantry	19.84	Fortress artillery	13.0*
Grenzer	5.02†	Train	9.1
Train	3.42	Infantry	7.7

Source: *Militär-Statistisches Jahrbuch für das Jahr 1870*, Part I (Vienna, 1872), p. 222; and *Militär-Statistisches Jahrbuch für das Jahr 1904* (Vienna, 1905), p. 146.

*By 1904, the field and fortress artillery were listed separately.

†By 1904, the Military Border no longer existed.

familiarity with these languages was also widespread there. Slavic officers and men and, hence, a knowledge of Slavic languages were conspicuous among the infantry, Grenzer, Train, and medics. German and Czech speakers predominated in the artillery and other technical units. Between 1870 and 1904, however, there was a remarkable increase in the number of Magyars in the artillery, reflecting the spread of education in Hungary and the growing interest of Magyars in all branches of service, not simply the cavalry, their traditional preserve.

The Habsburg military also kept track of its officers' familiarity with the major foreign languages. Few things provide a better indication of the differing social and

Table 4.3. Familiarity of Career Officers with English, 1870 and 1904 (Percentages)

1870		1904	
Officer Category	Percentage	Officer Category	Percentage
General staff	18.75	General staff	18.9
Cavalry	8.29	Cavalry	8.0
Artillery	3.85	Field artillery	6.2*
Jäger	2.53	Fortress artillery	5.6*
Infantry	2.29	Train	4.2
Grenzer	0.20†	Jäger	1.8
Train	0.00	Infantry	1.2

Source: *Militär-Statistisches Jahrbuch für das Jahr 1870*, Part I (Vienna, 1872), p. 222; and *Militär-Statistisches Jahrbuch für das Jahr 1904* (Vienna, 1905), p. 146.

*By 1904, the field and fortress artillery were listed separately.

†By 1904, the Military Border no longer existed. Note that in 1870, only two Grenzer career officers (0.2 percent) out of a total of 996 spoke some English.

educational standing of officers in the various service arms than statistics on their knowledge of French and English. Not surprisingly, a familiarity with these two languages was most widespread, in 1870, among the highly educated officers of the general staff and in the wealthy cavalry; it was less common among the officers of the elite Jäger and the gunners, and even less so among infantry officers. A knowledge of French, and of English especially, was virtually nonexistent among the Grenzer officers and the Train. It was as if the officers of the latter two branches had little connection, in terms of education and social standing, with the general staff, the cavalry, and the artillery.

Remarkably, despite the higher educational qualifications needed for an officer's commission in 1904, as compared to 1870, general familiarity with French declined from 22.91 percent to 14.7 percent. While it is true that the knowledge of English had increased from 3.1 percent to 7.9 percent during the same period, it is nonetheless clear that proportionately fewer officers spoke a foreign language in 1904 than in 1870. The reason for this must be sought in the increasing technical specialization at the military schools and in a decreasing aristocratic and upper-middle-class presence among the officers. This is confirmed by the stable percentage of foreign language speakers in the cavalry, the aristocrats' preserve.

Against all odds, the old multinational army succeeded, more or less, in solving the language problem in its ranks even after length of service for ordinary soldiers was reduced from eight to three years in 1868. It achieved this unique success by devoting a considerable amount of time in military schools to the study of languages and by forcing its officers to become veritable artists in linguistic inventiveness.

Later, however, as warfare became more complex and technical, the difficulties inevitably increased. What is worse, command over the smaller units during World War I would gradually pass into the hands of reserve officers who were linguistically unprepared, in part at least because of the growing nationalism of Hungarian, Croatian, Polish, and even German high-school education. As I shall subsequently show, the typical reserve officer in World War I would know how to die for the monarchy, but he often lived like a deaf-mute among his men.

Officers and Men

An infantry lieutenant was usually in charge of a platoon, which numbered fifty men in wartime, and perhaps thirty in peacetime. A captain had a hundred fifty to two hundred fifty men under his command, a colonel several thousand, a general tens of thousands, or even more. Yet whether commanding a small group or an enormously large one, the Habsburg officer seemed to live in blissful ignorance of the lives, pleasures, hopes, and sufferings of his soldiers. He rarely, if ever, discussed their fate, addressed them in private, or remembered them in his writings. Only exceptionally does a poorly defined individual face emerge from an officer's memoirs: a particularly stupid or exceptionally valuable batman, a devoted sergeant, a heroic enlisted man. The officer gave orders, the men obeyed; this seems to have been the level of understanding between the two groups.

What we find are mainly stereotypes: the Austrian mountain peasants were seen as fine soldiers and, among them, the Tyroleans as excellent marksmen but also as slow moving and stubborn; the Magyars as brave but unruly and violence prone; the Czechs as reliable but unimaginative; the Italians as reluctant warriors; the Serbs, Croats, and Bosnians as the finest of all but only if held firmly in hand; the Poles as heroic but wild; the Ruthenes as meek and dumb; and the Romanians as backward and primitive. The overall picture is one of the common soldier as a child: eminently malleable if well led; useless and even dangerous if left to his own devices.[12]

No doubt, the peasant recruit of yore was often illiterate and ignorant of the world. Yet, this simplified image of the average recruit persisted in officer circles even after the introduction of universal conscription in 1868, and the massive influx of urban elements. In any case, however, the Habsburg officer at least did not regard the urban recruits, especially industrial workers, with the same profound suspicion as did his Reich German colleague.

One reason for this collective ignorance was indifference, but there was also the army's ban on private contacts with the men. The Austrian socialist Otto Bauer, who had been to reserve officer training school just before World War I, cites the words of his school commander:

> The noncommissioned officers are peasants; an educated person has no social contact with a peasant. If I should learn that one of you talks to a noncommissioned officer outside of military duty, shakes hands with him or even joins him in a pub, he will lose eligibility to become an officer![13]

Bauer holds that the Prussian officers were closer to their men than the Habsburg officers, and he argues that the Austro-Hungarian officers, who, at least in the later period, were often of lower-middle-class background, had to create artificially the social prestige which came naturally to their Junker counterparts.[14] Bauer could have added that the Habsburg officer of noble background—the Austro-Hungarian nobility being a very varied group indeed—did not always enjoy the same social prestige as his well-established Prussian counterpart.

Unfortunately, ordinary soldiers tell us next to nothing of their lives, and I have come across only one memoir by an enlisted man. Published posthumously, it is the story of one Leo Schuster, an ethnic German from Bohemia, born in 1889, who served as a career noncommissioned officer, first as an artillerist under Francis Joseph and then as a gendarme, in the first Austrian republic, in the Third Reich, and in the second Austrian republic. Having experienced dire poverty in his childhood, Schuster was a happy soldier; he dutifully served any regime that offered him a modicum of respectability.[15]

While individual officers may have been heedless of the enlisted men, the army was not. Countless regulations prescribed the proper way to treat, educate, discipline, and train the men, as well as the quantity and quality of the food, drink, and tobacco they were to be given, and the space they were to occupy in the barracks. Some of these regulations read to us now as if coming from a bureaucracy gone mad, yet we must consider that when the military bureaucracy formulated in minute detail, and in the name of the emperor, the precise way to prepare the soldiers' morning soup or the number of floggings that officers of various ranks were permitted to dispense (in the prereform age only, of course), it was attempting to prevent unnecessary brutality, corruption, and theft.

The Rank and File in the Prereform Period

The pre-1868 soldier was either a volunteer or a draftee. In practice there was little difference between the two, since even in lands where recruitment was theoretically voluntary, such as Hungary, men were generally dragooned into the forces.

Service was alternately a nightmare to some but quite tolerable to others who had known starvation or the cane of the estate supervisor at home. The soldiers slept two to a bed, then as well as later; they were given enough food to still their hunger, although required to cook for themselves.* Provisioning was at first the responsibility of private entrepreneurs, the so-called *Commis* or *Kommis,* and later of the army commissariat. (The word *Kommis,* incidentally, entered the Hungarian language to denote "shabby, vile."). Service was onerous, sometimes running from 4:00 A.M. to 7:00 P.M., under the often brutal supervision of NCOs. Training in the prereform army consisted mainly of efforts to teach incredibly complex mass-formation maneuvers, the handling of musket and bayonet, and the no less complex system of trumpet and drum signals. All this necessitated many years, which made the long-service soldier a truly valuable and expensive commodity. Training was regularly interrupted, however, by the army's inability to feed all the soldiers. Furloughed for months at a time, an enlisted man did agricultural labor or developed artisanal skills. When crippled or no longer needed, he was discharged, which meant that he had to fend for himself once again. Only the war-wounded might receive a pittance as a pension, and even fewer made it into one of the veterans' homes founded by Maria Theresa. Since it was invariably difficult to return to the family farm, the old army veteran often used the skills he had acquired in the military to earn a living as a craftsman or a village scribe.[16]†

The most heinous aspect of military life in the prereform era was corporal punishment. As a progressive measure, the army reform of 1838 limited to twenty-five the number of strokes with a cane that a company commander could order. Battalion commanders were permitted forty strokes, and regimental commanders fifty. The 1855 reform further reduced the permissible number to twenty, thirty, and forty, respectively.

The law of 1838 limited to thirty the number of soldiers involved in administering the punishment known as *Gassenlaufen* (running the gauntlet), and it reduced to one hundred the maximum number of times a victim was to pass between the two

---

*For instance, in 1848, a soldier at Komárom fortress, Hungary, received two pounds of bread daily, as well as nearly a pound of meat, a pint of wine, and, less frequently, flour, rice, barley groats, peas, beans, lentils, sauerkraut (to ward off scurvy), smoked meat, garlic, onions, salt, vinegar, pepper, and tobacco. (Royal Hungarian Ministry of War to the National Defense Committee. Országos Levéltár [National Archives, Budapest], OHB, 1848: 3318.)

†In fact, the eight years' service usually meant only three years in the 1850s. (*Sechzig Jahre Wehrmacht* [Vienna, 1908], p. 44). The discharge paper or *Abschiedsbrief* was such an important document that its name entered, usually in some wildly distorted form, into the language of most peoples of the monarchy. In Hungarian, the veteran with an *Abschiedsbrief* was known as an *obsitos.*

parallel rows of soldiers, each armed with a cane. Such extreme punishment was to extend over several weeks, yet as late as 1841 Fenner complained of an occasional victim having to run the gauntlet ten times in a day, always between three hundred men. If he refused to run, he was laid on a bench, and the soldiers marched past him (this was called the *Contremarsch*), caning him up to a total of six thousand times. What outraged Fenner in particular was the utter callousness of the soldiers administering the punishment. He conceded, however, that the Austrian practice of caning the buttocks was more humane than the Prussian practice of aiming at the back. Soldiers (but never officers or cadets) had to run the gauntlet for both common and political crimes. Following the 1848–1849 revolution, one horrified young officer in the 16th Venetian Zanini regiment witnessed the caning of rebellious Italian soldiers, some up to several thousand times. Those who cried were caned some more.[17] The law of 1855 finally forbade the hideous practice of running the gauntlet.

The murder of officers was not unknown, and suicide by enlisted men was quite common (on suicide, more later). The penalty for threatening an officer was seventy strokes with the cane, for attempted suicide, twenty-five strokes.[18]

In 1848, the Hungarian revolutionary army abolished corporal punishment, much to the indignation of that army's Habsburg career officers. The result, as General Görgey emphasized, was a vast increase in the number of executions.[19]

The soldiers occasionally engaged in passive resistance, by feigning not to understand orders, by shirking, and by deserting. The latter was a capital offense, at least in wartime, as were countless other violations listed in the *Kriegsartikel*, the articles of war. Yet the military courts were generally more humane than individual officers. In an extremely complicated procedure (of which more later), the courts attempted to protect the dignity and the natural rights of enlisted men.

The Common Soldier in the Dual Monarchy

Despite some similarities, the life and treatment of ordinary soldiers in the postreform period differed fundamentally from those in the first half of the nineteenth century. As living standards and general education improved, so did the quality of recruits. That many were still utterly alien to the world of discipline, timetable, and hygiene remains without doubt. A relatively unprejudiced observer, General Anton Lehár, notes in his memoirs that in 1893 Romanian recruits of the 50th k.u.k. Infantry Regiment in Transylvania arrived with their long, heavily greased hair parted in braids, and that they had never heard of soap.[20]

Universal military service brought highly systematized conditions. The annual recruit contingent arrived in the barracks on October 1; for the next nine months training was within the company, to be followed by one month in battalion, and another three weeks in regimental formation; the latter in preparation for the annual fall maneuvers. Then came two more years on active duty.

The hair of the recruits was cut to a regulation 6.5 cm (two and a half inches) in front, and 2.5 cm (one inch) in the back. (In 1908, this was modernized, respectively, to 7 cm and 3 cm.) Enlisted men were allotted a space of 4.5 square meters in the barrack room; corporals and the like were entitled to 6.2 square meters, with the additional privilege of a curtain around the bed. Noncommissioned officers lived two or three to a room. The pallets of soldiers were filled with exactly 22.4 kgs (50 lbs.) of straw, to be refreshed every four months with a further 11.2 kgs. The daily bread ration was nearly two pounds; the meat ration about 7 ounces. Breakfast consisted of a soup, always the same recipe, which had to contain nearly one ounce of flour, 0.4 ounce of fat, and 1.5 grams of caraway seed per man. The monthly ration of *Kommis* tobacco was eight packages, for which 4 kreuzer were deducted from the soldier's pay. I have mentioned earlier that the enlisted man's daily pay amounted to 6 kreuzer and that, following deductions, he was left with 0.75 kreuzer, equal to about 0.3 U.S. cent. The daily pay of ranks varied from 10 kreuzer to a sergeant's 35 kreuzer, plus some emoluments.

In their higher ranks, noncoms earned more than a lieutenant. This was still very little, especially if they had a family, but the NCOs also spent less money because their food and lodging were inexpensive, and because, unlike the officers, they were not expected to live elegantly. Theirs is no easy life—writes Danzer in 1889—but still better than being a factory worker or a hired hand. After eighteen years of service, NCOs were entitled to a pension, and after thirty years, to admission in a veterans' home. Most important, after twelve years of service, a noncommissioned officer was entitled to a low-level public service position, such as doorman, courier, or policeman.

The required height of a recruit in the Joint Army was set at 155 cm (a bit over five feet), yet in the infantry he was expected to carry sixty-six pounds on his back and march forty or more kilometers in one day.[21]

Military writers give markedly different accounts of how the soldiers were treated. Caning having been abolished after 1868, company commanders were still left with a range of disciplinary and punitive measures at their disposal, all the way from scolding to five days of "aggravated arrest" and tying up the culprit for two hours. Regimental commanders could order harsher punishments, and military courts meted out penalties ranging from dishonorable discharge to death by shooting or hanging.[22] Official statistics show the courts to have been amazingly lenient, at least in peacetime. Moreover, the number of sentences declined steadily. In 1878, for instance, 1,607 soldiers* were sentenced to imprisonment in the stockades (*Kerkerstrafe,* as opposed to a mere *Arreststrafe,* the latter to be spent in the barracks) for a period exceeding six months; in 1884, the number was 1,538; in 1904, 1,270; and in 1911, 938. In 1878, forty-six soldiers were given the death sentence, and seven of them were actually executed, six by hanging and one by shooting. In 1884, there were nineteen death sentences but only one soldier was executed, by hanging. (Apparently the more numerous and more honorable sentences of death by shooting were almost never translated into reality.) In 1904, nine were sentenced to death, and one was hanged; in 1911, there were nineteen death sentences, and no one was executed. In fact, no one sentenced to death in the Joint Army between 1905 and 1911 was subsequently executed.[23]

*This figure includes both officers and men, but officers made up only a very small proportion of this number, as we shall see later. The above figure represents about 0.6 percent of the total effectives in active service at that time.

Central European peoples have always suffered from a very high suicide rate. The reasons for this are the subject of continuous scholarly debate which need not concern us here. Contemporary statistics for Communist Hungary and Czechoslovakia as well as for non-Communist Austria show that the area's high suicide rate is not a corollary of economics and politics. The suicide rate in the Habsburg army was proportionally much higher than in the civilian population, a natural phenomenon for a body of young men suffering from loneliness, mistreatment, inadequate financial provision, sexual privation, or, the opposite of the last, venereal disease and sorrows of love. In 1878, for instance, there were 399 suicides among the rank and file, and in 1882, also 399.[24] Without going into detail about this extremely complex phenomenon, we should nonetheless note that the military suicide rate in Austria-Hungary was the highest in Europe. Between 1876 and 1890, the average number of suicides per 10,000 men was 12.53 in the Joint Army and only 8.11 in the next highest, the Saxon army. The rate among British soldiers, the lowest, was only 2.09. In 1903, the suicide rate per 10,000 men in the Joint Army was 10.5; in the German army, 2.6; and in the British, 2.3. Most suicides were committed by shooting.[25]

Austrian military statistics refused to attribute any suicides to mistreatment, but there is enough evidence to show that it was one of the major reasons that soldiers killed themselves. However, the social acceptability of suicide in central European society cannot be neglected either.

Since the days of Maria Theresa and Archduke Charles, military regulations stipulated that the rank and file be treated with dignity. It does not seem that the rule was very much respected. Officers, and especially drill sergeants, cursed, humiliated, and often hit the men so as to break their individuality and spirit. Opposition newspapers and politicians, in turn, spoke of infinite sufferings visited upon the recruits. To give a single example, in 1893 the Hungarian parliament was in an uproar over an incident in the 62nd k.u.k. Infantry Regiment, whose Transylvanian (hence Hungarian) recruits had been led on a forced march in extreme cold, resulting in 114 cases of frostbite. The fact that the Hungarian (and Croatian) regiments were still wearing the tight "Hungarian" trousers contributed to this appalling statistic. The colonel responsible for the incident was forced into retirement.[26]

Amazingly, military courts more than occasionally came out in defense of the rank and file. In October 1900, for instance, the garrison court at Olmütz, Moravia, sentenced a Dragoner lieutenant to one month's arrest in the barracks for having slapped and horsewhipped some recruits during riding instruction (note that officers sometimes suffered the same fate in a similar situation), and for having called them such names as "Bohemian swine" and "filthy Bohemian." In November 1913, the same garrison court gave a first lieutenant in the artillery four months of "rigorous arrest" (*strenger Profosenarrest*) for "pulling the ear, hitting the head with his cap, and choking the neck with both hands" of a cannonier. And in January 1913, the garrison court at Cracow sentenced First Lieutenant Gustaph Rab to six weeks' rigorous arrest, aggravated by one week in solitary confinement, for having insulted six artillerists, on diverse occasions, by using such terms as "idiot, dumbbell, cattle, swine, sea lion, moron, onanist, and cretin." Interestingly, Rab was not even accused of physical violence. What gave these soldiers the courage to report on their superior, and how they succeeded in doing so, remains a mystery.*

Seeking Happiness in the Army

Happiness in the army depended on where one served. Up until 1859, a large part of the armed forces was stationed in northern Italy and in the monarchy's central Italian client states. On the positive side, Italy was beautiful; the almost continuous military activity there could mean promotion and glory; the Army of Italy's near-eternal commander, Field Marshal Radetzky, was immensely popular among his officers; and the Austrians won every armed conflict in Italy, at least until 1859. On the negative side, service in that country meant social isolation. The better classes boycotted the Austrian military, in part for nationalist reasons, and in part because of threats from Italian irredentists. Hence, the officers congregated in a few select cafés, regaling each other with stories of largely imaginary conquests among Italian beauties. Italy could also be unbearably hot: the army high command at first seemed to take no notice of this other than to order its soldiers to hang a white kerchief from the back of their monstrously heavy and hot shakos or busbies. A light summer uniform was introduced only after 1850, a short time before the Austrians were booted out of Italy.

Following the loss of Venetia in 1866, the South Tyrol served as the main defense line against Italy. For the officers, this was a delightful place; it was clean and civilized, with a friendly population, whether *Welsch* (Italian) or German-speaking.

The Alpine provinces and the Czech lands were likewise favorites, even after conflicts arose with German and Czech nationalists in the last decades of the nineteenth century. The best place was, of course, Vienna, and graduating students at the military schools played with magic formulae to calculate when their chosen unit was likely to be transferred to the capital for the five-year stay that was every regiment's due. Vienna meant, among other things, a ten-kreuzer (four U.S. cents) ticket to the Hofoper or the Burgtheater, in a restricted area reserved for officers. This was a special favor granted by the emperor (legal owner and chief patron of

---

*(1) Case of Lt. Stanislaus Ritter von Dunin-Koeplicz, Garnisonsgericht Olmütz. Kriegsarchiv, Vienna, 1900, IA, 67-63. (2) Case of Oblt. Rudolf Hein, Garnisonsgericht Olmütz. Kriegsarchiv, Vienna, 1913, IA 67-127/3. The *Qualifikations-Liste* of First Lieutenant Hein, F 1075, notes that his was an "unruly character," that he had large debts, and that, in 1910, he had been sentenced to four weeks' arrest, "for failing to protect a secret document." Altogether, there were eleven disciplinary and court proceedings against Hein during his career. In 1915, he was sentenced to five years of "aggravated imprisonment" (*schwerer Kerker*) for embezzlement. He was cashiered in 1917, at the age of thirty-seven, and one wonders why this had not happened much earlier. (3) Case of Oblt. Gustaph (or Gustav) Rab, Garnisonsgericht Krakau. Kriegsarchiv, Vienna, 1914, IA 67-22. Rab's *Qualifikations-Liste,* F 2370, says that he was born in Vienna, and that his father was a sculptor. He completed a civilian high school and in 1902 transferred from the artillery reserve officer corps into the career corps. He was described as "very intelligent, very devoted, and a very good teacher and instructor" (a B+ average), but also as of "irritable temperament." First Lieutenant Rab was pensioned off in 1915, at the age of thirty-three.

these theaters), though it is true that one had to stand there, in full parade uniform. Vienna also meant the unique privilege for officers, without distinction of rank, of attending the annual Hofball (court ball), where they could catch a glance of the emperor, watch the highest dignitaries of the realm, eat unrestrainedly at the buffet table and, if extremely lucky, dance with a young countess or a baroness. (Usually, subalterns were ordered to dance with older ladies.) Entry to the Hofball was a favor originally granted by Maria Theresa, and it was as much appreciated by the officers as was their sacred right to request an audience with the emperor.[27]

Metternich's dictum that Asia began just east of Vienna was a view widely shared by the Habsburg officers. They found the hotels and inns in Hungary infested with bedbugs, the roads abominable, and the country gentry haughty and nationalistic. Still, garrisoning in that country had its rewards, both because of the legendary passion and beauty of its women and because of Hungarian hospitality. Alternately oppressed or treated as equal partners with their Austrian counterparts, the Magyar elite professed to hate the Joint Army yet generally welcomed its officers. The Hungarian word *mulatság* (merriment) became part and parcel of the Habsburg officers' vocabulary; conjugated in German, *mulatieren* meant to drink, sing, and listen to rousing Gypsy music.

Transylvania and Croatia were viewed as less civilized parts of only moderately civilized Hungary; Bosnia-Hercegovina was a hardship post with the compensatory features of Oriental exoticism and military adventure; and the Bukovina, at the eastern confines of the monarchy, was surprisingly popular because of its rich cultural life and the extraordinary ethnic harmony of its mixed Jewish, Ruthene, and Romanian population. Finally, Galicia, where a large part of the army was stationed beginning in the 1880s, was perceived as a place of exile and the ultimate hardship post.

Galicia, it was purported, contained the highest number of muddy and dusty roads, flies, and lice, as well as the greatest incidence of venereal disease, drunken peasants, and cunning Jews. The Polish landowners would have nothing to do with the Habsburg officers, nor would their daughters. Galicia was a place to get drunk and to stay drunk; to spend the night in shabby cafés, gambling and whoring; to long for civilization; and to make pilgrimages to the railroad station to watch the passing through of the Lemberg-Cracow-Vienna express.[28] Of course, not even Galicia was all horror: several memoirists mention exhilarating rides in open country, and at least one favorably recalls the officers' obligation to attend Jewish and Orthodox weddings as well as other festivities. The same officer, Lieutenant (and later general staff member) Franz Xaver Schubert, relates with delight his services in Galicia as a "Shabesgoy" (a Gentile helping out Orthodox Jews on the Sabbath) in the house of the lawyer from whom he rented a room.[29]

One amused oneself as one could. Those in Vienna and other big cities complained, or perhaps boasted, of having to attend too many balls, and of becoming veritable *Tanzmaschinen*. One young officer tallied up thirty-two balls in twenty-eight days, a remarkable achievement considering that most lasted until dawn, and that, come what might, one had to report to duty at 7:00 A.M. the next day. Another officer writes of nude balls, "veritable orgies," in the artillery riding school. Others recount more sedate amusements in the circle of bourgeois families, always with an eye to landing a fiancée with enough money for a marriage bond (of which more later). Theater and vaudeville were extraordinarily popular among the officers, but for the majority the main amusement was the café, where they sat, often all night, playing cards or listening dutifully to anecdotes told by the regimental commander (it would have been unforgivably impolite to leave the café before the "Old Man").[30] Gambling was a near-obligation and, for many, an addiction; its consequences will be discussed later.

Every regiment had a library, but, in the preliberal era, the list of forbidden books and newspapers was long, and the average troop officer did not read much in any case.[31] Reading was considered rather unmanly, and bookworms were encouraged to try for the general staff school. In fact, sending an officer to a higher training school was one way of getting rid of a man who did not fit into the community. In the liberal period, the Ministry of War fostered the creation of officers' clubs in the larger garrisons. The Vienna officers' club contained a fine library made up, in 1889, of 15,000 professional and 9,500 other books. By the end of the century, every regiment had an officers' association or club, which administered the officers' mess, maintained the library and the regimental music band, provided for loans at a low interest, and maintained savings accounts.[32]

Officers' everyday behavior was, of course, strictly regulated. In addition, there were scores of books on officer's etiquette, describing, for example, the proper day to pay a visit to a family, how to thank a family in advance for a dinner invitation and again eight days after a party (the so-called *Reconnaissance-Visite*), the correct procedure for depositing one's *Visite-Karte* in a household without setting an eye on anyone except the servants, where and how to place one's sword and shako while visiting, what and what not to say (avoid politics!), how to converse with the host and the hostess (as little as possible with the daughter), how to hold the silver, how long to stay after dinner, and so on and so forth.[33]

In the final analysis, whether life was bearable or unbearable was a question of money. Those who had the means rented luxurious apartments, consorted with expensive call girls, and, most important for men in faraway garrisons, traveled to big cities. The army was generous with furloughs, and those who could afford it, especially aristocrats, spent more time away from their unit than with it. Unfortunately for the officers, relatively few had private means and their pay allowed them scant luxuries.

Escape from the Regiment

In due time, every officer was temporarily detached from his unit to attend divisional riding, rifle, or gunnery courses, or to be taught to become a supply officer. For those, however, who could not take life in the garrison and for the ambitious, a long-term way out resided in the higher training courses which the army offered in increasing abundance as military science became more technical and complicated. There was the central rifle or gunnery school, the higher fencing and gymnastic courses, the riding instructor's school, the advanced engineering and construction courses, and, in the last decades before World War I, the automobile course, the telegraph and telephone course, the balloon-flying course and, finally, the aeroplane pilot's course.

It was unquestionably difficult to gain access to these courses and schools, some admitting no more than a dozen students annually, but each brought rewarding assignments and faster promotion. The most prestigious and rewarding of all higher training opportunities was the Kriegsschule, or general staff school. Because most military memoirists attended this school, and because it was the general staff that made military history, we have no want of information concerning its accomplishments and shortcomings.

The general staff itself was considerably older than the school. Known at first as the General-Quartiermeister-Stab, it had been active at least since Napoleonic times, but its main functions then had been topography and map-making. It was long overshadowed, particularly in the 1850s, by the corps of adjutants, and only after this group of amateurish aristocrats had completely disgraced itself in the wars of 1859 and 1866, did the general staff, now called Generalstab, become the supreme planning and operational office of the armed forces. By the 1880s, as we have seen, the chief of the general staff had become the unofficial head of the armed forces of the monarchy. Under Beck, the general staff made military policy, and under Conrad, it also began to make foreign and domestic policy. Its members wore a distinctive bottle-green uniform and, when in gala, a cocked hat with falling plumes of green vulture feathers that made them resemble generals. No wonder that they were the objects of much admiration, envy, suspicion, and contempt.

Inspired by the Prussian example, the general staff school was created in 1852, with an initial class of twenty-four students, or as they came to be called, *Frequentanten*. [34] Joining the school began with a written admission test, for which permission from one's colonel and long preparation were needed. Up to one thousand lieutenants and first lieutenants presented themselves for this anonymous examination at divisional or corps headquarters, and the approximately two hundred (later four hundred) who passed could then start preparing for the subsequent written and oral tests, held annually in Vienna. This round of examinations lasted many days and, our memoirists insist, was marked by perfect decorum and irreproachable objectivity. High aristocrats were turned down without much ado, even if recommended by an august personage. Around 1880, perhaps fifty candidates came to be accepted by the school annually; later, the number grew somewhat larger, but by 1907 had fallen to forty.

What particularly galled those who had been rejected was that, due to Hungarian pressure, eight honvéd officers were admitted to general staff school annually without an admission test. Upon graduation, these officers returned to the Hungarian National Guard to serve there as nominal members of the one and only Austro-Hungarian general staff.

School lasted two years, and under Conrad, three years, with a terrifying curriculum in which equal emphasis was placed on physical fitness (horseback-riding every morning), languages, and military science. There was, at least until Conrad's time, too much concentration on theory, and too little on naval power, political science, or the economy. Nor was there time, under the crush of the curriculum, for the kind of independent thinking which allegedly characterized the Prussian war college.

Graduates of the school were seconded to the general staff for two or three years, and if rated high enough, were made regular general staff officers, with a starting rank of captain. From there, the road led rapidly to field-grade officer and then to general. Service in the general staff was interrupted, however, more frequently than in Prussia, by assignment to the troops, in order to maintain an inevitably uneasy contact between field and general staff officers.

What made this process so harrowing was that in a given year, no more than thirty officers were admitted to the general staff, and those who had waited in vain for this sublime appointment, were obliged to return to their regiments. There they found themselves lower on the seniority list than those who had never left the unit. That this was an intolerable development for some is shown by what happened during the so-called Hofrichter affair.

The affair began in 1905 when an unusually large number of students graduated from the Kriegsschule, but of them only thirty finally made it into the general staff. The majority were forced to return to their units. One of the lucky ones was Captain Richard Mader who, on November 17, 1909, in Vienna, received a letter as well as a small package from a pharmacist with a French name. The contents consisted of two capsules, described by the letter writer as a sample from a new medicine designed to "fortify the male potential." The capsules were to be taken half an hour before an amorous encounter, and Mader, who was looking forward to precisely such an encounter, decided to make a try. Within a few minutes, he suffered an agonizing death, for—as it was later established—the capsules had been heavily laced with cyanide.

Military authorities were at a loss to unravel the mystery; it devolved on the Austrian police to determine that dozens of other young general staff officers had also been sent the capsules, but only Mader had fallen for the temptation. Suspicion centered on the waiting list for a general staff appointment, and the police soon decided that the crime must have been committed by a First Lieutenant Adolf Hofrichter of the 14th Infantry Regiment, at Linz. A fine officer, he had been with Mader at the general staff school and was very high on the waiting list. The lengthy investigation, which caused no end of jubilation to the left-wing press, resulted in the sentencing of Hofrichter on June 25, 1910, to twenty years of hard imprisonment. Because he had never admitted his guilt, despite rather convincing evidence against him, Hofrichter could not be sentenced to death. He was amnestied by the Austrian republic in 1927, joined the illegal Nazi movement and died in Vienna, a free man, in 1945. Hofrichter's act was understandable, in view of General Conrad's sudden decision, in 1907, to reduce admission to the general staff to only thirty, writes Otto Wiesinger, a former general staff officer, in his memoirs.[35]

The general staff was indeed a select body, with 276 regular members in 1880, and 434 in 1911.[36] There were, in addition, an artillery staff, an engineering staff (90 and 120 officers, respectively, in 1910), and a few other small, select institutions. When on a special assignment, a captain of the general staff could overrule even a general; when attached to a unit, as chief of staff of a brigade, a division, or an army corps, he could issue orders in the name of the commanding general. General staff officers were financially enabled to travel abroad; they consorted with members of the dynasty, and they often reported in person to the emperor.

In retrospect, there can be little doubt that these elite institutions, modeled after those of Prussia, may have been very efficient, but they also harmed the morale of the officer corps. The chasm between the elite and nonelite was simply too great in terms of responsibilities, career opportunities, and, above all, living standards.

5

From Payday to Payday

From Unpaid Service to Poorly Paid Service

The cost of living and officers' pay had only the vaguest relationship to one another in the old dynastic armies. Pay scales were arbitrarily determined, for eternity as it were, with no provision for price increases. The practice of paying an officer a salary worthy of his education, social standing, and needs originated with a few eighteenth-century enlightened monarchs, but it became customary only in nineteenth-century bourgeois-liberal societies. Characteristically, when the near-sovereign Hungarian liberal state was established in the spring of 1848, and a national army created, its officers and men were given considerably better pay than their comrades serving the same Habsburg prince in the Austrian army.

The old monarchies expected administrators and military commanders to cover their own expenses and even those of their underlings, in exchange for some past or future favor, for the opportunity to make money out of the office, or simply for power and glory. The medieval practice of unpaid military service had been partially undermined by the Renaissance custom of hiring mercenaries, but the mercenary captain or colonel was a businessman, not an official. His contract provided him with a lump sum from which he had to remunerate himself and his men. Only with the creation of the standing armies in the seventeenth and eighteenth centuries did the princes begin paying their soldiers a regular salary, but the pay was rarely adequate, in part because the military establishment was always grander than the financial means of the state, and in part because the military establishment was reluctant to see its ranks swamped by penniless commoners or even by impoverished noblemen.

The concept of military service as a noble obligation and privilege persisted long after the nobility had lost its fighting mettle or the means to finance its campaign expenses. The officer of the eighteenth-century dynastic army was a professional, yet, as a nobleman, he was loath to admit to being a salaried state servant. Hence, he accepted his salary as grudgingly as the state disbursed it.

In Austria, the first radical innovator was—as in so many other cases—Maria Theresa, who, having learned from her defeats by Frederick the Great, sought to reform the pay scale of the officer corps. Typically, she ruled in 1748 that a junior lieutenant or Fähnrich, appointed merely to "wave the flag vigorously and to beat the drum,"[1] was to be paid enough to "enable him to live at a level commensurate with his social standing (*standesmässig*) and to buy his own equipment (*Equipage*)."[2] This was calculated at sixteen gulden (or florins) per month, a sufficient amount then.

During the Napoleonic Wars, the Austrian officers were at the height of their patriotic enthusiasm and public prestige, yet this was not reflected in their pay, which reached its nadir in 1809, at the time of Archduke Charles's victory over Napoleon at Aspern, and again in 1813–1815, during the great wars of liberation against France. In 1809, a *Fähnrich*'s pay amounted to 19 gulden per month, and that of a colonel, 150 gulden, nearly the same as under Maria Theresa. Meanwhile, however, there had been a devastating inflation, which was only seldom compensated for by special subsidies. Worse still, the officers were not paid in bullion (except for those fighting abroad) but in depreciated paper currency. Only in 1815, during the Vienna Congress, were those officers stationed in the capital given double pay so as to assure their "worthy appearance" (*standesmässiges Auftreten*) in the presence of foreign rulers.[3]

The Metternichian state was not interested in the misery of its ten thousand-odd officers, nor would it have been able to help much, given its catastrophic finances following the Napoleonic Wars. Table 5.1 shows the average annual basic pay (monthly breakdown in parentheses) of the Austrian officers just before the salary reform of 1851.[4] Note that pay scales varied by province and by branch of service. Thus general staff and field artillery officers were paid more than infantry officers, and the latter more than those in the cavalry. The low pay of cavalry officers was, of course, a further guarantee of their exclusivity.*

By computing their annual income at between 450 and 600 gulden, the Austrian economic historian Roman Sandgruber equates the income of a lieutenant and a first lieutenant in 1850 with that of the lowest category of master artisans and the highest category of journeymen.[5] But Sandgruber seems too optimistic regarding the income of subalterns, for—as shown in table 5.1—not even a first lieutenant earned 450 gulden, unless the housing allowance (96 gulden) and other minor special emoluments are added to his basic pay. On the other hand, Sandgruber is correct in estimating the annual income of a captain at between 600 and 900 gulden, and in equating this with the income of the second-lowest category of master artisans.[6] Incidentally, the income of a district judge in Lower Austria more or less equaled that of a captain II. class in that period.[7]

---

*The currency was the gulden, written as "fl." for florins, and it was worth about 40 U.S. cents of the same period. Each gulden contained 60 kreuzer, written as "kr." The gulden that is meant here was the fl. CM (or KM), for "*Conventions-Münze*," which was worth 2 fl. 50 kr. WW ("*Wiener-Währung*"), a much depreciated form of paper currency. In 1858, the two currencies were replaced by the fl. Ö.W., for *Österreichische Währung*. The new gulden related to the old as 100 fl. C.M. = 105 fl. Ö.W., and it was divided into 100 kr., rather than into 60 kr. as thitherto. (Monika Schmidl, "Überblick über die österreichische Münz- und Währungsgeschichte." Unpublished manuscript [Vienna, 1985].)

Table 5.1. Officers' Pay before 1851

	Rank category (*Rangklasse*)	Rank	Basic Pay, Gulden Per year (Per month)	Index
Subalterns	XI	Lieutenant II. class	300 (25)	1.0
	XI	Lieutenant I. class	360 (30)	1.2
	X	First lieutenant	408 (34)	1.4
	IX	Captain II. class	600 (50)	2.0
	IX	Captain I. class	900 (75)	3.0
Field-grade officers	VIII	Major	1,116 (93)	3.7
	VII	Lieutenant colonel	1,329 (110 fl.45 kr.)	4.4
	VI	Colonel	1,790 (149 fl.10 kr.)	6.0
Generals	V	Generalmajor	4,000 (333 fl.20 kr.)	13.3
	IV	Feldmarschalleutnant	6,000 (500)	20
	III	Feldzeugmeister or General der Kavallerie	7,992 (666)	26.6
	I	Field marshal	10,000 (833 fl.20 kr.)	33.3

What were such salaries worth in mid-nineteenth-century Austria? Again according to Sandgruber, one pound (500 grams) of coarse bread cost 5 kr. in Vienna between 1851 and 1860, and one pound of beef 13.8 kr. This means that a lieutenant II. class was able to convert his basic pay (36 gulden monthly or 1 gulden 12 kr. daily in 1855) into 24 pounds of bread or into 8.6 pounds of beef per day. Undoubtedly, this was much more than the pay of a day laborer in Vienna, whose daily average wage of 34.9 kreuzer was worth only 7 pounds of bread or 2.5 pounds of beef per day.[8] Nor did a lieutenant usually have a family to worry about, or, if he did, then his income was more or less doubled from the interest on his marriage bond. Finally, a lieutenant enjoyed a steady income whereas a worker had to worry about unemployment.

Leaving aside the generals, the pay differential between the lowest subaltern, the lieutenant II. class, and the highest-ranking field-grade officer, the colonel, yielded a ratio of 1 : 6 before 1851, a ratio that would undergo some interesting variations later on. Most remarkable is the big jump in salary between captain II. class and captain I. class: it was held, not without reason, that a captain of the higher category could live quite comfortably, whereas the other subalterns could not. Note, however, that the average waiting period for each promotion in the Metternichian period was six to eight years; thus, a newly promoted captain I. class was likely to be close to fifty years old, and the majority of officers never reached that rank.

In addition to his basic pay, the Habsburg officer received a number of special emoluments in cash and kind, most importantly a housing allowance (*Quartiergeld*) averaging eight gulden monthly, but this was paid only if the officer was unable or unwilling to find accommodation in the barracks (*Naturalquartier*). A small sum was deducted from the pay of officers who did live in the barracks. The housing allowance varied according to garrison and rank, but it was never enough to cover the real cost of living "on the economy," to use the modern U.S. Army term. The officer was also provided with wood for fuel (one cord of softwood, or three-fourths of hardwood per month), but only in the cold season. In addition, he could avail himself of the services of a batman, selected from among the semi-invalids (or alleged semi-invalids, since the regimental doctors were invariably cooperative) in the regiment. Finally, generals and regimental commanders received a substantial *Tafelgeld,* literally table-money, for entertainment, and all officers entitled to keep a horse were given a special allotment of fodder—again insufficient in quantity.

All this was very little when compared even with the miserly pay of officers in other German states. In 1840, for instance, officers in the armies of Baden and Württemberg earned about 50 percent more than those in the Austrian army.[9]

It might have been bearable, presuming that the officer at least received his full salary on payday at the end of the month, but this was never the case. The army provided him with his basic uniform and sword, but withheld one-fourth of his pay until the full cost had been repaid. Another three gulden were deducted monthly for the regimental library and the regimental band, indispensable luxuries demanded by regimental pride and financed entirely by the officers until the last decades of the nineteenth century. The unpaid debts of fellow officers were occasionally shouldered by the regimental officer corps, and there were other deductions as well. All of this meant that, in Metternich's time, an Austrian lieutenant II. class did not take home much more than ten gulden ($4) per month, and a first lieutenant perhaps twenty gulden. This had to suffice for food and all other expenditures. Because there were as yet no mess halls, the officer had to eat in restaurants, where a dinner cost about one gulden, unless he set up his batman as a cook. Such clothing "extras" as caps, shoes, underwear, gloves, and parade uniforms were his responsibility, as were tobacco, private travel, entertainment, drinks, gambling losses, and visits to the theater or to a prostitute. Even travel to and from maneuvers or on official missions—and the number of the latter was legion—was either reimbursed inadequately or not at all. Officers regularly complained about bureaucratic haggling over "excess" food or fodder consumed on an official mission. The military bureaucracy was relentless: it demanded accounting down to a fraction of a kreuzer, and failure to return a few overspent pennies led to endless correspondence and dire official warnings.

The white uniform of the Austrian soldier was quite beautiful, but its upkeep presented horrendous difficulties. The uniform had to be spotless, of course, and it was to emanate a light-blue shimmer which could be achieved only through assiduous brushing. The slightest wear or tear led to a reprimand and the order to purchase a new uniform immediately, a devastating expense.[10] In the late 1850s, General Count Franz Gyulai ordered every officer and man in his Army of Italy to sport a black moustache. This miraculous transformation could be achieved only with the help of generous doses of black shoe-polish, but when it rained, the shoe polish ran, the white uniform was ruined, and with it, the officer's financial stability.[11]

Another source of worry was the enormously heavy and ornate officer's shako. We know from the correspondence of Arthur Görgey, a young cavalry officer in the early 1840s, what it meant to carry a parade shako, in a huge hatbox, from one faraway army post to another.[12] A first lieutenant in 1841, Görgey was admitted to the 12th Hussar Regiment, but had to beg a loan of 2,000 gulden from his family to buy the ornamental uniforms and fine horses indispensable in the cavalry.[13] For that matter, he had applied to the 12th in the first place because its uniform, unlike those of the other eleven hussar regiments, was decorated in silver, not in the more expensive gold. To pay back the debt he owed to his family, Görgey "ate as a first course, army-issue bread; as a second and third course, the same, and for dessert, a little piece of the same bread."[14] In 1845, he was made a regimental adjutant, which meant free meals at the colonel's table but involved extra expenses which he was unable to bear. Görgey soon resigned his commission and, in the spring of 1848, joined the newly created Hungarian national army, where he was immediately made a captain, with a higher salary than that of a captain in the old army. Within the same year, at the age of thirty, Görgey became the commanding general of the largest Hungarian army.

Young Görgey's case of near-starvation was not unique. Reminiscing about his days as a lieutenant in Budapest in 1855, Baron Potier des Échelles wrote in his memoirs: "By then, I had eaten nothing for three days but snacks consisting of a glass of beer, two salted rolls, and a small piece of cheese. Instead of lunch and dinner, I went for walks on the Danube shore."[15] Small wonder that some officers resorted to selling their allotment of wood. This meant freezing in the winter, but at least there was food. In the warmer months, there was no allotment of wood and hence no food either.[16]

Compared to all this, the common soldier's lot seemed almost enviable: he was given free lodgings and clothes and received two pounds of bread, some meat, and five kreuzer daily. True, three kreuzer were deducted from his pay for food, which left him with no spending money. But he ate heartily and well.[17]

Because the officer corps had saved the dynasty in 1848–1849, the emperor tried to be grateful: in 1851, and again in 1855, pay scales were revised upward. No definite pattern emerges from the changes introduced in this so-called absolutist period; very important, however, is that the new pay scales were now uniformly established, without regard to garrison or the arm of service.

Bourgeois Comforts in the Bourgeois Age

A clear pattern of change in the living standards of officers would emerge only following the Compromise of 1867. Thereafter, the monarchy took measures to bring the officers' pay abreast of rising prices and to improve the relative position of the subalterns. This resolve was once again weakened, however, no longer by the poverty of the state but by the intermittently hostile attitude of the two parliaments toward the military establishment. Table 5.2 outlines the pay scales for the period between the introduction of universal military service in 1868 and the outbreak of the First World War.[18]*

*Note that the distinction between lieutenant I. class and II. class had disappeared after 1867, and that the distinction between captain I. class and II. class was abolished in 1907. By the latter year, the unit of currency was no longer the gulden but, beginning in 1892, the krone. Because two kronen equaled precisely one gulden, even the 1907 figures are computed here in gulden. (Incidentally, 1 krone consisted of 100 Heller.)

Table 5.2. Officers' Pay in 1868 and in 1907

Rank Category	Rank	1868 Basic Pay, Gulden Per Year (Per month)	Index for 1868*	1907 Basic Pay, Gulden Per Year (Per month)	Index for 1907 (minimum–maximum)
XI	Lieutenant	600 (50)	1	840–1,000 (70–83.33)	1
X	First lieutenant	720 (60)	1.2	1,100–1,400 (91.66–116.66)	1.3–1.4
X	Captain II. class	900 (75)	1.5		
X	Captain I. class	1,200 (100)	2.0	1,500–1,800 (125–150)	1.8–1.8
VIII	Major	1,680 (140)	2.6	2,200–2,400 (183.33–200)	2.6–2.4
VII	Lieutenant colonel	2,100 (175)	3.5	2,700–3,100 (225–258.33)	3.2–3.1
VI	Colonel	3,000 (250)	5.0	3,600–4,400 (300–366.66)	4.3–4.4
V	Generalmajor	4,200 (350)	7.0	5,700–6,500 (475–541.66)	6.8–6.5
IV	Feldmarschalleutnant	6,300 (525)	10.5	7,008–8,000 (584–666.66)	8.3–8.0
III	Feldzeugmeister or General der Kavallerie	8,400 (700)	14.0	8,400–9,000 (700–750)	10.0–9.0
II	Minister of war	—		10,000 (833.30)	11.9–10.0
	Field marshal	10,000 (875)	17.5	12,000 (1,000)	14.3–12.0

Sources: Ulf Sereinigg, "Das altösterreichische Offizierskorps 1869–1914. Bildung, Advancement, Sozialstruktur, wirtschaftliche Verhältnisse," unpublished doctoral dissertation, University of Vienna, 1983, p. 110; and Karl F. Kurz, ed., *Militär-Taschenlexikon*, 10th ed., Part I (Vienna, 1911), pp. 100–101.
Note that the pay scales established in 1868 remained in effect until 1900.

As shown by the statistics in Table 5.2, the difference between the pay of a lieutenant and a colonel had diminished from 1 : 6 in Metternich's time to 1 : 4.4 in the twentieth century, and the difference between the pay of a lieutenant and of a field marshal from 1 : 33.3 in Metternich's time to 1 : 12. During these sixty-odd years, the wages of a freshly commissioned lieutenant had almost tripled, whereas the wages of a colonel had merely doubled. The pay of a three-star general barely grew at all.

Because price increases in the long period between 1851 and 1907 amounted to a modest 30 percent, we are talking about an increase in real wages. By 1907 a lieutenant earned considerably more than an industrial worker. His minimum annual basic pay of 840 gulden compared favorably with that of a worker in the Vienna food industry, who earned an average of 550 gulden, or a worker in the Vienna machine industry, who made 687 gulden. The 1907 pay of a lieutenant looked even better when compared with the salary of a worker in the food industry in Galicia (the poorest part of the monarchy), who earned a mere 275 gulden, or a worker in the machine industry in Galicia, whose annual income amounted to 412 gulden.[19]

It is curious how strongly historians and contemporary observers disagree on the question of the living standard of the officers. The Austrian historian Ulf Sereinigg argues in his recent doctoral dissertation that after 1868 the officer had little to complain about, partly because of his increased pay and partly because his lunch or dinner at the new officers' mess (*Offiziersmenage*) cost only ⅓ gulden, making his monthly food expenditure no more than 10–15 gulden. According to Sereinigg, after 1868 the total monthly income of a lieutenant amounted to about 72 gulden (salary, plus housing allowance, and 2 gulden for furniture rental), while his basic expenses totaled only 55 gulden. He was left with enough money for modest entertainment and other amenities. The pay of a lieutenant, writes Sereinigg, matched that of a teacher (60–70 gulden) or a commercial employee (70–80 gulden) of the same age group, but the lieutenant was better off because of such fringe benefits as inexpensive meals in the officers' mess. Sereinigg calculates that an officer earned about 14 percent more than a civil servant (Beamter), even though the latter was better educated.[20] A somewhat propagandistic military publication issued in 1889 argues in the same vein, stating that a lieutenant stationed in Vienna or Budapest—the monarchy's most expensive cities—enjoyed a total monthly income of 104 gulden (basic pay, 50 gulden; special supplement for living in the capital, 10 gulden; housing and furniture allowance, 36⅔ gulden; and 8 gulden for hiring a private servant), more than enough for a lifestyle commensurate with an officer's social standing, to say nothing of such extra benefits as job security and life in the "bright and hospitable barracks."[21]

A semiofficial handbook for "freshly commissioned infantry officers," pub- lished in 1899, was even more specific in its discussion of the income and expendi- tures of a young lieutenant. According to its author, an unmarried lieutenant earned a total of 66 gulden monthly (it is hard to tell how this accords with the 104 gulden mentioned in the other army publication), while required to spend no more than 53 gulden (see table 5.3).

Contemporary military critics of the officers' financial lot would have objected violently to such optimistic conclusions. In fact, as the monarchy's economy ex- panded in the second half of the nineteenth century (despite a long period of depression following the stock market crash of 1873), military commentators be- came more and more exasperated. Writing under an assumed name in 1910, a general staff officer calculated the officer's monthly existential minimum at 67 gulden in the Austrian part of the monarchy and, surprisingly, at a much higher 83 gulden in Hungary. In theory, his pay should have enabled the lieutenant to make ends meet but, the writer argued, the young officer was under psychological pres-

Table 5.3. Lieutenants' Required Monthly Expenditures, 1899

Expenditure Category	Gulden
Uniform	10.0
Music band	1.05
Regimental library	0.35
Officers' casino	1.05
Lunch	15.0
Dinner	10.0
Breakfast	4.5
Utilities	3.0
Heating	3.0
Laundry	3.0
Batman's pay	2.0

Source: [Captain] Arthur Iwanski von Iwanina, *Az újonnan kinevezett gyalogsági tiszt (hadapród) szolgálata és magánélete fölötti alkalmazó megbeszélések* (Practical considerations about the service and private life of the freshly appointed infantry officer [cadet]); translated from the German by Captain István László (Budapest, 1901), pp. 59–60.

Table 5.4. Annual Pay of Officers and of Civil Servants in 1899 (Gulden)

Rank Category	Officers (in Austria–Hungary)		Civil servants (in Austria only)		
XI		600	800	900	1,000
X		720	1,100	1,200	1,300
IX	900	1,200	1,400	1,500	1,600
VIII		1,680	1,800	2,000	2,200
VII		2,100	2,400	2,700	3,000
VI		3,000	3,200	3,600	4,000
V		4,200	5,000	6,000	
IV		6,300	7,000	8,000	

Source: *Armeeblatt*, October 25, 1899:2.

Note: Remember that, beginning in 1892, the unit of currency was the krone, not the gulden. However, for the sake of uniformity and because two kronen equaled one gulden, post-1892 salaries and pensions are computed here in gulden.

sure to "enjoy life," in other words to overspend. The result was a devastating burden of debt.[22] The writer complained about the many obligatory deductions from the officer's pay, a situation confirmed by the individual payrolls (*Gagezettel*) available in the Vienna War Archive. For instance, the *Gagezettel* of a first lieutenant in the cavalry shows, for January 1907, a gross income of 125 gulden but a net payment of only 28 gulden. The rest had been withheld for such things as the upkeep of his horse, payments on the horse as well as on his riding equipment and his uniform, meals at the officers' mess (21½ gulden), drinks at the mess (a modest 8 gulden), tobacco from the commissary, membership in the officers' casino, and debt payments (25 gulden).[23]

The Fatherland has ample money for its civil servants, wrote an anonymous military commentator in 1899, but not for its officers. Where was a captain II. class to find the money to keep a horse, as required by his rank? And what can one say about the per diem of ½ gulden paid a captain I. class for marching at maneuvers "in dust and mud," six to eight hours daily (the so-called *Marschzulage*)? And as for the officers' pension plan, it is a "national scandal."[24] "The professional officer corps, recruited from among the best elements in the people, is the flesh of the people's flesh, and the blood of its blood. In a sense, it represents the flowering of the nation: it is the pride of the people," exclaimed the *Armeeblatt*, a military journal, in 1899.[25] And yet, the number of officer's candidates was declining steadily as the middle classes found better outlets for their energies than the poverty-stricken existence of the officer. As if contradicting the modern historian Sereinigg, the 1899 edition of the *Armeeblatt* demonstrated, through detailed statistics, that a civil servant in Austria enjoyed a much higher income than an officer. The journal did not mention Hungary but, in fact, civil servants were even better paid there. A few excerpts from the data listed in the *Armeeblatt* appear in table 5.4.

It seems clear that, whereas in 1868 the officer's pay more or less equaled that of a civil servant, it had fallen behind by the end of the century. The *Armeeblatt* also demonstrated that by 1899 the bureaucrats enjoyed higher pensions, higher per diems, higher subsidies for moving expenses, and higher tuition subsidies for their children than the officers. The *Armeeblatt* neglected to mention, however, that high-

ranking Beamten were university graduates, which most officers were not, and that
the officers' sons had absolute priority for tuition-free admission to military schools,
whereas the sons of civil servants had fewer schools and fewer free places available
to them. Nonetheless, it is still true that the liberal state was more favorably
disposed toward its civil servants than toward its officers.

The officers enjoyed no public support for improvement of their condition, and
it did not occur to them to make their voice heard collectively. Much of the educated
public, particularly the left-wing politicians and the Hungarian and Slavic national
leadership, viewed the officers of the Joint Army with extreme suspicion. Turning on
the army's tormentor in the left-wing press, the *Armeeblatt* wrote in 1899:

> We . . . reject with indignation the exceedingly brutal utterances of the Vienna
> *Arbeiter-Zeitung* [the chief socialist newspaper], which has waxed ironical on the
> question of [the officers'] pay, calling it the most useless thing in the world. . . . In
> an article dripping with venom, the paper writes, among other things, that the
> taxpayers (to whom the officers have the honor of belonging, just like any other
> citizen) have no obligation to waste money on the decorum and private pleasures of
> the officers. This is just what we need, to have the guardians of "the people's
> interest" begin supervising the lifestyle of the officers![26]

Needless to say, not all officers were impecunious, but it is extremely difficult to
determine the proportion of well-to-do individuals within the corps. The officer's
Qualifikations-Liste included a rubric on his financial situation, but this listed
mainly his debts and the monthly subsidy he received from his parents during his
years as a very junior subaltern. Only seldom do we find such entries as "independently wealthy," or "came into a substantial [or modest] inheritance," or "fairly
well-to-do." Even less frequent are precise data on the extent of wealth or private
income. Most officers undoubtedly preferred to declare themselves as "without a
private income." Our random sample of two generations of lieutenants shows that
those with a declared private income were but a small minority.

The distinction between those who were independently wealthy and those of a
modest private income has been determined, perforce arbitrarily, by the nature of
the relevant entry in their *Qualifikations-Liste* (see table 5.5). Surely, the proportion
of wealthy and fairly-well-to-do career lieutenants had not increased from a total of
16 percent to 36.2 percent between 1870 and 1900. Rather, the reason for the

Table 5.5. Private Income of Lieutenants in the Joint Army, Based on a Random Sampling
of 1,000-Odd Career Lieutenants

	1870 Cohort		1900 Cohort	
	Absolute Number	Percentage	Absolute Number	Percentage
No private income	406	83.5	329	63.8
Modest income	56	11.5 } 16.0	111	21.5 } 36.2
Wealthy	22	4.5	76	14.7
No information	2	0.5	—	—
Total	486	100.0	516	100.0

discrepancy between the two sets of figures must be sought either in more honest reporting on the part of the officers or in improved methods of inquiry. Certain it is that the majority of officers were not independently wealthy.

Finally, let me attempt a comparison of the Habsburg officers' income with those of French and German officers. According to Douglas Porch, a French lieutenant's annual pay in 1908 amounted to 2,340 francs; that of a captain between 3,942 and 5,004 francs; and that of a colonel, 8,136 francs. In the German army, the respective figures were 2,813 francs for a lieutenant; 5,333–7,003 for a captain; and 12,767 for a colonel. One Austro-Hungarian krone being more or less equal to one pre-World War I French franc, we arrive at the following figures for the Habsburg officer's pay, according to the pay scales of 1907: lieutenant, 1,680–2,000 francs; captain, 3,000–3,600 francs; and colonel, 7,200–8,800 francs.[27]

Even by conceding that prices were lower in the Dual Monarchy than in economically more advanced Germany and France, there can be no doubt that the Habsburg officer was paid much less than his French or German counterpart. For instance, the pay of an Austro-Hungarian captain was just over half that of a captain in the German army. Incidentally, French officers complained of the same kinds of deductions from their pay—for mess dues, receptions, military charities, inadequately reimbursed garrison changes, costly maneuvers, and equally costly strike duty (!)—as did their Habsburg colleagues.[28]

On Debtors and Usurers

Few things troubled the military writers more than the enormous debts shouldered by many officers. Such complaints were endemic, although the situation did improve toward the end of the century, after the two governments, the emperor, and the officers themselves had taken matters in hand.

Officers contracted debts to pay for their horse and uniform, to set up a household, to educate their daughters, to entertain in style, to settle their gambling losses, and, last but not least, to bail out a comrade. There were many types of debts, the worst being those of the "dirty" variety (*schmutzige Schulden*), contracted from such unworthy types as innkeepers, landlords, sergeants, and ordinary soldiers. Dirty debts, if disclosed, almost inevitably led to an officer's expulsion from the corps by the regimental officers' assembly. And small wonder, since these debts had to be shouldered by the comrades of the offender.[29] Ordinary debts were treated with more indulgence, although an officer's personal record made a careful distinction between "carelessly" accumulated debts (*leichtsinnige Schulden*) and the more acceptable variety. The most respectable debts were when the officer signed as a guarantor for his comrade (called *kavieren*).

Debts varied, of course, from a few gulden to astronomical sums, all carefully recorded (when known) in the personal records. One memoirist's father, a colonel, had accumulated a debt of 52,000 gulden by 1883, in part to fulfill his societal obligations as a regimental commander, and in part to support his drinking habit. Meanwhile, his extra income amounted to 180 gulden monthly, from the interest on his marriage bond.[30] Another officer, a captain, took out a loan of 1,200 kronen from a military fund, more than one-third of his annual pay, to pay for his daughter's education at the fashionable Sacre Coeur School.[31]

As a rule, officers borrowed at usurious rates. True, by the end of the nineteenth century, scores of organizations existed, from regimental savings associations to semiprivate and private foundations, to provide low-interest loans. The emperor himself often bailed out deserving officers from his private funds. Yet, if one is to believe the military critics, all this did not help the majority of officers. A former general staff officer, writing under an assumed name in 1910, held that his comrades had been spoiled in the military schools, that no one had prepared them for the real world, and that, as members of an elevated caste, they were obliged to overspend. Yet their chances of marrying into a well-to-do family were close to nil. Usurers were causing the officers more harm, he wrote, than the enemy could. Instead of helping their underlings, regimental commanders played the role of enforcers on behalf of the moneylenders. They did not care where the money came from, as long as the debt was paid, and the regiment's honor saved. And where else could the money come from, the writer queried, if not from other usurers? Enforcement usually began with an open postcard to the officer;* it continued with a direct letter to the colonel, threatening with denunciation to the minister of war. To avoid such embarrassment, the author explains, regimental commanders often imposed thirty days' garrison arrest on the officer, thereby resurrecting the long-lost practice of debtors' jails. The victim had no choice but to sign another series of promissory notes, from which 10 percent was deducted at the outset. A debt of 500 kronen could easily grow in this way to 1,500 in a year, and then to 2,000. By then, a large part of his pay was being withheld to cover at least the interest on the debt. In theory, such a predicament should not have affected his promotion; in reality it did. And the final outcome of it all? Dishonor, resignation from the corps, and often suicide.[32] Yet death itself did not help, for if the officer died leaving behind an unpaid debt, then even his sword and portepée would be auctioned off, an anonymous pamphlet complained, wondering aloud why a life insurance policy could not be created for the officers. Surely, the 6-gulden annual expense would be more manageable than the 120 gulden he had to contribute to the upkeep of the regimental music band![33]

My random sample of 487 lieutenants in the 1870 generation shows that 341 (70 percent) owed no money; 83 (17 percent) owed relatively modest sums when compared to their pay; 26 (5.3 percent) were heavily in debt but were paying it back step by step; and 34 (7 percent) were foundering. (There was no information on three officers.) These statistics, although far from comforting, seem nevertheless to contradict the apocalyptic picture drawn by the military writers. But, of course, the

---

*On July 18, 1898, Lieutenant Gustav Stumpf (born in Bohemia, former cadet school student, age twenty-five) of the 40th k.u.k. Infantry Regiment received such a postcard from his moneylender, one Josef Hopfinger. The lieutenant subsequently went to Hopfinger and shot him dead. The k.u.k. Festungskommando (fortress command) at Przemyśl cashiered Stumpf and sentenced him to two years in prison, aggravated by solitary confinement in the second and eighth month of his imprisonment. (Kriegsarchiv, Vienna, Kriegsministerium 1 A 67-72.)

Qualifikations-Listen knew nothing of debts kept in secret, a predicament possibly shared by a sizeable number.

While the pay of the officers may well have been in accordance with their relatively modest social origin and education, it contradicted their high social standing and the requirements of their lifestyle. To a certain extent, the officers were the victims of their own pretensions: the hostile picture painted by the liberal and socialist press of the officers as womanizers, gamblers, and drinkers was, to a large degree, the officers' own creation. It mattered little that those who smashed the mirror in the town's best hotel during a night of drinking, beat up the night watchman, shot out the gaslights in the street, took a nude bath in the public fountain with squealing dance-hall girls, lifted the figure of the Christ-child from the Christmas manger on the town square and lay down in it instead (all actual case histories) were either wealthy cavalry officers or individual rowdies bored to tears with garrison life. The public did not differentiate among officers, nor were officers willing to tolerate such a differentiation. Even the poorest of them tried to appear elegant and carefree, and each stood ready to draw his sword to defend the honor of a comrade. Officers were forbidden to eat in a low-class restaurant, to ride an omnibus (at least until the twentieth century), to travel third-class, or to carry the smallest of packages (unless it appeared to contain chocolate or candies): this is what the public saw, not the simple, modest, withdrawn life of the vast majority of the corps.

Curiously, the officers were their own worst enemies, at least financially, when they asserted that they were volunteers freely attaching themselves to the person of a prince. Their insistence on the fiction of membership in a special noble estate militated directly against their economic interest as paid servants of the state. The state, too, was ambivalent about the place of the officer in state and society, and thus, too, about its financial obligation to him. The emperor wanted to see a contented officer corps but, at least after 1867, he had no constitutional means to increase their pay; nor was he willing to part with the fiction of the officers' being his liege vassals. Both the Austrian and Hungarian governments, and the two parliaments, required a competent army for the realization of their domestic and foreign policy goals, but they also held the officers in suspicion. Hungarian politicians accused them of being pro-German; the Austro-Germans of not being pro-German enough; and the Slavic politicians of being pro-German, pro-Hungarian, and anti-Slav. In the long run, neither the two governments nor the two parliaments could avoid raising the officers' pay to a level at least approximating that of the two well-paid civil services. Thus, the officers ultimately benefited from the respected social position of the bureaucracy, a caste they held in disdain.

6

Latter-Day Knights

On July 1, 1900, lieutenants Augustin Weigel and Anton Bonkowski of the 22nd Dalmatian Franz Moritz Graf von Lacy k.u.k. Infantry Regiment entered a house of pleasure in the Dalmatian city of Zara to cap an evening of drinking. There, as the Zara military command later reported to the minister of war in Vienna,[1] Weigel got into an argument, at pleasure's end, with an equally drunk local civilian of Italian nationality, Cirillo Cristo, who heaped abuse on him. In accordance with army regulations concerning the defense of honor, Weigel attempted to draw his sword to put a violent end to the insults, but his arm was pinned down by a number of prostitutes and patrons. Nor was Lieutenant Bonkowski any more successful in rescuing the honor of the corps when he subsequently appeared on the scene. Ejected from the brothel, the two lieutenants, rather surprisingly, reported the incident to the local military command, but a quickly dispatched patrol found no trace of either Cristo or the other culprits.

Lieutenant Weigel now attempted to redeem himself. Since neither the lower-class Cristo nor the other guests were worthy of offering satisfaction in honorable combat, except for one, who refused to fight, Weigel waited for Cristo on the street several months later, and hit him in the face with a dog whip. But this was of no help to the two lieutenants: in the meantime, their colonel had ordered the regimental honor commission (*Ehrenausschuss*) to look into the matter, and the latter voted three to one to convoke the regimental officers' assembly (*Offiziersversammlung*). Meeting on September 21, the assembly voted fourteen to eleven in favor of instituting honors proceedings against the lieutenants, which culminated in the unanimous decision of the divisional court of honor (*Ehrenrat*) of the Zara military command on January 17, 1901, that, having violated his honor (*Verletzung der Standesehre*), Weigel should be deprived of his rank. The minister of war subsequently reduced him to private in the reserve and transferred him to another regiment. Lieutenant Bonkowski was given a warning.*

*Anton Bonkowski, a member of my 1900 sample cohort, was born in the Bukovina in 1880; his

126

The argumentation of the court of honor well reflected the philosophy of the army: Weigel was not castigated for having been inebriated, for having been in a brothel, or, finally, for having done battle with a dog whip, but solely and most decidedly, for not having used his sword to put an end to Cristo's vile invectives. From the point of view of the army, Weigel's honor had been put in extreme danger in the brothel encounter, and this had entitled, nay obliged, him to take far-reaching measures. His case clearly involved the principle of *Ehrennotwehr*, or "urgent defense of honor," yet Weigel had done nothing, resulting in the loss of his caste honor (*Verlust der Standesehre*); it made him unworthy to remain an officer. His comrade-in-arms had endangered his caste honor (*Gefährdung der Standesehre*) when he failed to rush to Weigel's rescue.

A question of honor was also involved in the case of First Lieutenant Anton Schmidt of the 14th Field Artillery Regiment at Pressburg in Hungary, who, sometime around 1910, gambled away the *Batteriegeld*, a small money reserve customarily set aside in each artillery unit for such special occasions as a birthday or an emergency. The *Batteriegeld* in Schmidt's unit amounted to some thirty kronen ($6), and he had been made its custodian by his battery commander, who had gone on a short leave. Having lost his own cash at a card game, the first lieutenant was persuaded by his comrades to gamble the battery money: this seemed innocent enough, for Schmidt was quite wealthy. He lost again and, on the following morning, while on his way to withdraw thirty kronen from his bank account, he encountered the battery commander. The loss of the money was duly acknowledged but his attempt to make amends was promptly rejected with the words: "You have appropriated the battery's money; it makes no difference whether provisionally or lastingly. . . . You must therefore know your duty." First Lieutenant Schmidt subsequently restored the missing funds, wrote a letter of apology to his comrades, and shot himself dead on the same day. The ensuing official inquiry fully vindicated the battery commander's action.[2]

Behavior of Habsburg army officers, like that of officers of other dynastic armies, was regulated by a code of honor and by service rules. Reiterated interminably in official handbooks and professional commentaries, the code and service rules merely provided an outline of what the officer owed himself, his unit, the army, and the ruler. "The basic principle remains the same in all conditions," a popular Austrian military commentary stated in its conclusion, "the officer's honor must be protected at all costs."[3] The manuals were, however, less clear with regard to implementation; at best they presented illustrative examples. When, for instance, was a commander entitled to recommend suicide to an underling? This inevitable lack of clarity was a source of great anxiety and concern; after all, it was not the individual but the court of honor which decided whether or not his behavior had been proper. Nonetheless, these often revised and never truly final regulations had a

---

father was a servant in the employ of the army (*Armeediener*), and he himself completed the cadet school at Łobzów in Galicia. According to his *Qualifikations-Liste*, Bonkowski was a mediocre soldier, frequently set back on the promotion list ("*zur Zeit nicht geeignet*"). He spoke German, Polish, Ruthene, Serbo-Croatian, and Romanian, none of them fluently. He was unmarried. By 1908, he had accumulated a debt burden of 4,335 kronen and, in that year, he transferred to the army construction office as an accountant (*Militär Baurechnungsoffizial 3. Klasse*).

more profound influence on the life of an officer than the laws of his state, the precepts of his religion, or the traditions of his family and nation. The code of honor greatly restricted the officer's freedom of action; at the same time, it raised him above ordinary mortals. The officer's honor was said to transcend individual happiness, career, or even life; it made him a special person who, like his supreme commander, the emperor, was above the law in many respects. In the words of a contemporary handbook: "The strict interpretation of military honor ennobles the officer corps in its entirety and endows it with the character of knighthood."[4]

Military writers customarily described the life of an officer as a near-Calvary: poor pay and an even poorer pension, onerous and dull service, exile from home, involuntary celibacy and loneliness, a wandering, restless existence, social isolation, public hostility, and, last but not least, the prospect of a violent death. For all these sacrifices there was but a single compensation: the officer's privileged status. Yet this was not a privilege of luxury, pleasure, or power, but one of noble obligation. Referring to a German Reichstag debate, on November 19, 1896, when one of the main speakers argued that "there could be only one type of honor for all human beings, the honor of the worker and of the merchant having the same value as that of an officer," an Austrian military writer protested that the extraordinary sacrifices demanded of an officer clearly entitled him to a special status. The writer contrasted the civilian's *jus communale* (common right) with the officer's *jus singulare* (*Sonderrecht,* or special right), and claimed privileges for the officer as "the bearer and the leader of all the spiritual and moral forces in the military estate."[5]

Ehrennotwehr

Of all the officer's privileges, the most onerous and most dangerous was the *Ehrennotwehr,* most accurately rendered as the urgent necessity to defend one's honor. It was endorsed categorically by all military writers with the argument that whereas the state law gave every citizen the right to defend his life, the lives of his family, his freedom, and his private property, military law gave the officer the additional right and duty to defend his honor. Paragraph 114 of the army's criminal code, drawn up in 1855, stated: "The *Ehrennotwehr* with the aid of a weapon is legal when the honor of the officer . . . is under attack, without provocation and in the presence of one or more persons."[6] This urgent or emergency right was limited to "genuine" officers, that is, to those of the combat forces, as well as to judge advocates, medical officers, and troop accountants. Other military administrative officials and all military students were excluded. However, the handbooks warned, the civilian or general criminal code knew nothing of an *Ehrennotwehr* and, by exercising his right and duty, the officer would inevitably come into conflict with the law of the very state he had sworn to defend.

The question of *Ehrennotwehr* arose whenever someone insulted an officer, the officer corps as a whole, the armed forces, or the emperor, in the presence of one or more persons (insults launched in a tête-à-tête counted for nothing), and when the application of force seemed to be the only way to put an end to the insults. Thus, if the insulting person were a gentleman, and he promptly and quietly accepted a challenge to a duel, there was no need for *Ehrennotwehr*.* Nor would such a need arise if there were a policeman present who could be called upon to arrest the culprit. In all other cases, the officer's honor was to be defended, on the spot, with the weapon he was wearing. The use of a service revolver was acceptable, but only barely so (some said it was not acceptable at all, and in any case, Austro-Hungarian officers practically never wore revolvers), for the only noble weapon of the officer was his sword, the symbol of his membership in the knightly estate. The sword had to be on the officer's person at the time of the offense, or it was no longer a noble weapon. Lifting it hastily from a coat rack would have exposed the officer to severe punishment as, incidentally, would the use of a hunting rifle. The sword was to be wielded, at least in theory, for the sole purpose of silencing the insulter (*um der Fortsetzung solcher Beleidigungen ein Ziel zu setzen*), but military commentators disagreed on whether "first blood" was sufficient, or whether the sword should be wielded until the offender was unable to resume his insults or was properly chastized.

After 1867, the liberal, socialist, and nationalist press turned increasingly against the institution of *Ehrennotwehr*, calling it a barbarian instrument in the hands of arrogant and reactionary officers, and military commentators grew more and more cautious and dejected. Referring to the perpetual martyrdom of the "Great Silent One," the army, they warned that because an officer in mufti was not entitled to the defense of his honor, he should wear his uniform at all times. Furthermore, they argued, he should never take off his sword in a public place, and in general, should avoid all such places as cafés, where hostile civilians might gather. Or, if he had no choice but to go there (and where else could he eat when not at home or in the barracks?), he should leave at the first suspicion of a possible provocation. Nevertheless, if insulted, he had to go ahead with the whole nightmarish process, for the honor of an officer was "like a golden ring with a perfect diamond in the center," or "like pure, freshly fallen snow; to besmirch it only once meant to besmirch it forever."[7] No matter that every act of *Ehrennotwehr* was followed, inevitably, by a public outcry and a criminal investigation.†

---

*What complicated matters immensely was that the insulted officer had to make an immediate, on-the-spot evaluation of the "duel-worthiness" (*Satisfaktionsfähigkeit*) of his opponent. If he drew his sword and cut down his opponent, who subsequently proved to be a gentleman, then the court of honor was very likely to punish him for not having challenged his opponent to a duel; if, on the contrary, the officer challenged his attacker, who subsequently proved to be unworthy of giving satisfaction in personal combat, then he could be punished for having failed to exercise his right of *Ehrennotwehr*.

†What, indeed, was an insulted officer supposed to do? One case, somewhat similar to that of Lieutenant Weigel but with far more serious political consequences because it occurred in Hungary, began with the Hungarian nationalist politician Miklós Bartha's scathing critique, in November 1880, in his Kolozsvár newspaper *Ellenzék* (Opposition), of First Lieutenant Edmund Dienstl. In the article, Bartha accused the first lieutenant, himself born in Hungary but in all other respects a typical *Soldatenkind*, of having called some Hungarian one-year volunteers in the regimental reserve officer training school, "Hungarian dogs." Anxious to save his honor and thus his job, Dienstl challenged Bartha to a duel but was refused satisfaction. Dienstl thereupon rushed to his opponent's editorial office, accompanied by a fellow officer, and cut up Bartha's face with his sword, inflicting lasting injuries. The ensuing tumult—in the streets of Kolozsvár and in the Budapest Chamber of Deputies—might have been the reason for a military court's sentencing Dienstl to seven months' imprisonment. Amnestied by Francis Joseph, Dienstl was subsequently "exiled" to a Galician garrison. (Tibor Hajdu, "A tisztikar társadalmi

Cases of *Ehrennotwehr*, also called *Säbelaffäre*, because they involved the officer's use of his sword, were very rare indeed, and they became even rarer in the decades before World War I. The dramatist Arthur Schnitzler exaggerated a good deal when he described them as typical occurrences in his well-known story, *Leutnant Gustl* (1900). But the army's reaction to Schnitzler's story was far more typical: in a court of honor procedure, Schnitzler was deprived of his rank as a reserve medical officer.

Duelling

The military regarded *Ehrennotwehr* as a necessary evil; by contrast, duelling (*Rencontre* or *Zweikampf*) was seen as an ennobling process, a part and parcel of the officer's lofty lifestyle, and yet the laws and rules governing duelling were at least as contradictory as those governing *Ehrennotwehr*. Whereas the urgent defense of honor was forbidden only by the civilian criminal code, duelling was also forbidden by the criminal code of the army. In fact, the military code generally envisaged harsher punishment for duelling than the civilian code. Nonetheless, the officers of the Habsburg army went on duelling through several centuries of the army's existence; for them it was not only a question of honor but also one of professional survival. Since a refusal to accept a proper challenge could easily lead to the loss of one's commission, duelling was a bread-and-butter issue.

Duelling, as we define it today, seems to have been unknown in ancient civilizations, although there were analogous procedures in many primitive cultures. The modern form of duelling is of Germanic origin and stems from the tribal custom of judicial combat (ordeal) to determine the guilt or innocence of the accused.[8] The *Sachsenspiegel*, the oldest Germanic collection of laws, regulated the modalities of the duel, including the use of lethal but equal weapons, and the required presence of witnesses (at first a jury, later seconds). The old Germanic custom exempted ecclesiastics, women, boys under eighteen, and men over sixty from the obligation to fight a judicial combat. The nineteenth-century central European duelling codes recognized the same exemptions, and like the ancient Germanic codes, demanded that male relatives between eighteen and sixty take the place of those exempted. Women were never allowed to fight; rather, it was the duty of men to fight in defense of a woman's honor.

The Germanic tribes carried the custom of judicial combat to many parts of Europe, including France, Spain, and England. Because the swearing of judicial oaths led to an endless series of perjuries, judicial combat was the preferred method of establishing guilt or innocence. The defeated contestant was judged guilty, and if he was still alive, he was often put to death. The papacy forbade judicial combat as early as 887; in England it was abolished in 1215, but then it was renewed and declared legal as late as 1818. It was finally abolished by Parliament in the following year. In France, King Henry II abolished judicial combat in 1547.

helyzetének változásai [1849–1914]" [Changes in the social position of the officer corps (1849–1914)] *Valóság*, 87/4 [Budapest, April 1987]; 70–71.)

Francis Joseph (1830–1916) around 1850 in general's uniform. Pencil drawing by Franz Eybl. Historical Art Gallery of the Hungarian National Museum (Budapest).

Francis Joseph during World War I. Note the Order of the Golden Fleece hanging from his collar. Drawing by Eugen Wieland. Bildarchiv der Österr. Nationalbibliothek (Vienna).

Crown Prince Rudolf (1858–1889), at the age of three, as colonel-in-chief of the Imperial and Royal 19th Hungarian Kronprinz Erzherzog Rudolf Infantry Regiment. Bildarchiv der Österr. Nationalbibliothek (Vienna).

Archduke Francis Ferdinand (1863–1914) in the uniform of an Austro-Hungarian admiral. Bildarchiv der Österr. Nationalbibliothek (Vienna).

Feldzeugmeister Ludwig Ritter von Benedek (1804–1881), who fell into disgrace after the Austrian defeat at Königgrätz in 1866. Eduard Kaiser's lithograph shows Benedek in 1857 when he was still a Feldmarschalleutnant. Bildarchiv der Österr. National-bibliothek (Vienna).

Feldzeugmeister (later Generaloberst) Count Friedrich Beck-Rzikowsky (1830–1920), who was Francis Joseph's favorite chief of the general staff. Bildarchiv der Österr. Nationalbibliothek (Vienna).

Hungarian hussars battling Austrian infantry and dragoons at Komárom fortress on February 24, 1849. Lithograph by Vincenz Katzler. Historical Art Gallery of the Hungarian National Museum (Budapest).

Officers of the Imperial-Royal 2nd Kaiser Franz Joseph Hussar Regiment in Galicia, 1860/1862. Composed of three group scenes with painted background, this is among the earlier photographs of Habsburg officers. Bildarchiv der Österr. Nationalbibliothek (Vienna).

The Military Academy at Wiener Neustadt, south of Vienna, in the 1860s. Drawing of the front entrance by Wilhelm von Doderer. Bildarchiv der Österr. Nationalbibliothek (Vienna).

Cavalry attack at the Imperial Maneuvers (*Kaisermanöver*) in the Waldviertel, Lower Austria, September 1891. Drawing by R. von Ottenfeld. Bildarchiv der Österr. Nationalbibliothek (Vienna).

Court Ball (*Ball bei Hof*), Vienna, January 19, 1898: "The last quadrille." Note Francis Joseph to the far left and a Hungarian nobleman in the left corner. Bildarchiv der Österr. Nationalbibliothek (Vienna).

Ensign (later First Lieutenant) Stephan (István) Deák, father of the author, as artillery observation officer at the Russian front, 1914. In the background, the commander and the first officer of Ensign Deák's howitzer battery.

Generaloberst Baron Sámuel Hazai (1851–1942), at left, Hungary's minister of defense from 1910 to 1917 when he became chief of mobilization and supply for the Austro-Hungarian armed forces. Born Kohn, Hazai was of Jewish origin. To the right, the Hungarian minister of agriculture in gala costume. Austrian Ministry of Defense/Army Museum (Vienna).

Austro-Hungarian infantry in the trenches during World War I. Bildarchiv der Österr. Nationalbibliothek (Vienna).

The famous Austro-Hungarian 30.5 cm. Škoda heavy mortar during World War I. Bildarchiv der Österr. Nationalbibliothek (Vienna).

The staff of the 16th Austro-Hungarian Army Corps in 1915. Seated, second from the right, is the corps commander, Feldzeugmeister Wenzel Wurm; first to the right is Captain in the Reserve Count Leopold Berchtold, who was Austria-Hungary's foreign minister in 1914. Seated at the small table, fourth from the left, is Captain of the General Staff Johann Friedländer, who later became a Feldmarschalleutnant in the army of the Austrian republic. Of Jewish origin, Friedländer died in a Nazi concentration camp. Bildarchiv der Österr. Nationalbibliothek (Vienna).

Catholic field mass in 1917 held to commemorate a Captain Hensel who died fighting the French in 1809. Bildarchiv der Österr. Nationalbibliothek (Vienna).

Jewish religious service for Austro-Hungarian soldiers at the Lublin military synagogue in occupied Russian Poland around 1916. Austrian Ministry of Defense/Army Museum (Vienna).

In the later Middle Ages, a new form of duel arose in the knightly tournament. Here adversaries fought not to settle a judicial question but for honor. In Renaissance Italy, private encounters between young noblemen multiplied rapidly, and from there the custom spread to all of Europe. By the sixteenth century, duelling had become a veritable epidemic, and it persisted despite repeated interdicts.[9] Duelling was forbidden in the Germanic lands as early as 1582, and thereafter, the ban was reiterated with amazing regularity.[10] In 1752, Maria Theresa's law against duelling ordered the decapitation of duellers, as well as of their seconds (*Sekundanten*).[11] In 1790, the punishment for duelling in peacetime was reduced to loss of commission and detention in a fortress, but the death penalty was upheld for duelling in wartime. In 1813, execution by the sword was changed to hanging. The military code of 1855 declared duelling a felony (*Verbrechen*) and threatened with harsh punishment not only the duellers but also their seconds and the commanding officer who had failed to prevent the encounter. The penalties foreseen by Section XVI of the 1855 military criminal code were incredibly complex but were generally harsher than those listed in Section XIX of the Austrian criminal code (in Hungary, Law V of 1878). Penalties ranged from six months to one year in prison for an encounter in which neither duelist was wounded, and from five to ten years of severe imprisonment for the survivor of a mortal duel. Seconds could go to prison for up to twenty years if they had not tried to prevent the duel. Ironically, they were not to be indicted if they had gone through the formal process of calling for a reconciliation just before the encounter.

The attitude of the Habsburg rulers with regard to duelling, like that of all rulers and most states, was a farrago of contradictions. Maria Theresa and Joseph II looked on duelling with particular disfavor, partly because as absolute rulers they were loath to let their subjects take the law into their own hands, and partly because they resented the perpetual self-decimation of their expensive officers. But because these enlightened despots were also the first aristocrats and first soldiers of their land (Maria Theresa can be quietly masculinized in this respect), they were reluctant to deprive their favorite subjects of this important privilege and duty. As a result, the tough laws remained mainly on paper: only a few officers were indicted, even fewer were sentenced, and the sentences were almost invariably commuted. Nineteenth-century rulers did not behave differently from those of the eighteenth century. Fenner von Fenneberg tells of a young officer who, after being sent to prison for challenging his own commander to a duel, was amnestied almost immediately by Francis I.[12] Instead, the emperor sent the commander into early retirement because he had refused to accept the challenge. "This state," Fenner exclaims, "does not have the power to protect those who obey its laws as well as the precepts of humanity and reason."[13] Worse still, adds Fenner, those who refused to fight a duel were systematically hounded out of the officer corps by their fellows.

Nothing really changed between Fenner's description in the 1830s, and the turn of the twentieth century; it even appears that the army went out of its way to assure its officers that duelling was more advantageous than not duelling. In 1900, Lieutenant Carl Smerczek, of the 60th k.u.k. Infantry Regiment, a member of my sample cohort stationed in Hungary, was blinded in one eye in a pistol duel with a regimental comrade. Military court proceedings were subsequently instituted against his opponent for the "felony of personal combat," but the garrison court at Miskolc soon quashed the proceedings with the argument that the officer had acted under "irresistible compulsion" (*unwiderstehlicher Zwang*) when he challenged Smerczek to a duel. As for the wretched Smerczek, he petitioned the emperor for permission to remain in active service, despite his physical handicap. Permission was granted in 1901, even though Smerczek's personal record describes him as a bad soldier. He was cashiered two years later, for reasons unconnected with the duel.[14]

The army did not tolerate even theoretical opposition to duelling. General Bardolff, a confidant of Francis Ferdinand, tells in his memoirs of Count Ledóchowski, a brilliant officer from an Ulan regiment who had been Bardolff's colleague in general staff school and, as a captain, was serving directly under General Beck.[15] Ledóchowski declared, in the course of a dispute, that he was opposed as a matter of principle to duelling and he subsequently put his views into writing. The court of honor of the general staff (with Bardolff as a member of the court) investigated the affair, and even though the defendant invoked a papal bull damning duelling, and stated that, for him, religious precepts outweighed lay customs, the court of honor ruled unanimously that the captain had violated his honor when he had entered the corps with a mental reservation. Therefore he should be cashiered. Beck took the matter directly to Francis Joseph, but this devout Catholic ruler fully agreed with the court's findings. As a consequence, the captain was reduced to the rank of sergeant and had to enter civilian service.

The Catholic church consistently opposed duelling, as did the Freemasons, Social Democrats, and bourgeois liberal parties.[16] All this amounted to nothing, for not even the bourgeois and socialist politicians hesitated to take up the sword or the pistol to defend their honor or that of their party. The German socialist leader Ferdinand Lassalle, for example, was killed in a duel in 1864. Moreover, because the officer's code of honor applied not only to career officers in active service but also to those on pension, those not in active service, and those in the reserve, and because the latter category grew by leaps and bounds following the introduction of universal military service in 1868, the obligation to duel encompassed ever-larger sections of civilian society. What had once been a noble pastime, became increasingly a middle-class pursuit. Officers in the reserve, even ensigns and other officer candidates, whether teachers, doctors, lawyers, civil servants, businessmen, or students in civilian life, wielded the sword or raised the pistol in thousands of encounters to defend the honor of their golden portepée, which, incidentally, they wore on only the rarest of occasions. Educated civilians without a reserve officer's commission took to duelling to prove that they were the equal of an officer. The Anti-Duelling League, founded in Vienna in 1902, had over a thousand members, among them high-ranking aristocrats, but it made no serious headway.[17]

For certain thitherto second-class strata, the institution of duelling brought significant benefits. Officers from some of the monarchy's poorer nationalities, such as the Ruthenes, Slovaks, or Romanians, fought to be equal to the Germans, the Magyars, or the Poles. Officers of peasant or artisanal background fought to be treated as gentlemen. Perhaps the greatest social beneficiaries of the system were the Jews. In fact, Theodor Herzl considered duelling an excellent means to combat anti-Semitism. In Joseph Roth's *The Radetzky March*, Demant, a Jewish medical captain (*Regimentsarzt*), himself the grandson of an orthodox Jewish tavern keeper, does not hesitate to challenge an aristocratic fellow officer for a few drunken anti-Semitic remarks. Sensing that he will be killed in the encounter, Demant says to his friend, the principal character of the novel:

> Tomorrow I shall die like a hero, a nice little hero. Quite contrary to my nature, and the nature of my ancestors, and that of my race, and against my grandfather's wish. In the big old books he used to read there is the saying, "Whosoever raises his hand against his brother is a murderer." But tomorrow someone is going to raise his pistol against me, and I shall raise my pistol against him. And I shall be a murderer. But I'm short-sighted, I shall not take aim. I shall have my little revenge. If I take off my glasses, I can see nothing at all, nothing at all. I shall fire without seeing. That will be more natural and more honest and quite fitting.[18]

Later the doctor says: " 'I haven't the strength to run away from this idiotic duel. I shall be a hero out of sheer stupidity, all according to the code of honor and the rules of the book. A hero!' He laughed."[19] In the novel, the duel takes place the next morning, with the contestants firing at each other simultaneously: both are killed.

By 1900, 18.3 percent of the Austro-Hungarian reserve officer corps were of the "Mosaic confession" (not including the Jewish medical officers in the reserve), many times more than the proportion of Jews in the monarchy (4.5 percent), and many times more than the percentage of Jewish officers in any other army.[20] True, anti-Semitism was rampant in German and Slavic middle-class circles, but even the most rabid anti-Semite had to think twice in Austria-Hungary before insulting a Jew who could possibly be an officer, for, if challenged by the latter, he had to fight or risk his status as an officer and a gentleman.

In 1896, in the so-called Waidhofen Program, the German nationalist student fraternities (*Burschenschaften*) of Austria resolved never to fight a duel or a student *Mensur* (the athletic version of a duel) with a Jew, on the grounds that the latter "is completely void of honor according to our German concepts."[21] The resolution had dire consequences for the anti-Semitic students, since those among them who were reserve officers or reserve-officer candidates, as most university students were, soon discovered that the army would tolerate no exception to its rules.* In decision after decision, regimental honor commissions ruled against these students, ordering them to fight their Jewish challengers or risk losing their rank. A "Guide for Reserve Officers," published in 1915, offers, as an illustrative example, the case of a German nationalist student, an ensign in the reserve, who, having hit a Jewish student on the head (the Jewish student had insulted the German student in the first place), was challenged to a duel. Basing his position on the Waidhofen Program, the German student refused to give satisfaction and had to suffer the consequences: he lost his rank in the army. Summing up the case, the reserve officer's guide states: "It

---

*The resolution would have been meaningless in Prussia because there, in contrast to southern Germany and Austria-Hungary, no Jew could obtain an officer's commission.

is against the army's notion of honor to refuse chivalrous satisfaction (*ritterliche Genugtuung*) to a person simply because he belongs to another nation or religious community."[22]

The officer corps had more trouble with university students than with any other social group. Incidents involving Hungarian, Polish, or Italian nationalist students were no rarity, but the greatest number of conflicts were with German Austrian students. Particularly dangerous to the army were those students who belonged to the duelling fraternities (*schlagende Verbände*) of Pan-German persuasion. During the Badeni language law riots in 1897, German nationalist students repeatedly insulted Habsburg officers in the street.* This led to scores of duels in which the officers fared very badly, the students being far more experienced duellers. The losses among the officers were so great that special fencing schools had to be set up for them in such hardship posts as Vienna and Graz, and when this proved to be of no help, the army was driven to decree that duels with students ought to be fought not with swords but with pistols. This was all the more remarkable given the fact that pistol duels, being considered more lethal than sword duels, were specifically forbidden in the army. In Joseph Roth's novel, Doctor Demant receives a special dispensation from his colonel to fight with the pistol because of his hopeless ineptitude with the sword. Not that most officers were such skilled marksmen, but the smoothbore duelling pistol, lacking an aim, was such an unreliable weapon that the officers stood at least an even chance in the encounter.

The Rencontre

As elite social customs became more elaborate in the seventeenth and eighteenth centuries, the rules governing duelling also became more complicated, until they assumed their ultimate ritualistic rigidity in the nineteenth century. The slightest deviation from the rules—and they varied from country to country—exposed the violator to dishonor and judicial pursuit. Small wonder, then, that the officers and other gentlemen anxiously consulted such famous guides to the art of duelling as Ludwig Berger's *Der Waffengebrauch des Offiziers* (Linz, 1903); Franz von Bolgar's *Regeln des Duells* (Vienna, 1822, with many further editions, in several languages); Gustav Hergsell's *Duell-Codex* (Vienna-Budapest-Leipzig, 1891); Friedrich Teppner's *Duell-Regeln für Offiziere und Nachschlagebuch in Ehrenangelegenheiten* (Graz, 1898); and—just to mention one post-World War I publica-

---

*The German students' provocation of Habsburg army officers was discussed by Carl Freiherr von Bardolff in *Soldat im alten Österreich. Erinnerungen aus meinem Leben* (Jena, 1938), pp. 38–41 (rather indignantly, because Bardolff, too, was a German nationalist), and, in the same vein, by the Austrian military writer Rudolph von Eichthal in *Die Goldene Spange. Ein Roman aus Altösterreich* (Vienna and Leipzig, 1941), pp. 88–119. Writing during the Nazi period, Eichthal felt obliged to turn the rowdiest of the German nationalist students into a Serb in disguise. In the novel, the pseudo-German is taught a lasting lesson in a duel with the hero of the story, an ethnic German Habsburg officer. On the conflict between the German students and the officers, see also Mailáth-Pokorny, "Memoiren," unpublished manuscript, Kriegsarchiv, Vienna, B/700 Nr. 2, pp. 33–34; and Colonel Kurt von Schmedes, "Jugend- und Kriegserinnerungen," unpublished manuscript, Kriegsarchiv, Vienna, B/1044: pp. 2, 17.

tion—Caesar de Sgardelli's *Párbaj zsebkódexe* (The pocket code of duelling) (Budapest, 1922).

The basic principles enunciated by these guides were always the same: duels had to be sufficiently motivated by an insult (no duels for pleasure or for the sake of the art!); they were to be fought with equal and lethal weapons; they had to follow specific, previously agreed upon rules, and they required the presence of a specific number of witnesses. The Austro-Hungarian codes differentiated between three degrees of insult leading to a "chivalrous affair" (*ritterliche Angelegenheit*): (1) light insults, such as impolite behavior; (2) heavy insults, such as verbal abuse; and (3) physical assault, such as a box on the ear (*Ohrfeige*), the vilest form of abuse to a Central European gentleman. The severity of the duel was determined by the degree of the insult, but also by the wishes of the insulted person and the decision of the seconds. The role of the latter was crucial, for as Alphons Karr, an expert on duelling, has said: "It is not the bullet and not the blade of the sword that kill, but the seconds!"[23] And, in fact, the outcome of the chivalrous affair was greatly influenced by the negotiating skill, experience, and presence of mind of the seconds. They determined whether or not the duel should take place and, if so, under what conditions it should be fought and when it should be stopped.

It is impossible to describe in detail the complex ritual that preceded, accompanied, and followed the actual *Rencontre*. The affair began with the silent exchange of visiting cards, continued with the selection of the seconds (two for each contestant), their repeated meetings, and the drawing up of a formal protocol. Often there would be a consultation with an honor commission and/or experienced older duellers. The place and the time of the *Rencontre* were selected and finally the duel would take place, conducted, ideally, in an atmosphere of impeccable politeness and impartiality, with the presence of two surgeons to treat the wounded, and of the coaches, waiting at a respectable distance. The ritual of the duel itself was no less elaborate: the breaking of the seals on the box containing the pistols; the careful examination of the weapons; the reading of the agreed-upon rules; the formal call for a reconciliation, a new attempt at a reconciliation following the duel (provided that the opponents were still able to shake hands); and the drawing up of a final protocol.

Austro-Hungarian military experts recognized two types of duelling weapons; the sword and the pistol. The use of rifles, revolvers, or the foil was discouraged.

Duels with the sword could take two different forms: those involving slashes only, and those permitting both slashes and thrusts. The latter was far more dangerous, of course, and it was theoretically forbidden to officers. One could fight until "first blood," or for a specific time, or until "total exhaustion," or until one of the contestants was dead (the latter form of prearrangement was also strictly forbidden). Pistol duels could take place from a fixed position, the opponents firing at each other freely or on command, or with the contestants moving toward each other (*Avance*), either stopping from time to time or not stopping at all. The number of bullets to be fired was also predetermined. The worst form of duel was the one in which the duellers walked freely toward one another until, in the end, only fifteen paces separated them.

Today it seems incredible what flimsy reasons sufficed for a challenge and, often, for a duel: an arrogant look; failure to greet a lady in the company of a gentleman; an involuntary push in a crowded tramway; a derogatory remark about someone's profession or professional association, all were sufficient reasons to send the "insulter" to a hospital or to a cemetery. The 1915 edition of the Austro-Hungarian "Guide for Reserve Officers" offers fourteen case studies; they range from calling someone a "liar," or an "ordinary person," to "staring at someone (*fixieren*) while playing with a dog whip."[24]

Paradoxically, whereas "ladies of impeccable reputation" were put on a pedestal, and the defense of their honor, if insulted by a man, was an absolute obligation for their male relatives and friends, insults exchanged by the same impeccable ladies were considered meaningless: a clear case of females being treated as the valuable property of men.

Naturally, not every affair of honor was constructed on flimsy grounds. One example should suffice here. In 1908, honor proceedings were instituted at Pola in Istria against First Lieutenant Wilhelm Ritter von Rosner for adultery with the wife of a fellow officer. Rosner's personal record describes him as a brilliant officer. Seconded to the elite engineering staff, he was serving at the fortress artillery directorate in Pola at the time of the incident. The court of honor found him guilty of endangering his honor as an officer: he lost his general staff assignment and was ordered transferred to a fortress artillery regiment in Galicia. General Conrad intervened on behalf of Rosner on March 1, 1909, requesting that he not lose the seniority earned by serving on the general staff, but the minister of war turned down the request. In any case, Rosner's case was put *ad acta* soon thereafter because, on March 11, 1909, he died of injuries suffered in a duel with the husband, a naval lieutenant.[25]*

The Rosner case, incidentally, clearly illustrates the difference between the German and the Austro-Hungarian military practice on duelling. In Germany, duelling in the army began to decline at the end of the nineteenth century for the simple reason that, in that country, military honor commissions increasingly found those officers who had committed such reprehensible acts as adultery with the wife of a fellow officer unworthy of giving satisfaction. Therefore, in the Reich, many more officers were cashiered for acts that in Austria-Hungary would have led honor commissions virtually to order a duel. (Because duelling was theoretically a felony, no direct order to fight a duel was actually ever given.) Ironically, then, the Austro-Hungarian practice of exposing the culprit to mortal danger—a duel under the most severe conditions—was more humane than the German practice. In Germany the officer was denied the opportunity to save his commission by fighting a duel; in Austria-Hungary, he had a chance to save his job by risking his life.

No one knows how many duels were fought in Austria-Hungary in the nineteenth and early twentieth centuries: statistics were not kept and, anyway, most

*A member of my 1900 sample cohort, Rosner was born in 1880 in Bohemia. His father was manager on a Schwarzenberg princely estate; he himself completed the Technical Military Academy and the general staff school, both with "very good" grades. Fluent in German and Czech, Rosner also had some knowledge of Italian, Serbo-Croatian, French, and English. See his *Qualifikations-Liste*, F 2476, in the Vienna Kriegsarchiv.

duels went unreported. The nineteenth-century Austrian expert Albert Wiesinger lists fifty "famous duels" (fourteen of them lethal) fought by Habsburg officers, but this list is in no way representative, and chronologically it ranges from 1529 to 1893. The same author estimates that a total number of 2,500 duels were fought in Austria (Hungary excluded?) between 1800 and 1893.[26]

In 1917, under Emperor-King Charles, a more democratic and even more devout ruler than Francis Joseph had been, duelling was forbidden again for the officers of the Austro-Hungarian army, but even then duelling continued, although on a diminished scale. The postwar Austrian republic took strict, even if not always efficient measures against duelling. In traditionalist Poland and Hungary, on the other hand, duelling continued unabated. Interestingly, however, fewer and fewer officers were involved, and the *Rencontre* became the favorite pastime of young professionals and politicians. These duels tended to be rather harmless: "first blood," usually a small scratch, was sufficient for the seconds to declare that honor had been safeguarded. Characteristically for the Hungary of Admiral Horthy, the *Ehrennotwehr* of officers was made legal, in an unprecedented parliamentary move, by Law II of 1930.[27]

According to Wilson D. Wallis, duelling had disappeared in England, Scandinavia, Holland, and even Germany* by the end of the nineteenth century.[28] It continued, however, in the Latin countries as well as in Hungary, Poland, and Russia—in the latter, of course, only until 1917. The fascist states soon rediscovered the attraction of duelling as a mark of masculinity and individual heroism. In Italy, Mussolini encouraged the practice, and in Nazi Germany, duelling was made legal in 1936. In fact, dueling continued in West Germany even after World War II, although as a regularized fraternity procedure (*Mensur*), and not as a means of seeking "chivalrous satisfaction."†

The notion of honor is probably as old as society itself. In the Middle Ages, the defense of personal honor was restricted, at least in theory, to the elevated estates, but there is no reason to believe that peasants were less keen about defending their own honor. Poets, jurists, and ecclesiastics idealized the "knight" as one delegated by the Lord to defend the Church, Christianity, the poor, and the defenseless. The officer corps of the nineteenth century borrowed almost verbatim the ideology of the medieval writers, and attempted to make it effective in a modern society. The Christian soldier of the Middle Ages, the *miles christianus,* wielded his sword in

---

*Wallis errs with regard to Germany, as we have seen above.

†As defined by the High Court of the Federal Republic, the student *Mensur,* of early nineteenth-century romantic origin, is an athletic event because it involves no insult and no challenge. I had the pleasure to witness, in 1961, at Heidelberg, a series of *Mensuren,* or encounters, between the members of two student fraternities, "Vandalia" and "Borussia." The contestants wore goggles, and nose and ear guards; their necks were bandaged, and they wore a heavy blood-soaked apron that protected the entire body. They slashed away at each other with what seemed to be monstrously heavy swords, aiming at the head and the cheeks. And even though the *alte Herren* (alumni) who were present ridiculed the whole thing as child's play, they were pretty bloody affairs indeed. As if in a caricature of the traditional duel, the winner of the *Mensur* is not the one who makes mincemeat of his opponent, but the one who receives the greater scars (*Schmisse*) on his head or face, and who winces less when his scars are being stitched without anesthesia, and with a deliberately crude hand.

defense of the virtues of honor, loyalty, service, justice, courage, and moderation. The officer of the modern dynastic armies sought to uphold these same virtues all the more fervently as the modern world turned to different goals and ideals.

The nineteenth-century state succeeded almost everywhere in putting an end to self-administered justice among the lower classes. Only where the state was weak, as, for instance, in southern Italy, did the lower classes continue to pursue their own form of justice and uphold their own interpretation of individual honor. The nineteenth-century dynastic state was far more ambivalent toward self-administered justice among the elite. The result was a mass of contradictions, with the state both forbidding and requiring that its elevated strata take the law in their own hands, under certain circumstances. The reasons for this are very complex but, undoubtedly, the interdiction stems from the absolutist tradition, whereas the requirement to fight a duel originates from the feudal custom of carefully differentiating among the several estates and endowing each one with special privileges and obligations. Considering, for instance, that members of the Jewish community never had the right to defend their individual honor and were to rely instead, like women or priests, on the protective arm of the nobles, it is miraculous how easily nineteenth-century Austro-Hungarian society, or at least the officer corps, accepted the notion that a Jew too could have "honor."

The officers of the Habsburg monarchy served the most traditionalist of all dynasties in one of the most rapidly developing areas in Europe. As anational and apolitical representatives of that dynasty, they had a strong interest in preserving values different from those of the rest of the population. This alone protected them from the nearly irresistible influence of nationalist and social-political agitation. Duelling served them as a mark of their caste differentiation. Their strict interpretation of the concept of honor made the officers less corrupt and more conscientious than is normally the case among the members of a privileged institution, but the concept of honor also prevented the officers from grasping the significance of modern political and social currents. Their ideology of service, honor, and loyalty seemed then to clash directly with Europe's new ideology of liberty, equality, and fraternity. It is a testimony to the officers' prestige, but also to the ambivalent nature of the monarchy, that the officers' traditional ideals made at least as much headway among the educated classes as the new political and social movements. The result was an enormous ideological confusion.

7

Marriage, Family, Sexual Ethics, and Crime

Wives and Children

The ideals of medieval chivalry demanded that the knight be chaste or, if married, that he spend long spells away from hearth and home in pursuit of some noble goal. Nineteenth-century officers liked to subscribe to these ideals and often compared the corps to the ancient fighting orders, but like most knights of old, they had little desire to live according to these precepts. Yet dire necessity and army policy held down the number of marriages and caused thousands of officers who did attain marriage to live a nomadic existence, not unlike that endured by the medieval knight.

As in so many other cases, such as pay and duelling, the Habsburg army was of two minds regarding matrimony. On the one hand, it regarded the family as a nuisance, a burden on the military bureaucracy (if not at first on the treasury, as we shall see), and an impediment to the free use of the officers' talents and services. On the other hand, officers' sons were known to be the best and often only reliable source for perpetuating the corps. In any case, the army severely limited the proportion of those in each unit who could have a family, and it ruled that marriages ought to be contracted only with women who would neither be a drain on the treasury nor demean the lofty social status and dignity of the corps. Overcoming the triple obstacle of *numerus clausus,* financial requirements, and acceptable social standing made a nightmare of an officer's existence.

Not surprisingly, it was Maria Theresa who first regulated officers' marriages, in 1750. Her measures were subsequently extended to officers not in active service or in retirement, on the basis of the argument that the latter two categories could, at any time, be reactivated.[1] The empress's decree made marriage conditional upon a permit from the regiment's owner, commander, and officers' assembly. It also demanded the deposit of a marriage bond (*Heiratskaution*), which was to provide for an officer's widow. The lower the officer's rank, the higher the marriage bond: nearly ten years' pay for a lieutenant, five years' for a captain.

Joseph II's decree of 1777 extended the *Kaution* to all the officers, not only those with the troops; it also provided for the possibility of marriage without a *Kaution*, on permission from the emperor and renunciation of any claim to a widow's pension. In keeping with Joseph's etatist policy, and in flagrant violation of the tenets of the church, a marriage concluded in violation of these regulations was declared null and void.[2]

Many more decrees followed. That of 1812 prescribed, in place of the deposit of a set sum, a guarantee of a certain annual income, which could also be drawn from real estate or some other source. The income was to be used during the married officer's lifetime, more or less doubling his pay. The same decree limited the proportion of married officers in each regiment to one-sixth.[3]

The 1861 regulation increased the amount of income required, and it placed an even greater burden on members of the combat branches, arguing that, because of the greater probability of such officers' dying in war, their widows had to be better provided for. Officers under thirty years of age had to double their bond, irrespective of rank. At least an exception was made for the poor Grenzer officers, allowing them to post a lower bond and letting half the officers in each Grenzer regiment to marry. In 1887, the required bond was again increased, but more officers were allowed to be married as well: in the line regiments, one-fourth of the unit and in the general staff, half. Finally, the regulation of 1907 permitted half of each regiment's officer corps to be wed, but it also increased the *Kaution*. A lieutenant was to deposit 60,000 kronen (30,000 gulden), more than thirty times his average annual basic pay; in the higher ranks, the amount decreased drastically, to the point that a major had to deposit only 30,000 kronen (15,000 gulden), about five times his annual basic pay. Those above major needed no marriage bond.[4]

The result of all this was late marriage or no marriage at all. First Lieutenant Arthur Görgey resigned his commission in 1845 because both he and his bride were impoverished. Görgey's resentment over his broken career undoubtedly helped lead him into the Hungarian national army in 1848.[5] Among some of the memoirists cited in my book, Stillfried married at the age of thirty-five, Auffenberg at thirty-eight, Hirsch at forty-four, and Miščević at fifty-four.[6] The Austrian historian Müller estimates that, on an average, officers married ten years later than other members of the monarchy's male population.[7]

At first, the marriage bond was meant to provide an income for retired officers and their widows, an absolute necessity at a time when there was no pension system. Later, it was also to supplement family income. But, as we shall see, pensions and even widows' benefits were introduced in the nineteenth century and became quite adequate, at least for those officers who had made a decent career. Officer's pay also improved, as we have already seen, to a point where it was no longer impossible to have a family, assuming one married at the rank of captain or above. Then why the ever-increasing cost of the marriage bond? The purpose must have been to prevent socially unacceptable marriages. But even so, the army's policy made little sense, because the officers' assemblies and regimental commanders achieved the above objective in any case.

Young officers were constantly on the lookout for the right *Partie*, the family rich and foolish enough to part with such an enormous sum and to entrust their daughter to a nomad, possibly a stranger, with a modest income and the prospect of an early death. For that matter, he might soon be out of a profession if the monarchy collapsed, as it frequently threatened to do.

When social encounters brought no results, officers sometimes humbled themselves to place an ad in the papers, like this one, in the *Neues Wiener Tagblatt* on November 29, 1900:

Gallant young man, member of a privileged estate, desires marriage with a kind young woman ready to deposit a marriage bond (*cautionsfähiges Fräulein*). Replies under "Three Stars."[8]

Needless to say, such things were strictly forbidden, and if the captain ("Three Stars") had been caught, he would surely have been indicted by a court of honor for having violated, or at least endangered, the honor of an officer. Such strict guardians of the honor code as A. Kielhauser protested bitterly but vainly against this widespread practice.[9]

The majority of officers remained unmarried. In 1872, for instance, only 3,628, or 29.2 percent, of the Joint Army's 12,436 active field-grade and subaltern officers (no reserve officers as yet) were married or widowed.[10] In my 1870 sample cohort of 487 officers, 284 or 58.4 percent remained unmarried during their military career. In the 1900 cohort of 516 officers, 370 or 71.7 percent were unmarried, but here we must consider that the youngest of these officers were only thirty-four years old when their personal records ceased to be kept at the outbreak of World War I. We must also remember that many officers in my two samples left the army early in their lives, some undoubtedly because of the restrictions on marriage.

There were a few ways out of this predicament. Marriages concluded before commissioning were not invalidated by the army; an officer could also request a dispensation from the emperor, especially if his bride was the daughter of another penniless officer. Anton Lehár received such a dispensation in 1900 following an audience with Francis Joseph, even though Lehár, as a first lieutenant seconded to the general staff, was forbidden to marry.[11] One could also use influence. In 1850, Mollinary was on the waiting list for obtaining permission to marry, with five or six candidates in the regiment ahead of him. He applied directly to the chief of the general staff and the local army commander, however, which brought him a promotion to lieutenant colonel and thus the liberty to marry a beautiful Italian aristocrat, Beatrix Torresani. But Urbański, an officer in the same position as Mollinary, had to wait until promoted to captain in the general staff.[12]

Finally, if no *Kaution* was available, one could risk inventing one. Fenner noted in the 1840s that some officers in his regiment had persuaded relatives and friends to invest their money in 5 percent government bonds. The latter then transferred the bonds to the young couple in exchange for the promise that the interest would be secretly surrendered to the donors.[13]

I have found some information in my sample on the marriage bonds posted by officers. In the 1870 cohort, out of a total of 133 officers about whom we have reliable information, 9 officers (6.8 percent) were wealthy enough to provide their own bonds; 74 (55.6 percent) relied on their bride's family; and 50 (37.6 percent) received a dispensation to marry without depositing a bond—an amazingly high proportion indeed. In the 1900 cohort, the numbers and proportions were 13 (17.1 percent), 62 (81.6 percent), and 1 (1.3 percent), making a total of 76 officers.

The life of the officers' families could not have been easy, especially before the reform period, when the pay was abysmal, and regiments changed garrisons almost annually. Often the family tagged along, transporting baggage and furniture, practically without compensation, and, once at the new place, had to hunt for an apartment that was something more than a hovel. After the 1880s, things improved somewhat, since units moved less, and housing conditions improved. It was unthinkable for the wives to work; in any case, they had more than enough trouble managing the household, batman, servants, and children, the problems of a closed society, and the occasional terror of the Kommandeuse, the colonel's wife. Needless to say, not all wives led an unhappy existence; moreover, divorce was almost unknown, at least until the turn of the century.

Officers had relatively few children, probably because of the lateness of their marriages.* In 1872, for instance, of the 3,628 married field-grade and subaltern officers in the Joint Army, 969 (36.5 percent) had no children. The total number of officers' children in that year was 6,058, less than 2 per family.[14]

Concubines, Mistresses, Prostitutes, and Sexual Offenses

If only these Victorian gentlemen had been less secretive about their private affairs! There is, of course, belletristic testimony, especially Arthur Schnitzler's, about ballerinas, midinettes, and whores, but the officers' memoirs speak mainly of chaste courtships: the more fiery and exotic the object of admiration, the less likely for the affair to end in matrimony. Wives are almost invariably described as generous, patient, loyal, and saintly, which makes one suspect that few among them had been married for love. Only Gründorf confesses to his wife's having left him for a fellow officer, with all of their jewels. Her desertion led Gründorf to fall upon the lover with his sword in, of all places, the corridors of the Ministry of War. The incident occurred in 1866, and it ended with both Gründorf and the lover drawing six-month prison sentences. The lover actually went to jail; Gründorf did not, but he was forced into retirement in the middle of a highly successful career.[15]

Gründorf seems to have had fewer Victorian prejudices than most. In his entertaining memoirs, he describes how, as a bachelor officer in Galicia, he and his fellows ordered some girls from a tobacco factory into their bedrooms. Later, even though wildly anti-Semitic, he had a "beautiful love affair" with a Jewess. Again, when in Vienna at general staff school, he had a long lasting affair with "Mizzi, the pastry-shop girl from Michaeler Platz."[16]

Concubinage must have been widespread, although evidence is hard to come by because, even though illegal in the corps, the practice was widely tolerated. Glaise notes that, in the 1870s at Salzburg, half the officers in his father's 59th Infantry Regiment lived in *Konkubinat*.[17]

---

*In my 1870 cohort, the average age of the officers at matrimony was thirty-six, and in my 1900 cohort thirty.

Military bordellos, called *Feldbordellen,* were introduced by the high command only during World War I, but in peacetime officers visited the private establishments frequently, as did other nineteenth-century gentlemen. Despite police registration of prostitutes and regular medical supervision, venereal disease was the nearly inevitable concomitant of such activity, as shown by the many entries to that effect in the officers' personal records.

A particularly tragic case, and the gravest crime I have found next to the Hofrichter affair mentioned in chapter 4, was that of Ensign Heinrich Schmidt, aged twenty-one, who, in July 1912, at Gyulafehérvár, Transylvania, concluded a suicide pact with the young prostitute named Maria Jenuleszk. Schmidt used his pistol to kill the girl, and then fired two bullets into his own chest but survived. The local garrison court sentenced him to death by hanging and, in May 1913 the High Military Court (Militär Obergericht) in Vienna confirmed the verdict. The High Court noted, however, that Schmidt had killed the girl at her own request and recommended him for mercy. Francis Joseph subsequently changed the sentence to five years of aggravated hard imprisonment (*verschärfter schwerer Kerker*). One wonders to what degree the emperor's leniency was influenced by the fate of his own son, Rudolf, who, in 1889 had successfully carried out the same type of suicide pact.[18]

Although lenient on cohabitation and mistresses, the court of honor came down hard on adultery, especially in cases involving fellow officers' wives. The military courts were, in turn, ruthless in dealing with rape. In 1874, the court of the Budapest General-Commando cashiered an officer in my 1870 sample for rape and gave him two years in a severe-regime prison, with the addition of two days each month on bread and water only.[19]

Homosexuality was a crime in the eyes of the law, both civilian and military. It must nevertheless have been widespread in the army, as one could expect in an all-male society where women were either absent, unapproachable, or possibly infected. Some officers may well have entered the army in the first place because it was made up of males. But one looks in vain for evidence in the memoirs, the only available source of information being court records. The following three cases, selected at random from a contemporary index of court-martial proceedings between 1896 and 1915 in the Vienna war archive, shed some light on the subject.[20]

In 1901, the garrison court at Komárom in Hungary cashiered First Lieutenant Cornelius Ritter von Hafner of the 19th Infantry Regiment and sentenced him to two months of imprisonment with severe regime for having engaged, while drunk, in unnatural behavior with one of his subordinates. What aggravated matters was that Hafner had performed the deed behind "incompletely obscured windows." In 1900, the garrison court at Theresienstadt, Bohemia, cashiered First Lieutenant Curt Josef Mayer, a teacher at a cadet school, and sentenced him to two years in a severe-regime prison, compounded by periodic fasting and solitary confinement, for having attempted to seduce one of the students and for having had an affair with an ensign. The ensign was given five months in prison. Finally, there was the case of Lieutenant Johann Kautek of the 48th Infantry Regiment, who was tried by the garrison court at Sopron in Hungary, for having engaged in homosexual activity with two soldiers of his own regiment, and for having attempted to seduce six others. Perhaps because this trial took place in 1908, in a more enlightened era, the proceedings against Kautek were quashed, on the argument that he had acted under an "irresistible compulsion." Kautek resigned his commission the same year.[21]

The best known homosexual in the Habsburg army was Colonel Alfred Redl, the master spy for Russia, who committed suicide in 1913. The Redl Affair has been obscured by the destruction of many documents in the general staff's intelligence bureau (Evidenzbüro) and by the fertile imagination of popular historians and film directors.* The basic outlines of the case are nevertheless clear. By origin, Redl was a most typical Habsburg career officer and not, as the fictionalized accounts would have it, an exceptional phenomenon. His father was a former officer who became a clerk at the Karl-Ludwig Railway Company in Galicia. The family was German. Born in 1864 at Lemberg, Redl at first followed the traditional road for becoming an officer by entering the army at the age of fifteen as a cadet but then attended one of the new cadet schools. He was commissioned a lieutenant in the 9th Galician k.u.k. Infantry Regiment in 1887, at the age of twenty-three. As his *Qualifikations-Liste* shows, he contracted syphilis in 1891, but a year later the personal record cheerfully noted that he had fully recovered from his illness. (The autopsy in 1913 showed that he had not.)

Uncommonly diligent and talented, Redl successfully passed the admission tests to general staff school in 1892, proving thereby what was well known in the army but not by the public, that it was not necessary to have attended a military academy and to have excellent connections to gain admittance into that elite institution. No doubt, the clean bill of health given to him in the same year was intended to facilitate his entry into the school.

Having completed the school in 1894 with a "very good" grade, Redl was seconded to the general staff and, in 1899, he became a full-fledged general staff officer. Because he spoke fluent Polish and Ukrainian, Captain Redl was sent to Russia in the same year, in an exchange of general staff officers. The ostensible purpose of his trip was to learn Russian, but in reality both sides used this friendly arrangement to train spies. Back in Vienna in 1900, Redl was posted to the Evidenzbüro of the Austro-Hungarian general staff and put in charge of intelligence activities vis-à-vis Russia. Enormously dedicated, he pursued Russian and other spies with extraordinary success, but then he too became a Russian spy, an activity into which he had been blackmailed by Russian military intelligence, which exploited Redl's homosexuality, his crushing debts, and his love of luxury. From at least 1903 on, he provided the Russians, but then also the Italians, with important Austro-Hungarian military documents. He also gave the Russians the names of scores of Austro-Hungarian spies operating abroad, and in numerous spy trials held in the monarchy, in which he acted as a much-respected expert, he skillfully shifted his own responsibility onto others. He may have consoled himself with the fact that, in the lenient monarchy, convicted spies were never given more than a few years in prison.

Over the years, decorations and promotions were heaped on Redl; up to the year of his death, he was described in his personal record as a "man of noble thinking

---

*It should be noted that István Szabó's celebrated film, *Colonel Redl*, which was released in the 1980s, is even less related to the real Colonel Redl than the two earlier film versions.

[*vornehme Denkungsart*] and great tact: all in all an excellent general staff officer."
He was made a full colonel in 1912 and became general staff chief of the 8th Prague
Army Corps. On May 24, 1913, he was finally unmasked, thanks to the vigilance of
the intelligence bureau of the German Great General Staff and of the Austrian state
police. He killed himself that same night, with a revolver handed over by fellow
officers in the Austro-Hungarian intelligence bureau, at the express orders of General Conrad, the chief of the general staff.

Although Redl had admitted his guilt, no attempt was made to elicit any details
from him. The order for him to commit suicide actually marked the beginning of a
lengthy attempt at obfuscation, in which both Conrad and the emperor were deeply
involved. There ensued, nevertheless, a public scandal, which severely damaged the
reputation of the general staff, the army, and the monarchy. It is also quite likely that
the catastrophic military defeats the monarchy suffered in 1914 on the Russian and
Serbian fronts were caused at least in part by Redl's activity.

How could Redl get away with so many years of spying, combined with his
extremely active homosexuality (which included transvestism), and his ostentatious
living? (He owned, among other things, one of the most expensive custom-made
automobiles in the monarchy.) These questions have intrigued many observers and
writers, but the explanation is actually not too complicated. There was the typical
Austrian *Schlamperei* (slackness), and, more important, there was the feudal mentality of the army which coincided, strangely, with the liberal mentality of the
period. Both required that one not pry into the private affairs of an officer and
gentleman, and that one accept without question Redl's spurious claim that he had
come into a large inheritance. That he was still a bachelor at the age of forty-nine
was not at all exceptional, as we have seen. Even if some of his colleagues knew
that Redl was a homosexual—as they must have, for he subsidized dozens of
lovers—this was tolerated because it involved consenting adults, most of them
officers. The army prosecuted only homosexual affairs involving minors or subordinates from the rank and file. Not untypically, one of Archduke Francis Ferdinand's
main concerns following Redl's death was that Conrad had ordered the man to
commit a mortal sin, suicide, which may have doomed him to eternal damnation.
Besides, suicide was a crime in the eyes of the state and of the army, as was, of
course, causing someone to kill himself. Finally, we should note that Redl's protégé
and the object of his unmitigated passion, Lieutenant Stefan Horinka of the 7th
Ulanen, was given three months of hard labor and discharge from commissioned
rank by a military court in July 1913 for the crime of "unnatural prostitution," a
very mild sentence indeed. Horinka served as a sergeant in World War I.[22]

All in all, the military courts were not preoccupied with sexual crimes. An index
of court-martial proceedings for the period 1896–1915 shows the following: in the
sample years 1896–1897, out of a total of 181 cases listed, 10 (5.5 percent) dealt
with sexual offenses; in 1912–1913, out of 254 cases, there were 11 (4.3 percent);
and in 1914, out of 164 cases, there were only 3 (1.8 percent).[23]

Other Crimes and Military Court Procedures

The basic principle of the Habsburg military jurisdiction was that all infractions of
the code of behavior as well as all crimes ought to be settled within the "family,"

including crimes against civilians. The relevant military penal code was first systematized under Maria Theresa and was reformed several times, most significantly in 1884.

The theory was that courts of honor made up of fellow regimental (later also divisional) officers should handle all matters concerning an officer's honor, such as duels, drunkenness, failure to pay debts, insults, refusal to offer satisfaction, lack of discretion, concubinage, adultery, tactless behavior, keeping unsuitable company, making false reports, and so on.[24] Gradually, however, more and more of these problems were taken over by regular military courts, which had always handled the more serious crimes, such as espionage, treason, incitement to mutiny, murder, assault, and crimes against property.

In time, the exclusivity and unusual procedures of the military courts came under public attack as an anomaly in a society and state where even the Catholic church had lost most of its ancient jurisdictional privileges; still, the army managed to prevent any serious tampering with its privileges.

The practices of the Austro-Hungarian military courts were so complex (frankly, I have been unable to understand them fully) as to preclude a detailed analysis. Perhaps it is enough to state here that both investigation and trial were held in secret (even noninvolved members of the armed forces being excluded); that, at least before the reform era, the court included two representatives of each rank, from private up; and that voting always began with the two privates, so as to prevent their intimidation by the opinion of their superiors.* The examining magistrate, prosecutor, counsel, and expert judge was one and the same judge advocate (*Militärauditor*), the only qualified lawyer in court. Clearly, his recommendation was crucial, especially as long as there were rank-and-file judges, who may not have fathomed the meaning of the whole procedure. The defendant was entitled to an interpreter but never to a civilian lawyer. The verdict was announced with the sound of trumpets, actually, the only way for friends and relatives assembled in the courtyard to know that the proceedings were over. The verdict was then passed on to the commander of the garrison, who could, but rarely did, mitigate or even reverse the sentence. An appeal was seldom possible.[25]

If all this sounds arbitrary, it was. If it also sounds unjust, it should be noted as well that the Auditore generally took their task very seriously, and that they did in effect plead for the defense as well as for the prosecution. We have seen already that, in the postreform period at least, verdicts pronounced on enlisted men were surprisingly mild, and that death sentences and executions were very rare indeed.

---

*The involvement of rank and file in the trials even of officers harked back to the egalitarian, mercenary (*Landsknecht*) tradition of the dynastic Habsburg army. In 1849, for instance, the Hungarian rebel officers were tried at Arad by a court composed of fourteen judges: a president who was a field-grade officer, the judge advocate, two majors, two captains, two lieutenants, two sergeants, two corporals, and two privates. It is unclear to me when this practice was abandoned but, certainly, by the turn of the century, officers were judged by a court composed of their peers, none of whom was to be of a lower rank than the defendant. (Tamás Katona, ed., *Az aradi vértanúk* [The Arad martyrs], 2 vols. [Budapest, 1979], 1:29, and documents. Also, Walter Wagner, "Die k.(u.)k. Armee—Gliederung und Aufgabestellung," in Adam Wandruszka and Peter Urbanitsch eds., *Die bewaffnete Macht* ["Die Habsburgermonarchie," vol. 5; Vienna, 1987], pp. 268–77, 539–60.)

Table 7.1. Officers and Ensigns Tried by the Military Courts
of the Joint Army in a Few Sample Years
(Percentages)

Nature of the Crime	1896–1897	1912–1913	1914
Political	0.6	2.4	14.6
Military	2.2	6.3	37.2
Sexual	5.5	4.3	1.8
Mistreatment of subordinates	20.4	29.9	3.0
Against property	34.3	26.8	8.5
Other	37.0	30.3	34.8
Total	100.0	100.0	100.0
In absolute numbers:	181	254	164

Source: "Strafuntersuchungsprotokolle 1896–1915," unpublished manuscript, Kriegsarchiv, Vienna. The statistical data represent my own computations based on the entries
in this index.

As for the officers, so few were tried as to defy an in-depth analysis. In 1911, for
instance, courts of honor cashiered only nine officers, and military courts sixteen
officers (ten lieutenants, three first lieutenants, and three captains). Incidentally, in
the same year, five officers—three lieutenants, one first lieutenant, and one captain—deserted.[26]

Table 7.1 is a statistical breakdown of the cases listed in the above-mentioned
comprehensive court-martial index. It should be noted that the tables 1896–1897
and 1912–1913 figures include only career officers. In 1896–1897, ten reserve
officers were tried, and in 1912–1913, twenty-three reserve officers, whereas the
1914 figure includes both career officers and reservists (eighty-six and seventy-
eight, respectively). Political crimes include espionage, treason, and lèse-majesté;
military crimes comprise desertion, disobedience, and cowardice; the much more
numerous crimes against property consist mostly of embezzlement and an occasional theft; and the "other" category is made up of such things as drunkenness and the
mysterious entry "general offenses against military discipline." Eighty percent of
the defendants were ensigns and subalterns; the occasional higher ranks were never
combat officers but medical officers and other military officials. Nearly half of the
defendants belonged to the infantry; the rest were proportionally distributed among
the other arms of service. About one-third of the trials ended in acquittal, a little
over one-third resulted in the officer's being cashiered, and less than one-third in
both a prison sentence and dismissal from the officer corps. In 1914, the nature of
the crime was not always registered. In that year, one encounters a number of Serbo-
Croatian names among the defendants, but only one or two of them received a
sentence. Finally, the lower the rank of the defendant, the more likely he would be
sent to prison and also cashiered.

Clearly, in peacetime, the courts dealt by and large with ordinary crimes, including an amazing number of cases involving brutality against subordinates. In the first
year of the war, the emphasis changed to desertion, espionage, disobedience, incitement to mutiny, and treason; in other words, to military and political crimes. All in

all, relatively few officers appeared before the military courts: in 1896 and 1897, 0.45 percent of the entire corps; in 1912 and 1913, 0.48 percent; in other words, fewer than five out of a thousand in any given year. The inescapable conclusion is that the vast majority of officers were basically decent and loyal, unless we make the unreasonable assumption that many more got away with their crimes.

8

Pensioners, Widows, and Orphans

Hoping for a Pension

If life in active service was not easy, life in retirement could be even harder, although it is true that the officers' pension system improved considerably between the 1850s and 1914.

An officer's right to a pension was even more of a novel idea than his right to regular pay. At first, pensions were but a manifestation of princely munificence, granted to victorious generals, wounded soldiers, or war widows. Until 1855, the Habsburg army knew nothing of a retirement age: officers served as long as they wished or could, which resulted in such extraordinary scenes as a seventy-year-old captain riding at the head of his company, or Field Marshal Radetzky commanding the Austrian army in Italy at ninety. Nonetheless, the vast majority of officers had to quit at a much earlier age, often because of such service-connected disabilities as war wounds, pneumonia, arthritis, malaria, or, in the case of gunners, deafness. In 1770 a system of pensions was introduced for all officers whom the military arbitration commission certified as disabled. The commission included medical officers, but because it was open to all sorts of outside pressure, its decisions were often unjust. The commission distinguished between total and partial disability: those certified as semi-invalids were put on half pay (*mit Wartegebühr beurlaubt*) for up to a year and could still hope to be recalled to active service or, if lucky and well connected, to be transferred to a garrison battalion or some other less demanding post.[1] Totally disabled officers were entitled to a regular pension, the sum of which was sometimes based on the pay of the next-highest rank at the time of their retirement. The pension bore no relation to the length of service, as it would later. Field-grade officers and generals could be pensioned off at their own request or at the command of the emperor even without being disabled. Table 8.1 shows the pension scale of the officers between 1770 and 1855. The differential ratio between the pension of a junior lieutenant and a colonel was the same as the difference between their regular pay, namely, 1:6.

Table 8.1. Officers' Annual Pension before 1855

Rank Category	Rank	Pension (Gulden)	Index
XI	Lieutenant II. class and I class	200	1
X	First lieutenant	200	1
IX	Captain II class	400	2
IX	Captain I class	600	3
VIII	Major	800	4
VII	Lieutenant colonel	1,000	5
VI	Colonel	1,200	6
III–V	General (1 to 3 stars)	1,500–4,000	7½–20
I	Field marshal	5,000	25

Source: [Daniel] Fenner von Fenneberg, *Österreich und seine Armee* (Leipzig, 1842), pp. 322–23.

Impecunious retired officers (that is, the vast majority) took up a job or, if that proved impossible, starved. J. K. Mayr, the chronicler of Viennese history, notes the sorry fate of Unterleutnant (Lieutenant II. class) Németh, whom his French captors had thrust into a fire in 1815 and who had, as a consequence, lost his left eye, his nose, and a part of his upper lip. He was rewarded for his pain with an annual pension of 200 gulden ($80).[2] Other officers committed suicide or died of starvation in a city celebrating the Austrian victory over Napoleon. Even a captain II. class, enjoying an annual pension of 400 gulden ($160), must have faced terrible hardships. Yet the majority of officers retired at this rank, or at that of a captain I. class, and this after many years of service. These officers were still lucky because many others turned down by the arbitration commission had to retire without any pension.

There was a remedy, however, for some, although certainly not all of the officers: the sale of their position. This was a private transaction, not involving the authorities, whereby an older officer agreed to resign from active service in exchange for payment by those below him on the regimental roster. If such a transaction, called *Convention,* met with the approval of both the regimental commander and the regiment's owner, then the negotiated retirement was followed by a whole series of promotions, with a newly commissioned lieutenant gaining a foothold in the regiment at the bottom of the list. The price for the transaction varied widely: in the best case, the retiring officer was paid something like 10,000 gulden by those below him in line for promotion. The annual interest on 10,000 gulden being 400 gulden, the retiring officer could face his declining years with some confidence, especially if the arbitration commission had also played its part in the deal, certifying him as an invalid and thus providing him with an official pension.[3]

The situation changed in 1855, when the pension system was reorganized, making all those officers who had completed at least fifty years of active service eligible for a pension. Their pension equaled their full pay before retirement. Officers of less phenomenal endurance still had to be invalided in order to receive a pension, but now they were paid according to the length of their service. A disabled officer with ten years of service received 10 percent of his last regular salary; for each five years of additional service another 10 percent was added. Thus a disabled officer with forty-one years on active duty received 80 percent of his original salary. Length of service was computed from the date of entry into the army, at whatever rank. This benefited those who had come up through the ranks or had begun as regimental cadets but not those who had studied at a military academy. War years counted as double, and campaign-connected injuries or illness, particularly the loss of an arm or a leg, were rewarded with an impressive number of additional service years. Finally, no retired officer was to receive less than 200 gulden annually.[4]

The post-1868 period brought further improvements in the pension system. Most important, the minimum service required for an automatic pension was reduced from fifty to forty years. Also, officers qualified for automatic pension when they became sixty years of age. The size of this pension was, as before, equivalent to the officer's last pay when on active duty. Earlier retirement still depended on the goodwill of the arbitration commission, but the minimum pension was increased from 200 to 300 gulden per annum. More important, because the average waiting period for a promotion to a higher rank had gradually decreased from six to eight years to five to six years, the average officer could now retire, not as a captain II. class but as a captain I. class or even a major.[5]

All of this was still far from satisfactory, however, especially when compared with the pension plan of the Austrian civil servants. While an officer's minimum pension was set at 300 gulden, that of a Beamter was 400 gulden, and while a retiring captain I. class received half his regular pay after twenty years of service, the civil servant got 60 percent.[6]

A final military pension revision after 1900 improved the situation of both earlier and current retirees. A few examples are shown in table 8.2.

War years still counted as double, and years spent in military school were still not counted. Also, it became customary to pension off deserving officers at a rank one step higher than the one they had last held in active service. This *ad honorem* rank brought no higher pension, however, only a little more glory.

Vast improvements in hygiene, health care, nutrition, and living conditions, as well as the absence of war enabled an ever-increasing number of officers to serve a full forty years, and to retire, at sixty, on a full pension. Earlier retirement had also become easier, thanks to the growing willingness of the arbitration commission to cooperate. Nothing else can explain the vast number of officers who were pensioned

Table 8.2. Annual Pension for Officers Retiring after 1900 (Gulden)

Service Years	Category IX (Captain II. Class; Regular Pay, 1,200) Pension	Category VIII (Major; Regular Pay, 2,004) Pension	Category VI (Colonel; Regular Pay, 3,600) Pension
20	600	1,002	1,800
30	900	1,503	2,700
40 (or 60 years of age)	1,200	2,004	3,600

Source: Karl F. Kurz, ed., *Militär-Taschenlexikon*, 10th ed., Part I (Vienna, 1911), p. 200.

off as invalids on grounds of "impaired hearing," "impaired vision," "nervous breakdown," or "general exhaustion."

Since the beginning of the nineteenth century, the state had endeavored to find alternative sources of income for its disabled officers, such as office work in the military or state bureaucracy, the postal service, and the railways. Unfortunately, however, there were never enough of these alternative sources, which caused the officers to fall back on their own pensions. Because of this reliance, the pension plan steadily improved throughout the century, both in terms of its real value and in terms of the number of its beneficiaries.

Pale Widows and Hungry Orphans

Military literature is awash in heartrending stories of the sufferings of an officer's widow and orphans, too proud to beg for food but too poor to survive. In the words of the *Armeeblatt* in 1899:

> Who has not seen them, these pale women, with their tired walk and desperately sad eyes, dim from crying and red from nightly labor; they display the traits of painful resignation. . . .These unfortunates, who once followed the dictates of their heart and thought the world to be theirs, are now paying for every hour of past happiness with grief, freezing, and misery.[7]

Widows' petitions for financial support, a standard feature in the military archives, tell the same story over and over: an unfortunate widow from a good family, herself the daughter of an officer, now without any source of income, yet with a great number of small children, begs His Imperial Majesty on her knees for assistance. The alternative is a broken heart, illness, starvation, and death. Was all this true, or were these tales simply the manifestations of a sentimental age? Or perhaps the accepted tone for such a petition was to suggest that the bereaved widow was near extinction, just as discharged soldiers applying for reenlistment were expected to write that their greatest joy would be to die for Throne and Country. The stereotypical form of letters, memoirs, and official petitions can sometimes hide the truth from us, although it does appear that the widows' stylized and formalized expressions of distress often coincided with genuine misery.

At first, widows' pensions were as much a manifestation of princely benevolence as were the officers'. Widows were expected to live on the interest of their marriage bond. If it was not available (because the officer had married before being commissioned a lieutenant, or for some other reason), an officer was expected to contribute to a special widows' fund (*Offizierswitwenkasse*) during his years of active service. Only if even the latter sum was unavailable did the state step in, either by granting a mercy pension (*Gnadengabe*) to the widow or by procuring her a concession to sell tobacco, which was a state monopoly. Austrian cities had plenty of these small state-owned tobacco shops (*Tabaktrafiken*), operated by widows who seemed forever dressed in black. That all this still left many officers' widows without a source of income is proven by the fact that a great number were supported from local paupers' funds (*Armenfond*), which during the Napoleonic era in Vienna provided the lordly sum of eight to ten kreuzers daily.[8]

Following the Napoleonic Wars, regular pensions were paid to war widows and to those who had married without depositing a marriage bond. Moreover, now even their children were given a small subsidy, but only if there were at least three of them, and only so long as the boys were under twenty and the girls under eighteen.

In the second half of the nineteenth century, the widow's situation gradually improved. In 1887, for instance, all widows whose husbands had been killed in battle or had died of campaign exertion (*Kriegsstrapazen*), service-connected accidents, or epidemics ravaging the region where he was stationed were judged worthy of a pension. In 1896, benefits were at last extended to the widows of officers who had died of certain types of peacetime casualties, such as service-connected exertions, rheumatism, heatstroke, sunstroke, and certain kinds of tuberculosis. Curiously, the widows of those officers who had died of the flu were specifically excluded from the pension plan. Also, in 1887, all widows whose husbands had been over sixty years of age at the time of retirement, or had served forty years and thus earned the right to a pension, were themselves judged worthy of a pension. On the other hand, the widows of officers who had died of non-service-connected illnesses or accidents, married without permission, resigned their commission, emigrated, or been sentenced by a criminal court were excluded.[9]

At the end of the nineteenth century, however, the pensions of officers' widows still trailed far behind those of the widows of civil servants, as revealed by table 8.3. Thus a captain's widow (IX) with two children had to make ends meet with a total monthly pension of 29.2 gulden, and a colonel's widow (VI) with 50 gulden. War widows received 50 percent more; they were also given an educational subsidy for each child, even if they had fewer than three children (as opposed to other military widows). As an indication of just how inadequate these pensions were, note that the widow of an usher I. class (*Amtsdiener I. Klasse*) with two children, whose husband had served a full term, received a higher annual pension (373 gulden, 32 kr.) than the widow of a captain with two children (350 gulden).[10]

Table 8.3. Annual Pension of Widows at the End of the Nineteenth Century (Gulden)

Rank Category	Officers' Widows with Two Children (in Austria–Hungary)			Widows of Civil Servants with Two Children (in Austria)		
	Pension	Education Subsidy	Total	Pension	Education Subsidy	Total
XI	250	—	250	400	160	560
X	300	—	300	500	200	700
IX	350	—	350	600	240	840
VIII	400	—	400	700	280	980
VII	450	—	450	900	360	1,260
VI	600	—	600	1,200	480	1,680

Source: "Der Officiersmangel und seine Ursachen," *Armeeblatt* 18, No. 43 (October 25, 1899): 3.

Table 8.4. Annual Pension of Officers' Wives Widowed in or after 1907

Rank Category	Rank of Husband	Pension (Gulden)	Index	As Percentage of Officer's Maximum Peacetime Basic Pay
XI	Lieutenant	375	1	37.5
X	First lieutenant	450	1.2	32.1
IX	Captain	500	1.33	27.8
VII	Major	600	1.6	25.0
VII	Lieutenant colonel	750	2.0	24.2
VI	Colonel	1,000	2.66	22.7
V	Generalmajor	1,250	3.33	19.2
IV	Feldmarschalleutnant	1,750	4.66	21.9
III	Feldzeugmeister, General der Kavallerie	2,500	6.6	27.8
I, II	Field marshal and minister of war	2,700	7.2	27.0–22.5

Source: Karl F. Kurz, ed., *Militär-Taschenlexikon,* 10th ed., Part I (Vienna, 1911), pp. 306–7. Also *Statuten der Kaiser Franz Josef-Stiftung für Versorgung k.u.k. Offiziers-Witwen und Waisen* (Vienna, 1905).

Finally, in 1907, a new regulation set more acceptable standards for widows' pensions (see table 8.4). The widows of officers who died in battle or from wartime exertions again received 50 percent more. Note the sharp increase in the size of pensions compared to the earlier figures, and the institution of a sliding scale allowing a relatively higher pension for a subaltern's widow than for the widow of, let us say, a colonel. A widow's pension ceased if she remarried or took up employment.

The law of 1907 brought some relief to orphans as well. Educational subsidies were to be paid even to families with fewer than three children, but only so long as the orphans were minors. Remarkably, the age limit for both sexes was raised to twenty-four, which meant that the state was now willing to support the university education of both officers' sons and daughters. Naturally, the authorities were still very keen on seeing children who were "unprovided for" (*unversorgte Kinder*) become "provided for" (*versorgte*). The easiest way to achieve this was to place boys in military schools and girls in educational institutions created for the daughters of officers (*Offizierstöchter-Erziehungsinstitute*).

Set up by Maria Theresa in 1775, at St. Pölten in Lower Austria, the first publicly supported school for women in Austria trained the daughters of impoverished or deceased officers to become governesses for aristocratic families. Graduates were provided with a gift of 250 gulden, and if they stayed on as governesses for at least six years, they were permitted to marry an officer without depositing a *Kaution*. If they found no husband and grew too old to work as governesses, they received a lifetime annual pension of 150 gulden.

In 1786, the officers' daughters' institution moved to Hernals, near Vienna. It was complemented in the first half of the nineteenth century by two smaller schools for the orphaned daughters of enlisted men and noncommissioned officers; girls there were trained to become "maids for middle-class families." Finally, in the nineteenth century, a second officers' daughters' institution was set up at Sopron, in western Hungary, which after 1877 prepared students for Hernals.

After a while, Hernals came to train not only governesses but teachers as well, and by the end of the nineteenth century, its more talented students were encouraged to complete high school. In 1907, after the educational subsidy for officers' orphans had been extended to the age of twenty-four, Hernals graduates were able to study at the university. All in all, the daughters of officers had better educational possibilities than women in civilian life.

In 1905, Hernals had thirty-one regular and nineteen "outside" teachers, a good number for the fewer than two hundred pupils. A girl lost her right to an educational subsidy if she entered a convent, got married, or accepted employment.[11] In 1907, the educational subsidy for each child was set at one-fifth of the widow's pension. The total sum of orphans' subsidies paid to each family could not, however, exceed the sum of the widow's pension.[12]

Finally, it ought to be mentioned that widows received an immediate subsidy upon the death of their husbands. This *Sterbequartal* amounted to one-fourth of the husband's last annual pay (hence the term *Quartal*). Special provisions were also made for the widows of such officers who had been declared insane as well as for mentally ill widows and orphans.[13]

All this allowed for a modest standard of living only; still it was infinitely better than in the prereform age. The real tragedy would come later, after World War I, when pensioners, widows, and orphans would be left with no support at all, or would be paid in increasingly worthless currency.

There was one more gratuity which pre–World War I pensioners and their widows and orphans had enjoyed, and which the interwar successor states were either unwilling to recognize or unable to replace. That gratuity brought the officer and his family no financial benefits but was nevertheless very much appreciated: it was membership in the hereditary nobility, to which every long-serving Habsburg officer had a legal claim.

9

Nobles and Near-Nobles
in the Officer Corps

There is hardly a more complex story than that of the nobility in the various Habsburg possessions. In some lands, such as Hungary, Transylvania, Croatia-Slavonia, and Galicia, nobles numbered historically in the tens of thousands or even in the hundreds of thousands. In pre-1848 Hungary, they made up about 5 percent of the population. In other provinces, they numbered only a few hundred or a few thousand. Some noble families predated the Habsburgs; most others were Habsburg creations, but socially it made a big difference, of course, whether one's *Adelsbrief* (noble patent) dated from the sixteenth or the twentieth century. Nor was it socially negligible whether the patent had come from the Holy Roman Emperor, the king of Hungary, or, let us say, the princely count of the Tyrol; never mind that the three were one and the same person. The grandfather of the Marxist philosopher Georg Lukács was a barely literate Orthodox Jewish quilt maker in the Hungarian city of Szeged; Lukács's father became a successful banker and was ennobled, in 1901, by Francis Joseph in his capacity as king of Hungary. In his early German-language publications, Georg Lukács used the same "von" before his name as did, for instance, a descendent of imperial knights whose ancestors had been independent petty rulers under the emperor's nominal suzerainty.

The princes Esterházy traditionally owned nearly a million acres of land in Hungary and Austria, including over one hundred villages, forty towns and markets, and thirty castles or palaces.[1] Their neighbor in Hungary, a "sandaled" (poor) nobleman, might have owned a few acres of land or nothing at all, yet in Hungarian constitutional theory, the prince and the poverty-stricken peasant noble were part of the same noble estate and enjoyed identical political and social rights. Meanwhile, a rich Hungarian merchant or a wealthy peasant was not considered a member of the noble *Natio Hungarica*. In other provinces, however, sharp constitutional distinctions were drawn between the titled and the lesser nobility. True, after 1848, and particularly after 1867, all legal distinctions between nobles and commoners disappeared; yet patents of nobility continued to be granted from which their new owners derived some economic and social benefit.

What is of interest here are two basic questions. First, did the nobility lose most of its earlier economic and political power in the liberal, post-1867 age? The answer is that by and large it did, but only in the western provinces of the monarchy as well as in the Austrian bureaucracy and the Austro-Hungarian army. In Hungary, Croatia-Slavonia, and Galicia, the great landowning aristocracy and, in Hungary in particular, the gentry, preserved much of its influence and power. Second, did the nobility gradually abandon its ruler in the second half of the nineteenth century by failing to perform its traditional role in government service and the army? Many observers felt that this was indeed the case—Archduke Rudolf himself wrote a bitter anonymous pamphlet on the issue.[2] Yet, in reality, such a generalization is most difficult to make about a monarchy which was, after 1867, divided into two sovereign states. A Hungarian aristocrat, for instance, may well have been supremely loyal to Hungary and active in its public service or even its army, while being alarmingly disloyal to Austria-Hungary, as indeed many Hungarian aristocrats were. It is true, however, as we shall see shortly, that the number of titled noblemen in the Joint Army's officer corps was gradually declining.

Among all the strata of the nobility, only one group was unquestioningly loyal to the dynasty: the ennobled career officers. And it mattered little in their case whether they had inherited the title from a soldier ancestor or had received it in person.

How to Become a Nobleman

In the sixteenth and seventeenth centuries, when the rule of the Habsburgs over their manifold possessions was still extremely tenuous, the dynasty had no choice but to create a large coterie of well-endowed followers. Supplied with vast tracts of land and placed in charge of the army, administration, and church, this great Habsburg aristocracy of a few hundred families in turn helped to consolidate the monarchy. But the emperor himself became impoverished in the process, and the aristocracy, although politically loyal, was generally less than eager to contribute to expenditures. In 1740, the year Maria Theresa succeeded to the throne, the destitute monarchy nearly collapsed under the Prussian military onslaught. The empress quickly learned her lesson, and although she would never neglect the great nobility, she set out to create a new elite of imperial officers and bureaucrats drawn to a significant extent from the ranks of the commoners. She rewarded the latter for their services with elevation into the nobility, although generally without any accompanying material benefit.

At first, only officers and civil servants were ennobled without a land grant, but in the nineteenth century the practice came to be applied increasingly to bankers, industrialists, politicians, judges, professors, medical doctors, lawyers, journalists, writers, and artists. In all this, religion and nationality played no role whatsoever. In Hungary alone about 350 Jewish families were ennobled, and an additional 25 families received the baronial title between the 1840s and 1918.[3] Ennobled families were given the right to place a "von" before their name or to wear a decoration (which in some cases was the source of their elevation into the nobility); others were awarded such titles as Ritter (knight), Freiherr (baron), and very exceptionally, Graf (count). Only a handful of these distinctions, however, secured their bearers regular access to the imperial court and to "First Society," a most exclusive yet loosely defined group of hereditary great aristocrats and top-ranking bureaucrats. Moreover, as time passed, many of these titles became quite costly, no longer to the dynasty but to their beneficiaries.*

Of all the social groups in the monarchy, only the officer corps had a firm claim, rather than merely a vague hope, for accession into the ranks of the hereditary nobility. The noble patent of an officer came to him free of charge; and he received it in return for fulfilling a number of relatively simple obligations.

Well into the eighteenth century, noble and commoner officers lived separate lives and had different career opportunities. Then, however, Maria Theresa set out to create a unified military elite and, simultaneously, to rejuvenate the old nobility. Her goal was fulfilled only to a degree, for while the practice of ennobling commoner officers became the rule under her successors, the merging of the "old" nobility (*Altadel*) with the "new" or "service" nobility (*Neuadel, Dienstadel*) never really took place. Intermarriage between the old and new aristocracy remained the exception. To give but a single example: from among a sample of eighty-four military noble families between 1804 and 1918, only seventeen individuals married into old noble families. Of those seventeen brides, moreover, seven came from *Reichsdeutsche*—that is, non-Austrian German—families, while most of the others belonged to the Hungarian, Polish, or other "ethnic" nobility. Only one military nobleman succeeded in winning a bride from the old Austrian nobility.[4]

The ennobling of officers was regulated and systematized in 1821 by Francis I, who decreed that all officers who could prove thirty years of irreproachable conduct (*tadellose Conduite*) in active field service were entitled to a patent of nobility. Military officials, such as medical officers, who had not served "with sword in hand and in front of the line" (*mit Degen in der Faust und vor der Front*) were thus excluded from this privilege.

The use of the term "free of charge" (*taxfrei*) to describe the officers' special right to ennoblement was not entirely correct, for it still cost between 120 and 150 gulden to obtain the necessary papers and the noble patent, even if one was content simply to have a "von" before one's name. If an officer wished to call himself "Edler von" (a nobleman of) and attach a noble predicate to his name, he had to pay the treasury an additional 100 gulden CM (105 gulden ÖW).[5] On the other hand, he was then free to choose his own noble predicate and to devise his own coat of arms. The result was a good number of strange predicates that easily betrayed their owners as members of the new nobility. Some officers chose as their predicate the name of

---

*For instance, at the end of the nineteenth century, the tax on ordinary ennoblement in Hungary was 1,575 gulden; on a baronial title, 3,150 gulden; on a countship, 6,300 gulden; and on a princely title, 12,600 gulden. Add to this the cost of the noble patent itself, which ranged all the way from 72 gulden 89 kr. for an ordinary ennoblement to 1,437 gulden 45 kr. for a princely patent. (See Béla Kempelen, *A nemesség. Útmutató az összes nemesi ügyekben. Genealógiai és heraldikai kézikönyv* [The nobility. Guide on all matters regarding ennoblement. A manual on genealogy and heraldry] [Budapest, 1907], pp. 47, 51.) The cost of ennoblement in the Austrian half of the monarchy was approximately the same. In addition to the above expenses, wealthy businessmen were expected to contribute a considerable sum to a charitable foundation as a precondition for their elevation into the nobility.

the place where they had fought a battle or had been garrisoned; others strove to give proof of their vocation or their loyalty to the throne in their choice of name. Because battlefields and garrisons often lay in the Hungarian or Slavic areas of the monarchy, the officers' chosen predicates reflected the ethnic diversity of the Habsburg possessions. Among the famous military dynasties of the monarchy were names like Gründorf von Zebegény (the latter a small village in Central Hungary); Gyurits von Vitesz-Sokolgrada Belisar (a family of Croatian peasants whose members served as outstanding Grenzer officers); Nawratil, Edler von Kronenschild ("Shield-of-the-Crown"); Lenk von Treuenfeld ("Loyalfield"); Wagenbauer von Kampfruf ("Call-for-Battle"); Gross von Stahlborn ("Born-in-Steel"); and Waldstein, Edler von Heilwehr ("Defense of Good Health"), the latter the noble predicate of a Jewish medical general.

Such artificial concoctions compared poorly with such grand aristocratic names as Prince von Thurn und Taxis; Graf Wallis, Freiherr auf Carighmain; Graf Coreth von Coredo und Starkenberg; Graf Bigot de St. Quentin; the Polish Pieniążek, Ritter von Odrowaz; or the Hungarian Thomka de Thomkaháza et Falkusfalva; Gyömörey de Győri-Gyömöre et Teölvár; Görgey de Görgő et Toporcz; and Ghyczy de eadem et Assa-Abláncz-Kürth.*

Not all officers had to wait thirty years before obtaining the right to demand admission into the nobility. Outstanding service decorations, such as the Military Maria Theresa Order or the higher ranks of the orders of Leopold, St. Stephen, and the [Italian] Iron Crown automatically conferred hereditary noble status on their holders. Naturally, however, the number of such specially distinguished officers was very small.

After 1868, it became somewhat more difficult for an officer to obtain a patent of nobility. The thirty-year rule continued to apply only to officers who had served in a war—a rare occurrence between 1868 and 1914. All other officers had to prove forty years of untarnished service.[6] Considering that forty years of service also meant an impending retirement, very few freshly ennobled officers were able to play an active role in the army of the post-1867 Dual Monarchy. This did not, however, mean the gradual disappearance of the new or service nobility from the officer corps. On the contrary, since military families continued to form the backbone of the corps, the sons and grandsons of ennobled officers constituted the majority of all noble officers.

Old Nobles and New

The nobility of the Dual Monarchy was ethnically as heterogeneous as the general population. It included very old Austrian princely families such as the Khevenhüllers or Starhembergs; great Bohemian landowning families such as the Schwarzenbergs, whose rise to fame was due to Habsburg favor in the seventeenth century;

---

*With one exception, I have culled the names of the military noble families from among general staff and war ministry officers listed in the *Militär-Schematismus* of 1880. The names of the old noble families have been selected from among the cavalry officers listed in the same book.

knights and other aristocrats from the former Holy Roman Empire; and great Catholic magnate families from Poland, Hungary, Croatia, and Italy. Alongside these were the hundreds of thousands of petty nobles living in the eastern parts of the monarchy. In addition, there were those families whose ancestors had been officers or bureaucrats and those who had been personally ennobled for their services. Finally, there were the descendants of immigrant foreign aristocrats. In view of the above, all statements about the "noble-dominated" Habsburg army and all statistical data regarding the presence of nobles in the officer corps require qualification. What sense does it make, for instance, to identify a general whose baronial title was just one more feather in his cap with a retired captain whose "von" before his name was the sole reward for a lifetime of assiduous and unappreciated service? And why list an officer as a commoner simply because he had not completed forty years in the army, while considering another to be a nobleman simply because he had already served his forty years?

Yet most Habsburg histories and statistical compilations offer us just such unrefined data on the relative proportion of nobles and commoners in the Austro-Hungarian army. In the Prussian, Russian, or British armies, the members of the old nobility were relatively easy to locate, for they served mainly in elite guards regiments. The Habsburg army, as we have said, had no guards regiments. Its court guards (Hungarian and Italian Noble Guards, the First Arcièren Body Guards, the Trabanten Body Guards, and the Horse Guards) were minuscule forces made up of a few dozen—mainly aristocratic—officers. Clearly, then, we must proceed with caution when estimating the proportion of nobles in the officer corps as a whole.

The only modern historian prepared to distinguish between the old and new, or service, nobility in the Habsburg army is Nikolaus von Preradovich, but his statistical sample is so small (from 21 to 61 highest-ranking generals, depending on the historical period) as to make his data only moderately useful.[7] Even so, his figures for 1878 and 1918 show a jump of such magnitude in the number and proportion of new nobles and commoners among the top generals that, no matter how small the sample, it cannot be ignored (see table 9.1). Preradovich's figures are made credible by an anonymous Austrian military writer in 1903, who calculated that approx-

Table 9.1. Old and New Nobles among the Highest-Ranking Generals in the Habsburg Army

Year	High Nobility	Old Nobility	New Nobles and Commoners	New Nobles and Commoners
		(absolute numbers)		(percentages)
1804	14	20	3	8
1847	9	17	2	7
1878	7	3	11	52
1918	4	11	46	75

Source: Nikolaus von Preradovich, *Die Führungsschichten in Österreich und Preussen 1804–1918, mit einem Ausblick zum Jahre 1945* ("Veröffentlichungen des Instituts für Europäische Geschichte Mainz," vol. 11; Wiesbaden, 1955), pp. 56–58.

Table 9.2. Nobles and Commoners among the Career Officers
of the Habsburg Army in 1896

Status	Absolute Number
Prince	37
Count	257
Marquess	2
Baron	495
Knight	722
"Edler von"	647
"von"	1,374
Total nobles	3,534
Total commoners	12,346
Total officers	15,580

Source: Karl Kandelsdorfer, "Der Adel im k.u.k. Offizierskorps," *Militärische
Zeitschrift* (1897):248–49.

imately 200, or two-thirds, of the monarchy's 301 generals were of non-noble
origin.[8]

By the end of the nineteenth century, military writers were turning their attention
increasingly to the question of the noble presence in the officer corps as a whole, but
not a single one of these writers seems to have been able or willing to distinguish
between the old and new nobility. On the other hand, they had no trouble in
distinguishing between the titled and untitled nobility. The most detailed statistics
on this issue were provided by Karl Kandelsdorfer, whose analysis appeared in 1897
in the Austrian *Militärische Zeitschrift*.[9] Some results of his compilations are shown
in table 9.2. Kandelsdorfer's data indicate that, in 1896, 28.6 percent of the career
officers (3,534 out of 15,580) belonged to the noble estate. In an attempt to differentiate between titled and lower nobility, we might legitimately classify the "Edler
von's" and "von's" as belonging to the latter group; this gives us 1,513 aristocrats
and 2,021 officers of the lower nobility. In other words, in 1896, 42.8 percent of the
noble officers belonged to the titled nobility. Note, however, that a large part,
perhaps the majority, of the titled nobles (especially among the knights and the
barons) belonged to the new or service nobility and were therefore not genuine
aristocrats.

Kandelsdorfer also provides us with revealing statistics on the uneven distribution of nobles among the various arms of service, thus offering one more clue to the
class character of each of them (table 9.3). Even if we disregard the generals, who
could have been ennobled individually, there was a marked social discrepancy
between the cavalry, general staff, and Jäger on the one hand and the infantry,
medics, and Train on the other.

Even within the individual service arms there were socially elite and nonelite
regiments, or at least regiments that were respectively favored or avoided by the
nobility. In the infantry regiments, for example, the proportion of noble officers
varied from 2 percent to 33 percent, in the Jäger battalions from 7 percent to 50

Table 9.3. Nobles among the Various Service Arms in 1896 (Percentages)

	0	10	20	30	40	50	60	70	80	90	100
Generals								72%			
Cavalry							58%				
General Staff				37%							
Jäger			24%								
Technical Units			21%								
Artillery		16%									
Infantry		14%									
Medics	6%										
Train (Transport)	6%										

Source: Karl Kandelsdorfer, "Der Adel im k.u.k. Offizierskorps," *Militärische Zeitschrift* (1897), p. 249.

percent, in the artillery regiments from none at all to 41 percent, and in the cavalry regiments from 32 percent to 75 percent. In fact, the cavalry was the only branch of service with several regiments boasting an absolute majority of noble officers. Among them, the 7th Dragoner from Bohemia and the 7th Husaren from Hungary counted as the most exclusive, with three out of four officers belonging to the nobility.[10]

What is one to make of all this information? First, in contrast to the situation in Prussia, the socially prestigious regiments were not necessarily the ones with the greatest historical tradition. There were a number of famous old regiments with fewer noble officers than some newer formations. Second, a regiment's recruiting area (not its garrison) provides a satisfactory explanation. Units originating from provinces in which the population was reputed to be both loyal and relatively well educated, as for instance Lower Austria, Bohemia, Moravia, and the Tyrol, boasted a higher proportion of noble officers than regiments recruited from backward Galicia. Finally, there were many more noble officers in the more prestigious arms of service.

As usual, the artillery and other technical formations do not fit into the general picture. Because their officers had to be well educated, the artillery, engineers, sappers, and the Railroad and Telegraph Regiment attracted far fewer noblemen than the prestige of these services might otherwise have warranted.

How aristocratic, in the final analysis, was the officer corps, and did the proportion of nobles change over time? Using my random sample of lieutenants, I have established that 19.5 percent (95 individuals) of the 487 officers in the 1870 cohort were noblemen. Of course, it was impossible to determine the origin of every noble patent, but I did find data on 64 of the 95 (see table 9.4). Admittedly, 64 names is a small sample with which to address the problem of thousands of officers, but it still

Table 9.4. Origin of Noble Patents of Sixty-Four Officers
in the 1870 Cohort

Origin of Noble Patent	Number	Percentage	
Acquired the title in person	23	35.9	54.6% service nobility
Title acquired by father or grandfather	12	18.7	
Old untitled nobility	16	25.0	45.3% old nobility
Old titled nobility	13	20.3	

seems plausible to argue that more than half of the young noble officers in 1870 belonged to the new or service nobility.

The gradual embourgeoisement of the officer corps in the second half of the nineteenth century is more difficult to prove, even though it was a well-known fact.[11] Comparing our 1870 cohort with that of 1900 would yield no satisfactory results, since the careers of the 1900 cohort were broken off in 1918, and there is thus no way of telling how many of these officers would have been ennobled in the course of their military careers. However, some other data are available.

The Austrian historian Ulf Sereinigg, although unable to differentiate between the old and the service nobility, demonstrates that the proportion of noblemen as a whole among field-grade officers (major to colonel) declined between 1880 and 1910. More specifically, according to Sereinigg, the proportion of majors with a noble predicate decreased from 37.7 percent to 18.2 percent between 1880 and 1910; that of lieutenant colonels, from 38.7 percent to 26.8 percent; and that of colonels, from 46.7 percent to 27.0 percent.[12] These figures become all the more significant if one considers that back in 1850 more than half of the field-grade officers had been noblemen.

Finally, Nikolaus von Preradovich reports that, whereas 90 percent of the high-ranking generals in 1859 were noblemen, the proportion had decreased to 41 percent by 1908, and to 25 percent by 1918. This is a remarkable change even when taking into account the fact that, in the 1850s, the thirty-year rule had applied and in the 1900s, the forty-year rule. What is significant is that, by the end of World War I, three out of four commanding generals in the Austro-Hungarian army were commoners.[13] Note that the Russian imperial officer corps underwent a similar process in the last decades before World War I.

Characteristically, the Hungarian National Guard had a far heavier noble representation—genuine nobles at that, not service nobles—than the Joint Army. In 1869–1870, when the honvéd army was created, three-fourths of the newly appointed field-grade officers belonged either to the Hungarian aristocracy (14 percent) or to the lower nobility (60 percent); by 1881, the proportion of nobles in the honvéd army had declined to one-half (10 percent titled, 39 percent lower nobility), but even this exceeded by far the proportion of the old nobility in the Joint Army.[14] Again characteristically, only a very small proportion of the field-grade officers in the Hungarian National Guard were sons of soldiers. In fact, the great majority of the honvéd army's first field-grade officers had fought in the revolutionary ranks in 1848–1849. (The minority too had been at war in 1848–1849, but in the Austrian, not in the Hungarian, ranks).[15] This again proves that the 1848–1849 revolution had been, to a large degree, the affair of the Magyar nobility—in truth, a very large social class.

The gradual decline of noble representation—especially of the old historic nobility—in the officer corps of the Joint Army shows the availability of other, financially more rewarding careers but also the growing indifference of the great nobility to the Habsburg cause. As the Bohemian, Galician, Hungarian, Croatian, and Italian aristocracy increasingly embraced local nationalist ideologies, fewer and fewer of their sons were willing to serve the supranational Joint Army. In 1905, for instance, seventy-five great noble families were represented by only ninety-five career officers in the Joint Army and Navy, a much smaller number than a few decades earlier. Moreover, sixty-six of the ninety-five were in the cavalry, and only six in the infantry, ten in the artillery, and four in the general staff.[16] Without any doubt, by the first decade of the twentieth century, the great Austro-Hungarian aristocratic families had begun to abandon their emperor.

10

Religion, Nationality, Advanced Training, and Career

What factors determined the success of an officer's career? How important to advancement were religion, nationality, social origins, connections, schools, or the type of advanced training courses he had attended? Was it all a question of seniority? Some of these considerations are distinctive of the structure of the Habsburg army; others not.

As we have seen, the historic titled nobility possessed the unwritten privilege of congregating in the more prestigious arms of service and, within each of these, in specific regiments. Moreover, aristocrats were usually better able than others to purchase a position in a regiment (as long as that system existed); in the prereform era they also enjoyed preferential treatment in promotions. Much of this ended, however, in the second half of the nineteenth century, with the army's increasing professionalization. By the end of the century, promotion in the aristocratic cavalry had fallen into line with that in the other service branches; some even claimed that aristocrats were discriminated against in the admission to the general staff, the ultimate elite institution.

Only one select group of individuals was assured a brilliant military career at all times: members of the House of Austria and a few other related princes. Francis Joseph demanded that his relatives become soldiers; he then promoted them at lightning speed, not in accordance with their achievement and talent but in keeping with their position in the family hierarchy. For example, in 1880, the army's only field marshal was Archduke Albrecht. In addition to him, there were eighteen archdukes in the armed forces: twelve generals, three colonels (including Crown Prince Rudolf, then twenty-two years of age), two lieutenants (including Francis Ferdinand, then seventeen), and a first lieutenant in the navy.[1] Crown Prince Rudolf was made an honorary colonel and regimental proprietor when he was two days old; at the age of twenty, he became an active colonel in charge of an infantry regiment as well as a naval captain. When he killed himself at the age of thirty-one, he had already been a two-star general for seven years. Francis Ferdinand became a colonel in the active service at twenty-seven; he ended up as inspector general of the monarchy's armed forces.

Not that archdukes performed merely nominal functions: the emperor saw to it that they did their duty. Their ability to assume high-level command positions was thought to flow naturally from their having been born into the august House. Francis Joseph promoted his relatives because he conceived of the army as a family posses-sion; only such an ideology can explain why, in 1880, Archduke Albrecht was inspector-general of the army, Archduke William (Wilhelm) inspector-general of the artillery, Archduke Leopold inspector-general of the engineering corps, Archduke Joseph commander in chief of the Hungarian National Guard, and the twenty-eight-year-old Archduke John (Johann) Salvator commander of an infantry division.[2]

Up the Promotional Ladder

The military of all countries has always allowed for a wide range of careers harbor-ing aging lieutenants and young generals; the Habsburg was definitely no exception. Not only revolutionary armies but conservative monarchical forces, too, have seen the meteoric rise of brilliant individuals. Eugene of Savoy became a commanding general when he was thirty-four; Joseph Radetzky was made a general at forty; and even in the second half of the nineteenth century it was still possible for Friedrich Beck to become a captain at the age of twenty-four. What distinguished such revolutionary forces as the French in the 1790s or the Hungarian in 1848–1849 from those more conservative was the fact that in the revolutionary armies not merely a select few but the great majority of officers were speedily promoted. Arthur Görgey became a commanding general in the revolutionary Hungarian national army at the age of thirty, and György Klapka at twenty-nine; in the Habsburg army, by all rights, they would still have been first lieutenants.

Lacking any representation on behalf of his interests, forbidden by regulations as well as personal dignity from speaking up on his own behalf, the average Habsburg officer, at least until the great army reforms of the 1860s and 1870s, watched more fortunate comrades sail through the ranks while he waited unendingly for one more star on his collar. Yet in few public institutions did rank count for more than it did in the military. A brisk career brought an officer good pay, access at least to "second society," challenging assignments, posting in a big city, a shower of decorations, elevation into the titled hereditary nobility, elite military schools and enhanced marriage prospects for his children. A slow career, on the other hand, meant poverty, social isolation, the ennui of a remote garrison, the deadly routine of training raw recruits, second-rate military schools for his children, and unquestion-ing obedience to his superiors who were often former classmates.

In contrast to the rank inflation of our days or even the pre–World War I period, promotion was agonizingly slow in every early-nineteenth-century army; it was particularly slow in the Habsburg forces because of the penury of the state. Wars brought relief, of course; during the Napoleonic Wars in particular there was no shortage of promotions. But when peace set in, after 1815, the process of promo-tions fell into stagnation. No wonder that each war, whether major or minor, was viewed as heavenly ordained by the officer corps. Of the 487 lieutenants in my first statistical sample (1870 cohort), a total of 305 (62.6 percent) had been commissioned in the war year 1866; during the ensuing year of peace, only 2 members of this group were commissioned. However, since only six of the sixty-six years between 1848 and 1914 were war years, we are concerned here primarily with the socially, politically, and psychologically far more interesting problem of peacetime promotions.

Around 1850, the career of a Habsburg officer depended on such factors as social origin, the ability to purchase a place in a regiment, and the goodwill of the regimental proprietor, as well as talent, luck, ambition, and educational qualifications. By the eve of World War I, noble birth was no longer of much use, the purchase of a position had faded into historical memory, and the power of regimental proprietors had long ago been eliminated. Now there was systematic promotion, not merely within one's regiment but within a general rank list encompassing an entire arm of service. The infantry, cavalry, field artillery, and so on each had its own rank list and its own promotion practices.

The increasing standardization of the military system between 1850 and 1914 gradually eliminated extreme career discrepancies. Promotion as a whole was speeded up and durability in service became the ultimate key to success. A general equalization of conditions likewise emerged among the several arms of service. Changes came slowly, however. In 1870, when the Austro-Hungarian forces began publishing detailed statistics, there were 13,263 active officers in the Joint Army, including the as yet insignificant number of reserve officers. Of the 267 colonels in active service, the youngest was thirty-seven and the oldest seventy. The average age of the colonels varied significantly, depending on their service branch. On the general staff, for example, only about two out of every ten colonels (18.75 percent) were forty-five years of age or older; in the infantry, the number was eight out of ten (84.55 percent), and among the Grenzer, nine out of ten (92.86 percent).

Statistics concerning the age distribution of the lieutenants are no less revealing. In 1870, only one out of the sixteen lieutenants in the cavalry (6.33 percent) was thirty-five years of age or older, compared with one out of seven lieutenants in the infantry (14.24 percent) and more than one of every two lieutenants (60.42 percent) in the Train.

No doubt, by 1870 the age differentials had become less extreme than they had been in the first half of the nineteenth century; still, as late as 1870 there were four Grenzer lieutenants aged fifty or older. On the general staff, the youngest lieutenant-colonel was thirty-five years of age; by contrast, among the sappers, the youngest lieutenant-colonel was fifty-one.[3]

In 1875, the military began publishing data on the average age of its officers in the different ranks (see table 10.1). What is remarkable is not only the large age gap separating the lieutenants, first lieutenants, and captains (nine and seven years, respectively), but also the great speed with which the select few who had made it to field-officer rank (majors and colonels) had been promoted (three and two years, respectively).

The same statistical report provided information on variations in age among the several arms of service. For instance, the average age of a colonel on the general

Table 10.1. Average Age of Career Officers in the Joint Army in 1875

Rank	Average Age	Absolute Number		Percentage
Lieutenant	26.2	3,589		
First lieutenant	35.3	4,171	11,111	89.0
Captain	42.7	3,351		
Major	46.4	606		
Lieutenant colonel	49.0	282	1,160	9.3
Colonel	50.9	272		
One-star general	56.0	115		
Two and three-star generals	58.0	92	208	1.7
Field marshal		1		
Total		12,479		100.0

Source: Militär-Statistisches Jahrbuch für das Jahr 1875, Part I (Vienna, 1878), pp. 153, 172, 175.

staff was 45.6; in the cavalry, 46.2; in the infantry, 51.8; and in the artillery, 55.0. In 1875, the average age of captains in the Joint Army ranged all the way from 34.8 on the general staff and 39.3 in the cavalry to 45.7 in the artillery and 49.2 in the Train.[4]

What can explain these differences? It should be remembered that the 1875 statistics still reflected careers begun well within the prereform age. This accounts for the relative success of the cavalry officers and, at the other end of the scale, for the slow promotion rate in the Train, which often received rejects from the other services. Yet the role of the Train was crucial in a military campaign, and at the time of mobilization, every career officer in this service would be put in charge of hundreds of reservists and a huge number of horses and wagons. Nothing, however, really seems to explain the lack of promotion opportunities among the highly trained artillery, engineer, and sapper officers. A nineteenth-century ditty summed up the plight of the gunners:

> Zwei Greise zogen durch das Land,
> ein Ober- und ein Leutenant
> Hauptleute werden sie leider nie,
> Denn beide sind von der Artillerie.

> [Hobbled, two oldsters move along the road,
> One a second lieutenant—the other a first
> Captain neither will ever be
> For they are from the artillery.][5]

Military reform put an end to much of the arbitrariness and disorganization of the promotion system. All promotions were now in the hands of the emperor or, in the case of the lower ranks, the minister of war: the result was increasing equalization and standardization.

In 1865 it was decreed that no captain over fifty years of age could be promoted to major; officers of field-officer rank could no longer be promoted if they had reached fifty-eight. Promotion was to be on the basis of seniority (*in der*

Rangstour); only battle-tested and particularly brave officers could be advanced without waiting for their turn (*aussertourliche Beförderung* or *Beförderung ausser der Rangstour*), and the promotion of these few was carefully regulated.

A decree of April 13, 1867, set a minimum number of years to be spent in each rank (four years, for instance, for a first lieutenant) and established an upper age limit for each rank. The rules on seniority were even more strictly defined. On the other hand, extraordinary promotions could thenceforth be made not only on the basis of battlefield heroism but also for outstanding personal qualities and accomplishments. An extraordinary promotion necessitated a petition by the evaluating commission to the emperor,* who formally granted such promotions, merely as a mark of "special favor." Among the subalterns serving with the troops, every sixth position was to be set aside for the beneficiaries of such extraordinary promotions.

The reforms of 1867 and subsequent years made promotion to field-officer's rank conditional on the successful completion of a special preparatory course. Promotion to colonel was made even more difficult and complicated.

Ulf Sereinigg has demonstrated that the promotion of officers was considerably accelerated between 1880 and 1910.[6] In this period, the average number of years needed to reach the rank of lieutenant colonel decreased from 28.8 to 27.7 years; to reach the rank of colonel they decreased from 30.5 to 28. Increasingly, only those officers judged worthy of ending up as colonels or generals were promoted to major. The others remained captains, and because an upper age limit was set on this rank, they were eventually obliged to resign from the corps. More and more of the successful officers had been to general staff school and served on the general staff. For instance, in 1880 only 10 percent of the colonels had completed general staff school, but by 1910, the proportion had increased to 38 percent.[7]

All this made the officer corps more than ever resemble a steep pyramid that was exceedingly difficult to negotiate. In 1911, the last year when such statistics were published, the career officer corps was divided as is shown in table 10.2.

Clearly, this was no operetta army, top-heavy with brass. Nor were there too many career officers for the number of men in active service. The latter numbered 326,080 in 1911, giving us a career officer to enlisted man ratio of 1:18 (not counting the 603,368 men in the reserve and the 533,418 in the supplementary reserve [*Ersatzreserve*], whose periodic training also fell to the 18,506 career officers and 13,293 reserve officers).[8]

Religious Confessions

The Habsburgs were the quintessential Catholic dynasty, and their army was a traditional bulwark of Roman Catholicism. In the sixteenth and seventeenth cen-

---

*"Captain Alexander Dini is an officer of excellent character traits and intellectual qualifications, and he is imbued with the most serious strivings in military affairs as well as in the sciences," wrote a commission composed of four superior officers in the 16th k.k. Landwehr Infantry Regiment, on December 2, 1902, at Troppau, in its two-page report to the emperor. Captain Dini received his extraordinary promotion to major in 1906, when he was forty-five years of age. (*Qualifikations-Liste* of Alexander Dini, Kriegsarchiv, Vienna.)

turies, the dynasty fought its many wars either in the name of Christianity, against the Ottoman Turks, or in the name of Catholic restoration, against the Protestant German princes and domestic Protestants. Maria Theresa was, depending on the issue, an enlightened ruler and a bigoted Catholic. Under Joseph II, however, the Catholic church was put at the service of the state, rather than being able to use the state for its own ends. True, during the post-Napoleonic conservative restoration, and then again in the 1850s, the church regained some of its former influence and power, but this no longer affected the Habsburg army. At no tir ɔ in the nineteenth century was much significance attributed to an officer's confessional affiliation, even though such an affiliation and the concomitant payment of a church tax remained compulsory for all citizens in both halves of the monarchy. Only at the end of the century did it become possible to declare oneself to be "without a confession" (*konfessionslos*), in a wearying and complex procedure. Characteristically, an officer's confessional affiliation is almost never mentioned in the memoirs and biographies; we must look for it in his *Qualifikations-Liste*.

When he was in the United States as a revolutionary exile, Louis Kossuth insisted that the Hungarian revolution of 1848–1849 had been a Protestant struggle against the reactionary Catholic Habsburgs. Yet there is no evidence to show that his army had had a strong Protestant contingent. On the contrary, the composition of the Hungarian honvéd officer corps in 1848–1849 closely reflected the country's confessional makeup. The only group somewhat underrepresented among the field-grade officers and captains of the Hungarian national army was the Eastern Orthodox, for the simple reason that Orthodoxy was most common among Hungary's Romanian and Serbian minorities, ethnic groups that were generally opposed to the Hungarian revolution.[9]

After the introduction of universal conscription in 1868, the confessional makeup of the rank and file rather faithfully mirrored that of the monarchy's population in general. Only Muslims and Jews were somewhat underrepresented, the first because conscription began much later in Bosnia-Hercegovina, the home of most of the Muslims, than elsewhere in the monarchy, and the second for reasons that I shall

Table 10.2. Career Officers in the Joint Army by Rank in 1911

Rank	Absolute Number		Percentage	
Lieutenant	4,641		25.7	
First lieutenant	5,832	15,608	32.3	86.4
Captain	5,135		28.4	
Major	1,299		7.2	
Lieutenant colonel	548	2,203	3.0	12.2
Colonel	356		2.0	
One-star general	144			
Two-star general	69	245	1.4	
Three-star general	32			
Total	18,506		100.0	

Source: *Militärstatistisches Jahrbuch für das Jahr 1911* (Vienna, 1912), pp. 143–45.
Note: Includes only those in active service in that year.

Table 10.3. Confessional Distribution in Austria-Hungary and in the Joint Army in 1911 (Percentages)

Religious Affiliation	General Population	Joint Army		
		Rank and File	Reserve Officers	Career Officers
Roman Catholic	65.9	66.2	68.2	86.0
Greek and Armenian Catholic (Uniate)	10.6	10.9	1.2	1.0
Greek and Armenian Orthodox	8.7	9.1	1.7	2.7
Lutheran	3.5	4.3	8.6	7.8
Reformed (Calvinist)	5.4	5.5	3.0	1.8
Unitarian	?	0.2	0.1	0.1
Other Christian	?	—	0.1	—
Jewish	4.4	3.0	17.0	0.6
Muslim	1.2	0.8	—	—
No confession	?	—	0.1	—
Total	100.0	100.0	100.0	100.0

Source: *Militärstatistisches Jahrbuch für das Jahr 1911* (Vienna, 1912), pp. 145, 147, and Alexander Sixtus von Reden, *Österreich-Ungarn. Die Donaumonarchie in historischen Dokumenten* (Salzburg, 1984), p. 67.

analyze below, in the section on Jewish soldiers. At the same time, given their differing social and educational profiles, the several confessional groups were un-evenly distributed in the different service branches.[*10]

The confessional distribution of the officers reflected both the varying size of the educated elite in each group and the varying degree of their dynastic loyalty. Table 10.3 shows the confessional makeup of the officer corps in 1911, the last year when comprehensive statistics were published.[11] What is striking is the enormous over-representation of Roman Catholics among the career officers, testifying to the Habsburg army's special appeal to the Catholic elite. The significant underrepresen-tation of the Eastern confessions in the career and reserve officer corps shows the relatively small size of educated elites among the Serbs, Romanians, and Ruthenes. The situation with regard to members of the Reformed Church points to another problem. Clearly, the Calvinists were better represented among the reserve than among the career officers, which shows that an educated elite was available to fill the ranks of the career officer corps but that members of the Reformed Church were less likely to become career officers than, for instance, Catholics.

Calvinism was most widespread among the Magyar population, which tended to regard the Reformed Church as a Magyar national institution. The result was that, in 1900, when members of the Reformed Church constituted 12.7 percent of the

*In 1872, for instance, when Catholics (made up mostly of Germans, Magyars, Czechs, Poles, Croats, and Italians) constituted 67.7 percent of the Joint Army's rank and file, their proportion among the army engineers was 94.3 percent and in the Train only 56.5 percent. Conversely, whereas Greek Orthodox soldiers (that is, mostly Serbs, Romanians, and Ruthenes) constituted 9.3 percent of the Joint Army's rank and file, their proportion among the army engineers was only 0.2 percent and in the Train, 12.7 percent. (*Militär-Statistisches Jahrbuch für das Jahr 1872*, Part I [Vienna, 1875], pp. 171-72, 202-3.)

population in the lands of the Hungarian Holy Crown, Calvinists made up only 5.4 percent of the total in my 1900 sample cohort of Hungarian-born Joint Army lieutenants but 17.5 percent of the total in my sample cohort of honvéd lieutenants. In other words, by the turn of the century, the Calvinist elites much preferred the Hungarian national army to the Joint Army. Most dramatic is the extraordinary overrepresentation of Jews, in 1911, in the reserve officer corps, but I shall address that phenomenon later, in the section on Jewish soldiers.

The army remained generally indifferent to the confessional affiliation of its members as long as they performed their religious obligation, which meant no more than being led to church on Sunday or on the Sabbath. The handful who had been officially recognized as being without confession were usually dispatched by the platoon sergeants to a synagogue, a determination which was, one must admit, generally not far from the mark.

The army was provided with a generous contingent of chaplains, who were, as elsewhere, the subject of much ridicule. In 1910, the Joint Army roster included 178 career and 244 reserve chaplains, none of whom ranked below captain. We find among them 6 *Feldrabbiner in der Reserve* (by 1918, their number had grown to 76) and 4 *Militärimame,* the latter charged with serving the spiritual needs of Muslim soldiers.[12]

Jewish Soldiers

There was a unique relationship between a confessionally tolerant monarchy and the Jews, who were among its most loyal citizens. The Habsburg government had opened the way to the emancipation of its Jewish subjects with patents of toleration in the late 1780s; Austria as well as Hungary formally emancipated the Jews in the 1860s. The monarchy outdid the other European powers in admitting Jews into its officer corps; without it, the process of Jewish integration into business, industry, education, the arts, and the administration would have been decidedly more difficult. Yet, as we have seen, the process of Jewish integration was far more real in the reserve than in the career officer corps. Moreover, around the turn of the century, a declining Jewish presence among the officers began.

Four periods of development can be detected with regard to Jewish officers: the first half of the nineteenth century, when basically only converts could make a career; the liberal period, between the 1860s and the end of the century, when Jewish participation in the corps increased rapidly; a period of decline in the years before 1914; and the Great War, when the number of Jewish officers again rose rapidly until they constituted a very significant part of the corps.*

Early History

It all began with Joseph II's 1788 decree, which obliged Jews of military age to serve in the transportation corps. A year later, the Galician Jewish Regulation

---

*Altogether, 25,000 Jewish officers may have served between 1914 and 1918 (more attention will be devoted to this later, in the chapter on the officers in the First World War).

(*Judenverordnung*) opened the ranks of the infantry to Jewish volunteers.[13] At that time, there were about 70,000 Jews in the Austrian provinces; 100,000 in Hungary, and 170,000 in newly acquired Galicia, amounting altogether to close to 2 percent of the monarchy's population.[14]

At first, the notion of Jews performing military service was as abhorrent to the army high command as it was to Jewish religious leaders. The Court War Council objected that the Jews were by nature not fit for service, and that the Jewish dietary laws as well as the prohibition of work on the Sabbath would make Jewish soldiers worthless. For their part, the Jewish leaders worried about the corruption of young Jews in the military and about their being forced to kill their co-religionists in foreign armies. Nonetheless, "enlightened" Jews rejoiced over this significant step toward emancipation, and soon even the Orthodox relented. Thus, Rabbi Eszekiel Landau of Prague advised the first Jewish soldiers conscripted in that city:

> Serve your Emperor loyally but do not forget your religion either. . . . Grease the wheels of the waggons for your comrades on Sundays, so that they will do the same for you on the Sabbath. As long as you are not able to buy meat from Jews, eat only butter and cheese and whatever else we [Jews] are permitted to eat.[15]

Because the army was not yet cooking for its soldiers, the Jewish recruits could easily prepare their own meals. In any case, during the first years following the decrees of Joseph II, only a handful of Jews served in the army, since the laws on conscription allowed for many exemptions, and even those who had been called up were permitted to buy their freedom with a cash payment.[16]

During the Napoleonic Wars, cash redemption was suspended and, during the same period, the first Jewish officers were commissioned.[17] After 1814, however, a reactionary period began when only Jewish converts made it into the combat branches. On the other hand, Jews were allowed to enter the military medical academy, the famous Josephinum; thereafter, the Jewish Regimentsarzt (regimental medical officer; captain's rank) came to be a legendary figure in the Habsburg armed forces.[18]

In 1848–1849 many Jews participated in the Vienna revolution, and in Hungary the majority of Jewish communities embraced the cause of Louis Kossuth, partly because of the growing assimilationist trend among them, and partly because of the proemancipation policy of the Hungarian liberal leaders. In the war between Austria and Hungary, thousands of Hungarian Jews served in the national army. (It is true that at least as many Hungarian Jews served in the Habsburg forces.) The honvéd army commissioned a great number of Jews; one or two even made it to major, the highest rank awarded in the revolutionary forces to any nonprofessional soldier. This infuriated the Austrian high command, which subsequently imposed heavy fines on several Jewish communities. Other Jews were imprisoned.[19] Nonetheless, there seems to have been no discrimination against Jewish soldiers loyal to the dynasty.

One example of such a brilliant, if somewhat incomprehensible career, was that of the Jew Karl Strass (also spelled Strahs in the documents), who was born in Bohemia in 1828 and who volunteered for a Jäger battalion in December 1848.[20] Within four months, Strass was commissioned a lieutenant and was transferred to a Dragoner cavalry regiment. Five months later, in December 1849, he was made a first lieutenant in the emperor's 2nd Hungarian Hussar regiment. Although only twenty-one, he had already had a career worthy of an archduke. Nonetheless, he did not convert, either then or later. Strass had not earned his promotions on the battlefield: he had been attached, throughout the war, to the military chancellery of Field Marshal Windisch-Graetz. He was pensioned off in 1861 as a semi-invalid, at the age of thirty-three, with the rank of captain I. class and thereafter performed only garrison duty. We must assume that Strass was very wealthy and had been able to purchase his promotions.

Jewish Recruits after 1867

Even before the Compromise Agreement of 1867, the number of Jewish soldiers had grown steadily. Thus, in the wars of 1859 and 1866, between 10,000 and 20,000 Jews served in the Habsburg army.[21] Following the introduction of universal conscription, the number of Jewish recruits increased dramatically, approaching the proportion of Jews in the general population. In 1872 the Joint Army included 12,471 Jewish enlisted men in the reserve and on active duty, representing 1.5 percent of the total. By 1902, their number and proportion had grown to 59,784, or 3.9 percent of the total; this at a time when Jews constituted about 4.5 percent of the monarchy's population. Thereafter, however, the number and proportion of the Jewish rank and file declined steadily, falling to 46,064, or 3.1 percent, in 1911. I have no sure way to explain this decline, for even though the proportion of Jews in the general population declined slightly, to about 4.4 percent, the proportion of the Jewish rank and file decreased even more significantly.[22] One reason for the decline must have been the massive Jewish emigration to America, which depleted primarily the younger age group; another reason was the high number of Jewish "one-year volunteers." Perhaps also, proportionally more Jews than Gentiles evaded active service by claiming ill health, economic necessity, or head-of-family status. Finally, the draft boards may have become more reluctant to take in Jews. In any case, no contemporary source I know even makes note of this interesting development, to say nothing of proffering an explanation.

In the years before World War I, the Jewish rank and file continued to be unevenly distributed among the several arms of service, as were the other ethnic and confessional groups. In 1911, the Jewish rank and file were greatly overrepresented among the medics (6.4 percent), and considerably underrepresented among the Jäger (1.8 percent) and cavalry (1.4 percent), a state of affairs that requires no further explanation.[23]

Jewish Reserve Officers

The Austro-Hungarian system of selecting and training reserve officers, instituted in 1868, was virtually identical with that of Prussia and the other German states. Between 1885 and 1914, the Prussian army trained some 30,000 Jewish officer candidates, yet none was given a reserve officer's commission. Not that the law forbade such a thing; it was simply that the king, the Prussian Ministry of War, and the regimental officers' assemblies silently conspired to prevent the commissioning of Jews.[24] We have no data on the total number of Jews who completed "one-year volunteer" service in the Austro-Hungarian forces in the same period, but we have precise statistics on the number of Jewish reserve officers in any given year. Thus, in 1897, the first time Austro-Hungarian military statistics began to differentiate between career and reserve officers, the Joint Army had 1,993 Jewish reserve officers, representing 18.7 percent of the total reserve officer corps. In the same year, the Joint Army had 680 Jewish reserve military officials, representing 21 percent of that service group. The proportion of Jewish reserve officers and reserve military officials in the Hungarian National Guard was even higher. This meant that in 1897 every fifth reserve officer and nearly every fourth reserve military official of the Habsburg armed forces was a Jew. True, numbers began to decline thereafter to the point that, by 1911, there were only 1,871 Jewish reserve officers (17 percent) in the Joint Army. Still, the fact remains that, with nearly 2,000 reservists, the Joint Army included many more Jewish officers than any other army.

The distribution of Jewish reserve officers among the various service arms was uneven. In 1911, every third reserve officer (30.3 percent) in the Train was an Israelite, and in the fortress artillery, every fifth reserve officer (20.0 percent). In the cavalry, the proportion was only 6.2 percent, yet even this meant that there were 63 Jews among the 1,007 reserve cavalry officers.[25]

The large number of Jewish reserve officers and officials can be easily explained by the existence of a large Jewish educated stratum. In 1903–1904, for instance, Jews made up between 13 and 14 percent of the student body in Austrian high schools, and 15.6 percent of the students in Austrian universities and technical academies. The proportion of Jewish students in Hungarian high schools and universities was even higher: fully 23 percent of those who had completed secondary school in Hungary between 1909 and 1911 were Jews.[26] The fact that the proportion of Jewish reserve officers closely resembled that of the Jews in the monarchy's high schools and universities shows that the army was willing to commission Jewish one-year volunteers, and that the regimental officers' assemblies did not object to Jewish officers.

Jewish Career Officers

In 1897, the Joint Army had 178 Jewish career subalterns and field-grade officers, or 1.2 percent of the total. In the same year, Jewish career military officials numbered 369, or 12.7 percent of the total. It is true that, by 1911, the number of Jewish career subalterns and field-grade officers had declined to 109, or 0.6 percent of the total, and that of the Jewish career military officials to 251, or 7.4 percent, but even these figures were higher than the number and proportion of Jewish career officers in the Prussian peacetime army, which was zero.[27] The distribution of these officers among the several arms of service closely resembled the pattern we have seen among the reserve officers and the enlisted men: in 1911, 1.9 percent of the career officers serving as medics were Jews; in the infantry, their proportion was 0.8 percent; and in the cavalry, a paltry 0.1 percent (2 individuals).[28]

The question again is, what caused the decline between 1897 and 1911? One reason was the officer shortage in the 1870s, when educated young civilians, thus also Jews, were readily accepted in the corps, after a relatively brief training. These officers were still in service in 1897, but only exceptionally in 1911. We could also point to the gradual assimilation of educated Jews into the Hungarian, Czech, and Polish nations. As Jews embraced the patriotic ideology of their host nations, they may have become less enthusiastic about a career in the supranational Joint Army. Nor can anti-Semitism be excluded as a factor, though anti-Jewish attitudes in Austria-Hungary were certainly no more advanced in the first decade of the twentieth century than they had been in the 1880s, the worst period of popular anti-Semitism.

In 1901, that is, before statistics began to show a decline in the number of Jewish officers, *Dr. Bloch's Wochenschrift* in Vienna pointed out that while there were many Jewish doctors in the army medical corps, and while an earlier war minister, General Ferdinand Bauer, had not hesitated to promote four Jewish medical officers to general's rank, the new war minister, General Edmund Krieghammer, was systematically denying study stipends to Jewish doctors interested in pursuing a military career; he had made it nearly impossible for Jewish reserve medical officers to become career soldiers. The *Wochenschrift* drew the attention of Jewish physicians to the Austrian National Guard, where there was a great shortage of doctors and where the minister of defense, General Count Welserheimb, was free of any bias. Again, three years later, the *Monatsschrift der Österreichisch-Israelitischen Union* complained of a significant reduction in the number of Jewish combat and medical officers in the Joint Army, attributing it to anti-Semitism.[29]

Undoubtedly, there was something ominous about the decline in the proportion of Jewish career officers from 1.2 percent to 0.6 percent in only fourteen years, and in the simultaneous decline in the proportion of Jewish career military officials from 12.7 percent to 7.4 percent. Perhaps the decline in the latter group was caused as much by the growing reluctance of Jewish doctors to seek a financially unrewarding career in the army as by the anti-Semitism of an occasional war minister or by the well-known bigotry of Francis Ferdinand. One thing is certain: Francis Joseph himself never wavered in his religious tolerance and his appreciation of the loyalty of Jews.

It is another question whether the Gentile career officers ever truly accepted their Jewish comrades. In this respect, the reserve officers represented only a minor problem because, as a general rule, career officers maintained cordial relations with reservists only while in service. As for relations between Gentile and Jewish career officers, the few sources we have insist that they were absolutely proper.[30]

It would be good to know what prompted a Jew to become a professional officer in the Habsburg army. Unfortunately, no relevant memoirs appear to exist, and the biographical material written by Jewish authors recount only the achievements, not the motives of the Jewish career officers. On the one hand, there must have been the lure of a prestigious elite institution and the perceived opportunity to assimilate completely; on the other was a lifestyle completely alien to Jewish tradition. Clearly, the few Jewish career officers represented an exception to the general Jewish experience.

A biographical compendium on Jewish career officers was prepared by Lieutenant Moritz Frühling in 1911.[31] It does not list those officers who were still in active service in the year of publication and says almost nothing about the background and education of the officers. Nonetheless, Frühling offers data on individual officers' careers and indicates their birthplace. According to him, between 1848 and 1910, a total of 987 Jewish career officers served in the Joint Army (372 in the combat branches, 469 in the army medical corps, 61 as troop accountants of officer's rank, 55 in other branches of military officialdom, and 30 as naval officers). The highest rank achieved by a Jewish career officer in the combat branches was that of two-star general, but this particular promotion was made only after the individual's retirement. The highest rank reached by a Jew in the medical corps was that of Generaloberstabsarzt, a two-star general's rank; among the military officials, one-star general, the highest possible for that service; and in the navy, rear admiral, although this too was granted only upon the officer's retirement. Altogether, Frühling knew of 19 Jews who had been promoted to general before 1911: 11 of them were medical officers, and one another type of military official. Of the 7 Jewish generals in the combat forces (6, army; one, navy), only 2 achieved general's rank while on active duty; the others received their promotion following retirement.[32]

As stated before, Frühling says little about the social origin of the Jewish career officers, but it is still clear from his compendium that only a very few among them had attended such elite schools as the Wiener Neustadt Military Academy.*

No doubt these officers were assimilationist: of the twenty-three pre-1911 Jewish generals and colonels in the army's combat branches, fourteen converted at various points during their career, some only at the very end. Conversion was not, however, a must for becoming a general: the highest-ranking Jewish officer in the Joint Army, Feldmarschalleutnant Eduard Ritter von Schweitzer, never converted. Schweitzer, who was born in Hungary in 1844, entered the army as an enlisted man in 1865 and was commissioned in 1870. He fought in the war against Prussia and in 1878 participated in the occupation of Bosnia-Hercegovina. The latter brought him the Order of the Iron Crown, which elevated him to knighthood. He completed general staff school but, despite his fine record there, was not taken into the general staff. Nevertheless, he became a Generalmajor, in 1904, and was put in charge of an infantry brigade. He retired a year later and was subsequently awarded the title of a two-star general. Legend has it that the old Schweitzer regularly attended synagogue in Budapest, kept a kosher diet, and requested and received permission not to eat forbidden food when dining with the emperor.[33]

There was also a General Alexander Ritter von Eiss, who, rather than converting, became a Zionist in old age. Eiss, who was born in Moravia in 1832, volunteered for a Jäger battalion in 1848. Having participated in the Hungarian campaign, he was commissioned a lieutenant in 1855. He fought at Magenta in 1859 and at Custozza in 1866. For bravery in the latter encounter, he was decorated with the Iron Crown Order Third-Class and became a Ritter. In 1859, Eiss transferred to the Austrian Landwehr as a colonel and regimental commander. He remained in service until 1895. Eleven years later, he was given the title of one-star general. He subse-

---

*In the academic year 1909–1910, a total of fifteen Jewish students were enrolled in the military schools of the Joint Army. Of them, one was at the Technical Military Academy and none at the Military Academy. (*Österreichisches Statistisches Handbuch 1910* [Vienna, 1911], p. 461.)

quently appeared, dressed in his general's uniform, at several Zionist meetings. His three sons also became career officers: two were killed in World War I, and the third received the extremely rare Gold Medal for Bravery.[34]

The most successful officer of Jewish origin served in the Hungarian National Guard, which as I have said before, was particularly sympathetic to Jews. This was in part because of the shortage of qualified officer candidates in the Hungarian Landwehr, and in part because of the Hungarian desire to speed up the assimilation of Jews into the Magyar nation. In fact, many in the Hungarian Jewish elite were among the fiercest Magyar patriots. Baron Sámuel Hazai (his original name was Kohn) was born in Hungary in 1851, the son of a well-to-do spirits manufacturer. He and his two brothers entered the honvéd army as enlisted men. Hazai was commissioned in 1876 and soon thereafter converted. He attended general staff school and then taught at the Hungarian military academy. In 1900, he became a colonel of the general staff, attached to the honvéd army; by 1910 he was already a general; and between 1910 and 1917, he served as Hungary's minister of defense.

To be sure, Hazai was not the only Hungarian cabinet member of Jewish origin; one of them, the minister of justice, had not even converted. In 1917, Emperor-King Charles promoted Hazai to Generaloberst and made him chief of mobilization and supply. As such, Hazai was the second most important officer of the Austro-Hungarian armed forces after the chief of general staff.[35]

Nationality

In view of the Habsburg monarchy's complex ethnic webbing, it would be most important to know in what ways nationality influenced service in the armed forces, and what effect it had on careers. Unfortunately, such concrete questions cannot lead to concrete answers, in part because of the uncertainty of all ethnic statistics, and in part because of the army's official disinterest in the matter.

The military statistical yearbooks published for the years 1870 to 1911 contain numerous statistics on the ethnic makeup of the Joint Army, but the statistics (and the Vienna War Archive) provide no indication as to how these figures were arrived at. Recruits—and hence also the "one-year volunteers," destined to become reserve officers—had their mother tongue entered in the registers upon induction, and we must assume that this was the information the yearbooks used for their comprehensive nationality (*Nationalitäten*) statistics. We do not know, however, how mother tongue was determined. Even if we assume that it was the recruit himself who gave that information, the many thousands, or perhaps millions, who were bilingual might have given the kind of answer they believed the authorities wanted to hear. Moreover, unlike the Austrian and Hungarian civilian statistical compilations, army statistics allowed for no "other nationalities," alongside the standard ones. This means that those who spoke Friulian (a language spoken in what is today northeastern Italy), Armenian, Greek, Turkish, or Romani (Gypsy) were assigned arbitrarily to one of the major linguistic groups. Jews were registered as Germans, Czechs, Poles, or Magyars, depending on where they lived.

Military students were asked about their mother tongue upon entering, but

Table 10.4. Nationalities in Austria-Hungary and in the Monarchy's Joint Army, 1910

Nationality Group	General Population			Rank and File (Active and Reserve)	
	Absolute number (thousands)	Percentage		Absolute number	Percentage
Germans	12,007	23.4		375,015	25.2
Magyars	10,056	19.6		344,210	23.1
Czechs and	6,442⎫ 8,410	12.5⎫ 16.3		191,878⎫ 245,046	12.9⎫ 16.5
Slovaks	1,968⎭	3.8⎭		53,168⎭	3.6⎭
Poles	4,968	9.7		118,168	7.9
Ruthenes (Ukrainians)	3,998	7.8		113,931	7.6
Croats and Serbs	4,381	8.5		134,019	9.0
Slovenes	1,256	2.4		36,361	2.4
Romanians	3,224	6.3		103,814	7.0
Italians	768	1.5		19,510	1.3
Others	2,314	4.5	Bulgarians	385	—
Monarchy total	51,390	100.0		1,490,459	100.0

Sources: Militärstatistisches Jahrbuch für das Jahr 1910 (Vienna, 1911), pp. 145–46.

because their ethnic statistics differ so wildly from those of the career officers—as we shall soon see—we must suspect that some other method was used to determine the nationality of the latter group. Maybe career officers were asked to provide information about their *Umgangssprache,* the language they most commonly used in everyday affairs. Hence the relatively small proportion of Germans among the military students, and the enormously large proportion of Germans among the career officers in military statistics. It is inconceivable, after all, that non-German military students should have had three or four times the dropout rate of Germans. In fact, only an insignificant proportion of students dropped out of military schools.

Let us first turn to the only category on which we have specific ethnic data for the entire period between 1870 and 1911, namely, the ordinary soldiers.

The Rank and File

Table 10.4 clearly indicates that the army did not hesitate to enlist the services of all the nationalities. The somewhat elevated proportion of German and Magyar enlisted men relative to the representation of these groups in the general population may well reflect a lesser willingness on their part to use the loopholes available to those who wished to avoid military service. The opposite may apply to the Poles and Italians. In view of the small number of men actually inducted, the army could afford to be choosy; still, the poverty and poor health of the Galician population must be ruled out as a factor in the relative scarcity of Polish soldiers, as the even poorer Ruthenes (Ukrainians) were not underrepresented.

Since the statistics in table 10.4 tell us nothing of the army's possible bias against one or another ethnic group, let us turn to the ethnic distribution among the

Table 10.5. Rank and File in Selected Service Arms of the Monarchy's Joint Army, Active and Reserves 1911 (Percentages)

Nationality Group	Rank and File	Infantry	Jäger	Cavalry	Field and Mountain Artillery	Fortress Artillery	Train	Medics	Absolute Number
Germans	24.8	22.2	42.7	20.3	29.6	37.1	19.0	32.2	362,804
Magyars	23.3	24.6	7.1	33.6	22.5	13.6	33.1	23.4	340,042
Czechs	12.6	12.8	12.2	15.7	11.3	11.4	11.9	10.5	184,409
Slovaks	3.6	4.0	4.8	1.0	4.8	2.1	3.0	3.0	51,971
Poles	7.9	7.6	4.0	11.2	9.2	10.4	8.3	7.0	114,968
Ruthenes (Ukrainians)	7.8	8.5	3.1	10.3	8.8	8.1	6.4	6.0	114,741
Croats and Serbs	9.2	8.2	2.7	4.6	5.9	3.9	11.9	8.4	134,717
Slovenes	2.5	2.3	3.8	1.4	2.5	6.7	1.7	2.4	36,429
Romanians	7.0	9.5	3.7	1.9	4.8	3.4	4.5	5.8	102,795
Italians	1.3	0.3	15.9	0	0.6	3.3	0.2	1.3	19,528
Bulgarians	0	0	0	0	0	0	0	0	462
Absolute number		865,849	82,543	100,013	144,968	49,125	56,401	30,197	1,462,866

Source: *Militärstatistisches Jahrbuch für das Jahr 1911* (Vienna, 1912), pp. 146–47, 196–97.

various service arms. The uneven ethnic representation revealed in table 10.5 resulted from variations in the recruiting area, tradition, and educational as well as technical requirements of the several service branches. The infantry, for example, took in mostly young peasants—hence the overrepresentation of a "peasant nationality" such as the Romanian. The Jäger recruited primarily in the western provinces of the monarchy—hence the high proportion of Germans and Italians. The latter group, largely concentrated in the South Tyrol, tended to be drafted into the four regiments of the Tyrolian Kaiserjäger. The cavalry drew a disproportionate number of Magyars (Husaren), Poles and Ruthenes (Ulanen), and Czechs (Dragoner). By contrast, the mountain-dwelling Slovaks, Slovenes, and Italians scarcely figured in the cavalry lists. The artillery (and engineers) favored the better-educated and technologically trained Germans and Slovenes and looked askance at the generally-less-well-educated Serbs, Croats, and Romanians. The Magyars (including Hungarian Jews) were vastly overrepresented in the transportation corps, and Germans provided one-third of the medics. All in all, it can be argued that, far from being motivated by ethnic bias—as its critics contended—the Joint Army distributed its recruits among the various service branches on the basis of practical considerations.

Reserve Officers

Unlike the rank and file, officers were not recruited at all evenly from the various national groups. The number and proportion of the officers reflected the varying class structure, wealth, education, dynastic loyalty, and military tradition of each group. They might also have reflected the ethnic bias of the army leadership. Let us first compare the ethnic distribution of the Joint Army's rank and file with that of the reserve officers, a group whose ethnic statistics are far less problematical than those of the career officers (see tables 10.6 and 10.7).

The question is why Slovaks, Poles, Ruthenes, Croats, Serbs, and Romanians were so grievously underrepresented among the reserve officers. Statistics computed by the Hungarian historian László Katus shed some light on the situation (see table 10.8). However, even after taking into account the fact that the proportion of educated youngsters among the monarchy's Germans vastly surpassed the percentage among other ethnic groups (except for Magyars, Czechs, and Italians), we must still search for an explanation as to why Ruthenes, to give but one example, were virtually nonexistent in the reserve officer corps (0.3 percent in 1910, a total of thirty-four individuals).[36] Certainly, a much higher percentage of Ruthenes had finished high school and thus qualified for one-year volunteer service. Ethnic prejudice could be a partial answer, although such an explanation is contradicted by the enormous overrepresentation of Jews in the reserve officer corps. After all, in contrast to official policy, many officers certainly viewed the Jews as a separate, alien, and less than attractive race. Rather than ethnic bias, then, the explanation for the scarcity of Ruthenes and others is probably the following: (1) the eagerness of the educated elite among the Ruthenes to "pass" as Poles in Galicia, and among the Romanians and Serbs to "pass" as Magyars in Hungary; (2) the great advantage enjoyed by Jews and Czechs—almost all of whom spoke German—over educated Ruthenes, Croats, Serbs, and Romanians, whose second language was likely to be Hungarian, Czech, or Polish; (3) the increasingly dynamic nationalism, by 1910–1911, of the Slavic, Romanian, and Italian social elites, which led them to shun military service or, if that could not be avoided, to shun a reserve officer's commission. It was a strong political statement on the part of an educated Ruthene in

Table 10.6. Reserve Officers in the Austro-Hungarian Joint Army, by Nationality, 1910 (Percentages)

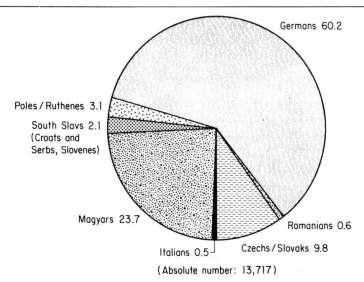

Germans 60.2

Poles / Ruthenes 3.1

South Slavs 2.1 (Croats and Serbs, Slovenes)

Magyars 23.7

Italians 0.5

Czechs / Slovaks 9.8

Romanians 0.6

(Absolute number: 13,717)

Table 10.7. Rank and File in the Austro-Hungarian Joint Army, by Nationality, 1910
(Percentages)

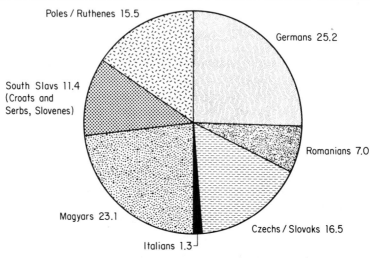

Poles / Ruthenes 15.5

Germans 25.2

South Slavs 11.4
(Croats and
Serbs, Slovenes)

Romanians 7.0

Magyars 23.1

Czechs / Slovaks 16.5

Italians 1.3

(Absolute number: 1,490,459)

Source: *Militärstatistisches Jahrbuch für das Jahr 1910* (Vienna, 1911), pp. 143, 145–46.

Galicia not to call himself a Pole, just as it was for an educated Slovak, Serb, or
Romanian not to identify himself as a Magyar in Hungary. Others of their national
group had long embraced the notion of assimilation to the locally dominant nationality. The situation in Bohemia was more complicated, since the Czechs had
become, for all practical purposes, the dominant nationality there. Hence, the

Table 10.8. High-School, Technical-Academy, and University Students Relative to Total
Population for Ethnic Groups Defined by Mother Tongue (Hungary) or by
Language of Communication (Austria)

Ethnic Group	Number of Students per 1,000 of Population
Germans	19.04
Magyars	17.20
Czechs and Slovaks	16.80
Poles	12.49
Ruthenes	3.63
Croats and Serbs	5.21
Slovenes	8.37
Romanians	4.46
Italians	18.17
Austria	16.19
Hungary	12.27
Monarchy as a whole	14.13

Source: László Katus, "Die Magyaren," *Die Völker des Reiches* ("Die Habsburgermonarchie 1848–1918," vol. 3,
Adam Wandruszka and Peter Urbanitsch, eds.; Vienna, 1980), p. 483.

relatively large number of self-confessed Czech nationals in the reserve officer corps. Finally, it must be remembered that in Austria-Hungary, unlike the German Reich, a reserve officer's commission was not indispensable for landing a good position in civilian life, nor did it enjoy universal respect.

Career Officers

All these meditations cannot obscure the fact that at least half of the Habsburg reserve officer corps consisted of Germans. If we are to believe the military statistics and the historians, the proportion of Germans in the career officer corps was much higher than half. Here, however, I would like to raise some objections, but let us first take a look at the official statistics (table 10.9).

According to these statistics, four out of every five career officers were Germans; all other nationalities were badly underrepresented, although the Magyars had made some headway between 1897 and 1910. The proportion of Czechs, Poles, and Croats and Serbs was declining, and the other nationalities were barely represented at all (a total of eight Slovak and thirty-three Ruthene career officers in 1910!).

Can this be true? If it were, then the multinational Habsburg army was—as its contemporary Magyar and Slavic critics and its later Nazi apologists claimed—just another German-led force, different from that of the German Reich only insofar as the majority of its rank and file consisted of subject races. Historical evidence, however, does not support the official military statistics.

Throughout its history, the Habsburg army was publicly and actively opposed to any manifestation of nationalism. It recruited its officers from all the provinces of the monarchy (after 1867, the number of foreign-born officers began declining

Table 10.9. Nationality of Career Officers and Enlisted Men in the Joint Army, 1897 and 1910

Nationality Group	1897		1910	
	Career Officers	Rank and File	Career Officers	Rank and File
Germans	77.7	28.3	78.7	25.2
Magyars	8.0	18.4	9.3	23.1
Czechs	5.5	14.4	4.8	12.9
Slovaks	0.1	4.3	—	3.6
Poles	3.0	9.5	2.5	7.9
Ruthenes	0.2	7.9	0.2	7.6
Croats and Serbs	3.6	7.0	2.4	9.0
Slovenes	0.6	3.0	0.5	2.4
Romanians	0.6	5.8	0.9	7.0
Italians	0.7	1.4	0.7	1.3
Absolute number	15,650	1,309,127	17,808	1,490,459

Sources: *Militär-Statistisches Jahrbuch für das Jahr 1897* (Vienna, 1898), pp. 143, 148; *Militärstatistisches Jahrbuch für das Jahr 1910* (Vienna, 1911), pp. 145–46.

Note: Officer category includes only the ranks from lieutenant to colonel.

rapidly). Officers born in German-Austria were not grossly overrepresented. In any case, place of birth was not decisive in a corps in which two-thirds of the officers were born to fathers in public service: bureaucrats, officers, NCOs, gendarmes, policemen, customs officials, employees of the state-owned railways, and Protestant ministers. These people often served in places far away from home. True, in 1867, all public services were divided between Austria and Hungary, and thereafter, only members of the Joint Army served throughout the monarchy. Still, it did little for a boy's national identity when, to give one example, his railway official father was transferred from Italian- and Croatian-speaking Trieste to Romanian-, Ukrainian- and Yiddish-speaking Bukovina. Both places were "Austria." In any case, the son might well have left home at the age of ten for a military school located, for example, in Hungarian- and Slovak-speaking Kassa, in northern Hungary. The fact is that an enormous number of Joint Army officers had, for all intents and purposes, no nationality.

In Franz Theodor Csokor's popular drama *3 November 1918,* published in 1936, a group of ill or wounded officers are recuperating at the end of the war in the mountains near Austria's Italian front. There they learn of the collapse of the monarchy from a passing revolutionary. The news brings joy to some reserve officers who have suddenly discovered their special "ethnic roots"; it brings fear to a Jewish reserve officer, who is the only true "Austrian" among the civilians in uniform; and it completely destroys the morale of the foremost professional among them, an army colonel. When asked about his nationality, the colonel invokes his regiment and, at the end of the play, he shoots himself dead.[37]

Csokor's dramatic presentation is corroborated by memoirs, letters, and other documents. Although to a lesser extent than in the first half of the nineteenth century, many career officers, as late as 1918, viewed the monarchy as their extended family and the regiment as their immediate one. Having been brought up in a regimental town, they attended military school in some other part of the monarchy and then served in yet another province. At all times, they were taught to view any expression of national sentiment as unbecoming of an officer or even as treasonous. Only the aristocratic Polish and Hungarian cavalry regiments represented an exception to this rule. In service, as in the mess hall, the officers used German and, consequently—unless their non-German ethnic identity happened to be particularly strong, as it was increasingly among the Magyars—they must have reported, when asked, that German was the language they used most frequently.

An analysis of my two sample cohorts of career officers shows that of the officers sampled, only 52.0 percent qualified as German in the 1870 cohort and 55.0 percent in the 1900 cohort. These are very considerable proportions, but still well below the figures indicated in the official statistics.

The fact is that the military did not know how to handle ethnic statistics. This becomes clear when we contrast the data taken from the military statistical yearbook with my data, and with those in the official Austrian statistical yearbook (see table 10.10). The latter calculated in 1891 that at the Joint Army's elite military schools (Militär-Realschulen and military academies) only 36.9 percent of the students were Germans. Remember also—from chapter 3 in this book—that at the Wiener Neustadt Military Academy those whose mother tongue was German constituted 63.3 percent of the class of 1912–1913! Yet at this elite institution, the proportion of

Table 10.10. Variations on a Theme: Ethnic Distribution of Career Officers in the Habsburg Monarchy's Joint Army, 1900 (Percentages)

Ethnic Group	According to the *Militär-Statistisches Jahrbuch für das Jahr 1900**		Calculated by Author[†]		Students in the Joint Army's elite military schools (*Militär-Realschulen* and the three military academies), 1890.[‡]
Germans	80.0		55.0		36.9
Magyars	7.6		9.1		22.1
Czechs	5.3	↑	8.1	↑	↑
Slovaks	0.1		0.4		
Poles	2.3	Slavs	3.3	Slavs	Slavs
Ruthenes	0.2	11.3	0.4	16.7	38.3
Slovenes	0.6		0.8		
Croats	2.8		2.1		
Serbs		↓	1.6	↓	↓
Romanians	0.6		1.6		0.5
Italians	0.5		0.2		1.9
Other	—		0.2		(Foreigners) 0.3
Mixed nationality	—		16.2		—
Undetermined	—		1.2		—

*Published in Vienna in 1901; pp. 180–81.

†Nationality calculated on the basis of the individual records of 516 lieutenants in active service in 1900 by taking into account name, religion, birthplace, legal residence, degree of familiarity with various domestic languages, and, whenever possible, family origin. The cohort represents 10 percent of all the career lieutenants, a random sample.

‡Calculated on the basis of statistics in *Österreichisches Statistisches Handbuch*, vol. 9 (Vienna, 1891), p. 273. It is presumed that these students had become lieutenants or first lieutenants by 1900.

Germans should have exceeded their proportion in the career corps as a whole. Clearly, I can do no better than to print these vastly contradictory statistics and to conclude that there is no reliable way to establish the nationality of career officers.

While there can be little doubt that Germans constituted an absolute majority of the career officers, others, particularly the Magyars, Czechs, and Serbo-Croats were also fairly well represented.

When it comes to the ethnic distribution of career officers in the various service arms—the reader will be spared the details here—it is clear that not only Germans but Magyars, Poles, and Czechs as well were overrepresented in those formations that required a considerable private income (cavalry), scientific training (artillery, engineers), a combination of both (field artillery), or good social and official connections (Jäger).

Career and Nationality

Even if we assume that the Habsburg army was truly "ethnic-blind" in recruiting its career officers—every military memoir insists that this was indeed the case, and there is no archival evidence to the contrary—the question still remains whether the

Table 10.11. Ranks of Officers after Fourteen Years of Service, 1870 Cohort
(Percentages)

Birthplace	Lieutenant	1st Lieutenant	Captain or Higher	Total
Austria	9.6	51.0	39.0	100 (N = 331)
Hungary	7.9	39.5	52.6	100 (N = 38)

Note: Given the fact that the lives and careers of the 1900 cohort were violently disrupted by the outbreak of World War I and then by the collapse of the monarchy in 1918, all career measurements both for the 1870 and the 1900 cohort refer to the first fourteen years of their service after 1870 and 1900, respectively.

Germans did not enjoy a distinct career advantage over the others. As a first step, I have decided to examine the military careers of my statistical sample in each half of the monarchy (see table 10.11). One is struck by the low proportion of officers born in Hungary but also by the remarkable success of this group in reaching higher ranks. While an absolute majority of those born in "Austria" were still first lieutenants after fourteen years of service, an absolute majority of the Hungarian-born officers had made it to captain or higher. Further investigation reveals that not all those born in Hungary enjoyed such an advantage but only those among them who could speak Hungarian. (Note that table 10.12 is based not on rank but on average level of pay, which depended upon an officer's rank and seniority.)

Clearly, the highest pay and, by implication, the highest ranks belonged to those who had been born in Hungary and were also of Magyar nationality or, at least, spoke the language. Officers from Hungary but who did not speak Hungarian did not fare any better than those born in Austria, and officers born in Austria who were familiar with the Hungarian language (probably because of service in a Hungarian regiment) did worst of all. Statistical data on the 1900 cohort indicate an even more favorable situation for Magyar-speaking Hungarians.

The reason for this is not difficult to determine. The honvéd army, created in 1868, aimed its recruiting efforts precisely at those officers who had been born in Hungary and spoke Hungarian. To counteract this drive, the Joint Army offered improved career opportunities to its Magyar officers. In addition, those Magyars who remained in the Joint Army were probably more talented and more dedicated to their vocation than those who went over to the less prestigious honvédség with its virtual guarantee of rapid promotion. Certainly, the honvéd army commanders complained repeatedly about the reluctance of the best-qualified Magyars in the Joint Army to join the Hungarian National Guard.[38]

All my attempts at a nationality analysis have produced only this one conclu-

Table 10.12. Average Annual Salaries after Fourteen Years of Service According to Place of Birth and Knowledge of Hungarian, 1870 Cohort (Gulden)

Birthplace	Hungarian-Speaking	Non–Hungarian-Speaking
Hungary	1,069 (N = 23)	836 (N = 14)
Austria	752 (N = 26)	811 (N = 283)

Note: The data refer only to those who completed fourteen years of service after 1870.

sion: if the Joint Army displayed any nationality bias in its promotions, it was in favor of its Magyar officers. This contradicts the incessant complaints of the Hungarian politicians, but is nevertheless true. The reason for this phenomenon was the particular situation created by the existence of a rival Hungarian national army, and by the monarchy's need to assure the presence of a substantial number of Magyar officers in its supranational force.

The real key to rapid promotion in the postreform Habsburg army was not confession, nationality, or social origin, but schooling and the higher training courses. In this respect, however, family background definitely played a role. For instance, as I shall try to demonstrate below, those born in the German-Austrian provinces—who were probably mostly Germans—were generally better educated and took more advanced training courses after being commissioned lieutenants than did those born, for instance, in the South Slav provinces of the monarchy.

Higher Training Courses

In the Joint Army, as in all late-nineteenth-century European armies, ever-increasing importance was attached to attending the "right" military schools and taking the "right" continuation courses, especially those offered by the general staff school. As my analysis of the 1870 cohort shows, those who completed one of the elite military schools and subsequently attended some of the more prestigious advanced training courses had a 53.4 percent chance of reaching the rank of captain or higher after fourteen years of service. In the 1900 cohort, the statistical chances of members of this select group reaching a high rank was an amazing 94.3 percent, meaning that virtually all those with an elite education and elite postgraduate training were rapidly promoted. Those who attended one of the less prestigious military schools and took lower-level continuation courses moved ahead more slowly. In fact, by the turn of the century, it was widely recognized that those who had gone to the Militär-Realschule (equal in quality to a Gymnasium) and subsequently attended one of the two military academies (as opposed to the much more numerous Kadettenschulen) had a distinctly superior chance of gaining admission to the Kriegsschule and then to the general staff, from which generals were ultimately selected.

My examination of the education and training of the officers in the two cohorts indicates that place of birth did make a difference in terms of elite or nonelite education and training, but only when comparing such extremes as officers born in German-Austria and those born in the South Slav provinces.

In the 1870 cohort, exactly one-half of the officers born to soldier-fathers in German-Austria attended elite military schools; in the 1900 cohort, the proportion was 41 percent. At the other extreme, only 14 percent of those in the 1870 cohort born in the South-Slav provinces of Croatia-Slavonia, Dalmatia, and Carniola attended elite military schools. In 1900, this figure had increased only slightly to 22.7 percent.

Let us now turn to the "postgraduate" training courses. Of those officers from military families in the 1870 cohort who were born in German-Austria, 75 percent attended elite continuation courses. This proportion diminished marginally to 66.7

percent in the 1900 cohort. Conversely, among such officers in the 1870 cohort who were born in the South Slav provinces, only 26.3 percent attended elite training courses and, in the 1900 cohort, a more respectable 45.5 percent.

What explains these differences? No doubt legendary German diligence and industry, the higher educational level of the German population, and the fact that the native tongue of these officers was the army's official language all had something to do with this phenomenon. The ethnic biases of those who decided on admissions to the military academies and elite training courses may also have been a factor. But the very low participation of the South Slavs in elite education and training requires some additional explanation. I would argue that the unfavorable situation of this group was due not so much to ethnic discrimination as to the peculiarities of their background.

Until the gradual dissolution of the Military Border in the late 1870s and early 1880s, most Serbian and Croatian officers hailed from that region and went back to serve in Grenzer regiments. This was reflected, among other things, in the extraordinarily high proportion of Serbian and Croatian officers who had been born into military families: in the 1870 cohort, 78.1 percent of the Serbs, and 66.7 percent of the Croats. Almost invariably of peasant origin, the average Grenzer officer was content to remain in his own regiment and lacked the ambition needed for a great career. At least so we are told by the memoir writers and the collectors of military anecdotes. The Grenzer officer was "Kamerad Krowatowitsch," a simpleminded but fiercely loyal soldier. The majority ended a life of service as junior captains or even lieutenants. The documented, near-total unfamiliarity of these officers with French and English (which we have seen in chapter 4) bears testimony to the group's lower-class background and limited education.*

Of course, not all South Slav officers ended their careers as lieutenants or captains. One of the principal Austrian commanders in the wars of 1848–1849, Josip Jelačić, was a Croat; the occupation of Bosnia-Hercegovina in 1878 was directed by a South Slav, General Philippović; and the 1882 uprising in that same province was suppressed by another South Slav, General Jovanović. There were many great South Slav military dynasties, and many famous Croatian and Serbian generals, such as Generaloberst Sarkotić, the military commander of Bosnia-Hercegovina and Dalmatia during World War I and conqueror of Montenegro.

Some further evidence may be adduced to demonstrate that the Habsburg army was more "ethnic-blind" than biased. According to the Austrian statistician Wilhelm Winkler, of the monarchy's 387 actively serving generals on November 1, 1918, 166 could be considered Germans, 94 Hungarians, 64 Czechs and Slovaks, 25 South Slavs, 24 Poles, 9 Italians, 1 Romanian, and 4 classified as "Other." It is true that Winkler based his computations mostly on the generals' legal place of residence, a doubtful procedure.[39] We know, however, that of the monarchy's 9 active field marshals during the World War, Friedrich, Eugen, and Joseph were Habsburg archdukes; Conrad was a German-Austrian; Böhm-Ermolli, born in Ancona, was part German, part Italian; Kövess and Rohr were born in Hungary, but in

---

*Because the Grenzer regiments had ceased to exist by 1900, it is impossible to determine whether humanistic education had made any headway by then among the Serbian and Croatian officers.

reality both were of local German stock; Krobatin, born in Moravia, was a Czech; and Boroević, a South Slav.[40]

Needless to say, all the field marshals viewed themselves as "Austrians," and their unconditional loyalty was to the emperor. After the war, only Conrad claimed to be a Great-German nationalist, while Archduke Joseph paraded as a Hungarian patriot. Most of the field marshals, like the great majority of the other career officers, never admitted to a specific nationality. Nor should we insist on assigning one to them.

What we should insist, however, is that in the Habsburg army officer corps education and postgraduate training were the key to promotion, not nationality or religion. Naturally, admission to a good school and academic achievement were inevitably tied, as elsewhere, to a candidate's social origin, the cultural milieu of his home, and his father's official connections. In other words, career was, however indirectly and by far not exclusively, also a function of class.

11

The Officers in the
Great War

Going to the Front

Historical memory has drawn two profoundly different portraits of the Habsburg army setting off to war in 1914. The first one is of a dedicated band of soldiers, marching away with flags flying and rifles decorated with flowers, confident of the imminent fall of Belgrade and the humiliation of "Dog Serbia." Bidding them farewell is a populace awash in enthusiasm and suddenly appreciative of the blessings of the monarchy. The second portrait is of a gloomy and disgruntled citizenry— Czechs, Serbs, Ruthenes, Magyar peasants, and Vienna factory workers—reluctantly donning the hated uniform of an unpopular monarch to fight an unwanted war. And the army into which they have been impressed appears as a motley mixture of anachronistic cavalry in suicidally handsome uniforms, overburdened infantrymen slogging along in clumsy outsize boots, and a once-famous artillery now mustering cannons inherited from the nineteenth-century wars. The instruments of modern warfare—entrenching tools, barbed wire, and machine guns—are almost nowhere in evidence.

The portraits drawn of the officers are no less contradictory. On the one side is Joseph Roth's young lieutenant, Baron Trotta, in *The Radetzky March,* quietly prepared to face his doom, which he will meet while fetching water for his men during a terrible retreat. On the other side are Lieutenant Lukash and his cronies in Hašek's *The Good Soldier Schweik,* at best stupid and at worst cynical, corrupt, cowardly, and vile.

No doubt, all these views are correct: in the vast multinational monarchy, much as in today's multiethnic United States, everything was possible, and no generalization was entirely valid. There were, in the early days of August 1914, valiant men in splendid uniforms, cheered on by delirious crowds, but there was also an extraordinary shortage of trained men and modern weapons. And while thousands went off to war with enthusiasm, others did not want to go at all.

The order for mobilization, partial on July 28, and full on August 1, was surprisingly well obeyed. However, mobilized reservists often discovered that they had no units to join, and others landed in brand-new units. Yet the value of a military formation is determined less by the zeal of the soldiers than by the degree of familiarity existing between leaders and followers, and by their common experience. In the Habsburg army of 1914, only about one in four members of an infantry company had been in active service before the war; the rest were reservists or men who had already completed service in the reserves and were now in the Landsturm. Ironically, after the decimation of the prewar standing army, the younger Landsturm soldiers, who were at least thirty-two years of age, would be regarded as some of the army's best. All the armies, German and French included, entered the war with almost incomprehensible handicaps, but the Habsburg army (and, of course, the Russian as well) clearly had more than the others. It was, moreover, poorly led from the very beginning. The worst mistake was that of Conrad, who, despite his gloomy prewar premonitions, did not want to believe that Russia would enter the war. As a result, he mistakenly sent an entire army of several hundred thousand men to the Serbian front, whence they could not be extricated and redirected against the Russians until it was almost too late. Meanwhile, the Austro-Hungarians had suffered terrible losses in Galicia and been forced into a precipitous retreat. Nor was any success achieved against the Serbs.*

The army began the war with truly grave shortcomings. It had, for example, only forty-two light and no heavy field guns for each infantry division, whereas the Germany army, for instance, had seventy-two light and eight heavy field guns in each division.[1] Likewise in the immediate prewar era, each Austro-Hungarian artillery battery had just 250 shells for training purposes (the same number as in 1866), as opposed to 500 to 600 in Russia, and 650 to 730 in France and Germany.[2] To inject a personal note, my father's unit, the 6th k.u.k. Fortress Artillery Regiment of Komárom, Hungary, went to the Russian front in 1914 without his battery's ever having fired a single live shell from its 15 cm howitzers. This meant that artillery observers, such as my father, had never viewed the explosion of a shell in the target area.

Armament production increased, at first slowly and then rapidly, but only until the third year of the war. Austria-Hungary produced 375,000 artillery shells in 1914, 950,000 in 1915, 1,400,000 in 1916, and 1,476,000 in the first half of 1917, but only 1,290,000 in the second half of that year, and 750,000 in the first half of 1918. Production figures for rifles and machine guns followed a similar curve.[3]

Victories Despite Weakness

We already know that the war began very badly for the Habsburg army. The attack against Serbia failed because troops were needed in Galicia and the Bukovina, and

---

*Indeed, an incident involving the Serbian chief of the general staff, General Radomir Putnik, makes one wonder why the Habsburg monarchy bothered to enter a modern armed conflict at all. When war broke out, Putnik found himself in Budapest; the Austrian high command wished to intern its much-feared enemy, the hero of the Balkan wars, but Francis Joseph, angry over such unseemly behavior, ordered a special train for the general, sending him back to Serbia, where he promptly proceeded to defeat the invading Austro-Hungarians. (Gunther E. Rothenberg, *The Army of Francis Joseph* [West Lafayette, Ind., 1976], p. 182.)

the offensive against Russia failed because of Russian numerical and material superiority and the initial weakness of the German army in the East. The magnificent hussars, in their blue attilas with golden breast cords, stormed the enemy lines and were mowed down by machine guns. By winter, the Russians had entered Hungary.

Hindenburg's and Ludendorff's victories in East Prussia, and the arrival of German reinforcements to bolster the Austro-Hungarians in Galicia, finally stabilized the front. The pattern was to remain the same until the end of the war. For a successful offensive, the Habsburg armies needed direct German support; they were capable, however, of dogged defense. Italy entered the war in 1915, but could make no headway in eleven major offensives on the Isonzo River because of determined Austro-Hungarian resistance. Unlike the war against Russia, the Italian war was popular among the troops because it was felt the Italians had stabbed the monarchy in the back.

Throughout the war, whenever the Germans were willing and able to turn their attention away from the stationary western front, great victories could be achieved in the east and southeast. In 1915, Serbia, Montenegro, and a part of Albania were invaded and occupied with Bulgarian help. But the Serbs went on fighting near the Greek border, where a new front was created with Franco-British assistance, and this front would prove fatal to the monarchy in the fall of 1918.

In 1915, the Russians were also driven back in the so-called Gorlice offensive of the Central Powers. True, there was a major Russian counterattack in 1916 at Luck (known as the Brusilov offensive in Western history books), which caused the near-collapse of the Habsburg army, with entire divisions surrendering to the enemy. Shortly thereafter, however, the Russian army entered into a fatal decline.

Romania, too, joined the war in 1916, another "stab in the back" by a nominal ally, but the Romanians were soon beaten, and most of their country was occupied by combined German, Austro-Hungarian, and Bulgarian forces.

Then came 1917, a miraculous year for Austria-Hungary, when the Italian army was driven back at Caporetto, and when the Russians were knocked out of the war. And so it came about that in 1917 and 1918, when the monarchy's population was suffering from hunger, the war economy was in decline, and desertions and revolutionary nationalist and socialist agitation were rampant, not a single enemy soldier stood on Habsburg territory. On the contrary, Austro-Hungarian armies were everywhere deep inside enemy territory. While the monarchy's political leaders quailed before the specter of immediate collapse, it seemed as if the country's war aims had been more or less accomplished: the defeat and humiliation of Serbia, Romania, and Russia, and now even the humiliation and near-defeat of Italy.[4]

The End of the Professional Army

The Dual Monarchy called up millions of half-trained soldiers and suffered losses to match. In the course of the war, over 8 million men, or nearly one-third of the total male population (and some 100,000 women) donned the uniform, a figure proportionally higher than the 11 million Germans in uniform. Losses were staggering: 1,016,200 dead and 1,691,000 captured or missing, representing 12.7 and 21.1

percent, respectively, of those in military service. These figures include neither the 437,000 officers and men rounded up by the Italians at the end of the war when the Austro-Hungarians were already on their way home, nor the 478,000 officers and men who died in Russian, Serbian, or Italian captivity. If we add to this the undetermined number crippled permanently by wounds, illness, or frostbite, we must conclude that well over half of those in service were lost to the army.[5] And considering that the majority of those in uniform never served at the front, it becomes clear that very few of the genuine combat troops emerged from the war unscathed, my father having been one of the lucky few.

Early on, the army regiments began to resemble gigantic meat grinders. In the first year of the war, 2,738,500 men were lost, permanently or temporarily, to death in battle, wounds, cholera, typhus, frostbite, and captivity: a number equivalent to six times the size of the peacetime army.[6] As active servicemen became casualties, their places were taken by youngsters, older reservists, and individuals formerly considered unfit for service. By the end of 1914, an average of five replacement battalions per infantry regiment, or a grand total of 750,000 men, had been sent to the front. As a rule, every infantry regiment (originally about 6,000 men) required one battalion replacement (about 1,000 men) each month. Even so, during the winter campaigns in the Carpathian mountains, infantry divisions were down from their normal complement of 12,000 rifles to something between 3,000 and 5,000 rifles.[7]

A particularly sore issue was the uneven social and ethnic distribution of battle casualties. It was no secret that certain social classes, particularly peasants, who made up the bulk of the infantry, paid a particularly heavy price in blood. Likewise, certain nationalities, particularly the German-Austrians, Magyars, Slovenes, and Croats, lost more men than the others. This was because the army high command had greater faith in these ethnic groups and tended to send their units to the more dangerous sectors. Criticism of this understandable policy was then blown all out of proportion by the newspapers and politicians (especially in Hungary, where censorship was lax and the parliament remained in session), contributing in no small measure to growing hostility among classes and nationalities.[8]

What concerns us most, however, is that, by the end of 1914, the bulk of the monarchy's trained soldiery had become casualties (82 percent of the original infantry complement, for instance) and that the rest of the war, therefore, had to be fought mainly by older and underage men, or by previously untrained civilians.[9] It is no great exaggeration to say that, by 1915, the traditional Habsburg army had been transformed into a militia, not too different from the citizens' army that fought the war for Great Britain. This new army was led, moreover, by a grossly inadequate number of civilians in uniform, rather than by career soldiers.

The War of the Reserve Officers

In 1914 it was expected that platoon and company commanders would march into battle ahead of their men, and that cavalry officers would ride in front of the line, all the while conspicuously displaying their insignia of rank. Select ensigns and NCOs were to carry the unit flag and protect it at the cost of their lives. The war taught a different lesson, but not before the bravest of the corps had died. Because of contradictory statistics, I cannot tell precisely how many officers served between 1914 and 1918, nor how many died, but there can be no doubt that the losses were very high.

Before the war, the Joint Army counted about 18,000 career and 14,000 reserve officers. Adding to this the number of officers who served in the National Guards, those who had been out of service and were now reactivated, and, finally, the able-bodied among the pensioners, we arrive at a grand total of less than 60,000. This would have been a ridiculously small number for an army of over 3 million, even assuming that so many officers had not been eliminated in the early months of the war. By the end of 1914, 3,168 officers had been killed, with total casualties amounting to 22,310, or almost half of the prewar corps of career and reserve officers.[10] The response was the rapid training and commissioning of a great number of young men, including some who had not qualified in the past because of poor health, inadequate social status, or less than complete high-school education. Even now, however, and throughout the war, the army steadfastedly refused to commission officers from the ranks, not even highly deserving NCOs experienced in leading platoons or companies (a not uncommon occurrence at a time when officers were falling in droves). At the end of 1915, there were a total of 130,000 officers, and on October 1, 1918, 188,000 officers, of whom perhaps 35,000 were professionals.[11] A glance at the changing composition of the corps in three regiments should tell the story (see table 11.1).

Clearly, the number of career officers actually declined in two out of three combat infantry regiments in my sample; this, despite the growing number of career officers in the armed forces as a whole. This does not mean that the professionals had become shirkers;* it means simply that there were not enough of them, and that many had been promoted to higher posts or were needed at home to train others and to administer the war.

The monarchy was now paying the price for its inadequate prewar military budgets, for the unpopularity of the military profession among the middle classes, and for the impossibility, after 1868, to rise from the ranks. Throughout the war, the task of commanding the smaller units at the front fell on the shoulders of the civilians in uniform. Because no reservist was promoted to a rank higher than captain, the command of larger units remained the responsibility of career officers.

What this meant in practice can be easily imagined. Among other things, the non-Germans among the newly commissioned officers had had no time to learn good German, let alone the language or languages spoken by their men. One officer described how he spent an entire week in a foxhole with an officer from a neighboring honvéd battalion without being able to understand a single word spoken by his Magyar companion.[12] The military historian Wilhelm Czermak surely exaggerates when he writes that problems of communication were the main reason for the failure of the Austro-Hungarian army, but they must have been an important factor.[13]

---

*Wilhelm Winkler has estimated that one out of every eight career officers died in World War I (*Berufsstatistik der Kriegstoten der öst.-ung. Monarchie* [Vienna, 1919], pp. 6–8).

Table 11.1. Career and Reserve Officers in Three Randomly
Selected Regiments of the Joint Army at the
Beginning of 1914 and at the End of 1916

Year	Career Officers	Reserve Officers
4. Hoch- und Deutschmeister Infantry Regiment, Vienna		
1914	112	93
1916	114	528
5. Freiherr von Klobučar Infantry Regiment, Eperjes, Hungary		
1914	94	75
1916	78	303
52. Erzherzog Friedrich Infantry Regiment, Pécs, Hungary		
1914	105	123
1916	100	310

Source: Figures computed by author from *Schematismus für das kaiserliche und
königliche Heer und für die kaiserliche und königliche Kriegsmarine für 1914* (Vienna, 1913), and from the same publication for the year 1917.

It is unclear just how many officers became casualties of the war: one reliable source speaks of 15,408 killed and 34,920 captured or missing.[14] Add to this the 8,000 who died in captivity, the 12,000 captured by the Italians at the end of the war, and the uncertain number of seriously ill and crippled officers, and we arrive at an approximate total of 100,000 officer casualties.

The overwhelming majority of officers served honorably in the war, although there were some famous instances of Italian, Serbian, and Czech officers going over to the enemy. True, the Czech and South Slav legions fighting on the side of the Entente were led mostly by former Austro-Hungarian officers, but these officers had been recruited into the legions from captivity, and the motivation of those officers or men who preferred service in the volunteer forces to languishing—and possibly dying—in a POW camp should at least be open to debate.

Jews and the Great War

World War I marked the apogee of Jewish participation in the life of Central Europeans. In the delirious enthusiasm of August 1914, Jews were among the greatest enthusiasts. They endorsed the war, in part because the enemy was the anti-Semitic Russian Empire, in part because the outcome of the conflict promised to bring their final and complete acceptance. Jewish writers and journalists did signal service as war propagandists, and thousands of Jewish reserve officers willingly assumed command of their troops. Never again would Jews be allowed to play such a dignified role in the history of German-Austrians, Magyars, and Slavs. Thereafter, their role would be increasingly that of victims. The cruelest irony in the history of Central European Jewry centers on the decorations and frontline photographs Jewish World War I veterans left behind on the walls of their looted apartments while forced to make their way, during World War II, to the gas chambers.

It must be stated nevertheless that the proportional representation of Jews in the armed forces, and especially at the front, remained lower than that of the proportion of Jews in the general population. The pro-Jewish military historian Ernst R. v. Rutkowski admits that "the percentage of those Jews who requested temporary or even complete exemption from military duty, especially during World War I between 1914 and 1918, was significantly higher than that of the members of other confessional groups."[15] And the anti-Semitic Hungarian statistician Alajos Kovács calculated, after the war, that only half as many Hungarian Jews had been killed at the front as would have been "normal" for their proportional representation in the country's population (Jews made up 2.57 percent of those killed, as opposed to 5.25 percent, which was the proportion of Jews among all Hungarian males between the ages of twenty and fifty). Going further, Kovács calculated that, whereas 2.8 percent of the Christian population of Hungary had been killed during the war, only 1.1 percent of the Hungarian Jews had suffered a similar fate.[16] But neither Rutkowski nor Kovács takes into consideration that the heaviest casualties were suffered by the infantry, which the army high command routinely filled with peasants; Jews, being German speakers and of solid education, were more likely to be sent to the more secure artillery, medical corps, or military administration. Moreover, a great part of the Jewish population, especially in Galicia and northeastern Hungary, became refugees during the war, and were thus less likely to be called up. Similar considerations might explain why only 1.66 percent of the Galician population was killed at the front, as opposed to 3.6 percent of the Carinthians or 2.87 percent of the Moravians.[17] All in all, Jews were as likely to become willing fighters, out of their loyalty to the monarchy or fear of the Russians, as they were to avoid service because of their pacifistic religious tradition, nonmilitary lifestyle, or trading and other nonphysical occupations.

It is more important, from our point of view, that about 300,000 Jews served in World War I, among them 25,000 Jewish officers.[18]

The war brought the rank of general to a number of Jews. There were, aside from Generaloberst Hazai, twenty-four other Jewish or converted Jewish generals.[19] Of the many military decorations earned by Jews, mention must be made, at the very least, of seventy-six Gold Medals for Bravery, and twenty-two Orders of the Iron Crown, Third-Class. Jewish officers served in the elite formations as, for instance, in the First Kaiserschützen Regiment of the Austrian National Guard, a famous Alpine unit.[20]*

Yet it appears that for the first time in the history of the monarchy, the valor of individual Jewish soldiers did not help to dampen anti-Semitism. As the situation worsened, the right-wing press increasingly attacked the Jews, despite censorship, for their alleged cowardice, war profiteering, and treason. The collapse of the monarchy, the misery, the confusion, and the outbreak of left-wing revolutions put an end to the general acceptance of Jews. It mattered little that the great majority of Austro-Hungarian Jewry wanted nothing to do with the radical revolutions. What

---

*One of the regiment's Jewish reserve officers was First Lieutenant Paul Kohn, whom I interviewed in New York when he was ninety-three years of age. Born in 1895 in Bohemia, Kohn fought in the Carpathian Mountains and the South Tyrol. He was twice wounded and ended World War I in charge of a company of storm troops. Because he left Austria in 1923, he escaped the fate of his two brothers, both decorated officers, who died in a Nazi concentration camp.

the public saw was the spectacle of Jewish socialist and communist leaders, particularly in the case of the people's commissars of the Hungarian Soviet Republic. It must be said, however, in defense of the former Austro-Hungarian career officers that they generally rejected racist anti-Semitism and insisted on defending the honor of "the brave Jewish officers and soldiers."

Nationality Strife in the Wartime Army

Besides exacerbating anti-Jewish feelings the war also vastly increased ethnic tensions, which now also affected the army. There had been a few ominous signs even before the war. In 1908, for example, after partial mobilization had been ordered in connection with the annexation of Bosnia-Hercegovina and after Czech politicians had violently protested the annexation, Czech soldiers of the 36th k.u.k. Infantry Regiment and of the 10th k.k. Landwehr Infantry Regiment refused to obey the orders of their superiors. They had no desire to fight, they declared, against brother Russians and Serbs.[21]

The 1908 mutiny was suppressed with relative ease, but not so the Pardubitz Mutiny of Czech soldiers in November 1912, which involved the reservists of the 8th Dragoner Regiment. About to be transported to Galicia to face the Russians during the great international crisis caused by the First Balkan War, the reservists suddenly refused to board the train. Forced into the wagons nonetheless, they battled intermittently (with no serious casualties) against loyal troops all along the unit's route from Bohemia to the cavalry barracks at Auschwitz.* Similar but less violent events took place somewhat later among reservists of the Czech 18th k.u.k. Infantry Regiment. The trial of the mutinous dragoons concluded in 1913 with the sentencing of thirty-eight men to prison terms ranging from one month to eight and a half years.[22]

Had the Habsburg army been able to win a few battles during the first months of the war, it is unlikely that as many soldiers would have gone over to the enemy; conversely, it is unlikely in such a case that Austro-Hungarian troops would have brutalized suspect populations as excessively. It must have been frustration and exasperation that drove entire battalions of Czechs, Ruthenes, and Romanians to surrender, and others to hang Orthodox priests, Slavic peasants, and other suspected spies. Yet one should be careful not to exaggerate the number of deserters or the number of atrocities. The Russians captured hundreds of thousands of the monarchy's soldiers in the first months of the war; even the Serbs captured tens of thousands, among them a huge number of Magyars and German-Austrians, but it is impossible to tell how many of these had come over voluntarily and if so, why. The Austro-Hungarians and Germans later captured an even greater number of Russian soldiers, whose motivation in surrendering remains equally unclear. Similarly, the brutality and hangings, gleefully attributed by some Austrian military writers to the Hungarian National Guards, were probably no worse than the atrocities committed by the Germans in Belgium or by the Russians on the eastern front.[23] Once the early period of hysteria was over and discipline had been restored, the Austro-Hungarians

*In World War II, these barracks served as the center for the infamous Nazi death camp.

behaved no better and no worse than the others. For Jews in the East and for most Poles, the Austro-Hungarians and Germans appeared as liberators from the Russian yoke, a sentiment unlikely to be shared by the Ruthene and Russian populations. And at no time did the Austro-Hungarians, or anyone else, treat captured enemy soldiers as cruelly as became common usage on the eastern front in World War II.

Developments in the Austro-Hungarian POW camps of Russia, Serbia, and Italy nevertheless helped exacerbate national and class strife within the monarchy.[24] Until 1918 the civilian population learned about these problems only through POW letters and from rumors, but after Russia's exit from the war, returning prisoners offered first-hand accounts. In accordance with prewar international agreements, the Russian, Serbian, and Italian authorities had strictly separated the captive officers from the men, and while the officers were given their peacetime pay, did not have to work, and were sometimes allowed to leave the camp on their word of honor to return, the rank and file were generally ill-fed, had to do heavy labor, and were locked up in the camps. Worse still, all the enemy armies attempted to separate out the German-Austrian and Magyar prisoners and treated them far worse than the others. It appears that an overwhelming majority of the hundreds of thousands who died in the Siberian forests, factories, and mines were prisoners of German and Magyar nationality.

As if that were not enough, all the enemy armies actively recruited Slavic, Romanian, and Italian prisoners into volunteer legions to fight against the monarchy. While their military importance should not be overestimated (only 10 percent of the South Slav prisoners responded to the call and, as for the famous Czech Legion, it never numbered more than 60,000 men), the psychological importance of these volunteer formations was very great indeed.[25] Legionnaires were given new uniforms, food, and good pay; whatever their motivation for joining, they fought well, for they were convinced that they would be executed as traitors if captured by the Austro-Hungarians. In May 1918, two months after the Bolsheviks had signed a peace treaty with the Central Powers, the Czech Legion attempted to cross Siberia to join the Entente Powers in the West. In the course of this legendary anabasis, the legion gained control of the Trans-Siberian Railroad and willy-nilly began to act as the chief anti-Bolshevik force in the region. On their way, the legionnaires also fought a running battle with former German-Austrian and Magyar POWs who had gained control of several Siberian cities and districts. In the end, there were as many as 100,000 Magyar prisoners in the Russian Bolshevik army. Thus, under the aegis of Red and White, the Central European nationality struggle was acted out in faraway Asia. It was even a kind of reenactment of the 1848 scenario, with the Magyars fighting in the name of new revolutionary ideology and the Slavs opposing the Magyars in defense of their own national rights. In fact, the dissolution of the monarchy into hostile national entities had begun in the POW camps.

Wartime Politics

It is impossible to treat in detail the complex and tragic domestic history of the Dual Monarchy during the war; the barest outline will have to suffice.[26]

There was, at the beginning, as everywhere else in Europe, a period of national unity or rather, this being Austria-Hungary, of dynastic unity. All political parties, including the Social Democrats, supported the war effort, and the Hungarian parliament vied with the Slavic politicians in declarations of loyalty to the House of Austria. The Hungarian honvéd divisions proved to be among the most reliable units in the army. Unlike the Austrian Reichsrat, which had been sent home before the war, the Hungarian parliament remained in session, under the determined leadership of Count István Tisza. This made Hungary a much freer place than Austria, and the Budapest government never allowed the army high command to extend its dictatorial powers to any part of the country. In the Austrian half, large areas, including parts of Bohemia, were declared a war zone.

Food rationing began in the hinterland in 1915, and it soon became clear that Hungary, the breadbasket of the monarchy, was much better off than the Austrian provinces. This led to endless haggling, only partly justified, over Hungarians' alleged unwillingness to share their riches with the Austrians. It is true that the Budapest government behaved increasingly as if it were independent of Austria; it concluded separate trade agreements with Germany and began to formulate its own war aims.[27] In Austria, left-wing socialists gradually turned against their authoritarian government, and in October 1916, the young socialist Friedrich Adler assassinated the Austrian prime minister Count Stürgkh.

Francis Joseph died on November 21, 1916, having labored at his desk almost until the last minute. An era had come to an end, yet the emperor's death created no great stir for, as far as the public was concerned, the Francisco-Josephian age had ended in 1914, or perhaps even earlier. The old emperor was succeeded by his grandnephew, Charles I (Charles IV, as king of Hungary), a young man of infinite goodwill, genuine democratic inclinations, absolute confessional and ethnic tolerance, and a weak personality. Charles was no more a friend of Hungarian sovereignty than Francis Ferdinand had been, yet he allowed himself to be crowned in Budapest in December 1916, which committed him to maintain, at all costs, the integrity of the "Hungarian Empire." Admittedly, it is difficult to see what else he could have done. Charles fancied himself a general and, like Nicholas II in Russia, he assumed personal command of the armed forces. He dismissed Conrad, which must be judged a good move, and appointed General Arz as chief of the general staff. Unfortunately, however, Arz was nothing more than a trustworthy and dedicated soldier.

Charles pardoned a number of traitors among the Slavic politicians, and he abolished the last vestiges of corporal punishment (tying up) in the army. Because soldiers at the front wanted nothing better than to be sent to prison, and because the young emperor also frowned on executions, this measure did not exactly improve discipline in the ranks. Charles positively disliked the Reich German leaders and, egged on by his Franco-Italian wife, he began secret talks with the Entente. But he was ready only to sacrifice Alsace-Lorraine, not a single part of Austria-Hungary, and the Italians would not hear of a compromise peace. When news of the secret talks leaked out, the Germans were understandably indignant, and Charles did not dare abandon the German alliance.[28] Instead, he placed his army under the supreme command of the German kaiser in the spring of 1918, which meant, in practice, under the command of Hindenburg and Ludendorff.

Charles wished to reactivate parliamentary life in Austria, but the Reichsrat, when convoked in May 1917, served only as a platform for nationalist agitation. The king also wished to strengthen democracy in Hungary; in May 1917, he forced the resignation of Prime Minister Tisza and entrusted a new government of moderates with the task of suffrage reform. Nothing came of that either, however, and the last Austrian and Hungarian cabinets served merely as caretakers.

By 1918, the domestic situation had become hopeless. Both the monarchy's leaders and the nationalist politicians had realized that, win or lose, the postwar situation would be critical for all. Victory would cause Austria-Hungary to lose her independence to an all-powerful Germany.[29] Defeat would inevitably lead to a Slavic preponderance in Austria and, most probably, civil war in Hungary. The longer the war lasted, the more the Austro-German and Hungarian elites clung to the German alliance, and the less interested the Slavic politicians became in the preservation of the monarchy. For the time being, everyone waited for the outcome of the great Ludendorff offensive on the western front, and its failure in the summer of 1918 marked the end of the "German Course" of the Austro-Hungarian leadership. The dissolution of the monarchy was now only a matter of time.

Toward Disaster

The trouble facing Austria-Hungary in 1918 seemed truly infinite, despite a victorious peace treaty with the Russian Bolsheviks at Brest-Litovsk. Much-hoped-for food shipments from the occupied Ukraine did not materialize, and in Vienna and other Austrian cities, the population was starving. In January 1918, a wave of industrial strikes rolled over Austria and Hungary. The Russian treaty also resulted in the return of hundreds of thousands of POWs, few of them willing to fight again. Some had even become Bolsheviks. The army felt obliged to quarantine the former prisoners and made clumsy efforts at their reeducation. In the West, self-exiled Slavic politicians such as the Czech Masaryk and the South Slav Trumbić had gained the ear of the enemy politicians, including Wilson, for the recognition of Czechoslovak and South Slav independence, and by the fall of 1918, a still nonexistent Czechoslovakia and a South Slav state had become Entente cobelligerents. This meant that Czech, Slovak, Serbian, Croatian, and Slovene soldiers fighting in the Austro-Hungarian ranks were now theoretically members of the Entente forces. Fortunately for them, most were spared this morally disturbing information, and it was only during the hours of their final defeat that they learned they had just won the war.

At home, food requisitioning alienated the theretofore generally loyal peasantry. The forests of Croatia and other places teemed with deserters, some of whom waged a guerrilla war on the gendarmes. In the Hungarian parliament, Count Mihály Károlyi and the radical wing of the Independence Party agitated for a break with Austria and a separate peace with the Entente, and in the larger cities radical socialist intellectuals were readying themselves for a revolution. But what finished off the monarchy, besides material exhaustion, was unrest among the noncombatant elements of the army, which spread to the soldiers at the front in October of that year.[30]

Mutiny began on the idle ships of the navy, a part of the armed forces of which I have said practically nothing so far, mainly so as not to make this book even longer. Traditionally, the navy was quite weak, as befitted a principally land-oriented monarchy. In the first half of the nineteenth century, it was manned chiefly by Italians, but after they joined the Venetian revolutionaries in 1848, the Austrian navy became much more multinational. In 1866 the navy proved itself, as we have seen, by destroying the numerically superior Italian fleet. After 1868, the navy functioned as an autonomous part of the Joint Army. Grossly neglected at first, it suddenly underwent an overambitious expansion program early in the twentieth century, in tune with the imperialist philosophy of the age and the belated expansionist dreams of some of the monarchy's leaders and arms manufacturers. By 1914, it disposed of a number of very modern dreadnoughts, and the construction of heavy ships continued during the war.[31]

Ethnically, the naval crews, totaling 34,150 men (active and reservists) in 1910, were as mixed as the land army, except for the heavy representation of Dalmatian Croats and Italians (in 1910, 29.8 percent and 18.3 percent, respectively). Interestingly, a sort of ethnic division of labor took place on the ships, with Italians and Croats usually serving on deck; Czechs and Germans running the engines; and Magyars (12.6 percent in 1910) and Germans manning the guns. The naval officer corps (numbering 830 active sea officers in 1910) was no less colorful, with Germans making up 51 percent of the corps in 1910; Magyars, 12.9 percent; and South Slavs and the Italians, 9.8 percent each.[32] All in all, both officers and sailors represented highly trained elites.

During the war, the heavy ships were bottled up, as in Germany and Russia, at the monarchy's great Dalmatian and Istrian naval bases. Only the submarines and smaller surface vessels were active against the Italians and the French. There was only one significant—and successful—naval engagement, involving three cruisers and two destroyers at Otranto in 1917 under the command of Captain (later Rear-Admiral) Miklós Horthy, who would become Hungary's regent in 1920.[33] Those on the big ships were poorly fed, overdisciplined, and bored, and they mutinied in February 1918, at Cattaro in Dalmatia.[34] The mutiny, at first highly successful, was subdued only by the determined action of the smaller ships, whose crews remained loyal to the end, as they would in Germany.

The Cattaro mutiny had both ethnic and social connotations, and it pointed the way to a whole series of army mutinies in the hinterland. In the last year of the war, the bulk of the army was no longer at the front, in part because the frontlines were now so short; in part because the rolling stock and the coal to send out more troops were missing, and in part because more and more soldiers were needed at home to control the population and, increasingly, other troops. In October 1918, the armed forces still carried 3,824,000 men and 188,000 officers on their rosters, but only 2,313,000 men and 101,000 officers were with the field armies, and of these, only a small fraction were facing the enemy. To be precise, on October 15, 1918, Austro-Hungarian forces on the Italian front numbered 256,700 rifles, 4,650 cavalry, and 7,800 guns, amounting to a total of perhaps 400,000 fighting men. In addition, there were about 50,000 combat soldiers on the Balkan front, and occupation forces numbering about 150,000 in Russia, Romania, Montenegro, and Serbia. Finally, 18,000 Austro-Hungarians were serving with the Germans on the western front and another few thousand in Turkey and Palestine. Thus, only half a million soldiers were actually involved in the fighting, while another 3 million were not.[35]

At home, at first it was only individual companies, made up of reservists or former POWs, who refused to board the trains to the front and had to be transported in sealed wagons. Later, however, entire regiments mutinied; they occupied garrison towns, going on a rampage and firing on loyal troops. Most of the mutineers were Slavs but, by the fall of 1918, they had been joined by Magyars and German-Austrians. At the front, the soldiers were starving, and they wore rags. Entire battalions went without shirts; thousands wore boots with paper soles. In January 1918, the daily food ration of a combat soldier on the Italian front was reduced to ten ounces of bread and six ounces of meat, and on June 15, when the army mounted its last great offensive on the Piave River, not far from Venice, some troops were sent forward with a daily ration of only eight ounces of almost inedible bread and three ounces of meat. The emaciated soldiers weighed an average of 120 pounds, and it is no exaggeration to say that they went forward in the hope of reaching the Entente trenches with their fabulous hoard of food, tobacco, and liquor.[36]

Going Home

On September 15, 1918, the Entente armies began a major offensive in the Balkans, and two weeks later Bulgaria surrendered. The southern front collapsed, and there were no locomotives and no trains to transport units to fill the gap left open by the Bulgarians.[37] In a last-minute effort, on October 16, Charles issued a manifesto announcing the federal reorganization of Austria, and he called on the ethnic politicians to form national committees. The manifesto did not apply to the lands of the Hungarian Holy Crown, but the Budapest government used the opportunity to declare the Compromise Agreement null and void. By the end of October, national councils had sprung up everywhere, including a Hungarian council under Count Károlyi. Sooner or later, each of them declared for complete national independence. After a bloodless revolution broke out in Budapest at the end of October, and even the German-Austrians had formed their own council, Charles lost the last vestiges of imperial and royal authority. There was no more Habsburg monarchy. Yet, strangely, there was still a fighting Habsburg army.

On October 24, the Italians, the French, and the British attacked in northern Italy with vastly superior forces. Many Austro-Hungarian units refused to move up to the front: first the 2nd Laibach k.k. Landwehr Rifle Regiment, made up of Slovene soldiers, then a Bohemian division, then two Hungarian divisions. Others, however, determinedly resisted the Entente forces, and it took the enemy two weeks to achieve the "Vittorio Veneto," the only Italian victory in the war. By then, most Hungarian units had rebelled and started for home to defend their country against the expected Serbian and Romanian invasion.* The remainder were recalled by the revolutionary Hungarian government.

---

*Romania, which—just like Russia—had been forced to sign a humiliating peace treaty with the Central Powers in 1918, rejoined the war at the last minute.

The Magyars were joined in their insubordination by Czech and Croatian units. Finally, even the 3rd Tyrolean Edelweiss Division, the best of the best, refused to go up to the line. Incredibly, even after these events, some units continued to resist the Italians, and they were made up by no means only of German-Austrians.[38] At last, the Habsburg high command succeeded in contacting the Italians, and on November 3, signed an armistice, which, due to a misunderstanding, allowed the Italian command to capture a vast number of fleeing Habsburg soldiers. Of the hundreds of thousands rounded up past the day of the armistice, about 25 percent were German-Austrians; the rest were Slavs, Romanians, and Italians—that is, soldiers who were now seen as allies of the Entente forces. This did not prevent the Italian authorities from mistreating the captives; they were kept in open camps and forced to do hard labor; thirty thousand of them died.[39]

Those who had escaped capture flocked home; some on the principle of *sauve qui peut,* others in good order. To give only one example, the 104th Field Artillery Regiment of Vienna fought on until November 3. For another ten days the regiment held together and then, to the music of the regimental band and under the regimental flag, the colonel commander bade farewell to the troops.[40] Thereafter, each ethnic group marched off toward its new fatherland. Returning troops were stopped from time to time by former Austro-Hungarian officers wearing tricolor national armbands. They were chiefly reserve officers who had participated in, or often led, the national revolutions. With not too many exceptions, the career officers behaved passively. Bewildered, despised, their first concern was where to go, where to find employment or at least a pension. Suddenly, an officer's legal residence, in the past a nearly meaningless entry in his record, assumed crucial importance, for it made him an Austrian, a Hungarian, a Czechoslovak, a Romanian, a Pole, or a citizen of the new South Slav state.

As for Charles, he found himself alone. Deserted by the great Habsburg aristocracy, the Catholic high prelates, and the imperial bureaucracy, he also had to witness the sudden departure of his glittering Arcièren, Trabanten, and Hungarian Noble Guards, for whom this would have been the first genuine opportunity in history to defend their ruler. At the end, as has been noted before, teenaged cadets mounted guard at the Schönbrunn Palace to protect the ruler from the threatening Vienna mob. Finally, Charles agreed to renounce the right to exercise his power and went into exile. But he did not abdicate, and would later try to return.

The transition to new realities went relatively smoothly at first. All one needed to do was to replace the double-headed eagle with the national coat of arms, and a new state was born. Nearly everyone rushed to declare his loyalty to the new republican regimes and, in Hungary, Field Marshal Archduke Joseph even offered to change his name from Habsburg to Alcsúti, the village where his palace was located.

The Great War was long over, and troops were still flocking home from the Balkans, from Russia, and from Italy. It took weeks for the Austrian high-mountain units to descend from the lofty peaks of the Dolomites, where they had fought epic battles with equally adroit Italian high-mountain troops. By then, the peoples of the monarchy had began to fight their internecine wars. The Austrian high command itself survived for several more weeks, issuing orders that no one cared to obey. Its headquarters were in Vienna, in the building of the Habsburg War Archive, and when nothing else could be done, the high command transformed itself into the directorate of the War Archive, a fitting end for a defunct army.

I can do no better than to conclude this chapter with a quotation from Bruno Brehm's account of the end of the war where he writes of the valleys of northern Italy:

> Returning Italians marched through the villages, waving their caps, and calling out joyfully again and again: 'Pace! Pace! Pace!' The valleys emptied gradually. . . . Only the rags remained, the discarded clothing, the broken carts, the toppled wagons, and the poor horses. . . . They gathered in herds, and wandered along the countryside. . . . Until one day soldiers came again, without cockades, and rounded up the horses, bludgeoning to death those incapable of running and pressing the shaggy living skeletons into boxcars . . . which took them to the stinking slaughterhouses of the big cities. From there the meat was distributed to the empty stores, where a long line of starving humanity had already been patiently waiting. Advancing step by step, people paid for the horsemeat with crumpled, greasy banknotes.[41]

Habsburg Officers in the Successor States and in the Second World War

The revolutions which swept east central Europe in the fall of 1918 aimed variously at the achievement of national independence, independence combined with social equality, or unification with co-nationals in a neighboring country. The revolutionary leaders professed Wilsonian democracy and national self-determination on one hand, or Leninist proletarian internationalism on the other. Yet, in more ways than one, the upheavals were but a reenactment of the ethnic struggles of 1848–1849. This time, however, there was no powerful dynastic establishment able to put an end to the east central European civil war. The small successor states that emerged from the conflict reflected the failure of both the Wilsonian and the Leninist programs; none of them was socialist, nor was any of them truly based on the principle of national self-determination. Most were no less multinational than the old Habsburg Monarchy, but none practiced the latter's policy of ethnic toleration. In pretending to be national and unitary, and by insisting on the political hegemony of the "state-building" nationality, they closely resembled the post-1867 Hungarian kingdom.[1]

The least multiethnic of all the nation-states was German Austria. A small republic created to fill the vacuum left in the Alpine provinces by the defunct Habsburg monarchy, it had no desire to remain independent; rather, it would have preferred to unite with the new German republic. In Hungary—or what was left of the kingdom following its truncation by Romania, Czechoslovakia, the South Slav state, and the Austrian republic—minority groups were also less than substantial, but Hungary likewise could not become a factor of stability in the area either because of its insistent claim to the more than three million Magyars now living in neighboring states and to the kingdom's historic frontiers. The Paris peace treaties of 1919–1920 did indeed contain the seeds of their own destruction, as duly acted out in the Second World War.

In the 1918–1921 wars and local skirmishes that pitted Hungarians against Czechoslovaks, Romanians, and Austrians, Austro-Germans and Italians against South Slavs, and Poles against Czechoslovaks, Ukrainians, and Soviet Russians, former Austro-Hungarian officers and soldiers played a decisive role. Because the great majority of the returning soldiers wanted nothing more than to go home and forget about soldiering, the new armies were mere shadows of the imperial-royal army; still, there were enough unemployed officers and enlisted men to fill the ranks of these hastily created armed forces. The Hungarian Red Army, set up by the Republic of Councils in the spring of 1919, was led by Habsburg officers, the most famous of whom was a former colonel of the general staff, Aurél Stromfeld.[2]

The makeshift Czechoslovak army, which opposed the Hungarian Bolsheviks, was similarly commanded by former Habsburg officers, some of whom had served in the Czech Legion during the war, while others joined the Czechoslovak army after the collapse of the monarchy.*

Naturally, monarchistic sentiments were strong in former career officers' circles, manifesting themselves, among other things, in the attempt of former Habsburg officers of Ukrainian descent to set up an independent Ukrainian state under a Habsburg archduke in 1919, and in the efforts of General Anton Lehár and other Habsburg officers to reclaim the Hungarian throne for King Charles in 1921. However, the new Ukrainian state folded under the separate onslaughts of Soviet Russia and Poland,† and Charles's *putsch* attempts were successively fended off by the new Hungarian state, which was led, incidentally, by former Habsburg officers.

Of all the strange incidents in postwar east central Europe, the strangest was the dogged effort of the exiled Charles to return to Hungary. During his second attempt, in October 1921, pro-Habsburg Hungarian troops clashed with other units of the Royal Hungarian Army near Budapest, ending in victory for those who strove to prevent the restoration of the old dynasty in Hungary.[3]

Following the collapse of the Bolshevik revolution in August 1919 and the triumph of the counterrevolution in November of that year, Hungary became legally a kingdom again, but one without a king, under the regency of Rear-Admiral Horthy. Horthy never shed his Habsburg uniform and continued to proclaim his devotion to the memory of Francis Joseph and the monarchical principle, but he did not hesitate to send troops against his king, driving Charles into final exile. Nor did Regent Horthy recoil from assuming most of the rights and prerogatives of a monarch.[4]

Among the successor states, Hungary was definitely the most traditionalist despite the fact that the counterrevolutionary soldiers and politicians, who dominated the country until the end of World War II, rejected the liberal-conservatism of the prewar governments and preached and practiced a curious mix of chauvinism, racism, anti-Semitism, old-fashioned conservatism, and even liberalism.[5] The

---

*For example, Austro-Hungarian Feldmarschalleutnant Aloys Podhajský, who toward the end of World War I commanded an Austrian Landwehr infantry division, became, after 1918, the Czechoslovak military commander of Moravia. He made it to three-star general in the Czechoslovak army, but because after 1938 he accepted an increase of his pension from the German occupation forces, he was interned in Czechoslovakia after 1945 and died soon after his release. (See Miloš Sebor, *Alois Podhajský, voják. Život a rámec doby* [Rome, 1983].)

†The chief of staff of the Ukrainian army, General Alfred Samánek, had been a major in the Austro-Hungarian general staff during World War I. He was killed by brigands in 1920, following the collapse of the independent Ukrainian state. (Peter Broucek, ed., *Ein General im Zwielicht. Die Erinnerungen Edmund Glaises von Horstenau*, 3 vols. [Vienna-Cologne-Graz, 1980–1987], 1:132.)

honvéd army preserved its prewar command structure, insignia, and uniforms; outwardly it looked as if, through this independent armed force, the dreams of the 1848 revolutionaries had finally been realized. But the postwar peace treaty had limited the size of the Hungarian army to a measly thirty-five thousand volunteers, and rather than imitating the liberalism of the 1848-ers, the officer corps of the new army grew increasingly anti-Semitic, and partly even fascist. Because this tiny force could not accommodate all former officers, many were coopted into the administration while others turned to politics.

Curiously, even though the officer corps was extremely small, the Hungarian Ministry of Defense, the direct descendant of the prewar honvéd ministry, at first readily offered employment even to career officers who had had nothing to do with Hungary. Consequently, the interwar Hungarian national army contained an astonishing number of officers who spoke little or no Hungarian. Of the interwar state's 253 higher-ranking generals, only 69 (27 percent) had served exclusively in the prewar Hungarian honvéd army; 90 (36 percent) had served only in the Joint Army, and 75 (30 percent) had seen duty in both armies. Only one higher-ranking general had not been a career soldier before the war.[6]

The process of "Magyarization" began only in the early 1930s, under Prime Minister General Gyula (Julius) Gömbös, himself a former captain on the Habsburg army general staff. Even then, Magyarization consisted mainly of ordering the German and Slavic officers to assume Magyar-sounding names.

In addition to Gömbös, three other Hungarian prime ministers had been career officers in the Habsburg armed forces, and their story illustrates the ideological and political dilemmas plaguing the former Habsburg officers in the new states. Prime Minister Gömbös (1932–1936) had fascist leanings, and he prided himself on his friendship with Hitler and Mussolini. Prime Minister General Döme Sztójay, a Croat who had gone by the name of Demeter Stojákovics in the Habsburg army, had been a captain in the Habsburg general staff and was even more pro-Nazi than Gömbös. As prime minister between March and August 1944, Sztójay was responsible for the mass deportation of Hungarian Jews to the Auschwitz death camp. On the other hand, General Géza Lakatos, a former honvéd first lieutenant seconded to the Habsburg general staff, was appointed prime minister by the regent in August 1944 because of his anti-Nazi leanings, in the hope that he could help extricate Hungary from the German alliance and the war. Finally, there is Prime Minister General Béla Dálnoki Miklós (or Béla Miklós von Dálnok), who had also been a honvéd first lieutenant seconded to the Habsburg general staff, but as prime minister was not a Horthy appointee. Having gone over to the Russians in October 1944 following Horthy's unsuccessful attempt to conclude an armistice with the Allies, Miklós became prime minister of the new, antifascist Hungary, at the order of Stalin.[7]

Hungary's fascist führer, Ferenc Szálasi, who succeeded Horthy in October 1944, had served in World War I as a career first lieutenant in a Kaiserjäger regiment. His National Socialist government included a number of former Habsburg career officers, at least one of whom had also served in the Hungarian Red Army in 1919. The anti-German resistance movement also included a number of former Habsburg officers, all of whom were subsequently arrested and some of whom were executed at the orders of Szálasi. Finally, Hungary's post–World War II antifascist government included, in addition to Béla Miklós, two other former Horthy generals who had begun their military career under Francis Joseph. At the 1945–1946 trial of Ferenc Szálasi and other fascists in the people's courts, former Habsburg officers, now members of the new democratic army, testified against the defendants. Szálasi was hanged, as were many other fascist or collaborationist officers and civilians.[8] Only after 1948, following the Stalinist takeover and the complete sovietization of Hungary, were Habsburg-Horthy officers finally replaced by new cadres recruited from among the workers and peasants. In the Stalinist period, thousands of former Habsburg-Horthy officers were imprisoned or deported to the countryside. Because the state denied pensions to former officers, all were reduced to indescribable poverty. Communist Hungary persecuted its World War I and World War II veterans. Only recently has the process of their moral rehabilitation begun, under the aegis of national revival and a more humane socialism.

The life of former Habsburg officers was considerably more difficult in the other successor states: in the Austrian republic because of the early radical socialist character of the state, and especially of the Volkswehr, the new people's army; in Czechoslovakia, Romania, Yugoslavia, and Poland because these countries saw themselves as liberated from the Habsburg yoke and as Entente allies. But these countries, too, needed trained officers, and so they co-opted a surprising number of former Austro-Hungarian officers, sometimes eschewing the issue of nationality.

Habsburg officers fared best in the new Polish army, in part because the Poles were much less hostile to the memory of the Habsburg dynasty than the other Slavs, and in part because Austrian (Galician) Poles counted among the best-trained administrators and soldiers of the new Polish state. In 1922, of the new Polish army's ninety-six generals, forty-five were former Habsburg officers. The creator of modern Poland, Józef Pilsudski, had, in the early years of World War I, led a Polish legion within the Austrian army in the struggle against Russia.[9] At least three chiefs of the general staff of the new Polish army—Count Stanisław Szeptycki, Baron Tadeusz Jordan-Rozwadowski, and Count Stanisław Haller—had been career officers in the Habsburg army. General Stanisław Maczek, commander of the First Polish Armored Division in Normandy, where the unit closed the "Falaise Gap," thereby enabling General Patton to win a spectacular victory in the summer of 1944, had been a lieutenant in the 2nd Kaiserschützen Regiment of the Austrian Landwehr during World War I. Finally, General Tadeusz Bor-Komorowski, the heroic defender of Warsaw against the German SS in the fall of 1944, had once served Francis Joseph as a career cavalry officer in the Austrian Landwehr.[10]

The Czechoslovak state emerged directly and entirely out of the body of old Austria-Hungary. Inevitably, the first officers of the new Czechoslovak army were former Austrian officers, mostly Czechs, but also a number of Bohemian and Moravian Germans. However, unlike in Hungary and Poland, these men had no great future. Czechoslovakia, the most democratic and tolerant of the successor states, was intolerant in military matters. Though less than half of the population was Czech-speaking, the Czechoslovak army spoke Czech and Czech alone. It was as if the Czech state, once a part of the Austrian half of the Habsburg monarchy, had moved over to the former Hungarian half and adopted the pre–World War I nationalist practices of the Hungarian Landwehr, a practice which the Czech politicians of the monarchy had never ceased to excoriate.

Post–World War I Romania and Yugoslavia were but greatly expanded versions of the original Romanian and Serbian kingdoms. At first, both co-opted Habsburg officers originating, respectively, from the Romanian and South Slav provinces of the Habsburg monarchy. Later, however, these men were replaced, one by one, with officers originating from the mother kingdoms. Still, one can point to such strange careers as that of the Romanian General Artur Phleps, a Transylvanian German, who had been a major in the Austro-Hungarian general staff. In the interwar period Phleps rose to assume command of the Romanian mountain units, but in 1941 he joined the German Waffen SS, where he became a three-star general and commander of the German occupation forces in Southern Transylvania and the Banat. He died, or was perhaps killed or even executed, in September 1944.[11]

Habsburg officers of South Slav origin readily joined the new South Slave state; in fact, they were instrumental in its creation. But as the Kingdom of Serbia and the Serbs in general gradually asserted their predominance in the new multinational state, relegating the Croats and other nationalities to secondary status, the Habsburg officers, most of whom were Croats, were systematically hounded out of the army.[12] One of these officers, Slavko Kvaternik, a former major on the Habsburg general staff, quit the Yugoslav army and joined the Ustashe, the underground Croatian terrorist movement. During World War II, he was commander in chief of the army of independent Croatia, set up by the Germans, and deputy to Ante Pavelić, the Croatian head of state. He was executed in Belgrade in 1947.[13]

Following the collapse of the monarchy, most career officers flocked to Vienna, where they struggled to preserve the corps or, failing that, at least to obtain a pension. However, pensions were wiped out by the inflation, and officers were denied even such a minimal compensation if they could not prove that, before 1918, they had been legal residents of what was now the Austrian republic. Thus it came about that such high-ranking officers as Field Marshal Svetozar Boroević, a Croat, suffered from near-starvation in the Austrian republic. At the same time, the South Slav state denied Boroević an entry visa and even confiscated his personal belongings.[14]

Younger men tried to learn a new profession. They worked as waiters, traveling salesmen, or clerks. Former pioneers and sappers sought jobs as civil engineers. Many lived in desperate poverty.

At first, the Austrian republic experimented with a revolutionary armed force, the Volkswehr, which was as hostile to the Habsburg dynasty as it was to capitalism. But even the Volkswehr needed trained commanders, and so it was organized and led by Julius Deutsch, a Social Democratic politician and former artillery reserve officer, and by Theodor Körner, a former colonel of the Habsburg general staff. Körner was a devoted Social Democrat and after World War II became the second president of the reborn Austrian republic.[15] The great majority of former officers were, however, antirepublican, and many joined the conservative Heimwehr, a private army which fought the socialist party militia, the *Schutzbund*. As Austria grew increasingly conservative, the army too was reorganized along more traditional lines. Now called the Bundesheer, it again hoisted the old Habsburg regimental insignia. However, it was a tiny force of less than thirty thousand men, as dictated by the peace treaty of 1919, and it had a hard time maintaining even a semblance of order in a republic whose party militias vastly outnumbered the regular army. In the 1930s, more and more former officers as well as active officers of the Bundesheer joined the underground Nazi movement; others remained monarchists or were loyal to Engelbert Dollfuss's and Kurt Schuschnigg's clerical, anti-Nazi dictatorship. Dollfuss himself had been a first lieutenant in the reserve during World War I. Indeed, having been at least a reserve officer in the Habsburg army was now nearly a necessary precondition for a political career in central and east central Europe.

When the Anschluss threatened in 1938, General Alfred Jansa, the chief of the general staff of the Austrian army and a former Habsburg officer, was prepared, as were some other generals, to resist the Germans, but he and his colleagues were swept away by the tide of political events. Some of these officers landed in a German concentration camp, such as Feldmarschalleutnant Johann Friedländer, an Austrian general of Jewish origin, and Generalmajor Josef Stochmal, former military commander of Salzburg.[16]

The German annexation of Austria opened the way to a second career for former Habsburg officers, and many answered the call. Lothar Rendulić, the son of a Croatian Grenzer and a captain seconded to the Austro-Hungarian general staff during World War I, became a four-star general in the German Wehrmacht and commander of a group of armies. Another Wehrmacht Generaloberst was Erhard Raus, who had been a first lieutenant in the Austro-Hungarian army. At least 220 former Habsburg officers served Hitler as generals, among them the notorious Alexander Löhr, who was hanged by the Yugoslavs in 1947.[17]

Gentile officers at least had the choice of whether or not to serve a successor state. They could always take up a civilian profession or, if none could be found, live in dignified poverty. They could even attempt to resist the new authority, and some did: for instance, Anton Lehár, who opposed both Horthy Hungary and, later, the German Nazis, and who paid for his staunch monarchism with lifelong poverty. Only one group of officers was given no choice, except perhaps emigration: the Jewish officers and those of Jewish origin, whose fate was persecution and often death.

In the interwar period, former Austro-Hungarian career officers of Jewish origin were gradually weeded out from the armies of the successor states, mainly through attrition. Ironically, those in the Czechoslovak, Romanian, and Yugoslav armies were usually purged not as Jews but as Germans or Hungarians. But even in Austria and Hungary, where their nationality could not be used against them, Jewish officers were sometimes ill tolerated.

Jewish officers in the Austrian republic, mostly reservists, were permitted to keep their rank until the Anschluss in 1938. Thereafter, Nazi persecution descended on them with full fury. In that year, at least 238 "non-Aryan" officers were dismissed from service.[18] Additionally, it appears that Jewish officers suffered a worse fate than other Austrian Jews. Assimilated and trusting in their German brothers-in-arms, many elected not to leave Austria when it was still possible to do so. Then, in 1941, the local Gestapo commander demanded that the "Organization of Jewish War Invalids in Vienna" submit a complete list of its members and a separate list of highly decorated or invalid officers. The latter were deported to the model ghetto in Theresienstadt; the others were dispatched directly to the death camps. War heroes still did not escape death, however, since the road to Theresienstadt led ultimately to Auschwitz as well.[19]

In Hungary, Jewish reserve officers were particularly keen on disproving the Jewish stab-in-the-back legend; they edited and published a whole series of regimental histories making clear, without ever mentioning religion, that death at the front had been no respecter of confessional differences. There too, however, racial anti-Semitism gradually prevailed, and in 1939 military statisticians reported that there was not a single "full Jew" left in the career officer corps, meaning that converts, too, had been discharged. In 1940, the deployment of Jewish males for labor service was ordered, and on April 16, 1941, Decree No. 2870 deprived Jewish reserve officers of their rank. Subsequently, all former officers of even partly Jewish origin were called in for a renewal of their military booklets. The new identity card said nothing about their rank, decorations, wounds, or previous service record; instead, it classified them as liable to perform "auxiliary labor service." The card was stamped with a big "Zs," for *Zsidó* (Jew). Only Jewish war veterans with a Gold Medal for Bravery or two Great Silver Medals, or those with at least 75 percent disability due to injuries suffered in the Great War, were exempted from the decree or from the other anti-Jewish measures.

Generaloberst Hazai was allowed to die in peace in Budapest in 1942; others were less lucky. Many former Jewish officers died in labor battalions on the eastern front, and many more were deported and gassed on Adolf Eichmann's orders in 1944. Still, as noted in the preface, a handful of Jewish war heroes were spared even by the Arrow Cross regime, which had assumed power in October 1944, and I clearly remember a certain Jewish captain, a veteran of World War I, sitting in the administrative center of the Budapest Jewish community and receiving some Hungarian Nazi militiamen. They stood at attention, and he gave them only a casual salute. Moreover, because Jewish officers were among the best assimilated Hungarian Jews, they were better able to hide with Gentile families. And because so many of them lived in Budapest, from which Jews were generally not deported, a substantial proportion managed to survive the war.[20]

What is one to make of all this information? Austro-Hungarian training, to be sure, did not direct these officers toward any specific political orientation. Some served their new fatherland loyally, whatever its political and ethnic makeup; others, however, refused to labor for the enemy of their former emperor, choosing instead a poor living, preferably in Austria and Hungary, the two states which at least could not be accused of having done battle against Austria-Hungary. Many remained monarchists to the end, even refusing to shake hands with their renegade comrades. A few became socialists; many more flirted with the right-wing movements or became Nazis. Some died opposing Hitler; many more died for him. Most of those who rose to high rank in one of the successor states had served on the general staff of the Habsburg army. In fact, if any generalizations can be made, it is that the Habsburg war college and the general staff had trained successful military commanders, and that professionalism had a greater influence on these individuals than ideology.

Professionalism was the operative bond among officers—a bond that was eventually shattered. In the final analysis, the postwar political consciousness of the military was neither more nor less bewildering to decipher than that of ordinary citizens, millions of whom changed loyalties, voluntarily or involuntarily, during the most troubled decades in east central European history. At war's end, Habsburg officers found that gone forever was their sense of shared purpose in a professionalism directed chiefly toward preserving peace. Beyond this military professionalism built up over a century, no political ideology could claim them as an indissoluble fraternity in the far-flung region that was once the Habsburg monarchy.

In 1988, as these lines were being written, I received a letter from a Colonel Krzeczunowicz of the interwar Polish army, who had been a career lieutenant in His Imperial and Apostolic Royal Majesty's 1st Ulan Regiment. Writing from exile in London, his residence since World War II, the colonel referred to his experiences in the Joint Army as "the happiest years of my life." The calligraphic handwriting, barely trembling, bore unmistakable witness to Krzeczunowicz's training in an imperial-royal military school. Who can tell whether the sentiments he expressed were those of an old man longing for the days of his youth or whether they reflected genuine experience?

APPENDIX I

On Belles-Lettres, Memoirs, and Histories

Literature

Probably no armed force has entered into popular music, literature, and art as spiritedly as that of Austria-Hungary. Its gallant officers waltz across the stage and court handsome countesses; its ordinary soldiers sparkle with *bons mots,* polished boots, and good manners. "Háry János," the hero of Zoltán Kodály's eponymous operetta, combines the popular stage image of both officers and men when the irrepressible hussar captures the heart of a French princess and, with the same appealing artlessness, captures the great Napoleon as well.

In serious literature such novelists and playwrights as the Austro-Germans Franz Theodor Csokor, Robert Musil, Joseph Roth, Roda Roda, Stefan Zweig, and Arthur Schnitzler; the Hungarians Ferenc Herczeg, Sándor Márai, and Géza Ottlik; the Czech Jaroslav Hašek; and the Croatian Miroslav Krleža manifest their wonderment with the monarchy's multinational army.[1]

What explains this fascination? Certainly, in part it was the splendid spectacle of the soldiery in that uniform-mad but very unmilitaristic empire. Certainly too, the crucial role of the army in maintaining the cohesion of the variegated Habsburg possessions was a factor. But there was a third reason as well: most of the writers mentioned had been military students or even officers of the Habsburg army. Cadets Márai and Ottlik; Ensign Roth; Lieutenants Hašek, Krleža, and Roda Roda; Captain Musil—and one could go on—were all able to draw upon personal experience in writing about the military. The heroes and antiheroes of their novels, plays, and short stories, whether lonely adolescents aching under the harsh discipline and sexual repression of the military schools, seemingly carefree but in fact desperate officers, or simple but cunningly antimilitaristic enlisted men, tell us an enormous amount about life in the army and about relations between soldiers and civilians. The portraits these writers have drawn are much more somber than those of the operettas; they are also more ambiguous and contradictory. Was the peacetime army a dreadful prison that corrupted its inmates (both officers and men), as Hašek contends, or was it, as Joseph Roth suggests, a unique supranational institution that practiced ethnic and confessional tolerance on a scale unknown among the warring factions of civilian society? Did the wartime Habsburg army consist of men ready to die for a lost cause, or was it a soulless colossus that trampled on innocent peasants and Orthodox priests wherever it set foot?

The insight of the novelists and playwrights is valuable, but it is to memoir literature that we need turn to provide a more reliable perspective on the subject. We are in fact blessed with an abundance of such material, accumulated in part through the efforts of Dr. Peter Broucek, an Austrian military archivist and historian who persuaded scores of pensioned soldiers to pen their reminiscences and make them as complete as possible.[2]

Like retired officers everywhere, the former officers of the Habsburg monarchy were keen to record their recollections, if not as a form of self-justification, then as a lesson to others. Not all of these authors were commanding generals or important general staff officers; they also include individuals with more mundane careers. But even generals were often happier to relate their family background, education, and early years of service than to recount the campaigns they led and—this being the Austro-Hungarian army—often lost. Because a majority of Habsburg officers came from military families, where one's own career was closely bound up with those of fathers and sons, we find many a memoir writer proudly referring to himself as a *Tornisterkind,* a child "borne in the knapsack" of his soldier-father.[3] There also must have been some truth to the memoir writers' persistent assertion that theirs was a difficult but exciting youth, and that life at the military school and with the troops was a stimulating adventure. As a result of this broad perspective, these memoirs tell us even more about Habsburg society and the *mentalité* of the officers than they do about campaigns and wars.

Understandably, there is no clear-cut boundary between genuine memoir literature and the type of historiography that is based primarily on personal experiences and private papers. The memoirs of Field Marshal Conrad (1852–1925), for instance, are more than just an auto-biography; they represent an enormous (if biased and often erroneous) historical and documentary study of the last two decades in the life of the monarchy.[4] Similarly, the personal recollections of Generaloberst Arz (1857–1935), the monarchy's last chief of staff, served as a major source for his several historical studies of World War I.[5]

At the other end of the spectrum are the partly fictionalized reminiscences of such popular military writers as Rudolf von Eichthal, Ferdinand Fauland, Albert Lorenz, F. V. Schöffel, Oskar Teuber, and Carl von Torresani.[6] What distinguishes these writings from serious belles lettres is the fact that the popular accounts are usually written in the first person and employ fictionalized anecdotes merely to embellish the authors' personal recollections. By contrast, Musil's *Young Törless*—while based on the author's own experiences in military school—far transcends reality. To complicate matters, some of the popular, anecdotal writers, particularly Oskar Teuber, also dabbled in military historiography, mostly in order to defend the army against its critics.[7]

Memoirs

Remembering 1848–1849

The writing of Austrian military memoirs had some precedents in the seventeenth and eighteenth centuries, but it became a fairly popular pastime only in the first half of the nineteenth century. Thereafter, it waxed ever more common. The Napoleonic Wars inspired a few such writers, notably M. R. von Thielen (1781–1865),[8] but it was the campaigns of 1848–1849 that first evoked a whole series of reminiscences, among them, those of Moriz Edler von Angeli (1829–1904), Karl Bigot de Saint-Quentin (1805–1884), Leopold Kolowrat-Krakowsky (1804–1863), Anton von Mollinary (1820–1904), Carl von Schönhals (1788–1857), Carl von Torresani (1846–1907), and Ludwig von Welden (1780–1853). The memoirs of such Hungarian *Insurgentenführer* as Lajos Asbóth (1803–1882), Henryk Dembiński (1791–1864), Arthur Görgey (1818–1916), and György Klapka (1820–1902) provide

vide a valuable counterpart to those of the Austrians, particularly in light of the fact that the Hungarian revolutionary commanders (with the exception of Dembiński) were all former Habsburg officers.[9]

As with all war memoirs, one ought to distinguish between those that concentrate on military events and those that emphasize the human element. In the case of the texts dealing with 1848–1849, the first category includes the writings of Kolowrat-Krakowsky, Schönhals, Welden, and all the Hungarians, while the second includes the memoirs of Angeli, Bigot de Saint-Quentin, Mollinary, and Torresani. Those in the first group played leading roles in the Italian and Hungarian campaigns, and their primary reason for writing was to justify their actions. Generalmajor Kolowrat-Krakowsky commanded a brigade and earned the Order of Maria Theresa while in Italy. Feldmarschalleutnant Schönhals served as a deputy to Field Marshal Radetzky in the Italian war; he also wrote Radetzky's famous army orders. Ludwig von Welden, who was commander in chief of the Habsburg forces in Hungary and Transylvania between April and June 1849, the period of the worst Austrian defeats, takes pains to explain why the Austrian withdrawal was necessary, and how it prepared the way for the subsequent victorious campaign of General Haynau. Colonel Asbóth, once a senior captain in an Austrian *Kürassier* cavalry regiment, acted as a corps commander in the Hungarian national army. Dembiński, a Polish emigré general, was commander in chief of all the Hungarian forces at various points in 1849. Arthur Görgey's campaign descriptions display a remarkable professional detachment as well as a dual (and contradictory) commitment to both the notion of a just war fought for Hungarian constitutional rights and the ideal of dynastic loyalty. Görgey's memoirs clearly reflect his rigorous training in the Habsburg army, which brought him into repeated conflict with Louis Kossuth's concept of a revolutionary *levée en masse*. Finally, there are the voluminous memoirs of General Klapka, a former first lieutenant in the Habsburg army and Hungary's second most successful general during the war.

All these writers are rather short on autobiography and long on campaigns. Their recollections are informative but also apologetic and quite dry, with only occasional bursts of violent sentiment, as in General Welden's venomous remarks about the rebellious Viennese proletariat, Dembiński's contemptuous comments about the Hungarians, or Görgey's acerbic critique of revolutionary Hungary's civilian leadership.

More interesting, from a human and social point of view, are the 1848–1849 memoirs of lesser officers. Moriz von Angeli, an important military historian with two memoir volumes and a monumental study of Archduke Charles to his credit, was a young infantry lieutenant in 1848.[10] His *Wien nach 1848* is a withering indictment of the iron rule imposed by the Austrian military in the imperial capital after its recapture by Prince Windisch-Graetz in October 1848.

Unlike the gentle Angeli, the conservative Bigot de Saint-Quentin displays little concern for the plight of civilians. Descended from a leading military family, this future *General der Kavallerie* served as an adjutant to General Jelačić in 1848, an experience that only strengthened his already-well-developed conviction of the need for a total separation of the army ("the only pillar of the monarchy") from the rest of society. He first propounded his views in a book published in 1847 and continued to argue in the same vein in later works. He was, moreover, as J. C. Allmayer-Beck puts it, one of the army's decisive "opinion-makers."[11]

Anton von Mollinary, later one of the monarchy's most distinguished generals and a man of moderate-to-liberal convictions, was only twenty-eight when the revolution began. The son of a family of Grenzer officers in the Tschaikisten (Danube Flotilla) district of southern Hungary, Mollinary had been a general staff officer before the revolution, specializing in river warfare. During 1848–1849, he distinguished himself in several major northern Italian battles and was wounded twice; he later termed the events of 1848–1849 "the most important period in my life."[12] He became the army's youngest colonel after the war and the commander of the Austrian flotilla that plied the northern Italian lakes. Mollinary describes in detail the Italian events of 1848, but more important is his report of the tragedy that befell his family. During the war between Austria and Hungary that began in September 1848, his father, a lieutenant colonel of the Tschaikisten, as well as his uncle and two other close relatives ended up on the Hungarian side—the father and the uncle involuntarily, and the other two of their own free will. As a result, they were imprisoned and cashiered by the Austrians when the war ended. Mollinary never succeeded in having his father rehabilitated.

Finally, there is Carl von Torresani, who was just a little boy in 1848, but whose memoirs nevertheless contain a detailed account of the revolutionary events in northern Italy. The descendant of dynastically loyal Italian bureaucrats on his father's side and of Italian grandees on his mother's, Torresani witnessed the Milan uprising in March 1848, which was, to a great extent, directed against his own grandfather, the police president of Lombardy. He dramatically describes his family's flight from Milan as well as his grandfather's disgrace and forcible retirement after the war. The memoirs also tell of his widowed mother's encounter with and marriage to Anton von Mollinary: a rare union between the daughter of Italian patricians and the son of a Grenzer officer.

Unfortunately for us, the most important Austrian commanders of the 1848–1849 war—Radetzky, Windisch-Graetz, Jelačić, and Haynau—left no memoirs. There are some fragmentary reminiscences attributed to Field Marshal Radetzky, but as Peter Broucek has pointed-ed out, their authorship is doubtful.[13] The situation is somewhat better in the case of General Jelačić, whose campaigns were vividly described in the diaries of First Lieutenant Baron Hermann Dahlen and Major Count Wilhelm Hompesch, as well as in the memoirs of one of Jelačić's more important subordinates, Feldmarschalleutnant Joseph Freiherr von Neustädter. These and other writings on Jelačić have been compiled in a volume edited and introduced by Ferdinand Hauptmann.[14] As for Windisch-Graetz and Haynau, we must content ourselves with a few less-than-comprehensive biographies.

Memoirs Written while the Emperor was Alive

The most remarkable common characteristic of the pre-1918 memoirs is the political simplicity and optimistic worldview of the authors, at least when compared to some of the post-1918 memoir literature. One finds little if any trace of the religious and ethnic prejudice, political fanaticism, and "Walter Mitty-ish" fantasizing common in some twentieth-century memoirs.

Of the writers mentioned, Angeli, Mollinary, and Torresani were still alive and active well past the revolutions of 1848. Their memoirs embrace part or even all of the second half of the nineteenth century. To their work must be added that of such members of the older generation as Heinrich von Födransperg (1835–1909), Wilhelm Gründorf von Zebegény (1832–1920), Wilhelm Hirsch (1836–1935), Anton von Pitreich, Sr. (1838–1907), Rudolf Potier des Échelles (1836–1912), Baron Daniel Salis-Soglio (1826–1919), Andreas Thürheim (1827–1904), Ludwig von Wattman (1827–1907), and Karl Went von Römö (1831–1910).[15] All of these men witnessed dramatic changes and substantial reforms in the structure and life of the army. Most of them fought and were promoted in the catastrophic wars of 1859 and 1866, and then continued to serve in the long period of peace. Unfortunately, the commanders in chief of the 1859 and 1866 wars, Feldzeugmeisters Franz von Gyulai and Ludwig von Benedek wrote no memoirs. Nor did, incidentally, Archduke Albrecht, whose successful military career spanned more than fifty years.

What is admirable about this generation of memoir writers is their willingness to delve into minute details of their lives at military school and with the troops. The result is a series of enchanting reminiscences, especially those of Angeli, Födransperg, Hirsch, Mollinary, Potier des Échelles, Teuber, and Torresani. All these works are strikingly similar to one another in their description of specific aspects of military life, in their premodern ideology, and even in their style and topical structure. This, it might seem, should enable us to make far-reaching generalizations, yet it is precisely these remarkable similarities that warn us against hastily drawn conclusions. Behind the nearly identical accounts and experiences may lie some unwritten code for writing military memoirs. There seem to be only two exceptions to the rule: the early military historian Daniel Fenner von Fenneberg, who became a revolutionary in 1848 and even before the revolution had been extremely critical of military life, and Gründorf von Zebegény, a general staff officer who made a name for himself in the Danish campaign of 1864, only to be forced into retirement in 1866 as a result of an armed encounter, as we have seen in chapter 7, with his wife's lover. In his not always reliable memoirs, Gründorf goes so far as to hint at the political and military shortcomings and legendary ingratitude of Francis Joseph.[16] Basically, however, it is not the fundamental honesty of the older generation of memoir writers that one questions, but their ability or willingness to recall, at the end of a successful career, the personal doubts and discouragements that might have plagued their youths.

Practically without exception, the nineteenth-century memoir writers began their military careers as children, either through enrollment in a military school or by entering a regiment directly. They are at their best when describing the wild pleasures and monstrous discipline of the military schools, as well as the glories and miseries of the young officer's daily existence. Much in the former chapters was based on these often delightful early memoirs.

Remembering the Dual Monarchy

Those who wrote their reminiscences after the dissolution of the monarchy felt much freer to vent their sentiments. Trapped in a new political situation which the majority of former career officers rejected, poor, disoriented, and often cruelly neglected by the postwar regimes, some of these officers clung even more desperately to the conservative monarchist ideology of their youth. Others unconsciously combined their "Old Austrian" ideas with new, usually right-wing ideologies. The consequence was an often contradictory simultaneous longing for the old, tolerant, supranational state and for a new authoritarian or dictatorial nationalist system.

At the risk of oversimplification, we might divide the post–World War I memoir literature into three (obviously overlapping) categories: (1) memoirs devoted almost exclusively to the events of World War I; (2) autobiographies written by those whose military career ended more or less with the dissolution of the monarchy; and (3) reminiscences of soldiers who subsequently made a significant military career in one of the successor states or Nazi Germany.

The memoirs of Conrad and Arz are the most important of the works that deal primarily with World War I. To theirs, one must add the memoirs of August von Cramon (1861–1940), Germany's wartime military plenipotentiary in Vienna; Albrecht von Margutti (1869–1940), a member of the emperor's military cabinet; and Alfred Krauss (1882–1938), one of the monarchy's best generals.[17] Cramon and Margutti mostly discuss politics and personalities, while Krauss is concerned with strategy and the conduct of the war. Krauss's often legitimate critique of the monarchy's war effort must nevertheless be treated with caution, given the writer's right-wing views. There is a great contrast between the ideological underpinnings of his memoirs and those, for instance, of Conrad. The much older field marshal heaped abuse on the parliamentary system, liberalism, the Hungarians, the monarchy's Slavic subjects, the Italians, the Freemasons, and the "international Jewish conspiracy," yet he never failed to pay tribute to loyal soldiers, whatever their religion or nationality. General Krauss, on the other hand, represented a new type—a political soldier of the racist, National Socialist variety. Characteristically, most former Habsburg generals shunned Krauss precisely because of his ideology.

The second category of postwar memoirs, consisting of fairly complete autobiographies of military men who ended their careers around 1918–1919, is the most extensive. It includes, among others, the writings of such popular raconteurs as Rudolf von Eichthal (1877– 1974), Ferdinand von Fauland (1893–?), and Albert Lorenz (1885–1970), brother of the famous naturalist Konrad Lorenz. These writers are unanimous in their enthusiastic endorsement of the old army and its military schools in particular; they are at their best when discussing their adventures as military students. Eichthal and Fauland are also highly informative when describing their experiences as young subalterns in Galicia. Lorenz, the son of a famous orthopedic surgeon, vividly relates his much more comfortable experiences as a reserve officer, first in a cavalry regiment, then in the "Volunteer Automobile Corps," and, finally, as an army surgeon.[18] A creative artist of another type was Ludwig Hesshaimr (1872– 1956), who began his career at the Budapest Kadettenschule, went on to a Hungarian infantry regiment where almost everyone but he spoke Serbian, enjoyed a respectable military career, and ended up as a professional painter and illustrator in Rio de Janeiro. He was eighty-three when he wrote his reminiscences.[19]

Some military memoirs read like fiction, probably because they have been fictionalized, whether consciously or unconsciously. Two examples are the recollections of artillerist Hans Mailáth-Pokorny and of cavalryman Rüdiger Seutter. What they have to say is certainly not without value, but their accounts (particularly Mailáth's) are so full of enchanting tales about loyal subordinates, handsome horses, talented dogs, beautiful, fiery, yet chaste Hungarian and Polish baronesses, bungling superiors, and the authors' own heroic exploits that they ought to be read less for the sake of factual information than as testimony to the kind of image officers wished to project about themselves and their fellows.[20]

Because most of the post–World War I memoir writers had served on the general staff, it is a welcome change of pace to read the recollections of a member of the lowly Train. Captain Josef Leb (1874–1946), later a Catholic priest and writer, claims, perhaps correctly, to be the only author, within his service branch, of an autobiography. Writing in Austria in 1933, Leb is "up-to-date" enough to exult over the "Christian-German cultural mission" in southeastern Europe and boast, wrongly, that his branch of service had not known a single Jewish career officer. He is also sufficiently Old Austrian to praise the Jewish reserve officers and men who constituted a substantial part of the transportation corps.[21]

The great majority of memoirs in the Vienna War Archive are by officers whose mother tongue was German, all the more reason to appreciate the recollections of Gregor von Miščević (1856–1937), son of a family of South Slav Grenzer. He grew up in a peasant *zadruga* and ended his military career in 1918 as a Feldmarschalleutnant ennobled by the emperor. Like so many other military memoir writers, Miščević completed his informative and lucid recollections when he was more than eighty years old.[22]

The postwar memoirs of former general staff officers, many of whom had advanced to general before the dissolution of the monarchy, are quite naturally the most substantive. In particular, they are keen on reviewing in detail the hard struggle involved in acquiring admittance to and living through general staff school. Moritz von Auffenberg (1852–1928), one of the most talented products of the war college, served between 1911 and 1912 as the monarchy's minister of war and was one of the very few Austro-Hungarian generals able to inflict a defeat on the Russians in 1914. Even so, his was a controversial and tortured career, as he relates with vehemence in his memoirs.[23]

Some former general staff officers, such as Lieutenant Colonel Otto von Kiesewetter (1881–1962), presented their recollections in a series of lectures, addressed in Kiesewetter's case to a veteran's association.[24] Baron Anton von Lehár (1876–1962), one of the monarchy's most highly decorated officers, collected his papers and recollections over several decades. His was a truly Austrian family—Czech, German, and Hungarian, depending on the generation. Lehár considered himself a "Habsburg subject"—he had no nationality. The portion of his voluminous and often dramatic memoirs which has been published deals mainly with his forlorn attempt, in 1921, to restore Emperor-King Charles to the Hungarian throne.[25]

Almost all of the general staff officers devote considerable energy to attacking Hungarian politicians, whom they view as the gravediggers of the monarchy; particularly striking in this regard are the reminiscences of Baron Ernst Palombini von Jedina (1886–1979), a specialist in telecommunications.[26] Kurt von Schmedes (1877–1964), who, like most other general staff officers, came from a military family (his father and two uncles had been generals, and his brother was killed in 1914), offers much useful information, among other things on the Technical Military Academy at Mödling, where he was a teacher.[27] Franz Xaver Schubert (1883–1973) provides valuable insight into the postwar fate of his fellow students from the war college class of 1910. There were forty-four students in this group, and leaving aside those who had been killed in the war or had changed profession, Schubert was able to list eight who became generals in interwar Hungary, two who made a career in Czechoslovakia (one was subsequently executed by the Germans), one who became a general in the Polish army and was killed in Pilsudski's 1926 coup d'état, and one, Alfred Jansa, who became chief of staff of the Austrian Bundesheer in the 1930s. Schubert's class included Edmund Glaise von Horstenau, who became a general in the Wehrmacht, and the cavalryman Gustav Grabscheidt, who committed suicide following the Anschluss of Austria because he had a Jewish grandmother.[28]

One of the more recent autobiographies, written in 1940 when its author was eighty-four, would actually fit better into the category of older memoirs, partly because it concentrates on the events of the second half of the nineteenth century and partly because of its author's old-fashioned liberal inclinations. General Adolf Stillfried (1856–1946) is deeply concerned about the relations between officers and men, the army's neglect of the common soldier, the difficulties involved in training illiterate recruits from the monarchy's eastern provinces, and the language problems that plagued the military. Stillfried also deplores the devastating effect on morale caused by the army's obligation to assist civilian authorities in suppressing social and nationalist disturbances during the last decades of the monarchy.[29]

Two more important autobiographies, both by former high-ranking general staff officers, belong in the second category. August von Urbański (1886–1950) came from a Polish middle-class family but, as a typical soldier's son, he learned to speak several languages or rather language admixtures. In 1911 he was appointed chief of the Evidenzbüro, the military counterintelligence service. As such, he became deeply involved in the 1913 espionage affair of his former subordinate in the Büro, Colonel Redl. Although Urbański's responsibility for having failed to detect Redl's many years of espionage was clear to all, the continued protection of the emperor against the fury of Francis Ferdinand prevented that scandal from destroying him. Urbański ended his career in 1918 as a Feldmarschalleutnant.[30]

Theodor von Zeynek (1873–1948), a brilliant mind and a member of the general staff's all-important Operationsbüro, was a devoted follower of Conrad and of the latter's aggressive political strategy.[31]

There is only one category left for our consideration: the memoirs of soldiers who continued their military careers after the monarchy's dissolution. Three important sets of reminiscences need to be mentioned in this context—those of Carl Bardolff, Lothar Rendulić and, above all, Edmund Glaise von Horstenau—all of whom were Austro-Hungarian general staff officers in World War I and later became generals in National Socialist Germany.

Like Anton Lehár, Dr. Carl Freiherr von Bardolff (1865–1953), whose memoirs were published in Germany in 1938, was the son of a military band leader. His uncle was the memoirist Wilhelm Gründorf von Zebegény. Bardolff studied law at Graz University, where he belonged to a German nationalist student fraternity. He became a career officer in 1888 and earned his doctorate in law a short time later. His path led him through general staff school to the Operationsbüro of the general staff and from there to a teaching position back at the general staff school. In 1911, he was appointed head of Francis Ferdinand's military cabinet. A full-fledged anti-liberal, Bardolff easily fit into the Archduke's "Belvedere Cabal." During World War I, he occupied important general staff positions. In the interwar period, he was a businessman and president of the right-wing Austrian "Deutscher Klub." After 1938, he served as a General der Infanterie in the German Wehrmacht. Although highly intelligent and knowledgeable, Bardolff—as a racist and a Pan-German nationalist—represented the very opposite of the Old Austrian officer. Characteristically, he asserts in his memoirs that his parents were both "*rassestark*," that is, racially healthy and pure.[32]

Lothar Rendulić (1887–1971) came from a Croatian Grenzer family. During World War I, he was attached to the general staff, and in the interwar period he served in the army of the Austrian republic. Pensioned off in 1936 because of his National Socialist views, he joined the German Wehrmacht after the Anschluss and ended World War II as a Generaloberst. Rendulić's memoirs show him to be a neophyte German chauvinist and a convinced National Socialist.[33]

The most complex personality of the three was Edmund Glaise von Horstenau (1882–1946), whose enormous memoirs, edited and introduced by Dr. Peter Broucek, are an invaluable historical source.[34] Born at Braunau in Upper Austria, Hitler's birthplace, Glaise came from a family of officers. He wanted to become a priest, but because of his family's poverty, he was sent to military school. An excellent student at the Wiener Neustadt Military Academy ("the best years of my life"), he became a Jäger and then a general staff officer. Attached to the army high command during World War I, Glaise wrote the army reports, known as "*Höfer Berichte.*" By then, he was a confirmed German nationalist and a bitter critic of the Hungarians. He also wrote many military essays that, after 1918, led him to a job in the Austrian War Archive where he became director in 1925. In this capacity, he wrote or edited such important works as a biography of Feldzeugmeister Beck, and the multivolume *Österreich-Ungarns letzter Krieg.*[35] Politically, Glaise moved steadily to the right, ending up in March 1938 as vice-chancellor of Arthur Seyss-Inquart's pro-Nazi cabinet and, in 1941, as German military plenipotentiary in fascist Croatia. Captured by the Americans in 1945, he committed suicide. Glaise's memoirs, part of which were written in captivity, are important because of his interest in every conceivable aspect of military life, tactics, and strategy, his ability to recall correctly a myriad of names and events, and because of Peter Broucek's careful editing, which has turned this work into a veritable encyclopedia of central European military, political, and even cultural history. Glaise's extraordinary career and suicide, as well as the contradiction between his love for the old multiethnic army and his German nationalism, bear witness to the tragedy of Austria-Hungary's often brilliant but ideologically confused general staff officers. Even in Zagreb, as Hitler's emissary, Glaise hesitated between his wish to realize Nazi racial goals and his desire to protect the South Slav population to whom he was attracted as a former Habsburg officer.

The reminiscences by Austro-German and Hungarian army officers cited here are only a part of the memoir literature on the Habsburg armed forces. Naval officers, including Admiral Miklós Horthy (1868–1957), also recorded their recollections, as did Polish, Czech, and other army officers. Finally, some military diaries, such as that of Feldzeugmeister Franz Freiherr Kuhn von Kuhnenfeld (1817–1896), the monarchy's war minister between 1868 and

1874, are at least as informative as the genuine memoirs. Understandably, all of these authors were more favorably disposed toward the old army than most of the belletrists, particularly the non-German ones. The researcher looking for tales of oppression or of military persecution of Hungarians, Slavs, Romanians, Italians, democrats, and socialists, will be disappointed. Even when they do find something to criticize—military schools, service with the troops, the army leadership, or the conduct of wars—the memoir writers moderate their attack, either out of a sense of camaraderie or of nostalgia. Yet even if we take all these limitations into consideration, the picture that emerges is that of an extraordinarily complex, vital, and, at least until 1914, ethnically as well as religiously tolerant institution.

However, the memoirs also reveal one of the army's basic shortcomings: the inability or the unwillingness of the officers to become acquainted with the ethnic idiosyncrasies of the enlisted men. It is, without a doubt, one of the gravest criticisms that can be leveled at the multinational Austro-Hungarian army.

Histories and Historians

Habsburg military historiography is less well developed, for understandable reasons, than its French, German, or Russian counterparts. For several decades after the dissolution of the monarchy, what little serious research was done in the field was primarily the work of a few former Habsburg officers who had found refuge in the military archives of one or another successor state. The rest was simply a product of political passion, with Austrian or Hungarian monarchists and conservatives in one camp and Austrian socialists, Hungarian radical nationalists, and practically all the Czech, Romanian, and South Slav writers in the other. In the 1930s, the anti-Habsburg camp was powerfully reinforced by Austrian and German National Socialists, who regarded both the monarchy and its army as "Judeo-Hungaro-Slavic" abominations. At most, former Habsburg officers who became Nazi sympathizers saw a redeeming grace in the "solid German racial core" of the Austro-Hungarian army and its respectable performance on the German side during World War I. Nor did post–World War II developments help matters, as the Marxist-Leninists of east central Europe added their strident voices to the earlier nationalist critics of the monarchy.

Recently, however, things have begun to change. In Austria, newfound patriotism has led writers to appreciate the non-German characteristics and unique historical role of the multinational Habsburg army. In Hungary, the gradual rehabilitation of the Dual Monarchy has at last spilled over into military historiography, a field hitherto hobbled by strict dogmatic orthodoxy.[36] Stirrings of nostalgia and hence a growing sympathy for the Habsburg army can be detected in Poland, Yugoslavia, and Italy as well. Only Czechoslovak and, even more so, Romanian historians continue to glorify the liberation struggle of their respective nations against Habsburg oppression, ignoring the fact that Czech, Slovak, and Romanian soldiers once also marched under the Habsburg flag. Some of the best examples of this recent, more balanced approach can be found in the pages of a multivolume series, "War and Society in East Central Europe," edited by Béla K. Király, an American historian who served as a general in the post–World War II Hungarian army. The titles of some of these volumes, which are generally based on the papers of various international historical conferences, are listed in the notes, as are the names of a great many of the contributors.[37]

Even though there now exist a number of important essay collections on the Habsburg army, there are few comprehensive histories. The most attractive of the latter is a three-volume publication—each volume bearing a different title—by the Austrian historians Johann Christoph Allmayer-Beck and Erich Lessing, which covers the long period from the fifteenth century to 1918.[38] Essentially a popular history (and beautifully illustrated), the work goes far beyond the conventional record of military campaigns to include brief analyses of army organization, recruitment policy, the development of weaponry, and even the pay and living conditions of the officers and men. A semiofficial Austrian military publication, covering the last three hundred years of the Austrian army up to the 1960s, usefully complements the three volumes, as does Herbert Patera's fine study of the history of the Austrian army.[39] The older general histories, such as those of Hermann Meynert (1854) and the military journalist Oskar Teuber (1895), are today chiefly of antiquarian interest.[40] Finally, Alphons von Wrede's five-volume compendium on the regiments, independent battalions, and all other units and institutions of the Habsburg army, published between 1898 and 1905, is a most valuable encyclopedic reference.[41]

If there is relatively little on the pre-Napoleonic period, when Austria was truly a great power and its armed forces quite respectable, there is much more on the nineteenth century when, ironically, the monarchy was a great power in name only and its army markedly inferior to that of France, Prussia, or Russia. Clearly, decadence arouses interest, including— admittedly—my own interest.

A major new work on the Habsburg army from 1848 to 1914 is *Die bewaffnete Macht,* edited by the Austrian historians Adam Wandruszka and Peter Urbanitsch and representing volume 5 of a majestic series, *Die Habsburgermonarchie 1848–1918,* published under the sponsorship of the Austrian Academy of Sciences. *Die bewaffnete Macht* includes two comprehensive essays, one by Allmayer-Beck and the other by Walter Wagner, as well as more specialized discussions of the Austro-Hungarian navy and the Hungarian National Guard. These writings deal not with military campaigns but with army organization, military life, and civil-military relations.[42] A further volume in the series will discuss the Habsburg Monarchy in World War I, including, of course, a treatment of the army during those years.

The entire post-Napoleonic period is the subject of U.S. historian Gunther E. Rothenberg's valuable *Army of Francis Joseph,* so often cited in this book; it combines political with institutional and social history. The same author has produced two volumes on the history of the Military Border and another on the army under Archduke Charles, Napoleon's victorious opponent at the Battle of Aspern in 1809.[43]

Although not straightforward military histories, two older publications also provide detailed information on the army as a whole: *Sechzig Jahre Wehrmacht 1848–1908,* written and published in 1908 by unnamed members of the Vienna War Archive, is a candid account, among other considerations, of the army's earlier failures and shortcomings; *Unter den Fahnen. Die Völker Österreich-Ungarns in Waffen* (1889), by Alphons Danzer, was meant originally to promote enlistment and is, perhaps for that very reason, eminently entertaining and informative. It is at its best when discussing the peculiarities of the several branches of service.[44]

There are a good number of studies on specific problems or shorter periods in the army's history. The best account of the 1848–1849 wars is that of the prolific Austrian military historian and archivist Rudolf Kiszling. The war between Austria and Hungary is described in detail by a contemporary observer, the Swiss Wilhelm Rüstow, and in my *The Lawful Revolution.* Radetzky's Italian campaign, particularly its social aspects, is the subject of a monograph by British historian Alan Sked.[45] The army's history between the revolutions and the 1867 Compromise Agreement is analyzed in detail by the German historian Antonio Schmidt-Brentano; the disaster of 1866 has been investigated by the U.S. historian Gordon A. Craig; and the history of the Austrian War Ministry in this period is described, often in overwhelming detail, by the Austrian military archivist Walter Wagner.[46]

The number of military biographies is more limited than one might expect from a society profoundly dedicated to martial values and military heroes. Much of what does exist is pure hagiography, with such partial exceptions as Austrian historian Oskar Regele's biographies of Radetzky, Benedek, and Conrad.[47] The most comprehensive biography of Conrad, however, is by August Urbański, one of the general's former underlings. Feldzeugmeister Beck is the subject of an entertaining biography by Glaise von Horstenau.[48] A collective portrait of the monarchy's highest-ranking military commanders can be found in Nikolaus von Pre-radovich's comparative study of Austria-Hungary's and Prussia's highest-ranking diplomats, administrators, parliamentarians, and generals.[49]

There are, to add to this list, the specialized studies of Oskar Regele on the chiefs of staff of the Habsburg army between 1529 and 1918 and on the Austrian Court War Council between 1556 and 1848.[50]

World War I has, of course, inspired an enormous literature, some of which was discussed in the chapter on the officer corps during that period. The basis of all modern studies of that war is *Österreich-Ungarns letzter Krieg,* a compendium of seven volumes and ten supplements, edited and written (for the most part) by Glaise von Horstenau and Kiszling. It appeared in Austria in the 1930s. Two studies of the military and naval mutinies in Austria-Hungary during the final years of World War I have been produced by the contemporary Austrian historian Richard G. Plaschka and his colleagues.[51]

Worthy of mention is a very special literary genre, the commissioned regimental history, published primarily by the more historic infantry and cavalry regiments. Typically extracted from official regimental logbooks by some hapless captain commandeered to do the job, these histories generally make for dull reading, but they do provide a good deal of useful information. Their main emphasis is on battles heroically won or lost, individual acts of bravery, peacetime maneuvers and parades, regimental relics, pieces of furniture obtained for the officers' mess, and the periodic appearance of august visitors. Their style is invariably pompous and obeisant, although the earlier ones differ markedly from the later. Those published in the 1870s and 1880s, when the fashion for regimental histories seems to have first begun, are generally modest publications. More important, they pass over in silence such embarrassing episodes as when an entire regiment or at least some of its battalions fought against the emperor in the wars of 1848–1849. Alternatively, they seek to explain such deviations by blaming Hungarian or Italian coercion, demagogy, and bribery. The later histories, published around the turn of the century, are more lavish in appearance, reflecting the prosperity and stylistic vulgarity of the period. In tune with the rise of nationalism, they often relate with pride—especially in the histories of Hungarian regiments—the unit's heroic exploits in the anti-Habsburg camp in 1848–1849 or, more commonly, its exploits in both camps during that period.

The regimental histories published after World War I were once again quite different, chiefly because they attempted to combine devotion to the Old Austrian idea with loyalty to the new successor state in which the regiment now found itself. Based almost invariably on subscription drives, the post–World War I regimental histories are often richly illustrated with drawings and photographs and contain hundreds of individual biographies. They recount the agonies of World War I, offer data on casualties, and include statistics on the nearly incredible number of draftees who passed through the ranks between 1914 and 1918. To cite but one example, the "History of the 32nd Budapest Imperial and Royal Infantry Regiment" reports that a total of 120,000 men served in that unit during the war, and that 8,944 were killed.[52]

Because the Habsburg army is no more, interest in it seems academic. Yet there is much to be learned from the history of an armed force which, by dint of its lack of a cohesive ideology, its confusion of languages and cultures, and its inadequate war readiness, appeared to be doomed at the outbreak of World War I, yet which fought on to the bitter end. Social and psychohistorical studies of its rank and file would be as warranted as a monograph on its noncommissioned officers. The NCOs, after all, served not only as social and command liaisons between the officers and men, as has always been the case everywhere, but also as linguistic and cultural interpreters. Finally, modern and objective biographies of the top commanders are long overdue, if for no other reason than because we ought to know why highly trained and well-educated generals so often perform poorly in wartime.

APPENDIX II

Place Names

In parentheses are given, first, the kingdom or province in which the place was located within the Habsburg monarchy and, second, the state in which it now finds itself.

Abbreviations

E. English; G. German; H. Hungarian; Cz. Czech; I. Italian; P. Polish; R. Romanian; Ru-U. Ruthene or Ukrainian; SC. Serbo-Croatian; S. Slovak; Sl. Slovene

Arad H., R. (Hungary, Romania)
Aspern G. (Lower Austria, Austria)
Auschwitz G., Oświeçim P. (Galicia, Poland)
Budapest H., Ofen-Pest G. (Hungary)
Cattaro I., Kotor SC (Dalmatia, Yugoslavia)
Chłopy P. (Galicia, U.S.S.R.?)
Cracow E., Krakau G., Kraków P., Krakiv Ru-U (Galicia, Poland)
Custozza I., Custoza G. (Lombardy, Italy)
Eperjes H., Eperies/Preschau G., Prešov S. (Hungary, Czechoslovakia)
Fiume I., H., St. Veit am Flaum G. [archaic], Rijeka SC, Reka Sl. (Hungary, Yugoslavia)
Gitschin G., Jičin Cz. (Bohemia, Czechoslovakia)
Graz G., Gradec Sl. (Styria, Austria)
Győr H., Raab G. (Hungary)
Gyulafehérvár H., Karlsburg G., Alba Julia R. (Transylvania-Hungary, Romania)
Hernals G. (Lower Austria, Austria)
Innsbruck G. (the Tyrol, Austria)
Kassa H., Kaschau G., Košice S. (Hungary, Czechoslovakia)
Kolozsvár H., Klausenburg G., Cluj-Napoca R. (Transylvania-Hungary, Romania)
Komárom H., Komorn G., Komárno S. (Hungary, Czechoslovakia)
Königgrätz G., Hradec Králové Cz. (Bohemia, Czechoslovakia)
Lemberg G., Lwów P., Lviv/Lvov Ru-U (Galicia, U.S.S.R.)
Linz G. (Upper Austria, Austria)
Lissa I., Vis SC. (Dalmatia, Yugoslavia)

Magenta I. (Lombardy, Italy)
Mährisch-Weisskirchen G., Hranice Cz. (Moravia, Czechoslovakia)
Marburg G., Maribor Sl. (Styria, Yugoslavia)
Milan E., Mailand G., Milano I. (Lombardy, Italy)
Miskolc H. (Hungary)
Mödling G. (Lower Austria, Austria)
Olmütz G., Olomouc Cz. (Moravia, Czechoslovakia)
Pákozd H. (Hungary)
Pardubitz G., Pardubice Cz. (Bohemia, Czechoslovakia)
Pécs H., Fünfkirchen G., Peticrikve SC (Hungary)
Peterwardein G., Pétervárad H., Petrovaradin SC. (Slavonia, Yugoslavia)
Pola I., Pula SC., Pulj Sl. (Adriatic Littoral, Yugoslavia)
Prague E., Prag G., Praha Cz. (Bohemia, Czechoslovakia)
Pressburg E., G., Pozsony H., Bratislava S. (Hungary, Czechoslovakia)
Przemyśl P., Peremyshl' Ru-U (Galicia, Poland)
Ragusa I., Dubrovnik SC. (Dalmatia, Yugoslavia)
St. Gotthard G., Szentgotthárd H. (Hungary)
St. Pölten G. (Lower Austria, Austria)
Salzburg G. (Salzburg, Austria)
Schwechat G. (Lower Austria, Austria)
Solferino I. (Lombardy, Italy)
Sopron H., Ödenburg G. (Hungary)
Szeged H., Szegedin G. (Hungary)
Theresienstadt G., Terezín Cz. (Bohemia, Czechoslovakia)
Traiskirchen G. (Lower Austria, Austria)
Tulln G. (Lower Austria, Austria)
Venice E., Venedig G., Venezia I. (Venetia, Italy)
Vienna E., I., Wien G., Bécs H., Vídeň Cz., Wiedeń P., Viena R., Videnj Ru-U., Beč SC., Dunaj Sl. (Lower Austria, Austria)
Wiener Neustadt G. (Lower Austria, Austria)
Zagreb SC., Agram G., Zágráb H. (Croatia, Yugoslavia)
Zara I., Zadar SC. (Dalmatia, Yugoslavia)
Znaim G., Znojmo Cz. (Moravia, Czechoslovakia)

Notes

Kriegsarchiv, Vienna, will appear throughout as KA.

I have attempted to reproduce the original spelling of names and titles even if archaic and seemingly contradictory, as for instance in Glaise-Horstenau and Glaise von Horstenau, Görgei and Görgey, or *Militär-Statistisches Jahrbuch* and *Militärstatistisches Jahrbuch*. I have, however, consistently used "ä" instead of "ae" and "ö" instead of "oe" in reproducing the titles of books (but not of names).

Introduction

1. S. Enders Wimbush and Alex Alexiev, "The Ethnic Factor in the Soviet Armed Forces," (March 1982), *Rand,* R-2787/1, p. v.

2. For a history of the "Austrian concept," see Erich Zöllner, *Der Österreichbegriff. Formen und Wandlungen in der Geschichte* (Vienna, 1988).

3. The best brief history of the Habsburg dynasty in English is Adam Wandruszka, *The House of Austria: Six Hundred Years of a European Dynasty,* trans. Cathleen and Hans Epstein (Garden City, N.Y., 1964).

4. "Rangordnung der Offiziere und Zivilbehörden," in Karl Friedrich Kurz, ed., *Militär-Taschenlexikon,* 10th ed., Part I (Vienna, 1911), pp. 235–36. The military table of ranks is on pp. 235–236, and the proper forms of address to be used with the officers are discussed on p. 10.

5. On the units and service arms of the Habsburg army, see James Lucas's finely illustrated *Fighting Troops of the Austro-Hungarian Army, 1868–1914* (New York-Tunbridge Wells, Kent, 1987). The most comprehensive account, however, is Alphons Freiherr von Wrede, *Geschichte der k. und k. Wehrmacht. Die Regimenter, Corps, Branchen und Anstalten von 1618 zum Ende des XIX. Jahrhunderts,* 5 vols. (Vienna, 1898–1905).

6. See *Vorschrift zur Verfassung der Qualifikationslisten über Stabs-und Oberoffiziere des Soldatenstandes, dann Kadetten im k.u.k. Heere* (Vienna, 1908); and A. Tóth, *Kompendium aller Qualifikationslisten-Angelegenheiten mit Berücksichtigung aller bis Ende August 1905 erschienenen Erlässe und der einschlägigen Dienstbücher-Vorschriften,* 2nd ed. (Przemyśl, 1905).

Chapter 1

1. Gunther E. Rothenberg, *The Army of Francis Joseph* (West Lafayette, Ind., 1976), p. 1.

2. On the Military Border, see Gunther E. Rothenberg, *The Austrian Military Border in Croatia, 1522–1747* (Urbana, Ill., 1960), and *The Military Border in Croatia, 1740–1881: A Study of an Imperial Institution* (Chicago, 1966).

3. On the Court War Council, see Oskar Regele, *Der österreichische Hofkriegsrat 1556–1848* (Vienna, 1949).

4. Gustav Adolph-Auffenberg Komarów, "Das Zeitalter Maria-Theresias," in Herbert St. Fürlinger and Ludwig Jedlicka, eds., *Unser Heer. 300 Jahre österreichisches Soldatentum in Krieg und Frieden* (Vienna-Munich-Zurich, 1963), pp. 131–32. The best book on the military under Maria Theresa is Christopher Duffy, *The Army of Maria Theresa* (New York, 1977).

5. On Archduke Charles, see Gunther E. Rothenberg, *Napoleon's Great Adversaries: The Archduke Charles and the Austrian Army, 1792–1814* (Bloomington, Ind., 1982).

6. On the history of the Austrian general staff, see Oskar Regele, *Generalstabschefs aus vier Jahrhunderten. Das Amt des Chefs des Generalstabes in der Donaumonarchie. Seine Träger und Organe von 1529 bis 1918* (Vienna-Munich, 1966).

7. Rothenberg, *The Army of Francis Joseph*, p. 10.

8. Ibid., p. 16.

9. Johann Christoph Allmayer-Beck and Erich Lessing, *Das Heer unter dem Doppeladler 1718–1848* (Munich-Gütersloh-Vienna, 1981), p. 234; and Alphons Freiherr von Wrede, *Geschichte der k. und k. Wehrmacht. Die Regimenter, Corps, Branchen und Anstalten von 1618 zum Ende des XIX. Jahrhunderts*, 5 vols. (Vienna, 1898–1905), 1:105–8.

10. The only modern comprehensive history of the 1848–1849 revolutions in the Habsburg monarchy is Rudolf Kiszling, *Die Revolution im Kaisertum Österreich 1848–1849*, 2 vols. (Vienna, 1948), which, however, concentrates on military events. See also István Deák, *The Lawful Revolution: Louis Kossuth and the Hungarians, 1848–1849* (New York, 1979); Joseph A. Helfert, *Geschichte der österreichischen Revolution im Zusammenhange mit der mitteleuropäischen Bewegung der Jahre 1848–1849*, 2 vols. (Freiburg-Vienna, 1907–1909); C. A. Macartney, *The Habsburg Empire, 1790–1918* (London, 1968), ch. 9; Stanley Z. Pech, *The Czech Revolution of 1848* (Chapel Hill, N.C., 1969); R. John Rath, *The Viennese Revolution of 1848* (Austin, Texas, 1957); Priscilla Robertson, *Revolutions of 1848: A Social History* (Princeton, N.J., 1952), chs. 10–14; and Alan Sked, *The Survival of the Habsburg Empire: Radetzky, the Imperial Army and the Class War, 1848* (London-New York, 1979).

11. Oskar Regele, *Feldmarschall Radetzky* (Vienna-Munich, 1957), p. 262.

12. Deák, *The Lawful Revolution*, pp. 99–106 *et passim*.

13. Rudolf Kiszling, "Habsburgs Wehrmacht im Spiegel des Nationalitätenproblems 1815 bis 1918," in *Gedenkschrift für Harold Steinacker 1875–1965* ("Buchreihe des Südostdeutschen Historischen Kommission," vol. 16; Munich, 1966), p. 241.

14. On the Serbian political movement in 1848 and the anti-Hungarian revolt of the Serbs, see, among others, Vaso Bogdanov, *Ustanak Srba u Vojvodini i Madjarska Revolucija 1848–49* (The revolt of the Serbs in the Voivodina and the Hungarian revolution, 1848–49) (Subotica, 1949); and József Thim, ed., *A magyarországi 1848–49-iki szerb fölkelés története* (The history of the Serbian uprising in Hungary, 1848–49), 3 vols. (Budapest, 1930–1940). Text and documents.

15. Deák, *The Lawful Revolution*, pp. xvii–xviii, 140–41.

16. Blomberg to Baillet de la Tour, quoted by Thim, *A magyarországi 1848–49-iki szerb fölkelés története*, 1:167.

17. The best source on Croatian activity before 1848 is Gyula Miskolczy, *A horvát kérdés és irományai a rendi állam korában* (The history and documents of the Croatian question at the time of the feudal state), 2 vols. (Budapest, 1927–1928), which consists mostly of documents. See also, Rothenberg, *The Military Border in Croatia, 1740–1881*, chs. 7–8.

18. On the history of the Croatian campaign in Hungary in September 1848, see Deák, *The Lawful Revolution,* pp. 161–70; and Ferdinand Hauptmann, ed., *Jelačić's Kriegszug nach Ungarn 1848,* 2 vols. (Graz, 1975). Text and documents.

19. On Arthur Görgey, see his own *My Life and Acts in Hungary in the Years 1848–1849,* 2 vols. (London, 1852); and László Pusztaszeri, *Görgey Artúr a szabadságharcban* (Arthur Görgey in the war of independence) (Budapest, 1984). Also Deák, *The Lawful Revolution,* pp. 182–87.

20. On the Russian intervention in Hungary, see Erzsébet Andics, ed., *Das Bündnis Habsburg-Romanow. Vorgeschichte der zaristischen Intervention in Ungarn im Jahre 1849* (Budapest, 1963). Also Deák, *The Lawful Revolution,* pp. 285–91, 300–310; and Kiszling, *Die Revolution im Kaisertum Österreich,* 2:161–302, 329–30.

21. On the postwar trial of the Hungarian officers and politicians, see, among others, Deák, *The Lawful Revolution,* pp. 329–37; Kiszling, *Die Revolution im Kaisertum Öster-reich,* 2:291–94; and the following documentary collections: Gyula Tóth, ed., *Küzdelem, bukás, megtorlás. Emlékiratok, naplók az 1848–1849-es forradalom és szabadságharc vég-napjairól* (Struggle, defeat, and retribution. Memoirs and diaries from the last days of the 1848–49 revolution and war of independence), 2 vols. (Budapest, 1978); and Tamás Katona, ed., *Az aradi vértanúk* (The Arad martyrs), 2 vols. (Budapest, 1979).

22. Gábor Bona, *Tábornokok és törzstisztek a szabadságharcban 1848–49* (Generals and field-grade officers in the war of independence, 1848–1849) (Budapest, 1983), pp. 67–68 *et passim.*

23. The letters are in Katona, *Az aradi vértanúk,* 1:209–10, 227–28.

24. Quoted by Johann Heinrich Blumenthal, "Vom Wiener Kongress zum Ersten Weltkrieg," in Fürlinger and Jedlicka, *Unser Heer,* p. 234.

25. See Sked, *The Survival of the Habsburg Empire,* pp. 55–65.

Chapter 2

1. Much of my information on this historical chapter has been culled from the works listed in Appendix I, notes 37, 41, 43–44, and 46–50, especially from Gunther E. Rothenberg, *The Army of Francis Joseph* (West Lafayette, Ind., 1976).

2. See Adolph Schwarzenberg, *Prince Felix zu Schwarzenberg: Prime Minister of Austria, 1848–1852* (New York, 1946), ch. 3.

3. On Austria's controversial role in the Crimean War, see Heinrich Friedjung, *Der Kriemkrieg und die österreichische Politik* (Stuttgart-Berlin, 1907); Paul W. Schroeder, *Austria, Great Britain and the Crimean War* (Ithaca, N.Y., 1972); and A. J. P. Taylor, *The Struggle for Mastery in Europe* (Oxford, 1954), ch. 4. The Austrian military occupation of the Danubian principalities is amusingly described and intelligently analyzed by Moriz Edler von Angeli, an unenthusiastic participant, in *Altes Eisen. Intimes aus Kriegs- und Friedens-jahren* (Stuttgart, 1900), pp. 10–140.

4. Finally, Francis Joseph has a popular, modern biography in Jean-Paul Bled, *François-Joseph* (Paris, 1987). Of the older histories, Egon Caesar Conte Corti's three-volume history, *Von Kind bis Kaiser* (Graz, 1950), *Mensch und Herrscher* (Graz, 1952), and *Der alte Kaiser*

(Graz, 1955), reads like an informative and entertaining diary; Joseph Redlich's *The Emperor Francis Joseph of Austria: A Biography* (New York, 1929), and Karl Tschuppik, *The Reign of Emperor Francis Joseph,* trans. C. J. S. Sprigge (London, 1930), are most useful but concentrate on politics; Albert Freiherr von Margutti, *Kaiser Franz Joseph. Persönliche Erinnerungen* (Vienna-Leipzig, 1924), by the old emperor's former aide-de-camp, contains, among other things, a fine character analysis of Francis Joseph.

    5. On the history of the Austrian army in this period, see Antonio Schmidt-Brentano, *Die Armee in Österreich. Militär, Staat und Gesellschaft 1848–1867* (Boppard am Rhein, 1975).

    6. Except for a dated and quite superficial doctoral dissertation, Marianne Gräfin Szapáry, "Carl Graf Grünne, Generaladjutant des Kaisers Franz Joseph 1848–1859" (Vienna, 1935), there exists no biography of General der Kavallerie Grünne. For short biographical entries, the reader is advised to turn to Constantin Wurzbach, *Biographisches Lexikon des Kaiserthums Österreich,* 60 vols. (Vienna, 1856–1891), 5:394–96; *Österreichisches Biographisches Lexikon 1815–1950* (henceforward *ÖBL*), so far 10 vols. (Graz-Cologne, 1957–), 1:91; and *Allgemeine Deutsche Biographie* (henceforward *ADB*), 56 vols. (Leipzig, 1875–1912), 49:602–3. Walter Wagner, *Geschichte des k.k. Kriegsministeriums I, 1848–1866* (Graz-Cologne, 1966), discusses Grünne's politics in great detail.

    7. Cited in Moriz Edler von Angeli, *Wien nach 1848* (Vienna, 1905), pp. 142–43.

    8. See Schmidt-Brentano, *Die Armee in Österreich,* pp. 110–46.

    9. Franz Neubauer, *Die Gendarmerie in Österreich 1849–1924* (Vienna, 1925), is a substantial but much too laudatory history of the Austrian gendarmes.

    10. Like the obnoxious Grünne, the witless Count Franz Gyulai (or Gyulay) von Maros-Németh und Nádaska did not inspire a biography. Pensioned off immediately after the 1859 war, Gyulai died in 1868. There is a devastating evaluation of both Grünne and Gyulai in Anton Freiherr Mollinary von Monte Pastello, *Sechsundvierzig Jahre im österreichisch-ungarischen Heere 1833–1879,* 2 vols. (Zurich, 1905), 2:1–41. For short entries on Gyulai, see Wurzbach, *Biographisches Lexikon des Kaiserthums Österreich,* 6:70–77; *ABD,* 10:250–52; *ÖBL,* 1:114–15; and Wagner, *Geschichte des k.k. Kriegsministeriums, I,* p. 240.

    11. On the war of 1859, see, among others, Wilhelm Rüstow, *Der italienische Krieg 1859* (Zurich, 1859); Taylor, *The Struggle for Mastery in Europe,* ch. 6; Heinrich Friedjung, *The Struggle for Supremacy in Germany, 1859–1866,* trans. A. J. P. Taylor and W. L. McElvee (first edition in German, 1897; this edition: New York, 1966), pp. 11–21; and E. v. Steinitz, "Magenta und Solferino," *Militärwissenschaftliche Mitteilungen* 60 (1929):476–87.

    12. Johann Heinrich Blumenthal, "Vom Wiener Kongress zum Ersten Weltkrieg," in Herbert St. Fürlinger and Ludwig Jedlicka, eds., *Unser Heer. 300 Jahre österreichisches Soldatentum in Krieg und Frieden* (Vienna-Munich-Zurich, 1963), p. 246.

    13. Ibid., p. 248.

    14. István Deák, "Defeat at Solferino: The Nationality Question and the Habsburg Army in the War of 1859," in Béla K. Király, ed., *The Crucial Decade: East European Society and National Defense, 1859–1870* ("East European Monographs," No. 151; New York, 1984), pp. 496–516.

    15. On Archduke Albrecht, see Ludwig Jedlicka, "Feldmarschall Erzherzog Albrecht (1817–1895)," in *Gestalter der Geschicke Österreichs* (Vienna-Munich, 1962), pp. 389–95; J. J. Holzer, "Erzherzog Albrecht 1867–1895. Politisch-militärische Konzeption. Tätigkeit als Generalinspektor des Heeres," unpublished doctoral dissertation, University of Vienna, 1974; August Werkmann, "Erzherzog Albrecht und Benedek," unpublished doctoral dissertation, University of Vienna, 1946; and C. von Duncker, *Feldmarschall Erzherzog Albrecht* (Vienna, 1897), the latter a eulogy of limited value.

    16. On Benedek, see Werkmann, "Erzherzog Albrecht und Benedek"; Oskar Regele,

Feldzeugmeister Benedek. Der Weg nach Königgrätz (Vienna-Munich, 1960); and Gordon A. Craig, *The Battle of Königgrätz: Prussia's Victory over Austria, 1866* (Philadelphia-New York, 1964).

17. *Sechzig Jahre Wehrmacht 1848–1908* (Vienna, 1908), p. 102.

18. On the October Diploma in 1860 and the February patent in 1861, see, among others, C. A. Macartney, *The Habsburg Empire, 1790–1918* (London, 1968), pp. 506–27.

19. Regele, *Feldzeugmeister Benedek*, pp. 222–26; and *Sechzig Jahre Wehrmacht*, pp. 132–33.

20. Rothenberg, *The Army of Francis Joseph*, p. 61.

21. On the Danish War, see Heinz Helmert and Hans-Jürgen Usczeck, *Preussischdeutsche Kriege von 1864 bis 1871* (East Berlin, 1970), pp. 51–89, and a colorful although not always reliable eyewitness account by Wilhelm Ritter Gründorf von Zebegény in *Memoiren eines österreichischen Generalstäblers*, ed. Adolf Saager, 4th ed. (Stuttgart, 1913), pp. 174–307.

22. On the bravura tactics of the Austrians in the Danish War, see especially *Sechzig Jahre Wehrmacht*, p. 250; and Rothenberg, *The Army of Francis Joseph*, p. 65.

23. The Seven Weeks' War between Prussia and Austria boasts a substantial literature. My information has come mainly from Rothenberg, *The Army of Francis Joseph*, pp. 67–73; Craig, *The Battle of Königgrätz; Sechzig Jahre Wehrmacht*, pp. 251–56; and Edmund von Glaise-Horstenau, *Franz Josephs Weggefährte. Das Leben des Generalstabschefs Grafen Beck* (Zurich-Leipzig-Vienna, 1930), pp. 99–132.

24. See Rothenberg, *The Army of Francis Joseph*, p. 68; and Craig, *The Battle of Königgrätz*. Statistics regarding the respective strengths of the Allied and Prussian armies in Bohemia vary from source to source. However, [Hugo Kerchnave], *Die Vorgeschichte von 1866 und 19?? [sic] Von einem alten kaiserlichen Soldaten* (n.p., 1909), pp. i–vi, contains what seem to be reliable data on the organization, units, and total effectives of the contending forces.

25. Craig, *The Battle of Königgrätz*, pp. ix–x.

26. Ibid., p. 166. Casualty figures vary widely from source to source.

27. Hellmut Andics, *Das österreichische Jahrhundert. Die Donaumonarchie 1804–1900* (Vienna-Munich, 1974), p. 183. Again, these figures are as good or as unreliable as any others I could have cited.

28. Macartney, *The Habsburg Empire*, p. 542. See also Michael Derndarsky, "Das Klischee von 'Ces Messieurs de Vienne . . .' Der österreichisch-französische Geheimvertrag vom 12. Juni 1866—Symptom für die Unfähigkeit der österreichischen Aussenpolitik?," *Historische Zeitschrift* 235 (1982): 289–353.

29. See, for instance, Louis Eisenmann's pro-Slav and anti-Hungarian account, *Le Compromis Austro-Hongrois de 1867. Étude sur le Dualisme* (first ed., Paris, 1904; reprint: Academic International, n.p., 1971); Eduard von Wertheimer's pro-Hungarian *Graf Julius Andrássy. Sein Leben und seine Zeit, nach nachgedruckten Quellen*, 3 vols. (Stuttgart, 1910–1913); and a collection of some fifty essays on the subject by an international coterie of specialists in L'udovit Holotík, ed., *Der österreichisch-ungarische Ausgleich 1867* (Bratislava, 1971).

30. The military side of the Compromise Agreement is discussed by, among others, Glaise-Horstenau, *Franz Josephs Weggefährte*, pp. 135–52; Király, *The Crucial Decade*, pp. 519–50; Julius Andrássy, *Ungarns Ausgleich mit Österreich vom Jahre 1867* (Leipzig, 1897); and Walter Wagner, *Geschichte des k.k. Kriegsministeriums II, 1886–1888* (Vienna-Cologne-Graz, 1971), pp. 18–24. The early history of the Hungarian National Guard is discussed in Sándor Szurmay, *A honvédség fejlődésének története annak felállításától napjainkig 1868–1898* (The development of the honvédség from its establishment to our days, 1868–1898) (Budapest, 1898).

31. There is a fine summary of the 1867 Compromise in Macartney, *The Habsburg Empire*, pp. 551–64. For detailed presentations, see Ivan Zölger, *Der staatsrechtliche Ausgleich zwischen Österreich und Ungarn* (Leipzig, 1911); *Der österreichisch-ungarische Ausgleich von 1867. Vorgeschichte und Wirkungen* ("Forschungsinstitut für den Donauraum"; Vienna-Munich, 1967); and Eduard Bernatzik, *Die österreichischen Verfassungsgesetze mit Erläuterungen*, 2nd ed. (Vienna, 1911).

32. How the Dual Monarchy was actually governed has been explored by Péter Hanák in *Ungarn in der Donaumonarchie* (Vienna, 1984), pp. 240–80. See also Miklós Komjáthy, "Die Entstehung des gemeinsamen Ministerrates und seine Tätigkeit während des Weltkrieges," in Miklós Komjáthy, ed., *Protokolle des gemeinsamen Ministerrates der österreichisch-ungarischen Monarchie (1914–1918)* (Budapest, 1966), pp. 1–140.

33. The military laws of 1868, 1882, and 1889 are discussed in Alfons Danzer et al., *Unter den Fahnen. Die Völker Österreich-Ungarns in Waffen* (Prague-Vienna-Leipzig, 1889), pp. 10–19; and Wagner, *Geschichte des k.k. Kriegsministeriums, II*. See also *Corpus Juris Hungarici. Magyar Törvénytár 1000–1895*, vol. 7: *1838–1868 évi törvényczikkek* (Compendium of the laws of Hungary, 1000–1895: The laws of the years 1838–1868) (Budapest, 1896), pp. 470–79. Historical statistics on the annual intake of recruits are in *Magyar Statisztikai Évkönyv 1911* (Hungarian statistical yearbook, 1911) (Budapest, 1912), p. 528.

34. *A közös ügyek tárgyalására kiküldött magyar országos bizottság hadügyi albizottságának jelentései* (Reports of the military subcommittee of the Hungarian national delegation sent out to negotiate the joint affairs) (Budapest, 1882), pp. 122–23; and *A közös ügyek tárgyalására kiküldött magyar országos bizottság hadügyi albizottságának jelentései (1897 november 16, Bécs)* (same type of report, dated November 16, 1897, Vienna) (Budapest, 1898), pp. 254–55.

35. On the step-by-step dissolution of the Military Border, see Gunther E. Rothenberg, *The Military Border in Croatia, 1740–1881* (Chicago, 1966), chs. 9–10; and Mollinary, *Sechsundvierzig Jahre im österreichisch-ungarischen Heere 1833–1879*, 2:202–72, 309–14.

36. Danzer, *Unter den Fahnen*, p. 280.

37. On General John, see H. R. v. Srbik, "Erinnerungen des Generals Freiherrn von John 1866 und 1870," in *Aus Österreichs Vergangenheit. Von Prinz Eugen zu Franz Joseph* (Salzburg, 1949), pp. 43–105. On General Kuhn, see *Neue Österreichische Biographie 1815–1918*, 21 vols. (Vienna, 1923–1982), 13:57–67. Wagner, *Geschichte des Kriegsministeriums II*, contains brief biographies of both men on pp. 268–70.

38. On Feldzeugmeister Count Friedrich Beck-Rzikowsky, see Glaise-Horstenau, *Franz Josephs Weggefährte*.

39. On the Krisvosije campaign in 1869–1870, see Rothenberg, *The Army of Francis Joseph*, p. 86.

40. Literature on the occupation of Bosnia-Hercegovina will be presented in note 42. The 1881 military campaign is discussed in Charles Jelavich, "The Revolt in Bosnia-Hercegovina 1881–82," *Slavonic and East European Review* 31 (1952–1953):420–36. For personal reminiscences, see Adolf Stillfried von Rathenitz, "Erinnerungen aus meinem Leben," unpublished manuscript, KA, B/862, ch. 3.

41. Austria-Hungary's nonintervention in the Franco-Prussian War is discussed in Macartney, *The Habsburg Empire*, pp. 578–81; Glaise-Horstenau, *Franz Josephs Weggefährte*, pp. 165–73; István Diószegi, *Österreich-Ungarn und der französisch-preussische Krieg 1870–1871* (Budapest, 1974); [Archduke Albrecht], *Das Jahr 1870 und die Wehrkraft der Monarchie* (Vienna, 1870); Wertheimer, *Graf Julius Andrássy*, vol. 1, chs. 13–14; and János Decsy, *Prime Minister Gyula Andrássy's Influence on Habsburg Foreign Policy during the Franco-German War of 1870–1871* ("East European Monographs," No. 52; New York, 1979).

42. Austria-Hungary's role in the Balkan crisis of 1875–1878 is discussed in, among others, Taylor, *The Struggle for Mastery in Europe*, ch. 11; Macartney, *The Habsburg Empire*, pp. 590–93; Mihailo D. Stojanović, *The Great Powers and the Balkans, 1875–1878* (Cambridge, 1939); G. H. Rupp, *A Wavering Friendship. Russia and Austria, 1876–1878* (Oxford, 1941); W. W. Medlicott, *The Congress of Berlin and After* (London, 1963); and Glaise-Horstenau, *Franz Josephs Weggefährte*, pp. 179–217.

The military occupation of Bosnia-Hercegovina is dealt with by, among others, Mollinary, *Sechsundvierzig Jahre im österreichisch-ungarischen Heere 1833–1879*, 2:283–308; [Moritz von] Auffenberg-Komarów, *Aus Österreichs Höhe und Niedergang. Eine Lebensschilderung* (Munich, 1921), pp. 42–50; Milorad Ekmečić, *Ustanak u Bosni 1875–1878* (The Bosnian uprising) (Sarajevo, 1973); *Die Okkupation Bosniens und der Herzegowina durch die k.k. Truppen im Jahre 1878* (Vienna, 1879), a monumental study produced by the Vienna War Archive; and László Bence, *Bosznia és Hercegovina okkupáció-ja 1878-ban* (The occupation of Bosnia and Hercegovina in 1878) (Budapest, 1987).

On the Austro-Hungarian administration of the two provinces, see Ferdinand Schmid, *Bosnien und die Herzegowina unter der Verwaltung Österreich-Ungarns* (Leipzig, 1914); Kurt Wessely, "Die wirtschaftliche Entwicklung von Bosnien-Herzegowina," in Alois Brusatti, ed., *Die wirtschaftliche Entwicklung* ("Die Habsburgermonarchie 1848–1918," vol. 1, Adam Wandruszka and Peter Urbanitsch, eds.; Vienna, 1973), pp. 528–66; Peter F. Sugar, *Industrialization of Bosnia-Hercegovina, 1878–1918* (Seattle, 1963); and Berislav Gavranović, *Bosna i Hercegovina u doba Austrougarske okkupacije 1878 god* (Bosnia and Hercegovina at the time of the Austro-Hungarian occupation) (Sarajevo, 1973); and Ferdinand Hauptmann, *Die österreichisch-ungarische Herrschaft in Bosnien und der Hercegovina 1878–1918. Wirtschaftspolitik und Wirtschaftsentwicklung* ("Zur Kunde Südosteuropas," II/12; Graz, 1983).

43. Bence, *Bosznia és Hercegovina okkupációja 1878-ban*, p. 81.

44. Ibid., p. 220n.

45. On General Philippović, see *Neue Österreichische Biographie 1815–1918*, 16:183–87; and *ADB*, 53:54–55. On General Jovanović, see *ADB*, 50:705–6; and *ÖBL*, 3:138. On the Bosnian regiments of the Habsburg army see, among others, Fürlinger and Jedlicka, *Unser Heer*, p. 261.

46. The statistical data were culled from Brusatti, *Die wirtschaftliche Entwicklung*, pp. 16, 18, 22, 26, 237, 318, 476, 496, 563; Iván T. Berend and György Ránki, *Economic Development in East-Central Europe in the 19th and 20th Centuries* (New York-London, 1974), pp. 65, 78; and Alexander Sixtus von Reden, *Österreich-Ungarn. Die Donaumonarchie in historischen Dokumenten* (Salzburg, 1984), p. 106.

47. See *Statistische Rückblicke aus Österreich.* (Vienna, 1913), p. 98.

48. Ibid., p. 99. See also Rothenberg, *The Army of Francis Joseph*, p. 126; Oskar Regele, *Feldmarschall Conrad. Auftrag und Erfüllung* (Vienna-Munich, 1955), pp. 151, 163; and Georg Nitsche, *Österreichisches Soldatentum im Rahmen deutscher Geschichte* (Berlin-Leipzig, 1937), p. 217.

49. On the international crisis in 1885–1887, see Rothenberg, *The Army of Francis Joseph*, p. 114; Glaise-Horstenau, *Franz Josephs Weggefährte*, pp. 296–312 *et passim;* and Macartney, *The Habsburg Empire*, pp. 594–95.

50. The Hungarian military law debates in parliament and the accompanying street riots are discussed in Péter Hanák, ed., *Magyarország története 1848–1918* (History of Hungary, 1848–1918) (Budapest, 1972), pp. 250–51; and Gusztáv Gratz, *A dualizmus kora* (The age of Dualism), 2 vols. (Budapest, 1934), 1:244–50.

51. See *Schulthess' Europäischer Geschichtskalender*, 81 vols. (Munich, 1860–1940), 31 (1890):204.

52. Francis Ferdinand inspired several biographies. Of them, see particularly, R. A. Kann, *Erzherzog-Franz-Ferdinand-Studien* ("Veröffentlichungen des Österreichischen Ost- und Südosteuropa-Instituts," vol. 10; Vienna, 1976); Rudolf Kiszling, *Erzherzog Franz Ferdinand von Österreich-Este. Leben, Pläne und Wirken am Schicksalsweg der Donaumonarchie* (Graz-Cologne, 1953); Lavender Cassels, *The Archduke and the Assassin: Sarajevo, June 28th 1914* (New York, 1984); Victor Eisenmenger, *Archduke Franz Ferdinand* (London, 1931); and Friedrich Weissensteiner, *Franz Ferdinand* (Vienna, 1983). Also, Carl Freiherr von Bardolff, *Soldat im alten Österreich* (Jena, 1938), pp. 109–17 *et passim.* Margutti, *Kaiser Franz Joseph,* pp. 105–41, contains an excellent character analysis of Francis Ferdinand.

53. See, for instance, the *Revers* signed by Lieutenant Alexander Dini at Wiener Neustadt on August 18, 1881. *Qualifikations-Listen,* KA.

54. On the stationing of troops in 1894, see Alphons Freiherr von Wrede, *Geschichte der k. und k. Wehrmacht. Die Regimenter, Corps, Branchen und Anstalten von 1618 zum Ende des XIX. Jahrhunderts,* 5 vols. (Vienna, 1898–1905), 1:623–36. See also Rudolf Kiszling, "Habsburgs Wehrmacht im Spiegel des Nationalitätenproblems 1815 bis 1918," in *Gedenkschrift für Harold Steinacker* ("Buchreihe der Südostdeutschen Historischen Kommission," vol. 16; Munich, 1966), pp. 249–50.

55. Quoted in Oskar Freiherr von Mitis, *Das Leben des Kronprinzen Rudolf* (Leipzig, 1928), p. 353.

56. On the so-called Badeni language riots, see Berthold Sutter, *Die Badenischen Sprachen-Verordnungen von 1897,* 2 vols. (Graz-Cologne, 1965).

57. On the events in Graz, see ibid., 2:18–49, 176–230, 319–45.

58. Bardolff, *Soldat im alten Österreich,* pp. 38–40.

59. On the court of honor proceedings against the offending student reserve officers, see ibid., pp. 334–45.

60. Report of the French military attaché in Vienna, November 18, 1903, entitled, "La pénurie d'officiers hongrois pour l'encadrement de l'armée hongroise. Les causes de cette pénurie." Service Historique de l'Armée de Terre, Château de Vincennes. État Major de l'Armée, Attachés Militaires, Autriche-Hongrie 1903–1906. 7 N 1129.

61. Rothenberg, *The Army of Francis Joseph,* p. 132.

62. An excerpt from the Chłopy Army Order is contained in Glaise-Horstenau, *Franz Josephs Weggefährte,* p. 403. On the Hungarian events of the period, see Péter Hanák, ed., *Magyarország története 1890–1918,* (History of Hungary, 1890–1918), 2 vols. ("Magyarország története 10 kötetben," vol. 7; Budapest, 1978), 1:517–30.

63. On István Tisza, see Gábor Vermes, *István Tisza: The Liberal Vision and Conservative Statecraft of a Magyar Nationalist* ("East European Monographs," No. 184; New York, 1985).

64. On plans for the invasion of Hungary, see Kurt Peball and Gunther E. Rothenberg, "Der Fall U. Die geplante Besetzung Ungarns durch die k.u.k. Armee im Herbst 1905," *Schriften des Heeresgeschichtlichen Museums in Wien* 4 (1969):85–126. Also, Glaise-Horstenau, *Franz Josephs Weggefährte,* p. 406; and Auffenberg-Komarów, *Aus Österreichs Höhe und Niedergang,* pp. 90–92.

65. On universal suffrage and the 1907 elections in Austria, see, among others, Macartney, *The Habsburg Empire,* pp. 793–95; William A. Jenks, *The Austrian Electoral Reform of 1907* (New York, 1950); and Karl Ucakar, *Demokratie und Wahlrecht in Österreich. Zur Entwicklung von politischer Partizipation und staatlicher Legitimationspolitik* (Vienna, 1985).

66. Rothenberg, *The Army of Francis Joseph,* p. 127.

67. On the politics of the Belvedere Palace see, among others, Bardolff, *Soldat im alten*

Österreich, pp. 107–84; Peter Broucek, ed., *Ein General im Zwielicht. Die Erinnerungen Edmund Glaises von Horstenau*, 3 vols. (Vienna-Cologne-Graz, 1980–1987), 1:234–39 *et passim;* Robert A. Kann, *The Multinational Empire: Nationalism and National Reform in the Habsburg Monarchy, 1848–1918*, 2 vols. (New York, 1950), 2:187–207; and the Francis Ferdinand biographies listed in note 52.

68. Glaise-Horstenau, *Franz Josephs Weggefährte*, p. 403 *et passim*.

69. On Conrad, see Appendix I, notes 4, 47, 48.

70. On the annexation crisis in 1908–1909 see, among others, Rothenberg, *The Army of Francis Joseph*, ch. 10; and Bernadotte Schmitt, *The Annexation of Bosnia* (Cambridge, Mass., 1937).

71. Conrad von Hötzendorf, *Private Aufzeichnungen. Erste Veröffentlichungen aus den Papieren des k.u.k. Generalstabschefs*, ed. Kurt Peball (Vienna-Munich, 1976), pp. 148, 307.

72. On the monarchy's last peacetime foreign minister, see Hugo Hantsch, *Leopold Graf Berchtold*, 2 vols. (Graz-Vienna-Cologne, 1968).

73. On Austro-Hungarian domestic developments in the years before World War I, see Macartney, *The Habsburg Empire*, ch. 17.

74. Regele, *Feldmarschall Conrad*, p. 68.

75. Auffenberg-Komarów, *Aus Österreichs Höhe und Niedergang*, pp. 166–78.

76. On Tisza's crucial role in 1914, see Vermes, *István Tisza*, ch. 9.

77. Literature on the crisis of 1914 would fill libraries. Here is a small sampling: Luigi Albertini, *The Origins of the War of 1914*, 3 vols. (London, 1952–1957); Joachim Remak, *Sarajevo* (London, 1959); Vladimir Dedijer, *The Road to Sarajevo* (London, 1967); Wladimir Aichelburg, *Sarajevo, 28 Juni 1914* (Vienna, 1984); Cassels, *The Archduke and the Assassin;* and Friedrich Würthle, *Die Spur führt nach Belgrad. Sarajevo 1914* (Vienna-Munich, 1975).

Chapter 3

1. On the institution of regimental cadets, see Moriz von Angeli, *Wien nach 1848* (Vienna-Leipzig, 1905), pp. 117–20; [Daniel] Fenner von Fenneberg, *Österreich und seine Armee* (Leipzig, 1842), pp. 50, 114–20; Heinrich Ritter von Födransperg, *Vierzig Jahre in der österreichischen Armee. Erinnerungen eines österreichischen Offiziers von seinem Eintritte in die Armee bis zur Gegenwart 1854–1894*, 2 vols. (Dresden, n.d. [1895]), 1:5–93; Anton Freiherr Mollinary von Monte-Pastello, *Sechsundvierzig Jahre im österreichisch-ungarischen Heere 1833–1879*, 2 vols. (Zurich, 1905), 1:31–35; Franz Xaver Schubert, "Nachlass," unpublished manuscript, KA, B/833, Nr. 2, pp. 1–13, [Moritz Ritter von] Auffenberg-Komarów, *Aus Österreichs Höhe und Niedergang. Eine Lebensschilderung* (Munich, 1921), pp. 14–15; and *Sechzig Jahre Wehrmacht, 1848–1908* (Vienna, 1908), pp. 13–15. The cadets in the 3rd Infantry Regiment are referred to by Angeli, *Wien nach 1848*, p. 119, and the examination questions are related by Födransperg, *Vierzig Jahre in der österreichischen Armee*, 1:58–59. The educational system of the Military Border is discussed in, among others, Georg Edler von Miščević, "Der Werdegang eines Grenzerkindes als nützliches Glied des Staates und der menschlichen Gesellschaft," unpublished manuscript, KA, B/1146/1, pp. 1–5; Mollinary, *Sechsundvierzig Jahre im österreichisch-ungarischen Heere*, 1:10–30; and Walter Wagner in Adam Wandruszka and Peter Urbanitsch, eds., *Die bewaffnete Macht* ("Die Habsburgermonarchie 1848–1918," vol. 5; Vienna, 1987), pp. 183–99.

2. On the *Schul-Compagnien*, see Angeli, *Wien nach 1848*, pp. 115–17; and Mollinary,

Sechsundvierzig Jahre im österreichisch-ungarischen Heere, 1:21–30. Also, *Reglement für die kaiserlich-königlichen Militär-Bildungs-Anstalten* (Vienna, 1859).

   3. On the Austrian technical military academies, see Moriz Ritter von Brunner and Hugo Kerchnawe, *225 Jahre Technische Militärakademie 1717 bis 1942* (Vienna, 1942); F. Gatti and A. Obermayr, *Geschichte der k.u.k. Technischen Militärakademie 1717 bis 1942* (Vienna, 1942); Heinrich Schalk, *250 Jahre militärtechnische Ausbildung in Österreich* (Vienna, n.d. [1967]); and Ernst Palombini, Freiherr von Jedina, "Erinnerungen," unpublished manuscript, KA, B/959, pp. 83–104. A concise source on the history of Austrian military education is Otto Kainz, "Die Offiziersheranbildung in Österreich," *Militärwissenschaftliche Mitteilungen* 66 (1935):161–87; 67 (1936):776–88, 868–84. A more substantial account is G. Poten, *Geschichte des Militär-Erziehungs und Bildungswesens in Österreich-Ungarn* ("Monumenta Germaniae Pedagogica," vol. 15; Berlin, 1893). The tuition fee of 1,000 gulden (in 1810) is mentioned by Brunner and Kerchnawe, *225 Jahre Technische Militärakademie 1717 bis 1942,* p. 14.

   4. The most important source on the history of the Military Academy is J. Svoboda, *Die Theresianische Militär-Akademie zur Wiener Neustadt und ihre Zöglinge von der Gründung der Anstalt bis auf unsere Tage,* 3 vols. (Vienna, 1894–1897), with three supplementary manuscript volumes. Also recommended are Peter Broucek, ed., *Ein General im Zwielicht. Die Erinnerungen Edmund Glaises von Horstenau,* 3 vols. (Vienna-Cologne-Graz, 1980–1987), 1:107–37; Johann Jobst, *Die Neustädter Burg und die k.u.k. Theresianische Militärakademie* (Vienna-Leipzig, n.d. [1909]); Joseph Ritter Rechberger von Rechkron, *Das Bildungswesen im Österreichischen Heere vom Dreissigjährigen Kriege bis zur Gegenwart* (Vienna, 1878); and Carl Baron von Torresani, *Von der Wasser- bis zur Feuertaufe. Werde und Lehrjahre eines österreichischen Offiziers,* 2 vols. (Dresden-Leipzig, 1900), 1:40–42.

   5. Fenner, *Österreich und seine Armee,* p. 30.

   6. See Broucek, *Ein General im Zwielicht,* 1:96, 131; and Torresani, *Von der Wasser- bis zur Feuertaufe,* 2:79, 138.

   7. There are dozens of eyewitness accounts of life at the Military Academy. Of particular interest are Fenner, *Österreich und seine Armee,* pp. 28–43 *et passim;* Angeli, *Wien nach 1848,* pp. 114ff.; Födransperg, *Vierzig Jahre in der österreichischen Armee,* vol. 1; Wilhelm Hirsch, Edler von Stronstorff, "Erinnerungen," unpublished manuscript, KA, B/1003, Nr. 1, pp. 10–21; Anton Ritter von Pitreich, "Mein militärischer und politischer Werdegang," unpublished manuscript, KA, B/589, no. 3, pp. 8ff.; and Torresani, *Von der Wasser- bis zur Feuertaufe,* 2:3–172.

   8. Hirsch, "Erinnerungen," p. 15.

   9. Födransperg, *Vierzig Jahre in der österreichischen Armee,* p. 3; and Hirsch, "Erinnerungen," p. 11.

   10. *Reglement für die kaiserlich-königlichen Militär-Bildungs-Anstalten,* p. 12.

   11. Angeli, *Wien nach 1848,* pp. 114–15.

   12. Oscar Teuber, *Im Cadeteninstitut. Lose Skizzen aus dem militärischen Jugendleben,* 3rd ed. (Jena, 1881), pp. 52–53.

   13. Torresani, *Von der Wasser- bis zur Feuertaufe,* 2:91n; Teuber, *Im Cadeteninstitut,* pp. 22–26, 93–94; and Oscar Teuber, *Tschau! Lose Skizzen aus der Militär-Akademie,* 2nd ed. (Prague, 1881), p. 139.

   14. Broucek, *Ein General im Zwielicht,* 1:103; Hirsch, "Erinnerungen," p. 12; Torresani, *Von der Wasser- bis zur Feuertaufe,* 2:75–79, 107–8; Teuber, *Im Cadeteninstitut,* pp. 16–19 *et passim;* and Teuber, *Tschau!,* p. 33.

   15. Broucek, *Ein General im Zwielicht,* 1:102.

   16. Fenner, *Österreich und seine Armee,* p. 51.

   17. Teuber, *Im Cadeteninstitut,* pp. 7–13.

   18. Fenner, *Österreich und seine Armee,* p. 104.

19. Ibid., p. 42n. Also, Pitreich, "Mein militärischer und politischer Werdegang," p. 15; and Torresani, *Von der Wasser- bis zur Feuertaufe,* 2:172–89.

20. *Reglement für die kaiserlich-königlichen Militär-Bildungs-Anstalten,* pp. 6–7.

21. Ibid., p. 81.

22. Teuber, *Im Cadeteninstitut,* pp. 118–32. See also k.k. General-Commando in Graz to the Imperial War Ministry, February 7, 1867, KA. Unfortunately, the archive discarded the report of Feldmarschalleutnant Heinrich Rupprecht von Virtsolog, head of the investigating commission on the events (*Exzesse*) of February 1, 1867, at Marburg.

23. I have computed the statistical data on the Military Academy class of 1874 from the résumés contained in Svoboda, *Die Theresianische Militär-Akademie zur Wiener Neustadt,* 1:263ff.

24. I have computed the statistical data on the Militär-Oberrealschule at Mährisch-Weisskirchen from the *Classifikations-Listen* of that school for 1899, in the KA.

25. I have computed the statistical data on the Military Academy class of 1913 from the résumés contained in the 1909–1919 (unpublished) supplement to Svoboda, *Die Theresianische Militär-Akademie.*

26. On the post-1874 military academies and cadet schools, see Poten, *Geschichte,* pp. 335ff.; Broucek, *Ein General im Zwielicht,* 1:94–137; Alfons Danzer et al., *Unter den Fahnen. Die Völker Österreich-Ungarns in Waffen* (Prague-Vienna-Leipzig, 1889), pp. 415–57; Ludwig Hesshaimr, ". . . lass eine goldne Spur . . . mein Lebensweg vom Soldaten zum Künstler 1872–1954" (Rio de Janeiro, 1954), unpublished manuscript, KA, B/765, Nr. 1.; Otto von Kiesewetter, "Der Offizier der alten österr. ung. Armee," 4 pts., Donation Kiesewetter, unpublished manuscript, KA, B/1861; Anton Freiherr von Lehár, "Lehár Geschichten" (Vienna, 1942), unpublished manuscript, KA, B/600, Nr. 1/II, pp. 10–15; Adolf Stillfried von Rathenitz, "Erinnerungen aus meinem Leben," unpublished manuscript, KA, B/862, pp. 58–69; *Schwarz-Gelbe Armee—Sociale Fragen,* 2nd ed. (Dresden-Leipzig, 1899), pp. 15–60; Ulf Sereinigg, "Das altösterreichische Offizierskorps 1868–1914. Bildung, Advancement, Sozialstruktur, wirtschaftliche Verhältnisse," unpublished doctoral dissertation, University of Vienna, 1983, pp. 51–55; August von Urbański, "Das Tornisterkind: Lebenserinnerung," unpublished manuscript, KA, 5/58, Nr. 4, pp. 9–13; and Theodor Ritter von Zeynek, "Das Leben eines österreichisch-ungarischen Generalstabsoffiziers," unpublished manuscript, KA, B/151, Nr. 2, pp. 9–13. For a sampling of school histories, see *Historische Schilderung der k.u.k. Militär-Unterrealschule in Kismarton [Eisenstadt]* (Kismarton, 1909); Gotthold Krebs, *Die k.u.k. Militär-Oberrealschule zu Mährisch-Weisskirchen* (Vienna-Leipzig, 1906); *Lehrplan der k.u.k. Militärrealschulen* (Vienna, 1912); *Lehrplan der k.u.k. Militärakademien* (Vienna, 1918); and Adolf Proksch, *Geschichte der k.u.k. Artillerie-Kadettenschule in Wien* (Vienna, 1907).

27. On the reserve officer system, see Danzer et al., *Unter den Fahnen,* pp. 16–18, 112, 260–63; Kiesewetter, "Offizier," part 4; Sereinigg, "Offizierskorps," pp. 46–48; Anton Kainz, "70 Jahre Reserveoffiziere in Österreich," *Militärwissenschaftliche Mitteilungen* 68 (1937):353; Lorenz Seutter [Laurentius Rettues], "In goldenen Schnüren," unpublished manuscript, KA, B/139, pp. 220–32; *Dienstverkehr des Reserveoffiziers* (Vienna, 1915); *Der Weg zum Einjährigen-Freiwilligen-Begünstigung nach dem Wehrgesetze vom Jahre 1912* (Vienna, 1917); and H[ugo] Schmid, *Heerwesen,* vol. 2, *Österreich-Ungarn: Lehr- und Lernbehelf für Militärerziehungs- und Bildungsanstalten, sowie Reserveoffiziersschulen, dann für das Selbststudium* (Vienna, 1914), pp. 13–14. Statistical data on the number of infantry and Jäger reserve officers who joined the career officer corps are in Broucek, *Ein General im Zwielicht,* 1:19.

28. See Poten, *Geschichte,* p. 372. Also, *Lehrplan der k.u.k. Militär-Akademien* (Vienna, 1898), and *Lehrplan der k.u.k. Militärrealschulen* (Vienna, 1912).

29. Interview with the former Hungarian colonel Kálmán Kéri, who was at the artillery

cadet school at Traiskirchen, Lower Austria, between 1915 and 1918 (Budapest, December 4, 1984). Kéri's father was an engine-driver with the Hungarian State Railways.

30. "Mittheilung über die Studien-Erfolge," k.u.k. Infanterie-Kadettenschule in Wien, 1892–1893, Lehár Nachlass, KA, B/600.

31. *Historische Schilderung*, p. 63; and *Lehrplan der k.u.k. Militärrealschulen*, pp. 14, 42.

32. Percentages calculated from data in Mór Pásztory, *Az osztrák-magyar monarchia statisztikája*, (Statistics of the Austro-Hungarian monarchy) (Pozsony-Budapest, 1884), pp. 164–65; and Ungarische-Delegation, *A közös ügyek tárgyalására kiküldött magyar országos bizottság hadügyi albizottságának jelentése 1881*, no. 17 (Report of the military subcommittee of the Hungarian national delegation sent out to negotiate joint affairs) (Budapest, 1881), pp. 128–29.

33. See *Utasítás a pályázók felvételére nézve a m. kir. honvéd nevelő és képző intézetekbe* (Instruction regarding the admission of applicants to the Royal Hungarian honvéd educational and training institutions) (Budapest, 1898); *Aufnahmsbedingungen der Militär-Bildungs-Anstalten* (Budapest, 1906), pp. 50–90; Tibor Papp, "Die königlich ungarische Landwehr (honvéd) 1868–1914," in *Die bewaffnete Macht*, pp. 670–77.

34. Percentages calculated from "A Hadügyi Albizottság jelentése," in *A közös ügyek tárgyalására a magyar országgyűlés által kiküldött s Ő Felsége által 1912 évi szeptember 23-ra Bécsbe összehívott Bizottság irományai*, no. 20 (Budapest, 1912), p. 138.

35. Proksch, *Geschichte*, p. 17.

36. Pásztory, *Statisztikája*, pp. 164–65; and Ungarische-Delegation, *A közös*, pp. 128–29.

37. *Statistische Rückblicke aus Österreich* (Vienna, 1913), p. 99.

38. Statistics based on the biographies contained in the 1909–1919 (unpublished) supplement to Svoboda, *Die Theresianische Militär-Akademie*. Note that the sources disagree on the number of graduates. See also Broucek, *Ein General im Zwielicht*, 1:115.

39. See Rainer Egger, "Der Stand des österreichisch-ungarischen Militär-Erziehungs- und Bildungswesens 1918," *Österreichische Militärische Zeitschrift* 6 (1968):424–30.

40. Interview with Kálman Kéri, Budapest, December 11, 1984.

Chapter 4

1. Joseph Roth, *The Radetzky March*, trans. Eva Tucker (Woodstock, N.Y., 1974), pp. 119–20. See also Peter Broucek, ed., *Ein General im Zwielicht. Die Erinnerungen Edmund Glaises von Horstenau*, 3 vols. (Vienna-Graz-Cologne, 1980–1987), 1:126.

2. On the *Möbeljud* see, among others, Moriz Edler von Angeli, *Wien nach 1848* (Vienna-Leipzig, 1905), p. 139; Hans Mailáth-Pokorny, "Memoiren," unpublished manuscript, KA, B/700, Nr. 2, pp. 5–6; and Ferdinand Fauland, *Vorwiegend heiter. Von einem der auszog, General zu werden* (Graz-Vienna-Cologne, 1980), pp. 63–70.

3. Angeli, *Wien nach 1848*, pp. 137–38. On the officers' living quarters, see also Kurt von Schmedes, "Jugend- und Kriegserinnerungen," unpublished manuscript, KA, B/1044:2, p. 26; Franz Xaver Schubert, "Nachlass," unpublished manuscript, KA, B/833, Nr. 2, pp. 1–2.; and Fauland, *Vorwiegend heiter*, p. 72.

4. Joseph Burian, *Der kaiserlich-königlich österreichische Offizier. Systematische Darstellung der Pflichten, Rechte, Ansprüche und Gebühren der Offiziere im Allgemeinen*, 3 vols. (Prague, 1860–1861), 1:152.

5. Theodor von Zeynek, "Das Leben eines Ö.-U. Generalstabsoffiziers," unpublished manuscript, KA, B/151, Nr. 2, pp. 16–17.

6. On the loneliness of Military Academy graduates see, for instance, Anton Ritter von Pitreich, "Geschichte der Familie von Pitreich, II. Teil, (1928/32)," pp. 10–12, in "Pitreich Nachlass," unpublished manuscript, KA, B/589, Nr. 3.

7. Of the voluminous literature on the army *"Du"* see, among others, [Moritz von] Auffenberg-Komarów, *Aus Österreichs Höhe und Niedergang. Eine Lebensschilderung* (Munich, 1921), pp. 14–15, 36; Carl Freiherr von Bardolff, *Soldat im alten Österreich. Erinnerungen aus meinem Leben* (Jena, 1938), p. 54; Rudolf von Eichthal, *Kaisermanöver und andere Erzählungen* (Vienna, 1953), pp. 97ff.; Broucek, *Ein General im Zwielicht,* 1:145; and Josef Leb, "Aus den Erinnerungen eines Trainoffiziers," unpublished manuscript, KA, B/580, p. 8. Alfons Danzer et al., *Unter den Fahnen. Die Völker Österreich-Ungarns in Waffen* (Prague-Vienna-Leipzig, 1889), pp. 89–91; and Georg Auffahrt, *Inhalt und Form. Das Buch vom Offizier* (Vienna, 1910), reprinted in *Verein Alt-Neustadt. Mitteilungsblatt,* 4/1985, pp. 19–45, and 1/1986, pp. 21–22.

8. On the terrors of instructing the recruits in their mother tongue see, for instance, Otto von Kiesewetter, "Aus der goldenen Leutnantszeit," ("Vorträge vor dem Österr. Kameradschaftsbund ehem. Angehöriger des I.R. 17"; n.p., n.d.), in "Donation Kiesewetter," unpublished manuscript, KA, B/861, p. 2; Anton Freiherr von Lehár, "Lehár Geschichten," 2 vols., unpublished manuscript (Vienna, 1942), KA, B/600, Nr. 1/II, pp. 17–19; Ludwig Hesshaimr, ". . . lass eine goldne Spur" (Rio de Janeiro, 1954), unpublished manuscript, KA, B/765, Nr. 1, pp. 41–42; and Adolf Stillfried von Rathenitz, "Erinnerungen aus meinem Leben," unpublished manuscript, KA, B/862, pp. 70–73.

9. See Maximilian Ehnl, "Die öst-ung. Landmacht nach Aufbau, Gliederung, Friedensgarnison, Einteilung, und nationaler Zusammensetzung im Sommer 1914," Supplement 9 (1934) of Edmund von Glaise-Horstenau and Rudolf Kiszling, eds., *Österreich-Ungarns letzter Krieg 1914–1918,* 7 vols. and 10 supplements (Vienna, 1930–1938).

10. See, for instance, Schubert, "Nachlass," pp. 21, 29–30.

11. August von Urbański, "Das Tornisterkind. Lebenserinnerungen," unpublished manuscript, KA, 5/58, Nr. 4, pp. 16–17.

12. The ethnic characteristics of soldiers in the pre-1848 period are discussed, with above average insight, by [Daniel] Fenner von Fenneberg, *Österreich und seine Armee* (Leipzig, 1842), pp. 76–84. For the late Dualistic period, see Robert Nowak, "Die Klammer des Reichs. Das Verhalten der elf Nationalitäten Österreich-Ungarns in der k.u.k. Wehrmacht 1914–1918," 4 vols., unpublished manuscript, KA, B/726, Nr. 1 (1964), vol. 1, ch. 2.

13. Otto Bauer, *Die Offiziere der Republik* (Vienna, 1921), pp. 1–2.

14. Ibid., p. 5.

15. Leo Schuster, ". . . *Und immer wieder mussten wir einschreiten!" Ein Leben "im Dienste der Ordnung,"* ed. Peter Paul Kloss (Vienna-Cologne-Graz, 1986).

16. Fenner, *Österreich und seine Armee,* pp. 14–15, 21–25 *et passim.* The reference to the 4:00 A.M. to 7:00 P.M. schedule is on pp. 21–22. See also Johann Christoph Allmayer-Beck and Erich Lessing, *Das Heer unter dem Doppeladler 1718–1848* (Munich-Gütersloh-Vienna, 1981), p. 234; and *Sechzig Jahre Wehrmacht* (Vienna, 1908), pp. 17–19.

17. On corporal punishment and military court procedures in the prereform period, see Fenner, *Österreich und seine Armee,* pp. 251–304. He also cites the articles of war, both those of Maria Theresa and of the early nineteenth century, on pp. 253–73. See also Anton Freiherr Mollinary von Monte-Pastello, *Sechsundvierzig Jahre im österreichisch-ungarischen Heere 1833–1879,* 2 vols. (Zurich, 1905), 1:40–41. The lashing of Italian soldiers is related in Wilhelm Ritter Gründorf von Zebegény, *Memoiren eines österreichischen Generalstäblers,* ed. Adolf Saager, 4th ed. (Stuttgart, 1913), p. 51.

18. Fenner, *Österreich und seine Armee,* pp. 67–73.

19. See, for instance, István Görgey, *1848 és 1849-ből. Élmények és benyomások* (From 1848 and 1849. Experiences and impressions), 3 vols. (Budapest, 1885–1888), 1:158–61.

20. Lehár, "Lehár Geschichten," II:17.

21. The best source on the lives of recruits and on army regulations regarding their rights and duties, is Danzer et al., *Unter den Fahnen,* pp. 122–203, 255–83 *et passim.* On the NCOs, see especially pp. 200–203. The soldiers' diet, profoundly affected by their ethnic preferences, is well described in Christoph Tepperberg, "Mannschaftsmenage. Über das Essen und Trinken in den Kasernen der k. u. k. Armee," *Mitteilungen des Österreichischen Staatsarchivs. Festschrift Rudolf Neck* 39 (1986):90–113.

22. See Danzer et al., *Unter den Fahnen,* pp. 269–72. On the abolition of flogging, see Stefan Malfèr, "Die Abschaffung der Prügelstrafe in Österreich unter besonderer Berücksichtigung der Militärgrenze," *Zeitschrift der Savigny-Stiftung für Rechtsgeschichte* 102, No. 7 (1985):206–38.

23. See *Österreichisches Statistisches Handbuch, 1890* (Vienna, 1890), p. 272; *Magyar Statisztikai Évkönyv, 1882* (Hungarian Statistical Yearbook, 1882) (Budapest, 1882), pp. 24–25, 27–28; and *Magyar Statisztikai Évkönyv, 1911* (Budapest, 1911), p. 539.

24. *Magyar Statisztikai Évkönyv, 1882,* p. 26.

25. On civilian and military suicides, see Gerhard Füllkrug, *Der Selbstmord, eine moralstatistische und volkspsychologische Untersuchung* (Schwerin, 1919), pp. 87–105. See also Thomas G. Masaryk, *Suicide and the Meaning of Civilization* (Chicago-London, 1970). I am indebted to Alan Sked of the University of London for drawing my attention to these books, and for the information contained in his unpublished essay, entitled "Social Attitudes as Evinced in Army Life in the Monarchy."

26. See Országos Levéltár (National Archives, Budapest), K.26.-ME. 260/1893, "Question asked by Deputy Gábor Ugron in the Hungarian Chamber of Deputies," and the response of the k.u.k. Kriegsministerium, 685/1893. On the frostbite incident, see also Urbański, "Das Tornisterkind," p. 27.

27. On the officers' automatic access to the imperial court, see Alexander Hajdecki, *Officiers-Standes-Privilegien. System und Praxis des geltenden Officiersrechtes der k.u.k. bewaffneten Macht* (Vienna, 1897), pp. 58–61. On the officers' attending the Vienna opera and Burgtheater as well as the Hofball see, among others, Auffenberg-Komarów, *Aus Österreichs Höhe und Niedergang,* p. 38; Schmedes, "Jugend- und Kriegserinnerungen," p. 29; and Schubert, "Nachlass," p. 6.

28. On the officers' evaluation of different parts of the monarchy, see Hesshaimr, ". . . lass eine goldne Spur," pp. 50–51; Auffenberg-Komarów, *Aus Österreichs Höhe und Niedergang,* p. 39; Eichthal, *Kaisermanöver und andere Erzählungen,* pp. 31, 39ff.; Broucek, *Ein General im Zwielicht,* 1:126ff.; Lehár, "Lehár Geschichten," II:17–19; Pitreich, "Geschichte," pp. 38–39; Schmedes, "Jugend- und Kriegserinnerungen," p. 24; Schubert, "Nachlass," pp. 21–30; Stillfried, "Erinnerungen aus meinem Leben," pp. 70–73; and Carl Baron Torresani, *Von der Wasser- bis zur Feuerteufe. Werde- und Lehrjahre eines österreichischen Offiziers,* 2 vols. (Dresden-Leipzig, 1900), 1:199–230.

29. Schubert, "Nachlass," pp. 22.

30. On the different forms of amusement, see Auffenberg-Komarów, *Aus Österreichs Höhe und Niedergang,* p. 37; Bardolff, *Soldat im alten Österreich,* pp. 56–57; Gründorf, *Memoiren eines österreichischen Generalstäblers,* pp. 89–90; Pitreich, "Pitreich Nachlass," pp. 1–20; and Schubert, "Nachlass," p. 8.

31. A typical complaint on the officers' intellectual laziness can be found in Leb, "Aus den Erinnerungen eines Trainoffiziers," p. 10. On forbidden newspapers in the preliberal era, see Mollinary, *Sechsundvierzig Jahre im österreichisch-ungarischen Heere 1833–1879,* 1:60;

and István Görgey, *Görgey Arthur ifjúsága és fejlődése a forradalomig* (The youth and development of A. G. until the revolution) (Budapest, 1916), p. 182.

32. For an example of officers' associations, see *Statuten und Geschäftsordnung des Offiziersvereines des k. und k. Infanterie-Regiments Parmann Nr. 12. Dez. 1909* (Znaim, 1909). See also Danzer et al., *Unter den Fahnen*, pp. 121–35.

33. See, for instance, Adalbert Schneider, *Der Officier im gesellschaftlichen Verkehr*, 3rd ed. (Graz, 1895).

34. On the general staff and the general staff school see, among others, Danzer et al., *Unter den Fahnen*, pp. 54–87; *Die K. und K. Kriegsschule 1852–1902. Herausgegeben vom Kommando der K. und K. Kriegsschule* (Vienna, 1903); Oskar Regele, *Generalstabschefs aus vier Jahrhunderten. Das Amt des Chefs des Generalstabes in der Donaumonarchie. Seine Träger und Organe von 1529 bis 1918* (Vienna-Munich, 1966); and *Reglement für die kaiserlich-königlichen Militär-Bildungs-Anstalten* (Vienna, 1859). Of the very rich memoir literature, see particularly, Broucek, *Ein General im Zwielicht*, 1:168–206; Lehár, "Lehár Geschichten," II:38–52; Schmedes, "Jugend- und Kriegserinnerungen," pp. 30–36; Schubert, "Nachlass," pp. 31–55; Stillfried, "Erinnerungen aus meinem Leben," pp. 50–53; Urbański, "Das Tornisterkind," pp. 22–31; and Zeynek, "Das Leben eines Ö.-U. Generalstabsoffiziers," pp. 18–33.

35. On the Hofrichter affair, see Leomare Qualtinger, *K.u.K. Krimis. Berühmte Kriminalfälle aus dem alten Österreich* (Vienna-Munich, 1980), pp. 231–55; Broucek, *Ein General im Zwielicht*, 1:188; "Nachlass Otto Wiesinger," unpublished manuscript, KA, B/77, Nr. 24, p. 29; and Schmedes, "Jugend- und Kriegserinnerungen," p. 36. Young Captain Schmedes was one of those who received the poisoned capsules. On Hofrichter the military writer, see Erwin A. Schmidl, "From Paardeberg to Przemyśl: Austria-Hungary and the Lessons of the Anglo-Boer War, 1899–1902," in Jay Stone and Erwin A. Schmidl, *The Boer War and Military Reforms* ("War and Society in East Central Europe," 28; Lanham, Md.-New York-London, 1988), p. 261.

36. *Militär-Statistisches Jahrbuch für die Jahre 1880, 1881 und 1882*. Part I (Vienna, 1885), p. 149; and *Militärstatistisches Jahrbuch für das Jahr 1911* (Vienna, 1912), pp. 154–55.

Chapter 5

1. Quoted in [Daniel] Fenner von Fenneberg, *Österreich und seine Armee* (Leipzig, 1842), p. 4.

2. Quoted in Moriz Edler von Angeli, *Wien nach 1848* (Vienna-Leipzig, 1905), pp. 128–29. The term *"Equipage"* has been interpreted by some historians as "coach and horses"; in reality, it meant equipment.

3. Josef Karl Mayr, *Wien im Zeitalter Napoleons. Staatsfinanzen, Lebensverhältnisse, Beamte und Militär* ("Abhandlungen zur Geschichte und Quellenkunde der Stadt Wien, "VI; Vienna, 1940), pp. 223–24.

4. Quoted in Fenner, *Österreich und seine Armee*, pp. 240–42. Note that Angeli, *Wien nach 1848*, p. 130, gives somewhat lower salary figures for the same period. For instance, according to Angeli, a lieutenant II. class was paid 24 gulden monthly; a lieutenant I. class, 28 gulden; and a first lieutenant, 32 gulden. On the prereform pay of officers, see also Walter Wagner, "Die k.(u.)k. Armee—Gliederung und Aufgabestellung," in Adam Wandruszka and Peter Urbanitsch, eds., *Die bewaffnete Macht* ("Die Habsburgermonarchie 1848–1918," vol. 5; Vienna, 1987), pp. 302–7.

5. Roman Sandgruber, *Die Anfänge der Konsumgesellschaft. Konsumgüterverbrauch, Lebensstandard und Alltagskultur in Österreich im 18. und 19. Jahrhundert* ("Sozial- und Wirtschaftshistorische Studien," 15; Vienna, 1982), p. 227, table 43.

6. Ibid.

7. Monika Schmidl, "Überblick über die österreichische Münz- und Währungsgeschichte," unpublished manuscript (Vienna, 1985), p. 12.

8. Sandgruber, *Die Anfänge der Konsumgesellschaft,* table 20.

9. Fenner, *Österreich und seine Armee,* pp. 240–41. On the mid-nineteenth-century pay of the Württemberg and Baden officers, see also Heinz Helmert, *Militärsystem und Streitkräfte im deutschen Bund am Vorabend des preussisch-österr. Krieges von 1866* (Berlin, 1964), pp. 81–82.

10. Angeli, *Wien nach 1848,* pp. 133–34.

11. Heinrich Ritter von Födransperg, *Vierzig Jahre in der österreichischen Armee. Erinnerungen eines österreichischen Offiziers von seinem Eintritte in die Armee bis zur Gegenwart 1854–1894,* 2 vols. (Dresden, 1895), 1:107.

12. Quoted in István Görgey, *Görgey Arthur ifjúsága és fejlődése a forradalomig* (The youth and development of A. G. until the revolution) (Budapest, 1916), pp. 107–8.

13. Ibid., pp. 127, 139, 148.

14. Arthur Görgey to his brother, István (Svirotitz, June 3, 1843). Cited in Albert Görgei, ed., *Görgei Arthur 1818–1916* (Igló, 1917), p. 17. See also István Görgey, *Görgey Arthur,* pp. 82, 103.

15. Rudolf Baron Potier des Échelles, "Mein Leben," 2 vols., unpublished manuscript (1855), Theresianum, Vienna, 1:219.

16. Mayr, *Wien im Zeitalter Napoleons,* p. 231.

17. See Angeli, *Wien nach 1848,* p. 129; and Fenner, *Österreich und seine Armee,* pp. 230–50.

18. Data on the pay revisions were culled from Joseph Burian, *Der kaiserlich-königlich Österreichische Offizier. Systematische Darstellung der Pflichten, Rechte, Ansprüche und Gebühren der Offiziere im Allgemeinen,* 3 vols. (Prague, 1860–1861), 1:148; Antonio Schmidt-Brentano, *Die Armee in Österreich. Militär, Staat und Gesellschaft 1848–1867* (Boppard am Rhein, 1975); and Ulf Sereinigg, "Das altösterreichische Offizierskorps, 1869–1914. Bildung, Advancement, Sozialstruktur, wirtschaftliche Verhältnisse," unpublished doctoral dissertation, University of Vienna, 1983, pp. 105–7.

19. Data on workers' income are in Alexander Sixtus von Reden, *Österreich-Ungarn. Die Donaumonarchie in historischen Dokumenten* (Salzburg, 1984), p. 165. The most detailed sources on income and prices in Austria-Hungary are Sandgruber, *Die Anfänge der Konsumgesellschaft;* and Alfred Francis Pribram, *Materialen zur Geschichte der Preise und Löhne in Österreich,* 2 vols. (Vienna, 1938), 1:604, 608 *et passim.*

20. Sereinigg, "Das altösterreichische Offizierskorps," pp. 113–16.

21. Alfons Danzer et al., *Unter den Fahnen. Die Völker Österreich-Ungarns in Waffen* (Prague-Vienna-Leipzig, 1899), pp. 105–12. The quotation is on p. 105.

22. Salvator R. [*recte* Rudolf Hetz], *Die Verschuldung unseres Offizierskorps. Ihre Ursachen und Konsequenzen* (Vienna, 1911), pp. 7–9, 49–50.

23. *Gagezettel* of First Lieutenant Kurt Freiherr von Reden, January 1907. In "Nachlass Reden," unpublished manuscript, KA, Vienna, B/147.

24. *Schwarz-Gelbe Armee—Sociale Fragen!,* 2nd ed. (Dresden-Leipzig, 1899), pp. 108–13.

25. "Der Officiersmangel und seine Ursachen," Part I, *Armeeblatt* (Vienna) 8, No. 43 (October 25, 1899):1–3. See also Part II of the same article, ibid., 44 (November 1, 1899):4–5.

26. *Armeeblatt*, October 25, 1899: 3.

27. Douglas Porch, *The March to the Marne. The French Army, 1871–1914* (Cambridge, 1981), p. 89.

28. Ibid.

29. On "dirty" debts, see Angeli, *Wien nach 1848*, pp. 146–48.

30. Kurt von Schmedes, "Jugend- und Kriegserinnerungen," unpublished manuscript, KA, B/1044:2, pp. 1–4.

31. Adolf Stillfried von Rathenitz, "Erinnerungen aus meinem Leben," unpublished manuscript, KA, B/862, p. 88.

32. See Salvator R., *Die Verschuldung.*

33. *Schwarz-Gelbe Armee—Sociale Fragen!*, pp. 116–19.

Chapter 6

1. KA, Kriegsministerium 1901. Präs. 14-1/61 Militär-Commando in Zara. See also the *Haupt-Grundbuchblatt* of Augustin Weigel and the *Qualifikations-Liste*, F 274, of Anton Bonkowski.

2. See Major Hans Mailáth-Pokorny, "Memoiren," unpublished manuscript, KA, B/700, Nr. 2., pp. 23–27.

3. Captain Ludwig Berger, *Der Waffengebrauch des Offiziers. Ein Orientierungsbehelf,* 3rd ed. (Linz, 1903; first ed., 1898), p. 58. Among the many other publications on the same issue are Josef Burian, *Der kaiserlich-königliche österreichische Offizier. Systematische Darstellung der Pflichten, Rechte, Ansprüche und Gebühren der Offiziere im Allgemeinen, sowie der Obliegenheiten mit Bezug auf die Dienstsphäre im Besondern,* 3 vols. (Prague, 1860), especially 1:25ff.; [Judge-Advocate] Major Alexander Hajdecki, *Officiers-Standes-Privilegien. System und Praxis des geltenden Officiersrechtes der k.u.k. bewaffneten Macht* (Vienna, 1897), pp. 5ff.; Captain Adalbert Schneider, *Der Officier im gesellschaftlichen Verkehr,* 3rd ed. (Graz, 1895); *Vorschrift über die Behandlung unverbesserlicher Offiziere* (Vienna, 1862); *Dienstverkehr des Reserveoffiziers* (Vienna, 1915), pp. 215–44; Karl Friedrich Kurz, ed., *Militär-Taschenlexicon,* 10th ed., Part I (Vienna, 1911); and A. Kielhauser, *Die Vorschrift für das ehrenrätliche Verfahren im k.u.k. Heere und Ehrenrechtsfragen,* 4th ed. (Vienna, 1914).

4. Alfons Danzer et al., *Unter den Fahnen. Die Völker Österreich-Ungarns in Waffen* (Prague-Vienna-Leipzig, 1889), p. 91.

5. Hajdecki, *Officiers-Standes-Privilegien,* pp. 3–11, 188–96. The quotations are on pp. 5, 10.

6. See *Militär-Taschenlexikon,* p. 73; Berger, *Der Waffengebrauch des Offiziers,* p. 24; and *Dienstverkehr des Reserveoffiziers,* p. 228.

7. Berger, *Der Waffengebrauch des Offiziers,* pp. 12–13.

8. The information on the history of duelling has been culled, unless otherwise indicated, from Hubert Mader, *Duellwesen und altösterreichisches Offiziersethos* ("Studien zur Militärgeschichte, Militärwissenschaft und Konfliktforschung," 31; Osnabrück, 1983); Wilson D. Wallis's essay on duelling in the *Encyclopaedia of the Social Sciences,* 15 vols. (New York, 1959), 5:268–70; and V. G. Kiernan, *The Duel in European History: Honour and the Reign of Aristocracy* (Oxford-New York, 1988). The last-named book, although comprehensive in many respects, has unfortunately almost nothing to say on the Habsburg monarchy.

9. See Mader, *Duellwesen und altösterreichisches Offiziersethos,* p. 27.

10. Ibid., p. 113.

11. Hajdecki, *Officiers-Standes-Privilegien,* p. 197n.

12. [Daniel] Fenner von Fenneberg, *Österreich und seine Armee* (Leipzig, 1842), pp. 134–37.

13. Ibid., pp. 136–37.

14. KA, Kriegsministerium, 1901. 1 A 67. 28. See also Lt. Carl Smerczek's *Qualifikations-Liste,* F 2758.

15. Carl Freiherr von Bardolff, *Soldat im alten Österreich. Erinnerungen aus meinem Leben* (Jena, 1938), pp. 55–56. The Ledóchowski affair is also mentioned in Mader, *Duellwesen und altösterreichisches Offiziersethos,* p. 129.

16. The Catholic, Freemasonic, social democratic, and liberal opposition to duelling is discussed in Mader, *Duellwesen und altösterreichisches Offiziersethos,* pp. 119–28, 134–38.

17. On the Austrian and the Hungarian anti-duelling leagues, see ibid., pp. 129–34. See also D. Prokowsky, *Die Geschichte der Duellbekämpfung* (Bonn, 1965).

18. Joseph Roth, *The Radetzky March,* trans. Eva Tucker (New York, 1974), pp. 98–99.

19. Ibid., p. 103.

20. See *Militär-Statistisches Jahrbuch für das Jahr 1900* (Vienna, 1901), p. 145.

21. The Waidhofen student conference and the running conflict between the anti-Semitic students and the army are discussed in Peter Pulzer, *The Rise of Political Anti-Semitism in Germany and Austria* (New York, 1964), pp. 253–54. The quotation is from p. 253.

22. *Dienstverkehr des Reserveoffiziers,* pp. 236–37.

23. Quoted in Major Caesar de Sgardelli, *Párbaj zsebkódexe* (The pocket code of duelling) (Budapest, 1922), p. 20.

24. *Dienstverkehr des Reserveoffiziers,* pp. 231–44.

25. KA, Kriegsministerium, 1909. 1 A, 100–35. See also the *Qualifikations-Liste,* F 2476, of First Lieutenant Wilhelm Ritter von Rosner.

26. Albert Wiesinger, *Das Duell vor dem Richterstuhle der Religion, der Moral, des Rechtes und der Geschichte* (Graz, 1895), as cited by Mader, *Duellwesen und altösterreichisches Offiziersethos,* pp. 155–62. See also Wallis's essay on duelling, *Encyclopaedia of the Social Sciences,* p. 269.

27. See Sándor Némethy, *A tiszti fegyverhasználat* (The use of weapons by officers) (Szeged, 1936).

28. Wallis's essay on duelling, *Encyclopaedia of the Social Sciences,* p. 270.

Chapter 7

1. Much of my information on officers' marriages has been culled from Gerwin Müller, "Heiratsvorschriften und Heiratsverhalten im altösterreichischen Offizierskorps," unpublished doctoral dissertation, University of Vienna, 1980. On Maria Theresa's measures, see pp. 28–31.

2. Ibid., pp. 37–45.

3. Ibid., pp. 46–49.

4. Ibid., pp. 60, 102, 104. Müller seems to err here by vastly underestimating the officers' pay in 1907. For instance, he writes of 400 gulden annual pay for a lieutenant, when the legally prescribed basic pay amounted to 840–1,000 gulden. See chapter 5 in this book.

5. See István Deák, *The Lawful Revolution: Louis Kossuth and the Hungarians, 1848–1849* (New York, 1979), pp. 184–86.

6. Adolf Stillfried von Rathenitz, "Erinnerungen aus meinem Leben," unpublished manuscript, KA, B/862, pp. 66–69; [Moritz Ritter von] Auffenberg-Komarów, *Aus Österreichs Höhe und Niedergang. Eine Lebensschilderung* (Munich, 1921), p. 71; Wilhelm Hirsch, Edler von Stronstroff, "Erinnerungen," unpublished manuscript, KA, B/1003, Nr. 1,

p. 47; and Gregor Edler von Misčević, "Der Werdegang eines Grenzerkindes als nützliches Glied des Staates und der menschlichen Gesellschaft," unpublished manuscript, KA, B/1146/1, p. 10.

7. Müller, "Heiratsvorschriften und Heiratsverhalten im altösterreichischen Offizierskorps," p. 139.

8. Cited ibid., p. 145.

9. A. Kielhauser, *Die Vorschrift für das ehrenrätliche Verfahren im k.u.k. Heere und Ehrenratsfragen* (Vienna, 1914), p. 253.

10. *Militär-Statistisches Jahrbuch für das Jahr 1872,* Part I (Vienna, 1875), pp. 169, 208–9.

11. Anton Freiherr von Lehár, "Lehár Geschichten," unpublished manuscript, 2 vols., KA, B/600, Nr. 1/II, p. 49.

12. Anton Freiherr Mollinary von Monte-Pastello, *Sechsundvierzig Jahre im österreichisch-ungarischen Heere 1833–1879,* 2 vols. (Vienna, 1905), 1:193–94; and August Urbański von Ostrymiecz, "Das Tornisterkind. Lebenserinnerungen," unpublished manuscript, KA, 5/58, Nr. 4, pp. 29–34.

13. [Daniel] Fenner von Fenneberg, *Österreich und seine Armee* (Leipzig, 1842), pp. 60–61.

14. *Militär-Statistisches Jahrbuch für das Jahr 1872,* pp. 208–9.

15. Wilhelm Ritter Gründorf von Zebegény, *Memoiren eines österreichischen Generalstäblers 1832–1866,* ed. Adolf Saager, 4th ed. (Stuttgart, 1913), pp. 323–64.

16. Ibid., pp. 77–90.

17. Peter Broucek, ed., *Ein General im Zwielicht. Die Erinnerungen Edmund Glaises von Horstenau,* 3 vols. (Vienna, 1980–1987), 1:76.

18. Case of Fähnrich Heinrich Schmidt. Garnisonsgericht Gyulafehérvár, July 20, 1912, and Militär Obergericht, Vienna, May 2, 1913. KA, Kriegsministerium 1912, 1 A 67–93, and 1913 1 A 67–84.

19. Case of Oblt. Wenzel Hausmann, k.k. General-Kommando zu Ofen, Mil. Abt. Nr. 732. KA, Kriegsministerium, 1874, 1 A 67–6.

20. "Strafuntersuchungsprotokolle 1896–1915," KA.

21. (1) Case of Cornelius Ritter von Hafner, Festungs-Commando zu Komorn. KA, Kriegsministerium, 1901, 1 A 67–55/6; (2) Case of Curt Josef Mayer and Stanislaus Boicetta, Garnisons-Gericht zu Theresienstadt. KA, Kriegsministerium, 1900, 1 A 67–68; and (3) Case of Josef Kautek, Garnisons-Gericht zu Sopron. KA, Kriegsministerium, 1908, 1A 67–47/2.

22. The most famous work on the Redl affair is Egon Erwin Kisch, *Der Fall des Generalstabschefs Redl* (Berlin, 1924). Kisch, a young Prague journalist in 1913, was the first to question publicly the innocuous army statement published following Redl's suicide. The fullest account of the Redl affair is *The Panther's Feast* (New York, 1959) by Robert Asprey, a former U.S. intelligence officer posted to Austria after World War II. Asprey gained access to thitherto sequestered documentary collections in the Vienna War Archive, and he also interviewed many survivors. His exciting tale is marred, however, by Asprey's predilection for putting thoughts in the heads of his characters and for inventing both events and dialogues. See also Urbański, "Das Tornisterkind," pp. 94–101; Georg Markus, *Der Fall Redl* (Vienna-Munich, 1984); and Alfred Redl's *Qualifikations-Liste,* F 2399, in KA.

23. See "Strafuntersuchungsprotokolle 1896–1915," KA. The statistical data represent my own computations from this handwritten index.

24. See Hubert Mader, *Duellwesen und altösterreichisches Offiziersethos* ("Studien zur Militärgeschichte, Militärwissenschaft und Konfliktforschung," 31; Osnabrück, 1983).

25. On military court proceedings see, among others, Fenner, *Österreich und seine*

Armee, chs. 6, 9; Emil Dangelmaier, *Militär-rechtliche und militär-ethische Abhandlungen. Mit Berücksichtigung der Gesetzgebung Österreich-Ungarns, Deutschlands, Frankreichs und Italiens* (Vienna-Leipzig, 1893); Generalmajor Cleinow, *Zur Frage des Militär-Strafverfahrens in Deutschland und Österreich-Ungarn* (Berlin, 1894), which is very critical of the Austro-Hungarian procedures; Leo Geller, *Die Militär-Strafprozessordnungen for die gemeinsame Wehrmacht und die Landwehr* (Vienna, 1912); Ernst Franz Weisl, "Das Militärstrafrecht," *Österreichische Militärische Zeitschrift*, 1890:124–57, and, by the same author, "Zur Reform des Militärstrafprozesses," ibid., 1910:351–73, as well as his *Kommentar zu den Militär-Strafprozessordnungen für die gemeinsame Wehrmacht und für die Landwehren in Österreich und Ungarn vom 5. Juli 1912* (Vienna, 1913). Also, Leomare Qualtinger, *K.u.K Krimis. Berühmte Kriminalfälle aus dem alten Österreich* (Vienna-Munich, 1980): "Der Fall Adolf Hofrichter," pp. 231–55. Again, I have to express my thanks to Alan Sked of the University of London for having enabled me to look into his unpublished essay, "Social Attitudes as Evinced in Army Life in the Monarchy."

26. *Militärstatistisches Jahrbuch für das Jahr 1911* (Vienna, 1912), pp. 143, 154–61.

Chapter 8

1. Information on the pre-1855 system of pensions is very hard to obtain. The reader is referred to [Daniel] Fenner von Fenneberg's seminal work, *Österreich und seine Armee* (Leipzig, 1842), pp. 306–16, 322–25, and to Alan Sked, *The Survival of the Habsburg Empire: Radetzky, the Imperial Army and the Class War, 1848* (London-New York, 1979), pp. 24–26.

2. Josef Karl Mayr, *Wien im Zeitalter Napoleons. Staatsfinanzen, Lebensverhältnisse, Beamte und Militär* ("Abhandlungen zur Geschichte und Quellenkunde der Stadt Wien," VI; Vienna, 1940), p. 225.

3. On the negotiated retirements, see Fenner, *Österreich und seine Armee*, pp. 174–76.

4. On the 1855 pension regulation, see Antonio Schmidt-Brentano, *Die Armee in Österreich. Militär, Staat und Gesellschaft 1848–1867* (Boppard am Rhein, 1975), pp. 409–12.

5. See, Alfons Danzer et al., *Unter den Fahnen. Die Völker Österreich-Ungarns in Waffen* (Prague-Vienna-Leipzig, 1889), pp. 111–12; and "Der Officiersmangel und seine Ursachen," *Armeeblatt* 18, no. 43 (October 25, 1899):2.

6. Ibid.

7. "Der Officiersmangel und seine Ursachen," p. 3.

8. See Mayr, *Wien im Zeitalter Napoleons*, p. 225.

9. See Karl Ilming, *Die Versorgung der Militärwitwen und -waisen* (Vienna, 1907), pp. 9–11.

10. "Der Officiersmangel und seine Ursachen," p. 3.

11. See Erzsébet Gangel, *A soproni m.kir. "Zrinyi Ilona" honvédtiszti leánynevelőintézet története 1850–1936* (The history of the "Ilona Zrinyi" honvéd officers' daughters' educational institution) (Budapest, n.d.); and Adele von Arbter, *Aus der Geschichte der k.u.k. Offizierstöchter-Erziehungs-Institute* (Vienna, 1892). The data on teachers and pupils are in *Militär-Schematismus, 1905* (Vienna, 1905), p. 1064.

12. Ilming, *Die Versorgung der Militärwitwen und -waisen*, p. 69.

13. Ibid., pp. 43–56.

Chapter 9

1. C. A. Macartney, *The Habsburg Empire, 1790–1918* (London, 1968), p. 53. On pp. 49–58, the author treats the question of nobility in the Habsburg monarchy succinctly and

efficiently. Unfortunately, he errs with regard to the extent of the Esterházys' landed posses-
sions. Two other informative and brief sources on the nobility in the Habsburg lands are
Moritz Csáky, "Adel in Österreich," in *Das Zeitalter Kaiser Franz Josephs. I. Teil. Von der
Revolution zur Gründerzeit 1848–1880. Beiträge* (Schloss Grafenberg, 1984), pp. 212–19;
and László Deme, "From Nation to Class: The Changing Social Role of the Hungarian
Nobility," *International Journal of Politics, Culture and Society* (Summer 1988):568–84.
Also, Heinz Siegert, ed., *Adel in Österreich* (Vienna, 1971).

2. [Kronprinz Rudolf von Habsburg], "Der Österreichische Adel und sein constitu-
tioneller Beruf (1878)," in Brigitte Hamann, ed., *Kronprinz Rudolf, Majestät, ich warne Sie.
Geheime und Private Schriften* (Vienna, 1979), pp. 18–52.

3. See William O. McCagg, *Jewish Nobles and Geniuses in Modern Hungary* ("East
European Monographs," No. 3; New York, 1972), pp. 21–22.

4. See Johann Christoph Allmayer-Beck, "Die Träger der staatlichen Macht. Adel,
Armee und Bürokratie," in Otto Schulmeister, ed., *Spectrum Austriae. Österreich in
Geschichte und Gegenwart* (Vienna, 1957), p. 160.

5. See Josef Burian, *Der kaiserlich-königliche österreichische Offizier. Systematische
Darstellung der Pflichten, Rechte, Ansprüche und Gebühren der Offiziere im Allgemeinen,
sowie die Obliegenheiten mit Bezug auf die Dienstsphäre im Besondern*, 3 vols. (Prague,
1860), 1:213–16.

6. Ulf Sereinigg, "Das altösterreichische Offizierskorps 1868–1914. Bildung, Advancement, Sozialstruktur, wirtschaftliche Verhältnisse," unpublished doctoral dissertation, University of Vienna, 1983, pp. 98–99; also, Nikolaus von Preradovich, *Die Führungsschichten
in Österreich und Preussen 1804–1918, mit einem Ausblick zum Jahre 1945* ("Veröffentlichungen des Instituts für Europäische Geschichte Mainz," vol. 11; Wiesbaden, 1955),
p. 7.

7. Preradovich, *Die Führungsschichten in Österreich und Preussen 1804–1918*, pp. 56–
58.

8. "Die k. und k. Generalität," *Die Vedette* 35, no. 469 (Vienna, March 4, 1903):1.

9. Karl Kandelsdorfer, "Der Adel im k.u.k. Offizierskorps," *Militärische Zeitschrift*
(1897):248–69.

10. Ibid.:250–69.

11. See, for instance, Robert Nowak, "Die Klammer des Reichs. Das Verhalten der elf
Nationalitäten Österreich-Ungarns in der k.u.k. Wehrmacht 1914–1918," 4 vols., unpublished manuscript, KA, B/726, Nr. 1, vol. I, p. 11; and Kurt von Schmedes, "Jugend-
und Kriegserinnerungen," unpublished manuscript (1979), KA, B/1044:2, p. 3.

12. Sereinigg, "Das altösterreichische Offizierskorps 1868–1914," p. 97.

13. Preradovich, *Die Führungsschichten in Österreich und Preussen 1804–1918*, p. 44.

14. See Tibor Hajdu, "A tisztikar társadalmi helyzetének változásai (1849–1914)"
(Changes in the social position of the officer corps [1849–1914]), *Valóság*, 87/4 (Budapest,
April 1987):69.

15. Ibid.

16. These data represent my own calculations on the basis of the *Militär-Schematismus
für das Jahr 1905* (Vienna, 1905).

Chapter 10

1. I have culled these data from the *Kais. königl. Militär-Schematismus für 1880* (Vienna,
1879), pp. 10–22 *et passim*.

2. Ibid., pp. 113, 115.

3. Statistics culled from the *Militär-Statistisches Jahrbuch für das Jahr 1870*, Part I (Vienna, 1872), pp. 211–17.

4. See *Militär-Statistisches Jahrbuch für das Jahr 1875*, Part I (Vienna, 1878), pp. 172–75.

5. Quoted in August Urbański von Ostrymiecz, "Das Tornisterkind. Lebenserinnerungen," unpublished manuscript, KA, 5/58, Nr. 4, p. 16.

6. Ulf Sereinigg, "Das altösterreichische Offizierskorps 1868–1914. Bildung, Avancement, Sozialstruktur, wirtschaftliche Verhältnisse," unpublished doctoral dissertation, University of Vienna, 1983, pp. 80–85.

7. Ibid., p. 71n.

8. *Militärstatistiches Jahrbuch für das Jahr 1911* (Vienna, 1912), pp. 143–46.

9. See Gábor Bona, *Kossuth Lajos kapitányai* (The captains of Lajos Kossuth) (Budapest, 1988), pp. 57–58. On Kossuth's visit to the United States in 1851–1852 and his anti-Catholic stand there, see István Deák, *The Lawful Revolution: Louis Kossuth and the Hungarians, 1848–1849* (New York, 1979), pp. 342–45; and Donald S. Spencer, *Louis Kossuth and Young America: A Study of Sectionalism and Foreign Policy, 1848–1852* (Columbia, Mo.-London, 1977).

10. *Militär-Statistisches Jahrbuch für das Jahr 1872*, Part I (Vienna, 1875), pp. 171–72, 202–3.

11. See Alexander Sixtus von Reden, *Österreich-Ungarn. Die Donaumonarchie in historischen Dokumenten* (Salzburg, 1984), p. 67; and *Militärstatistisches Jahrbuch für das Jahr 1911*, pp. 145, 147. Not untypically, because of a lack of comprehensive statistics for the monarchy as a whole, Adam Wandruszka and Peter Urbanitsch, eds., *Die Konfessionen* ("Die Habsburgermonarchie 1848–1918," vol. 4; Vienna, 1985) does not contain a single statistical datum on its 859 pages regarding the overall confessional distribution of the monarchy's population.

12. See *Militärstatistisches Jahrbuch für das Jahr 1910* (Vienna, 1911), p. 147; and *Schematismus für das kaiserliche und königliche Heer und für die kaiserliche und königliche Kriegsmarine für 1910* (Vienna, 1909), p. 1216. For a venomous denunciation of the Joint Army's chaplains, see Jaroslav Hašek, *The Good Soldier Schweik*, trans. Paul Server (New York, 1962).

13. Much of the information on Jews in the Habsburg army has been culled from Erwin A. Schmidl's bilingual *Juden in der k.(u.)k. Armee 1788–1918. Jews in the Habsburg Armed Forces* ("Studia Judaica Austriaca," XI; Eisenstadt, 1989). On the *Judenverordnung* of 1789 see, among others, Joseph Karniel, "Das Toleranzpatent Kaiser Josephs II. für die Juden Galiziens und Lodomeriens," *Jahrbuch des Instituts für Deutsche Geschichte der Universität Tel Aviv* 11 (1982):55–89. The relevant passages are in paragraphs 48 and 49. See also Joseph Karniel, *Die Toleranzpolitik Kaiser Josephs II* ("Schriftenreihe des Instituts für Deutsche Geschichte Tel Aviv," Nr. 9; Gerlingen, 1986).

14. See C. A. Macartney, *The Habsburg Empire, 1790–1918* (London, 1968), pp. 37, 82, as well as Wolfgang Hansler, "Das österreichische Judentum im Zeitalter der josephinischen Toleranz," in *Österreich zur Zeit Kaiser Josephs II* (Vienna, 1980), pp. 166–69.

15. Cited in Wolfgang von Weisl, "Juden in der österreichischen und österreichisch-ungarischen Armee," *Zeitschrift für die Geschichte der Juden* 8 (1971):5.

16. For a detailed discussion of the special taxes paid by Jews in lieu of military service, see Schmidl, *Juden in der k.(u.)k. Armee*, pp. 40–42, 105–7.

17. Moritz Frühling, "Wiener Juden für die österreichisch-ungarische Monarchie," *Ost und West. Illustrierte Monatsschrift für das gesamte Judentum* 10 (1910):539–40.

18. Schmidl, *Juden in der k.(u.)k. Armee*, pp. 51–52, 115.

19. Weisl, "Juden in der österreichischen und österreichisch-ungarischen Armee," pp. 10–11; Jenő Zsoldos, ed., *1848–49 a magyar zsidóság életében* (1848–49 in the life of the Hungarian Jewry) (Budapest, 1948), pp. 189–90, 221–24 *et passim;* and Gábor Bona, *Tábornokok és törzstisztek a szabadságharcban 1848–49* (Generals and field-grade officers in the 1848–49 War of Independence) (Budapest, 1983).

20. See the *Qualifikations-Liste,* F 2874, of Karl Strass, KA.

21. Schmidl, *Juden in der k.(u.)k. Armee,* pp. 55, 118.

22. *Militär-Statistisches Jahrbuch für das Jahr 1872,* pp. 202–3; *Militär-Statistisches Jahrbuch für das Jahr 1902* (Vienna, 1903), pp. 186–87; and *Militärstatistisches Jahrbuch für das Jahr 1911,* pp. 188–97.

23. *Militärstatistiches Jahrbuch für das Jahr 1911,* pp. 192–93, 196–97.

24. Werner T. Angress, "Prussia's Army and the Jewish Reserve Officer Controversy Before World War I," *Publications of the Leo Baeck-Institute,* Yearbook 17 (London-Jerusalem-New York, 1972), pp. 19–42; Martin Kitchen, *The German Officer Corps, 1890–1914* (Oxford, 1968), p. 40; Rolf Vogel, *Ein Stück von uns. Deutsche Juden in deutschen Armeen 1813–1976. Eine Dokumentation* (Mainz, 1977), p. 38; and Peter Pulzer, "Die jüdische Beteiligung an der Politik," in Werner E. Mosse, ed., *Juden im Wilhelminischen Deutschland 1890–1914* (Tübingen, 1976), pp. 169–72 *et passim.* For a characteristic case of anti-Jewish collusion among several Prussian military bodies, see Isegrimm, "Vom Jahrmarkt des Lebens," *Dr. Bloch's Wochenschrift* (Vienna), Nr. 13 (March 25, 1904):201.

25. *Militärstatistisches Jahrbuch für das Jahr 1911,* pp. 149, 185–87, 193, 196–97, 213–15.

26. On Jewish high-school and university students in Austria, see Wolfdieter Bihl, "Die Juden," in Adam Wandruszka and Peter Urbanitsch, eds., *Die Völker des Reiches* ("Die Habsburgermonarchie 1848–1918," vol. 3; Vienna, 1980), Part II, p. 924. On Jewish high-school students in Hungary, see Victor Karády, "Jewish Enrollment Patterns in Classical Secondary Eduction in Old Regime and Inter-war Hungary," *Studies in Contemporary Jewry* 1 (Bloomington, Ind., 1984):232; and *A Magyar Szent Korona Országainak 1910. évi népszámlálása* (The 1910 census of the lands of the Hungarian Holy Crown), Part VI (Budapest, 1920), p. 95.

27. *Militär-Statistisches Jahrbuch für das Jahr 1897* (Vienna, 1898), pp. 191, 193, 217, 219; and *Militärstatistisches Jahrbuch für das Jahr 1911,* pp. 185, 187, 213, 215.

28. *Militärstatistisches Jahrbuch für das Jahr 1911,* pp. 149, 185, 213.

29. Eduard Beer, "Vom militärärztlichen Officierscorps," *Dr. Bloch's Wochenschrift* (Vienna), Nr. 52 (October 27, 1901):855–56; and *Monatschrift der Österreichisch-Israelitischen Union,* 16/4 (April 1904):2.

30. See, for instance, Weisl, "Juden in der österreichischen und österreichisch-ungarischen Armee," p. 3.

31. Moritz Frühling, *Biographisches Handbuch der in der k.u.k. österr.-ung. Armee und Kriegsmarine aktiv gedienten Offiziere, Ärzte, Truppen-Rechnungsführer und sonstigen Militärbeamten jüdischen Stammes* (Vienna, 1911).

32. This, and all other statistics relating to the career officers, have been calculated from Frühling, *Biographisches Handbuch der in der k.u.k. österr.-ung. Armee.*

33. On General Schweitzer, see Frühling, *Biographisches Handbuch der in der k.u.k. österr.-ung. Armee,* p. 3; Weisl, "Juden in der österreichischen und österreichisch-ungarischen Armee," pp. 11–12; E. Rubin, *140 Jewish Marshals, Generals, and Admirals* (London, 1952), pp. 67–68; Schmidl, *Juden in der k.(u.)k. Armee,* pp. 63, 125; and *Egyenlőség* (Equality), Budapest, May 27, 1938. See also Schweitzer's *Qualifikations-Liste,* F 2685, KA.

34. On General Eiss, see Frühling, *Biographisches Handbuch der in der k.u.k. österr.*

-ung. Armee, p. 4, and Weisl, "Juden in der österreichischen und österreichisch-ungarischen Armee," p. 12.

35. On General Hazai, see his *Qualifikations-Liste,* F 1064, KA, and in the Hungarian War Archive, Budapest, HM 2682. See also Bihl, "Die Juden," p. 941.

36. *Militärstatistisches Jahrbuch für das Jahr 1910* (Vienna, 1911), pp. 182–85.

37. Franz Theodor Csokor, "3. November 1918," in *Europäische Trilogie* (Vienna, 1972), pp. 5–78.

38. Tibor Hajdu, "A tisztikar társadalmi helyzetének változásai (1848–1914)" (Changes in the social position of the officer corps [1848–1914]), *Valóság* (Budapest), 87/4 (1987):55–80.

39. Wilhelm Winkler, *Der Anteil der nichtdeutschen Volksstämme an der öst.-ung. Wehrmacht* (Vienna, 1919), p. 3.

40. See Georg Živković, *Heer und Flottenführer der Welt,* 2nd ed. (Vienna, 1980), p. 76; and Johann Weidlein, "Ungarische Offiziere donauschwäbischer Herkunft," unpublished manuscript, KA, Brochure 1542.

Chapter 11

1. Wilhelm Czermak, *In deinem Lager war Österreich. Die österreichisch-ungarische Armee, wie man sie nicht kennt* (Breslau, 1938), pp. 38–39. On Conrad's incomprehensible strategic blunder at the time of mobilization, see Norman Stone, "Moltke and Conrad: Relations between the Austro-Hungarian and German General Staffs, 1909–1914," in Paul M. Kennedy, ed., *The War Plans of the Great Powers, 1880–1914* (Boston, 1979), pp. 222–51.

2. Czermak, *In deinem Lager war Österreich,* p. 36. Some of the major works on the Habsburg army's prewar armaments program and subsequent war effort are Gunther E. Rothenberg, *The Army of Francis Joseph* (West Lafayette, Ind., 1976), chs. 12–14; Alfred Krauss, *Die Ursachen unserer Niederlage,* 2nd ed. (Munich, 1921); Rudolf Kiszling, *Österreich-Ungarns Anteil am Ersten Weltkrieg* (Graz, 1959); and Edmund Glaise von Horstenau and Rudolf Kiszling, eds., *Österreich-Ungarns letzter Krieg 1914–1918,* 7 vols., with 10 supplements (Vienna, 1930–1938), which will hereafter be referred to as *ÖULK.*

3. *ÖULK,* vol. 7, Appendix 10.

4. There seems to be no short, comprehensive modern history of the Austro-Hungarian war between 1914 and 1918. Norman Stone's *The Eastern Front, 1914–1917* (London, 1975) discusses, as its title indicates, the conflict between the Central Powers and Russia. Robert A. Kann, Béla K. Király, and Paula S. Fichtner, eds., *The Habsburg Empire in World War I: Essays in Intellectual, Military, Political and Economic Aspects of the War Effort* ("East European Monographs," No. 23; New York, 1977), and Béla K. Király and Nándor Dreisziger, eds., *East Central European Society in World War I* ("East European Monographs," No. 196; New York, 1985), contain valuable essays on the army at the war. See also Franz Conrad von Hötzendorf, *Aus meiner Dienstzeit 1906–1918,* 7 vols. (Vienna-Berlin-Leipzig-Munich, 1921–1925); Oskar Regele, *Gericht über Habsburgs Wehrmacht. Letzte Siege und Untergang unter dem Armee-Oberkommando Kaiser Karls I—Generaloberst Arz von Straussenburg* (Vienna-Munich, 1968); and Cyril Falls, *The Battle of Caporetto* (Philadelphia-New York, 1966), as well as the other works listed in the historiographical essay in Appendix I.

5. See *ÖULK,* vol. 7, Appendix 37.

6. Ibid., 1:80, 7:46.

7. Fritz Franek, "Probleme der Organisation im ersten Kriegsjahre," *ÖULK,* Supplement 1 (Vienna, 1930), p. 20; and Czermak, *In deinem Lager war Österreich,* pp. 50–51.

8. On the uneven social and ethnic distribution of the war dead, see the pamphlets of the Austrian statistician Wilhelm Winkler: *Die Totenverluste der öst.-ung. Monarchie nach Nationalitäten* (Vienna, 1919), and *Berufsstatistik der Kriegstoten der öst.-ung. Monarchie* (Vienna, 1919).

9. Czermak, *In deinem Lager war Österreich*, pp. 50–51.

10. *ÖULK*, vol. 2, Appendix 3.

11. Ibid., vol. 7, Appendix 3.

12. Georg Nitsche, *Österreichisches Soldatentum im Rahmen deutscher Geschichte* (Berlin-Leipzig, 1937), p. 263.

13. Czermak, *In deinem Lager war Österreich*, p. 28.

14. *ÖULK*, vol. 7, Appendices 1, 37.

15. Dr. Ernst R. v. Rutkowski, "Das Schicksal des Oberleutnants in der Reserve Dr. Leon Lebensart im Weltkrieg 1914–1918," *Zeitschrift für die Geschichte der Juden* 4 (1967):231.

16. Alajos Kovács, *A zsidóság térfoglalása Magyarországon* (The expansion of the Jews in Hungary) (Budapest, 1922), pp. 22–25.

17. Winkler, *Die Totenverluste*, p. 6.

18. Maximilian Paul-Schiff, "Teilnahme der österreichisch-ungarischen Juden am Weltkrieg. Eine statistische Studie," *Jahrbuch für jüdische Volkskunde—Mitteilungen zur jüdischen Volkskunde*, 26/27 (1924–1925):153–54; Wolfdieter Bihl, "Die Juden," in Adam Wandruszka and Peter Urbanitsch, eds., *Die Völker des Reiches* ("Die Habsburgermonarchie 1848–1918," vol. 3; Vienna, 1980), p. 946; and Erwin A. Schmidl, *Juden in der k.(u.)k. Armee 1788–1918. Jews in the Habsburg Armed Forces* ("Studia Judaica Austriaca," XI; Eisenstadt, 1989) pp. 82–85, 142–145.

19. Bihl, "Die Juden," p. 945.

20. Ibid., p. 947. On Jewish officers in the First Kaiserschützen Regiment, see Heinz von Lichem, *Der einsame Krieg. Erste Gesamtdokumentation des Gebirgskrieges 1915/18 von den Julischen Alpen bis zum Stilfser Joch* (Munich, n.d.), p. 42. Also, interview with Paul Kohn, New York, November 22, 1988.

21. On the 1908 mutiny, see Robert Nowak, "Die Klammer des Reichs. Das Verhalten der elf Nationalitäten Österreich-Ungarns in der k.u.k. Wehrmacht 1914–1918," 4 vols., unpublished manuscript, KA, B/726, Nr. 1, 1:192–95.

22. On the 1912 mutinies, see ibid., 1:204–29; and Rothenberg, *The Army of Francis Joseph*, p. 170.

23. On the alleged brutality of honvéd units vis-à-vis the Ukrainian population, see Nowak, "Die Klammer des Reichs," 1:333–35, 357–63.

24. There are a number of fine studies of the Austro-Hungarian POWs in Samuel R. Williamson, Jr., and Peter Pastor, eds., *Essays on World War I: Origin and Prisoners of War* ("East European Monographs," No. 126; New York, 1983), pp. 105–264.

25. Ivo Banac, "South Slav Prisoners of War in Revolutionary Russia," ibid., p. 120, and Josef Kalvoda, "Czech and Slovak Prisoners of War in Russia During the War and Revolution," ibid., p. 225.

26. The political history of the Dual Monarchy between 1914 and 1918 is ably discussed by, among others, Z. A. B. Zeman, *The Break-Up of the Habsburg Empire* (London, 1961); Arthur J. May, *The Passing of the Hapsburg Monarchy, 1914–1918*, 2 vols. (Philadelphia, 1966); and Leo Valiani, *The End of Austria-Hungary* (New York, 1973).

27. See István Deák, "The Decline and Fall of Habsburg Hungary, 1914–18," in Iván Völgyes, ed., *Hungary in Revolution, 1918–19* (Lincoln, Nebr., 1971), pp. 10–30; and Gábor Vermes, *István Tisza: The Liberal Vision and Conservative Statecraft of a Magyar Nationalist* ("East European Monographs," No. 184; New York, 1985), chs. 10–18.

28. See Robert A. Kann, *Die Sixtus-Affäre und die geheimen Friedensverhandlungen*

Österreich-Ungarns im Ersten Weltkrieg (Vienna, 1966). On Emperor-King Charles, see Arthur Graf Polzer-Hoditz, *Kaiser Karl* (Zurich-Vienna, 1928); Reinhold Lorenz, *Kaiser Karl und der Untergang der Donau-Monarchie* (Graz, 1959); Ottokar Czernin, *Im Weltkrieg* (Munich, 1919); and Gordon Brook-Shepherd, *The Last Habsburg* (New York, 1968).

29. See Garry W. Shanafelt, *The Secret Enemy: Austria-Hungary and the German Alliance, 1914–1918* ("East European Monographs," No. 187; New York, 1985).

30. See Richard G. Plaschka, Horst Haselsteiner, and Arnold Suppan, *Innere Front. Militärassistenz, Widerstand und Umsturz in der Donaumonarchie 1918,* 2 vols. (Vienna, 1974).

31. On the pre-1914 history of the Austro-Hungarian navy, see Lothar Hobelt, "Die Marine," in Adam Wandruszka and Peter Urbanitsch, eds., *Die bewaffnete Macht* ("Die Habsburgermonarchie 1848–1918," vol. 5; Vienna, 1987), pp. 687–763. Also, Lawrence Sondhaus' pioneering study, *The Habsburg Empire and the Sea: Austrian Naval Policy, 1797–1866* (West Lafayette, Indiana, 1989).

32. *Militärstatistisches Jahrbuch für das Jahr 1910* (Vienna, 1911), pp. 149–51.

33. See Admiral Nicholas Horthy, *Memoirs,* with an introduction by Nicholas Roosevelt (New York, 1957), pp. 80–86.

34. See Richard G. Plaschka, *Cattaro-Prag. Revolte und Revolution* (Graz, 1963).

35. *ÖULK,* vol. 7, Appendix 3; and "Letzte Kriegsgliederung der öst.-ung. und der dem k.u.k. AOK unterstellten deutschen Streitkräfte am 15. Oktober 1918," ibid., vol. 7, Appendix 32.

36. See Márton Farkas, *Katonai összeomlás és forradalom 1918-ban. A hadsereg szerepe az Osztrák-Magyar Monarchia felbomlásában* (Military collapse and revolution. The role of the army in the dissolution of the Austro-Hungarian monarchy) (Budapest, 1969), pp. 76, 175. Also, Regele, *Gericht über Habsburgs Wehrmacht,* pp. 93–109.

37. On the final Balkan crisis, see Bogdan Krizman, "Der militärische Zusammenbruch auf dem Balkan," in Richard Georg Plaschka and Karlheinz Mack, eds., *Die Auflösung des Habsburgerreiches. Zusammenbruch und Neuorientierung im Donauraum* (Vienna, 1970), pp. 270–92.

38. On the final crisis in Italy, see Karel Pichlik, "Der militärische Zusammenbruch der Mittelmächte im Jahre 1918," in Plaschka and Mack, *Die Auflösung des Habsburgerreiches,* pp. 249–65. Also, Farkas, *Katonai összeomlás és forradalom 1918-ban,* pp. 271–98 *et passim;* Regele, *Gericht über Habsburgs Wehrmacht,* pp. 161–70; and Hanks R. Wayne, "The End of an Institution: The Austro-Hungarian Army in Italy, 1918," unpublished dissertation, Rice University, 1977.

39. Emil Ratzenhofer, "Der Waffenstillstand von Villa Giusti und die Gefangennahme Hunderttausender," in *ÖULK,* Supplement 2 (Vienna, 1931), pp. 29–55. See also Regele, *Gericht über Habsburgs Wehrmacht,* pp. 172–222.

40. Ernst Wengraf, ed., *Feuerbereit! Kriegsalbum des Feldartillerie-Regiments Nr. 104, Wien* (Vienna, 1919), p. 28 *et passim.*

41. Bruno Brehm, *Weder Kaiser noch König. Der Untergang der Habsburgischen Monarchie* (Munich, 1933), pp. 306–7. Translated by I. Deák.

Epilogue

1. Here are some titles, in English, on the central and east central European revolutions and the successor states: Francis L. Carsten, *Revolution in Central Europe, 1918–1919* (London, 1972); Arno Mayer, *Wilson vs. Lenin* (Cleveland-New York, 1964); Joseph Rothschild, *East Central Europe between the Two World Wars* (Seattle, 1974); Charles Gulick,

Austria from Habsburg to Hitler, 2 vols. (Berkeley, 1948); Barbara Jelavich, *Modern Austria: Empire and Republic, 1800–1986* (Cambridge, 1987), chs. 3–4; Ivan Völgyes, ed., *Hungary in Revolution, 1918–19: Nine Essays* (Lincoln, Nebr., 1971); Andrew C. János, *The Politics of Backwardness in Hungary, 1825–1945* (Princeton, 1982), chs. 5, 6; Jörg K. Hoensch, *A History of Modern Hungary, 1867–1986,* trans. Kim Traynor (London-New York, 1988), ch. 3; Rudolf Tőkés, *Béla Kun and the Hungarian Soviet Republic* (New York, 1967); Victor J. Mamatey and Radomir Luža, eds., *A History of the Czechoslovak Republic, 1918–1948* (Princeton, 1973); Ivo Banac, *The National Question in Yugoslavia* (Ithaca, N.Y., 1984); Fred Singleton, *A Short History of the Yugoslav People* (New York, 1985); Henry L. Roberts, *Romania* (New Haven, 1951); Norman Davies, *God's Playground: A History of Poland,* 2 vols. (New York, 1982), vol. 2; and Hans Roos, *A History of Modern Poland from the Foundation of the State in the First World War to the Present Day* (New York, 1966).

2. On Colonel Stromfeld, see Tibor Hetés, *Stromfeld Aurél* (Budapest, 1967). The Hungarian Red Army and its campaigns against the Romanians and the Czechoslovaks in 1919, are discussed in Sándor Tóth, ed., *Magyarország hadtörténete* (The military history of Hungary), 2 vols. (Budapest, 1984–1985), vol. 2, ch. 3; and Vilmos Boehm, *Im Kreuzfeuer zweier Revolutionen* (Munich, 1924). Also, Oscar Jászi, *Revolution and Counter-Revolution in Hungary* (London, 1924); Peter Pastor, *Hungary between Wilson and Lenin: The Hungarian Revolution of 1918–1919 and the Big Three* ("East European Monographs," No. 20; New York, 1976); and Peter Pastor, ed., *Revolutions and Interventions in Hungary and Its Neighbor States, 1918–1919* ("East European Monographs," No. 260; New York, 1988).

3. On the return of King Charles to Hungary in 1921, see Bruno Brehm, *Weder Kaiser noch König. Der Untergang der Habsburgischen Monarchie* (Munich, 1933), chs. 4, 5; Anton Lehár, *Erinnerungen. Gegenrevolution und Restaurationsversuche in Ungarn 1918–1921,* ed. Peter Broucek (Munich, 1973), ch. 4; Aladár von Boroviczény, *Der König und sein Reichsverweser* (Munich, 1924); and Gordon Brook-Shepherd, *The Last Habsburg* (New York, 1968), pp. 248–314.

4. On Admiral Horthy, see Admiral Nicholas Horthy, *Memoirs,* with an introduction by Nicholas Roosevelt (New York, 1957); Miklós Szinai and László Szücs, eds., *The Confidential Papers of Admiral Horthy* (Budapest, 1965); and Peter Gosztony, *Miklós von Horthy. Admiral und Reichsverweser* (Zurich-Frankfurt, 1973).

5. The ideology and practices of the Horthy regime are best described in C. A. Macartney, *A History of Hungary, 1929–1945,* 2 vols. (New York, 1956–1957). See also István Deák, "Historical Foundations: The Development of Hungary from 1918 until 1945," in K.-D. Grothusen, ed., *Ungarn* ("Südosteuropa Handbuch," vol. 5; Göttingen, 1987), pp. 36–66.

6. See Sándor Szakály, "Az ellenforradalmi Magyarország (1919–1944) hadseregének felső vezetése. Történelem-statisztikai tanulmány a katonai elitről" (The higher leadership of the army of counterrevolutionary Hungary [1919–1944]. A historical-statistical study of the military elite), *Hadtörténelmi Közlemények* 31/1 (Budapest, 1984):34–71; the relevant statistics are on p. 57.

7. On the generals who became Hungarian prime ministers, see Mathias Bernath and Felix v. Schroeder, eds., *Biographisches Lexikon zur Geschichte Südosteuropas* ("Südosteuropäische Arbeiten," 75; Munich, 1970–1981): 1:362–63; 4:263–64.

8. On Ferenc Szálasi, see ibid.; and Miklós Lackó, *Arrow-Cross Men. National Socialists, 1935–1944* (Budapest, 1969). Szálasi's personal record as a Habsburg officer is in KA, F 2932.

9. On József Pilsudski, see Joseph Rothschild, *Pilsudski's Coup d'État* (New York, 1966). The statistical data on Polish generals are in Jerzy J. Wiatr, *The Soldier and the Nation: The Role of the Military in Polish Politics, 1918–1985* (Boulder-London, 1988), p. 22.

10. On individual Polish generals, see *Wielka Encyklopedia Powszechna PWN,* 12 vols.

(Warsaw, 1967–1969), 4:539; 10:147; 11:214. Also, Peter Broucek, ed., *Ein General im Zwielicht. Die Erinnerungen Edmund Glaises von Horstenau*, 3 vols. (Vienna-Cologne-Graz, 1980–1987), 1:186–87 (Pilsudski); 185 (Szeptycki); 186 (Jordan-Rozwadowski); 447 (Haller).

11. On General Phleps, see Broucek, *Ein General im Zwielicht*, 1:204.

12. On Croatian officers in the Yugoslav army, see Banac, *The National Question in Yugoslavia*, pp. 150–53.

13. On General Kvaternik, see Broucek, *Ein General im Zwielicht*, 1:136; Bernath and Schroeder, *Biographisches Lexikon zur Geschichte Südosteuropas*, 2:537–38; and Ladislaus Hory and Martin Broszat, *Der kroatische Ustascha-Staat 1941–1945* ("Schriftenreihe der Vierteljahrshefte für Zeitgeschichte," 8; Stuttgart, 1964).

14. On Field Marshal Boroević, see Ernest Bauer, *Der Löwe vom Isonzo. Feldmarschall Svetozar Boroević de Bojna* (Graz-Vienna-Cologne, 1986). Boroević's postwar fate is described on pp. 128–31.

15. On General Körner, see Eric C. Kollman, *Theodor Körner. Militär und Politik* (Vienna, 1973); Hellmut Andics, *Der Staat, den keiner wollte. Österreich von der Gründung der Republik bis zur Moskauer Deklaration* (Vienna-Munich-Zurich, 1968), is an entertaining and accurate source on the history of the first Austrian republic.

16. On the Austrian army before and during 1938, and on General Jansa, see Erwin A. Schmidl, *März 1938. Der deutsche Einmarsch in Österreich*, 2nd ed. (Vienna, 1988); and Ludwig Jedlicka, *Ein Heer im Schatten der Parteien. Die militärpolitische Lage Österreichs 1918–1938* (Graz-Cologne, 1955), and Wolfgang Doppelbauer, *Zur Elend noch die Schande. Das altösterreichische Offizierskorps am Beginn der Republik* ("Militärgeschichtliche Dissertationen der österr. Universitäten," 9; Vienna, 1988).

17. On Generaloberst Lothar Rendulić, see the autobiographical *Gekämpft, gesiegt, geschlagen* (Wels, 1952), and *Soldat in stürzenden Reichen* (Munich, 1965). Also, Broucek, *Ein General im Zwielicht*, 1:136–37. On Erhard Raus, see Rudolf Sperker, *Generaloberst Erhard Raus, ein Truppenführer im Ostfeldzug* ("Soldatenschicksale des 20. Jahrhunderts als Geschichtsquelle," Nr. 7; Osnabrück, 1988). A general treatment of Austrian soldiers in the service of the Third Reich is Johann Christoph Allmayer-Beck, "Die Österreicher im Zweiten Weltkrieg," in Herbert St. Fürlinger and Ludwig Jedlicka, eds., *Unser Heer. 300 Jahre österreichisches Soldatentum in Krieg und Frieden* (Vienna-Munich-Zurich, 1963), pp. 342–75. The statistical data on the Austrian generals are on p. 359. On Generaloberst Löhr, see Broucek, *Ein General im Zwielicht*, 1:136.

18. See Erwin A. Schmidl, *Juden in der k.(u.)k. Armee 1788–1918. Jews in the Habsburg Armed Forces* ("Studia Judaica Austriaca," XI; Eisenstadt, 1989), pp. 90, 149.

19. See Raul Hilberg, *The Destruction of the European Jews* (Chicago, 1961), pp. 278–84 *et passim*. Also, Schmidl, *Juden in der k.(u.)k. Armee*, pp. 87–91, 146–50.

20. The lot of Jewish officers in Horthy-Hungary is discussed in Randolph L. Braham, *The Politics of Genocide: The Holocaust in Hungary*, 2 vols. (New York, 1981), 1:289–330 *et passim*.

Appendix I

1. Franz Theodor Csokor, *3 November 1918* (1936); Robert Musil, *Die Verwirrungen des Zöglings Törless* (1906) (*The Young Törless*, trans. E. Wilkins and E. Kaiser [New York, 1961]); Alexander Roda Roda, *Roda Rodas Roman* (1924); Joseph Roth, *Radetzkymarsch* (1932) (*The Radetzky March*, trans. Eva Tucker [Woodstock, N.Y., 1974]); Arthur Schnitzler, *Leutnant Gustl* (1900); Ferenc Herczeg, *A hét sváb* (The seven Swabians) (1916),

and *Herczeg Ferenc emlékezései* (Memoirs of Ferenc Herczeg) (1985); Sándor Márai, *Die Kerzen brennen ab* (Vienna, n.d.); Géza Ottlik, *Iskola a határon* (School at the border) (1959); Jaroslav Hašek, *The Good Soldier Schweik* (1920–1923) (trans. Paul Selver [New York, 1962]); and Miroslav Krleža, *Hrvatski bog Mars* (The Croatian God Mars) (1922). Also, Harro K. Kühnelt, "Dorothea Gerards Romane aus dem alten Österreich," in Otto Hieltsch, ed., *Österreich und die angelsächsische Welt* (Vienna, 1961).

2. See Peter Broucek's brief essay on Habsburg military memoirs in Peter Broucek, ed., *Ein General im Zwielicht. Die Erinnerungen Edmund Glaises von Horstenau*, 3 vols. ("Veröffentlichungen der Kommission für Neuere Geschichte Österreichs," vol. 67; Vienna-Cologne-Graz, 1980–1987), 1:15–17.

3. For instance, August Urbański von Ostrymiecz, "Das Tornisterkind. Lebenserinnerungen," unpublished manuscript, KA, 5/58. Nr. 4.

4. Franz Graf Conrad von Hötzendorf, *Aus meiner Dienstzeit 1906–1918*, 7 vols. (Vienna-Berlin-Leipzig-Munich, 1921–1925); *Private Aufzeichnungen. Erste Veröffentlichungen aus den Papieren des k.u.k. Generalstabschefs*, ed. Kurt Peball (Vienna-Munich, 1977), and *Mein Anfang. Kriegserinnerungen aus der Jugendzeit 1878–1882* (Berlin, 1925).

5. Arthur Arz von Straussenburg, *Zur Geschichte des Grossen Krieges 1914 bis 1918* (Vienna-Leipzig-Munich, 1924), and *Kampf und Sturz der Kaiserreiche* (Vienna, 1935).

6. Rudolf von Eichthal (*recte* Rudolf Pfersmann von Eichthal), *Die goldene Spange* (Vienna, 1950), and *Kaisermanöver und andere Erzählungen* (Vienna, 1953); Ferdinand Fauland, *Vorwiegend heiter. Von einem der auszog, General zu werden* (Graz-Vienna-Cologne, 1980), *In Kaisers buntem Rock* (Graz, 1973), *K.u.k. Raritäten* (Graz, 1974), and *Altösterreichischer Bilderbogen* (Graz, 1975); Albert Lorenz, *Schattenreiter* (Vienna, 1958), and *Alte Autos-junge Liebe* (Vienna, 1963); Oskar Teuber, *Im Kadetteninstitut! Lose Skizzen aus dem militärischen Jugendleben*, 3rd ed. (Jena, 1881), *Tschau! Lose Skizzen aus der Militär-Akademie* (Prague, 1881), *Grüss' Dich. Neue Skizzen aus dem militärischen Jugendleben* (Vienna, 1884), *Immer fesch! Neue Skizzen aus der militärischen Jugend* (Vienna, 1888), *Immer Jung! Neue Skizzen und Geschichten aus der Soldaten-Welt* (Vienna, 1894); F. V. Schöffel, *Servus Herr Zögling*, 2nd ed. (Vienna, 1957); and Carl Freiherr von Torresani, *Aus der schönen wilden Leutnants-Zeit. Roman aus dem österreichischen Cavallerieleben*, 2 vols., 3rd ed. (Dresden-Leipzig, 1894), and *Von der Wasser- bis zur Feuertaufe*, 2 vols. (Dresden-Leipzig, 1900).

7. Oscar Teuber, *Die österreichische Armee 1700 bis 1867*, 2 vols. (Vienna, 1895), *Historische Legionen Habsburgs* (Vienna-Prague-Leipzig, 1896), and *Feldzeugmeister Wilhelm Herzog von Württemberg. Ein Lebensbild* (Vienna, 1899).

8. Max Ritter von Thielen, *Erinnerungen aus dem Kriegerleben eines 82-jährigen Veteranen der österreichischen Armee, mit besonderer Bezugnahme auf die Feldzüge der Jahre 1805, 1809, 1813, 1814, 1815; nebst einem Anhang die Politik Österreichs vom Jahre 1808–1814 betreffend* (Vienna, 1863).

9. Moriz Edler von Angeli, *Altes Eisen. Intimes- aus Kriegs- und Friedensjahren* (Stuttgart, 1900), and *Wien nach 1848* (Vienna and Leipzig, 1905); [Carl Graf Bigot de Saint-Quentin], *Von einem deutschen Soldaten* (Leipzig, 1847), and *Unsere Armee. Vom Verfasser des "deutschen Soldaten"* (Vienna, 1850); both volumes republished as Bigot de Saint-Quentin, *Schriften*, ed. Hugo Kerchnawe, 2 vols., 2nd ed. (Vienna, 1911–1912); Leopold Graf Kolowrat-Krakowsky, *Meine Erinnerungen aus den Jahren 1848 und 1849*, 2 vols. (Vienna, 1905); Anton Freiherr Mollinary von Monte-Pastello, *Sechsundvierzig Jahre im österreichisch-ungarischen Heere 1833–1879*, 2 vols. (Zurich, 1905); Carl R. von Schönhals, *Erinnerungen eines österreichischen Veteranen aus dem italienischen Krieg der Jahre 1848 und 1849* (Stuttgart-Tübingen, 1852); Carl von Torresani, *Von der Wasser- bis zur Feuertaufe*, vol. 1, is partly on the events of 1848–1849 in northern Italy; Ludwig von

Welden, *Episoden aus meinem Leben. Beiträge zur Geschichte der Feldzüge der öster-reichischen Armee in den Jahren 1848 und 1849*, 2d. ed. (Graz, 1853), as well as *Asbóth Lajos emlékiratai az 1848-iki és 1849-iki magyarországi hadjárataiból* (The memoirs of Lajos Asbóth regarding the campaigns of 1848–1849 in Hungary), 2d. ed. (Pest, 1862); Alphons F. Danzer, ed., *Dembinski in Ungarn. Nach den hinterlassenen Papieren des Generals*, 2 vols. (Vienna, 1873); Arthur Görgei, *Mein Leben und Wirken in Ungarn in den Jahren 1848 und 1849*, 2 vols. (Leipzig, 1852); in English: *My Life and Acts in Hungary in the Years 1848–1849*, 2 vols. (New York, 1852); and General [George] [György] Klapka, *Memoirs of the War of Independence in Hungary*, 2 vols. (London, 1850); in German: *Memoiren von Georg Klapka* (Leipzig, 1850), and *Der Nationalkrieg in Ungarn und Siebenbürgen in den Jahren 1848 und 1849*, 2 vols. (Leipzig, 1851).

10. Moriz Edler von Angeli, *Erzherzog Carl von Österreich als Feldherr und Heeresorganisator*, 5 vols. (Vienna-Leipzig, 1896–1897).

11. Johann Christoph Allmayer-Beck, "Die bewaffnete Macht in Staat und Gesellschaft," in Adam Wandruszka and Peter Urbanitsch, eds., *Die bewaffnete Macht* ("Die Habsburger-monarchie 1848–1918," vol. 5; Vienna, 1987), p. 2.

12. Mollinary, *Sechsundvierzig Jahre im österreichisch-ungarischen Heere 1833–1879*, 1:112.

13. Broucek, *Ein General im Zwielicht*, 1:15–16n.

14. Ferdinand Hauptmann, *Jelačić's Kriegszug nach Ungarn 1848*, 2 vols. ("Zur Kunde Südosteuropas," II/5; Graz, 1975).

15. Heinrich Ritter von Födransperg, *Vierzig Jahre in der österreichischen Armee. Erin-nerungen eines österreichischen Offiziers von seinem Eintritte in die Armee bis zur Gegen-wart 1854–1894*, 2 vols. (Dresden, n.d. [1894]); Wilhelm Ritter Gründorf von Zebegény, *Memoiren eines österreichischen Generalstäblers 1832–1866*, ed. Adolf Saager, 4th ed. (Stuttgart, 1913); Wilhelm Hirsch, Edler von Stronstorff, "Erinnerungen," ed. Eugen Hirsch, unpublished manuscript, no date, KA, B/1003, Nr. 1 (Hirsch completed his memoirs shortly before his death in 1935 at the age of ninety-nine, but most of his "Erinnerungen" were penned between 1910 and the story's end in 1914); Rudolf Freiherr Potier des Échelles, "Mein Leben," 2 vols., unpublished manuscript, Library of the Theresianum, Vienna [1885]; Feldzeugmeister Anton Ritter von Pitreich, "Geschichte der Familie von Pitreich," unpublished manuscript in "Pitreich Nachlass," KA, B/589, Nr. 3 (the Pitreich military dynasty is discussed in Nikolaus von Preradovich, "Die Pitreich aus Marburg," *Neue Chron-ik*, 36, in "Pitreich Nachlass"); Daniel Freiherr von Salis-Soglio, *Mein Leben und was ich davon erzählen will, kann, und darf*, 2 vols., (Stuttgart-Leipzig, 1908); Andreas Graf Thürheim, *Memoiren, Licht- und Schattenbilder aus dem Soldatenleben und der Gesellschaft. Tagebuch-Fragmente und Rückblicke eines ehemaligen Militärs* (Prague-Teplitz, 1876); Ludwig Freiherr von Wattman de Maelcamp-Beaulieu, *53 Jahre aus einem bewegten Leben*, 2 vols., 2nd ed. (Vienna, 1904); and Karl Went von Römö, *Ein Sol-datenleben. Erinnerungen eines österreichisch-ungarischen Kriegsmannes* (Vienna, 1904).

16. [Daniel] Freiherr Fenner von Fenneberg, *Österreich und seine Armee* (Leipzig, 1842), and Gründorf, *Memoiren*.

17. August R. von Cramon, *Unser österreichisch-ungarischer Bundesgenosse im Weltkriege* (Berlin, 1922); Albrecht Freiherr von Margutti, *Kaiser Franz Joseph I und sein Hof. Erinnerungen und Schilderungen aus den nachgelassenen Papieren eines persönlichen Ratgebers*, trans. and ed. Dr. Joseph Schneider (Vienna, 1919), and *Kaiser Franz Joseph, Persönliche Erinnerungen* (Vienna-Leipzig, 1924); Alfred Krauss, *Die Ursachen unserer Niederlage* (Munich, 1920; 3rd ed., Munich, 1923), *Der Irrgang der deutschen Königspoli-tik. Die Lehren der Vergangenheit für Gegenwart und Zukunft* (Munich, 1927), and Krauss's "Schriftennachlass," in KA, B/60.

18. The titles of some of Eichthal's, Fauland's, and Lorenz's writings are listed in note 6.

19. Ludwig Hesshaimr, ". . . lass eine goldne Spur . . . mein Lebensweg vom Soldaten zum Künstler 1872–1954" (Rio de Janeiro, 1954), unpublished manuscript, KA, B/765, Nr. 1.

20. Hans Mailáth-Pokorny, "Memoiren," and "Der k.u.k. Generalstab. Erinnerungen und Betrachtungen," unpublished manuscripts (Vienna, 1965), KA, B/700, Nr. 12, and B/3700, Nr. 2.; and Laurentius Rettues (*recte:* Rüdiger Baron Seutter von Loetzen), "In guldenen Schnüren," and other writings in "Nachlass Seutter," unpublished manuscript, KA, B/139.

21. Joseph Leb, "Aus den Erinnerungen eines Trainoffiziers," unpublished manuscript (1933), KA, B/580.

22. Gregor Edler von Mišcević, "Der Werdegang eines Grenzerkindes als nützliches Glied des Staates und der menschlichen Gesellschaft," unpublished manuscript (Vienna, 1937), KA, B/1146/1.

23. Moritz Auffenberg, Freiherr von Komarów, *Aus Österreich-Ungarns Teilnahme am Weltkrieg* (Berlin-Vienna, 1920), and *Aus Österreich-Ungarns Höhe und Niedergang* (Munich, 1921). See also his "Schriftennachlass" in KA, B/677.

24. Otto von Kiesewetter, "Vorträge vor dem Österr. Kameradschaftsbund ehem. Angehöriger des I.R.17," unpublished manuscript (n.d.), in "Donation Kiesewetter," KA, B/1861.

25. Anton Freiherr von Lehár, "Lehár Geschichten," unpublished manuscript, 2 vols. (Vienna, 1942), KA, B/600, Nr. 1/I and II. Published in part as Anton Lehár, *Erinnerungen. Gegenrevolution und Restaurationsversuche in Ungarn 1918–1921,* ed. Peter Broucek (Munich, 1973).

26. Ernst Palombini, Freiherr von Jedina, "Erinnerungen," unpublished manuscript, KA, B/959.

27. Kurt von Schmedes, "Jugend- und Kriegserinnerungen," unpublished manuscript (1949), KA, B/1044:2.

28. Franz Xaver Schubert, "Mein Lebenslauf," unpublished manuscript, KA, B/833, Nr. 2.

29. Adolf Stillfried von Rathenitz, "Erinnerungen aus meinem Leben," unpublished manuscript (1940), KA, B/862.

30. August Urbański von Ostrymiecz, "Das Tornisterkind. Lebenserinnerungen," unpublished manuscript (n.d.), KA, 5/58, Nr. 4. See also his *Conrad von Hötzendorf. Soldat und Mensch* (Graz-Leipzig-Vienna, 1938; 2nd ed., 1939).

31. Theodor R. von Zeynek, "Das Leben eines Ö.-U. Generalstabsoffiziers," unpublished manuscript (1940), KA, B/151, Nr. 2.

32. Carl Freiherr von Bardolff, *Soldat im alten Österreich. Erinnerungen aus meinem Leben* (Jena, 1938). The specific quotation is on p. 21.

33. Lothar Rendulić, *Gekämpft, gesiegt, geschlagen* (Wels, 1952), and *Soldat in sturzenden Reichen* (Munich, 1965).

34. Broucek, *Ein General im Zwielicht.*

35. Edmund von Glaise-Horstenau, *Franz Josephs Weggefährte. Das Leben des Generalstabschefs Grafen Beck. Nach seinen Aufzeichnungen und hinterlassenen Dokumenten* (Zurich-Leipzig-Vienna, [1930]), and *Die Katastrophe. Die Zertrümmerung Österreich-Ungarns* (Vienna, 1929). Glaise was also coeditor, with Rudolf Kiszling, of *Österreich-Ungarns letzter Krieg 1914–1918,* 7 vols., with 10 supplements (Vienna, 1930–1938). A complete list of Glaise's work can be found in Broucek, *Ein General im Zwielicht,* 1:52–62.

36. Austrian military historiography of World War I is the subject of a brief essay by Kurt Peball, "Österreichische militärhistorische Forschung zum Ersten Weltkrieg zwischen 1918

und 1968," in Richard Georg Plaschka and Karlheinz Mack, eds., *Die Auflösung des Habsburgerreiches. Zusammenbruch und Neuorientierung im Donauraum* (Vienna, 1970), pp. 308–17. In Hungary, some of the foremost practitioners of Habsburg military history are Tibor Hajdu, Gábor Bona, and Sándor Szakály, all of whom specialize in the social history of Hungarian officers in the Joint Army and of the honvéd officers. In Austria, Manfried Rauchensteiner is currently researching this period.

37. See, for example, Béla K. Király and Gunther E. Rothenberg, eds., *War and Society in East Central Europe*, vol. 1, *Special Topics and Generalizations on the 18th and 19th Centuries* ("War and Society in East Central Europe," vol. 1; New York, 1979); Béla K. Király, ed., *East Central European Society and War in the Era of Revolutions, 1776–1856* ("War and Society in East Central Europe," vol. 4; New York, 1984); Béla K. Király, ed., *The Crucial Decade: East Central European Society and National Defense, 1859–1870* ("War and Society in East Central Europe," vol. 14; New York, 1984); Béla K. Király and Nándor F. Dreisziger, eds., *East Central European Society in World War I* ("War and Society in East Central Europe," vol. 19; New York, 1985); and Béla K. Király and Walter S. Dillard, eds., *The East Central European Officer Corps, 1740–1920s: Social Origins, Selection, Education, and Training* ("War and Society in East Central Europe," vol. 24; New York, 1988). Some of the most relevant contributions from the point of view of this book are by the Austrians Horst Haselsteiner and Richard G. Plaschka; the Hungarians József M. Borus, Zoltán Bárcy, Márton Farkas, Tibor Hajdu, István Nemeskürty, György Szabad, Zoltán Szász, and Aladár Urbán; the Poles Eligiusz Kozlowski, Leonard Ratajczyk, and Jerzy Skowronek; the Italians Raimondo Luraghi, and Paolo Santarcangeli; the Hungarian-Americans István Deák, János Decsy, and László Deme; the Yugoslav-American Dimitrije Djordjevic, and the U.S. historian Richard B. Spence.

38. Johann Christoph Allmayer-Beck and Erich Lessing, *Die kaiserlichen Kriegsvölker von Maximilian I bis Prinz Eugen 1479–1718* (Munich-Gütersloh-Vienna, 1978); *Das Heer unter dem Doppeladler. Habsburgs Armeen 1718–1848* (Munich-Gütersloh-Vienna, 1981); and *Die k.(u.)k. Armee 1848–1918* (Munich-Gütersloh-Vienna, 1974).

39. Herbert St. Fürlinger and Ludwig Jedlicka, eds., *Unser Heer. 300 Jahre österreichisches Soldatentum in Krieg und Frieden* (Vienna-Munich-Zurich, 1963); and Herbert Patera, *Unter Österreichs Fahnen. Ein Buch vom österreichischen Soldaten* (Graz, 1960).

40. Hermann Meynert, *Geschichte der k.k. österreichischen Armee, ihrer Heranbildung und Organisation sowie ihre Schicksale, Thaten und Feldzügen von der frühesten bis auf die neuere Zeit*, 4 vols. (Vienna, 1854); and Oskar Teuber and Rudolf von Ottenfeld, *Die österreichische Armee von 1700 bis 1867*, 2 vols. (Vienna, 1895).

41. Alphons Freiherr von Wrede, *Geschichte der k. und k. Wehrmacht. Die Regimenter, Corps, Branchen und Anstalten von 1618 zum Ende des XIX. Jahrhunderts*, 5 vols. (Vienna, 1898–1905).

42. Wandruszka and Urbanitsch, *Die bewaffnete Macht*.

43. Gunther E. Rothenberg, *The Army of Francis Joseph* (West Lafayette, Ind., 1976); *The Austrian Military Border in Croatia, 1522–1747* ("Illinois Studies in the Social Sciences," vol. 48; Urbana, Ill., 1960); *The Military Border in Croatia, 1740–1881: A Study of an Imperial Institution* (Chicago, 1966); and *Napoleon's Great Adversaries: The Archduke Charles and the Austrian Army, 1792–1814* (Bloomington, Ind., 1982).

44. *Sechzig Jahre Wehrmacht 1848–1908* (Vienna, 1908); and Alfons Danzer et al., *Unter den Fahnen. Die Völker Österreich-Ungarns in Waffen* (Prague-Vienna-Leipzig, 1889).

45. Rudolf Kiszling et al., *Die Revolution im Kaisertum Österreich 1848–1849*, 2 vols. (Vienna, 1948); Wilhelm Rüstow, *Geschichte des ungarischen Insurrektionskrieges in den Jahren 1848 und 1849*, 2 vols. (Zurich, 1860); István Deák, *The Lawful Revolution: Louis Kossuth and the Hungarians, 1848–1849* (New York, 1979); and Alan Sked, *The Survival of*

the Habsburg Empire: Radetzky, the Imperial Army and the Class War, 1848 (London-New York, 1979).

46. Antonio Schmidt-Brentano, *Die Armee in Österreich. Militär, Staat und Gesellschaft 1848–1867* (Boppard am Rhein, 1975); Gordon A. Craig, *The Battle of Königgrätz. Prussia's Victory over Austria, 1866* (Philadelphia-New York, 1964); and Walter Wagner, *Geschichte des k.k. Kriegsministeriums,* 2 vols.; vol. 1, 1848–1866, and vol. 2, 1866–1888 (Graz-Vienna-Cologne, 1966, 1971).

47. Oskar Regele, *Feldmarschall Radetzky. Leben-Leistung-Erbe* (Vienna-Munich, 1957); *Feldzeugmeister Benedek* (Vienna, 1960), and *Feldmarschall Conrad. Auftrag und Erfüllung 1906–1918* (Vienna-Munich, 1955).

48. Urbański, *Conrad von Hötzendorf;* and Glaise-Horstenau, *Franz Josephs Weggefährte.*

49. Nikolaus von Preradovich, *Die Führungsschichten in Österreich und Preussen (1804–1918), mit einem Ausblick bis zum Jahre 1945* (Wiesbaden, 1955).

50. Oskar Regele, *Generalstabschefs aus vier Jahrhunderten. Das Amt des Chefs des Generalstabes in der Donaumonarchie. Seine Träger und Organe von 1529 bis 1918* (Vienna-Munich, 1966), and *Der österreichische Hofkriegsrat 1556–1848* (Vienna, 1949).

51. Glaise and Kiszling, *Österreich-Ungarns letzter Krieg;* Richard G. Plaschka, *Cattaro-Prag. Revolte und Revolution* (Graz, 1963); and Richard G. Plaschka, Horst Haselsteiner, and Arnold Suppan, *Innere Front. Militärassistenz, Widerstand und Umsturz in der Donaumonarchie 1918,* 2 vols. (Vienna, 1974).

52. Sandor Varga (Tinódi), ed., *Budapest volt háziezredének, a cs. és kir. 32. gyalogezrednek története (1741–1918)* (History of Budapest's former house-regiment, the 32. imp. and royal infantry regiment), (Budapest, [1929]). Below a random sample of some regimental histories: Ludwig Kirchthaler, *Geschichte des k.u.k. Infanterie-Regimentes Nr. 2 für immerwährende Zeiten Alexander I Kaiser von Russland* (Vienna, 1893); Friedrich Mandel, *Geschichte des k.u.k. Infanterie-Regimentes Guidobald Graf von Starhemberg,* 2 vols. (Krakau, 1893); Karl Sirowy, *Kurze Geschichte des Warasdiner Infanterie-Regimentes Freiherr von Giesl Nr. 16* (Agram, 1903); Franz von Branko, *Geschichte des k.k. Infanterie-Regimentes Nr. 44 Feldmarschall Erzherzog Albrecht von seiner Errichtung in 1744 bis 1875* (Vienna, 1875); Leopold Freund, *Geschichte des k. und k. Feld-Jäger-Bataillons Nr. 25* (Mosty Wielkie, 1902); and Ernst Wengraf, ed., *Feuerbereit! Kriegsalbum des Feldartillerie-Regimentes Nr. 104, Wien* (Vienna, 1919).

Index